Zola's Painters

LEGENDA

LEGENDA is the Modern Humanities Research Association's book imprint for new research in the Humanities. Founded in 1995 by Malcolm Bowie and others within the University of Oxford, Legenda has always been a collaborative publishing enterprise, directly governed by scholars. The Modern Humanities Research Association (MHRA) joined this collaboration in 1998, became half-owner in 2004, in partnership with Maney Publishing and then Routledge, and has since 2016 been sole owner. Titles range from medieval texts to contemporary cinema and form a widely comparative view of the modern humanities, including works on Arabic, Catalan, English, French, German, Greek, Italian, Portuguese, Russian, Spanish, and Yiddish literature. Editorial boards and committees of more than 60 leading academic specialists work in collaboration with bodies such as the Society for French Studies, the British Comparative Literature Association and the Association of Hispanists of Great Britain & Ireland.

The MHRA encourages and promotes advanced study and research in the field of the modern humanities, especially modern European languages and literature, including English, and also cinema. It aims to break down the barriers between scholars working in different disciplines and to maintain the unity of humanistic scholarship. The Association fulfils this purpose through the publication of journals, bibliographies, monographs, critical editions, and the MHRA Style Guide, and by making grants in support of research. Membership is open to all who work in the Humanities, whether independent or in a University post, and the participation of younger colleagues entering the field is especially welcomed.

ALSO PUBLISHED BY THE ASSOCIATION

Critical Texts
Tudor and Stuart Translations • *New Translations* • *European Translations*
MHRA Library of Medieval Welsh Literature

MHRA Bibliographies
Publications of the Modern Humanities Research Association

The Annual Bibliography of English Language & Literature
Austrian Studies
Modern Language Review
Portuguese Studies
The Slavonic and East European Review
Working Papers in the Humanities
The Yearbook of English Studies

www.mhra.org.uk
www.legendabooks.com

RESEARCH MONOGRAPHS IN FRENCH STUDIES

The *Research Monographs in French Studies* (RMFS) are selected, edited and supported by the Society for French Studies. The series seeks to publish the best new work in all areas of the literature, language, thought, history, politics, culture and film of the French-speaking world and to cover the full chronological range from the medieval period to the present day. Proposals are accepted for monographs of up to 85,000 words, while proposals for 'short' monographs (50,000–60,000 words), a traditional strength of the series, are still welcomed.

PUBLISHED IN THIS SERIES

35. *The Subversive Poetics of Alfred Jarry,* by Marieke Dubbelboer
36. *Echo's Voice: The Theatres of Sarraute, Duras, Cixous and Renaude*, by Mary Noonan
37. *Stendhal's Less-Loved Heroines: Fiction, Freedom, and the Female*, by Maria C. Scott
38. *Marie NDiaye: Inhospitable Fictions*, by Shirley Jordan
39. *Dada as Text, Thought and Theory*, by Stephen Forcer
40. *Variation and Change in French Morphosyntax*, by Anna Tristram
41. *Postcolonial Criticism and Representations of African Dictatorship*, by Cécile Bishop
42. *Regarding Manneken Pis: Culture, Celebration and Conflict in Brussels*, by Catherine Emerson
43. *The French Art Novel 1900-1930*, by Katherine Shingler
44. *Accent, Rhythm and Meaning in French Verse*, by Roger Pensom
45. *Baudelaire and Photography: Finding the Painter of Modern Life*, by Timothy Raser
46. *Broken Glass, Broken World: Glass in French Culture in the Aftermath of 1870*, by Hannah Scott
47. *Southern Regional French*, by Damien Mooney
48. *Pascal Quignard: Towards the Vanishing Point*, by Léa Vuong
49. *France, Algeria and the Moving Image,* by Maria Flood
50. *Genet's Genres of Politics*, by Mairéad Hanrahan
51. *Jean-François Vilar: Theatres Of Crime*, by Margaret Atack
52. *Balzac's Love Letters: Correspondence and the Literary Imagination*, by Ewa Szypula
53. *Saints and Monsters in Medieval French and Occitan Literature*, by Huw Grange
54. *Laforgue, Philosophy, and Ideas of Otherness*, by Sam Bootle
55. *Theorizing Medieval Race: Saracen Representations in Old French Literature*, by Victoria Turner
56. *I Suffer, Therefore I Am: Engaging with Empathy in Contemporary French Women's Writing*, by Kathryn Robson
57. *Ying Chen's Fiction: An Aesthetics of Non-Belonging*, by Rosalind Silvester
58. *The Poetry of Céline Arnauld: From Dada to Ultra-Modern*, by Ruth Hemus
59. *The* Philomena *of Chrétien the Jew: The Semiotics of Evil*, by Peter Haidu, edited by Matilda Tomaryn Bruckner
60. *Louis-René des Forêts and Inner Autobiography*, by Ian Maclachlan
61. *Geometry and Jean Genet: Shaping the Subject*, by Joanne Brueton
62. *The Language of Disease: Writing Syphilis in Nineteenth-Century France*, by Steven Wilson
63. *The Living Death of Modernity: Balzac, Baudelaire, Zola*, by Dorothy Kelly
64. *The Holocaust in French Postmodern Fiction: Aesthetics, Politics, Ethics*, by Helena Duffy
65. *Contemporary French Poetry: Towards a Minor Poetics*, by Daisy Sainsbury
66. *Frantz Fanon: Literature and Invention*, by Jane Hiddleston
67. *Essay as Enabler in Yves Bonnefoy: Creating the Good Reader*, by Layla Roesler
68. *Zola's Painters*, by Robert Lethbridge

www.rmfs.mhra.org.uk

Zola's Painters

Robert Lethbridge

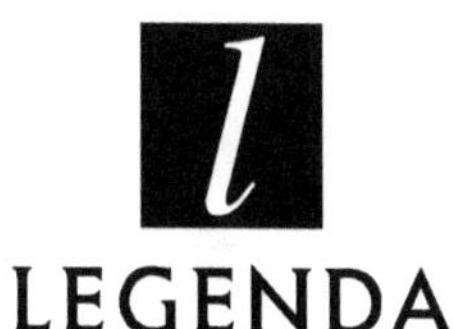

LEGENDA
Research Monographs in French Studies 68
Modern Humanities Research Association
2022

Published by Legenda
an imprint of the Modern Humanities Research Association
Salisbury House, Station Road, Cambridge CB1 2LA

ISBN 978-1-83954-079-0 (HB)
ISBN 978-1-83954-080-6 (PB)

First published 2022

Copy-Editor: Dr Katherine Shingler

CONTENTS

	Acknowledgements	ix
	Abbreviations	x
	List of Illustrations	xi
	Introduction	1
1	The Novelist as Art Critic	11
2	Cézanne	37
3	Courbet	71
4	Manet	95
5	Painters of the Landscape: From the Barbizon School to the Impressionists	127
6	From *La nouvelle peinture* to the Old Masters: Zola's Revisionist Art Criticism	173
	Afterword	209
	Bibliography	215
	Index	225

IN MEMORY OF
HENRI MITTERAND
1928–2021

ACKNOWLEDGEMENTS

My greatest debt is to the late Henri Mitterand: his friendship and encouragement over more than half a century have inspired my own work on Zola throughout my career, not least this book which I discussed with him during its preparation. My thanks also go to Richard Thomson: in kindly reading some of my chapters in draft, he has enriched my incursions into the art history of nineteenth-century France of which he is so authoritative an exponent. I am indebted to the late Barbara Wright, Michael Tilby, Terry Dolan and Freya Spoor, in respect of assistance with earlier published research which has been reconfigured here, as well as to Diana Knight and members of the RMFS editorial board who also offered valuable advice during the development of *Zola's Painters*.

R.D.L., St Andrews, January 2022

ABBREVIATIONS

References to Zola's works, with interpolated volume and page numbers, are abbreviated as follows:

RM	*Les Rougon-Macquart*, ed. by Henri Mitterand, 5 vols (Paris: Gallimard, Bibliothèque de la Pléiade, 1960–67)
OC	*Œuvres complètes*, ed. by Henri Mitterand, 15 vols (Paris: Cercle du livre précieux, 1966–70)
Corr.	*Correspondance*, ed. by Bard Bakker and others, 10 vols (Montréal: Presses de l'Université de Montréal/Paris: CNRS, 1978–95); vol. XI of this same edition was published as a supplement (*Lettres retrouvées*) in 2010, ed. by Owen Morgan and Dorothy E. Spiers
EsA	Émile Zola, *Écrits sur l'art*, ed. by Robert Lethbridge (Paris: Classiques Garnier, 2021)

Other abbreviations are:

Ms	References to Ms and folio numbers are to Zola's handwritten preparatory work-notes for his novels, conserved (in the Nouvelles acquisitions françaises) in the Bibliothèque nationale de France. These have been transcribed, opposite facsimile reproductions, in *La Fabrique des 'Rougon-Macquart'*, ed. by Colette Becker (Paris: Honoré Champion, 2003–17), eight volumes of which have been published to date.
LC	*Paul Cézanne, Émile Zola: lettres croisées, 1858–1887*, ed. by Henri Mitterand (Paris: Gallimard, 2016)
AJFS	*Australian Journal of French Studies*
CN	*Les Cahiers naturalistes*
FS	*French Studies*
GBA	*Gazette des beaux-arts*
NCFS	*Nineteenth-Century French Studies*
NGS	National Galleries of Scotland
RMN	Réunion des musées nationaux

LIST OF ILLUSTRATIONS

❖

Fig. I.1 (and cover). Henri Fantin-Latour, *Un atelier aux Batignolles* (1870), oil on canvas, 204 × 273.5 cm. Musée d'Orsay, Paris.

Fig. I.2. Henri Fantin-Latour, *Hommage à Delacroix* (1864), oil on canvas, 160 × 250 cm. Musée d'Orsay, Paris.

Fig. I.3. Bertall (pseud. of Charles-Albert d'Arnoux), *Jésus peignant au milieu de ses disciples, ou La Divine école de Manet, tableau religieux par Fantin-Latour* (*Le Journal amusant*, 21 May 1870).

Fig. 1.1. Édouard Dantan (1848–1897), *Un coin du Salon, en 1880* (1880), oil on canvas, 97.2 × 130.2 cm. Private collection.

Fig. 1.2. Paul Cézanne, *Portrait de Louis-Auguste Cézanne, père de l'artiste, lisant 'L'Événement'* (1866), oil on canvas, 198.5 × 119.3 cm. National Gallery of Art, Washington DC. Gift of Mr and Mrs Paul Mellon.

Fig. 1.3. Henri Gervex, *Une séance du jury de peinture* (1885), oil on canvas, 299 × 419 cm. Musée d'Orsay, Paris.

Fig. 1.4. Émile Zola, *Mes haines* (Paris: Achille Faure, 1866).

Fig. 1.5. Émile Zola, *Mon Salon* (Paris: Librairie centrale, 1866).

Fig. 2.1. Paul Cézanne, *La Pendule noire* (1869–70), oil on canvas, 55.2 × 74.3 cm. Private collection.

Fig. 2.2. Camille Pissarro, *Portrait de Paul Cézanne* (1874), oil on canvas, 73 × 59.7 cm. Private collection.

Fig. 2.3. Paul Cézanne, *Sucrier, poires et tasse bleue* (1865–66), oil on canvas, 30 × 41 cm. Musée Granet, Aix-en-Provence.

Fig. 2.4. Paul Cézanne, *Une moderne Olympia* (1869–70), oil on canvas, 46 × 55 cm. Musée d'Orsay, gift of Paul Gachet.

Fig. 2.5. Édouard Manet, *Olympia* (1865), oil on canvas, 130.5 × 190 cm. Musée d'Orsay, Paris.

Fig. 2.6. Paul Cézanne, *Le Punch au rhum* (rejected by the Salon of 1867), pencil, pen, watercolour and gouache on cardboard, 11 × 14.8 cm. Private collection.

Fig. 2.7. Paul Cézanne, *Vue de Bonnières* (1866), oil on canvas, 38 × 61 cm. Musée Faure, Aix-les-Bains.

Fig. 2.8. Paul Cézanne, *L'Enlèvement* (1867), oil on canvas, 90.5 × 117 cm. King's College, Cambridge, on loan to the Fitzwilliam Museum, Cambridge.

Fig. 2.9. Paul Cézanne, *Mur de jardin* (1867–68), oil on canvas, 23 × 38 cm. Private collection.

Fig. 2.10. Paul Cézanne, *Néréides et Tritons* (c. 1867), oil on canvas, 23.5 × 31 cm. Private collection.

Fig. 3.1. Gustave Courbet, *L'Aumône d'un mendiant à Ornans* (1868), oil on canvas, 210 × 175 cm. The Burrell Collection, Glasgow.

Fig. 3.2. Gustave Courbet, *La Femme au perroquet* (1866), oil on canvas, 129.5 × 195.6 cm. Metropolitan Museum of Art, New York. H. O. Havermeyer Collection. Gift of Mrs H. O. Havermeyer.

Fig. 3.3. Gustave Courbet, *La Remise des chevreuils au ruisseau de Plaisir-Fontaine* (1866), oil on canvas, 174 × 209 cm. Musée d'Orsay, Paris.

FIG. 3.4. Gustave Courbet, *Les Casseurs de pierres* (1849), oil on canvas, 165 × 257 cm. Formerly in Dresden but destroyed during World War II.
FIG. 3.5. Gustave Courbet, *La Mer orageuse (La Vague)* (Salon of 1870), oil on canvas, 116 × 160 cm. Musée d'Orsay, Paris.
FIG. 4.1. Zola's photograph of Manet's 1868 portrait of him (*c.* 1900).
FIG. 4.2. *Apothéose de Zola par Zola* (*L'Illustration*, 11 October 1902).
FIG. 4.3. Henri Fantin-Latour, *Portrait d'Édouard Manet* (1867), oil on canvas, 117.5 × 90 cm. Art Institute of Chicago. Stickney Fund.
FIG. 4.4. Édouard Manet, *Nana* (1877), oil on canvas, 154 × 115 cm. Kunsthalle, Hamburg.
FIG. 4.5. Édouard Manet, *Portrait de M. Émile Zola* (1868), oil on canvas, 146 × 114 cm. Musée d'Orsay, Paris.
FIG. 4.6. *Portrait de M. Émile Zola* (detail).
FIG. 4.7. *Portrait de M. Émile Zola* (detail).
FIG. 4.8. Émile Zola, *Éd. Manet* (Paris: E. Dentu, 1867), cover.
FIG. 4.9. Édouard Manet, *Portrait de Zacharie Astruc* (1866), oil on canvas, 90 × 116 cm. Kunsthalle, Bremen.
FIG. 4.10. Édouard Manet, *Jeune dame en 1866* (1866), oil on canvas, 185.1 × 128.6 cm. Metropolitan Museum of Art, New York. Gift of Erwin Davis.
FIG. 4.11. Édouard Manet, *Portrait de Théodore Duret* (1868), oil on canvas, 43 × 35cm. Petit Palais, Musée des Beaux-Arts de la Ville de Paris.
FIG. 4.12. Bertall, *Promenade au Salon de 1868* (*Le Journal amusant*, 6 June 1868).
FIG. 4.13. Bertall, *Promenade au Salon* (detail).
FIG. 5.1. Théodore Rousseau, *Sortie de forêt à Fontainebleau, soleil couchant* (1850–51), oil on canvas, 142 × 198 cm. Grand Palais, Paris.
FIG. 5.2. Jean-François Millet, *Un bout de village de Gréville* (Salon of 1866), oil on canvas, 81.5 × 100.5 cm. Boston Museum of Fine Arts. Gift of Quincy Adam Shaw.
FIG. 5.3. Camille Corot, *Forêt de Fontainebleau* (1834), oil on canvas, 175.6 × 242.6 cm. National Gallery of Art, Washington DC. Chester Dale Collection.
FIG. 5.4. Camille Corot, *Ville d'Avray* (*c.* 1865), oil on canvas, 49.3 × 65.5 cm. National Gallery of Art, Washington DC. Gift of Count Cecil Pecci-Blunt.
FIG. 5.5. Henri Harpignies, *Les Chênes de Château-Renard* (1875), oil on canvas, 167 × 109 cm. Musée des Beaux-Arts d'Orléans.
FIG. 5.6. Antoine Chintreuil, *L'Espace* (1869), oil on canvas, 102 × 204 cm. Musée d'Orsay, Paris.
FIG. 5.7. Léon Pelouse, *Une coupe de bois à Senlisse* (Salon of 1876), oil on canvas, 240 × 16 cm. Mairie de Pierrelaye (Seine et Oise).
FIG. 5.8. Charles-François Daubigny, *Les Champs au mois de juin* (1874), oil on canvas, 135 × 224 cm. Herbert F. Johnson Museum of Art, Cornell University, Ithaca, New York. Gift of Louis V. Keeler, Class of 1911, and Mrs Keeler.
FIG. 5.9. Charles-François Daubigny, *Le Verger* (1873), oil on canvas, 58.7 × 84.8 cm. Metropolitan Museum of Art, New York. Bequest of Collis P. Huntington.
FIG. 5.10. Charles-François Daubigny, *Lever de la lune, à Auvers (Seine et Oise)* (1877), oil on canvas, 106.5 × 188 cm. Montreal Museum of Fine Arts. Gift of Lady Drummond in memory of her husband, Sir George Drummond.
FIG. 5.11. Charles-François Daubigny, *La Neige* (1873), oil on canvas, 100.5 × 201.5 cm. Musée d'Orsay, Paris.
FIG. 5.12. Camille Pissarro, *Bords de Marne en hiver* (1866), oil on canvas, 91.8 × 150.2 cm. Art Institute of Chicago. Gift of Mr and Mrs Lewis L. Coburn.
FIG. 5.13. Camille Pissarro, *La Côte du Jallais* (1867), oil on canvas, 87 × 114.9 cm. Metropolitan Museum of Art, New York. Bequest of William Church Osborn.
FIG. 5.14. Johan-Bartold Jongkind, *Le Pont neuf* (1849–50), oil on canvas, 54.6 × 81.6 cm. Metropolitan Museum of Art, New York. Gift of Mr and Mrs Walter Mendelsohn.

Fig. 5.15. Johan-Bartold Jongkind, *Notre-Dame de Paris, vue du quai de la Tournelle* (1864), oil on canvas, 42.5 × 56.5 cm. Private collection.
Fig. 5.16. Claude Monet, *Le Bateau-atelier* (1876), oil on canvas, 54.6 × 65 cm. Musée d'art et d'histoire de Neuchâtel. Gift of Yvan and Hélène Amez-Droz.
Fig. 5.17. Claude Monet, *La Jetée du Havre* (1868), oil on canvas, 147 × 226 cm. Private collection.
Fig. 5.18. Claude Monet, *Effet d'automne* (1873), oil on canvas, 55 × 74.5 cm. Courtauld Institute of Art, London.
Fig. 5.19. Claude Monet, *Champ de coquelicots dans un creux près de Giverny* (1885), oil on canvas, 65.1 × 81.3 cm. Boston Museum of Fine Arts.
Fig. 5.20. Jules Bastien-Lepage, *Les Foins* (Salon of 1877), oil on canvas, 160 × 195 cm. Musée d'Orsay, Paris.
Fig. 5.21. Jules Bastien-Lepage, *Saison d'octobre* (Salon of 1877), oil on canvas, 180.7 × 196 cm. National Gallery of Victoria, Melbourne. Felton Bequest.
Fig. 6.1. Paolo Veronese, *Les Noces de Cana* (1562–63), oil on canvas, 667 × 994 cm. Musée du Louvre, Paris.
Fig. 6.2. Peter Paul Rubens, *La Kermesse* (*c.* 1635), oil on panel, 149 × 261 cm. Musée du Louvre, Paris.
Fig. 6.3. Raphaël, *The Triumph of Galatea* (*c.* 1512–1514), freso, 295 × 225 cm. Villa Farenisa, Rome.
Fig. 6.4. Nineteenth-century Rome: photo by Robert Turnbull Macpherson (1814–1872).
Fig. 6.5. Michelangelo, ceiling (1508–12) of the Sistine Chapel, Vatican.
Fig. 6.6. Michelangelo, *The Last Judgement* (1536–41), Sistine Chapel, Vatican.
Fig. 6.7. Michelangelo, *The Last Judgement* (detail).

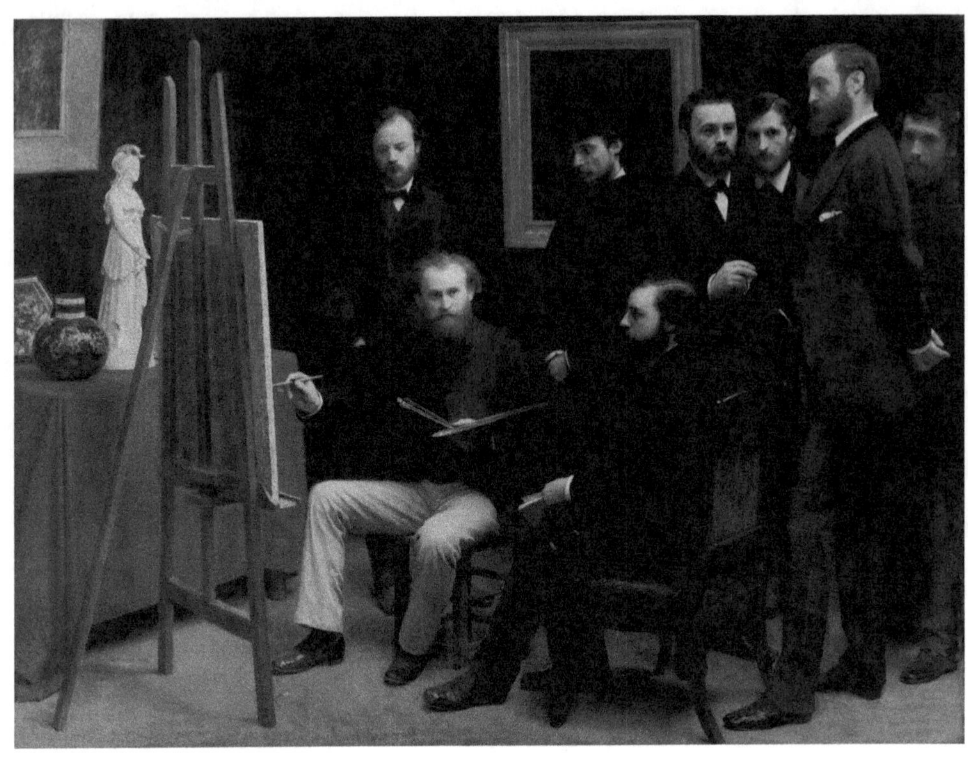

FIG. I.1. Henri Fantin-Latour, *Un atelier aux Batignolles* (1870), oil on canvas, 204 × 273.5 cm. Musée d'Orsay, Paris.

INTRODUCTION

The cover illustration of this book is emblematic of its concerns. Henri Fantin-Latour's *Un atelier aux Batignolles* (Fig. I.1) exhibited at the Salon of 1870, is consistent, in a literal sense, with Zola's earlier remark about the limits of his social intercourse during this period of his life, to the effect that 'Je ne suis entouré que de peintres'.[1] For the canvas includes some of the painters of his circle about whom he also wrote, as he did on Fantin-Latour himself: from the left, Manet with his palette, Renoir (set against the picture-frame behind him), the very tall Frédéric Bazille,[2] and Monet (recessed at the right-hand margin). It has been argued that Zola, looking right, seems to occupy a privileged position as the *only* writer in the midst of this apparent celebration, notwithstanding Fantin-Latour's denials of the picture's manifesto status,[3] of the artistic solidarity of the avant-garde grouped around Manet as the *de facto* leader of 'la nouvelle peinture'. In this reading of the painting, his presence is akin to Baudelaire's in Fantin-Latour's *Hommage à Delacroix* (1864) (Fig. I.2), with Zola's outward-looking gaze indexing, according to John House, his mediating role as the principal spokesman of pictorial innovation for this generation.[4]

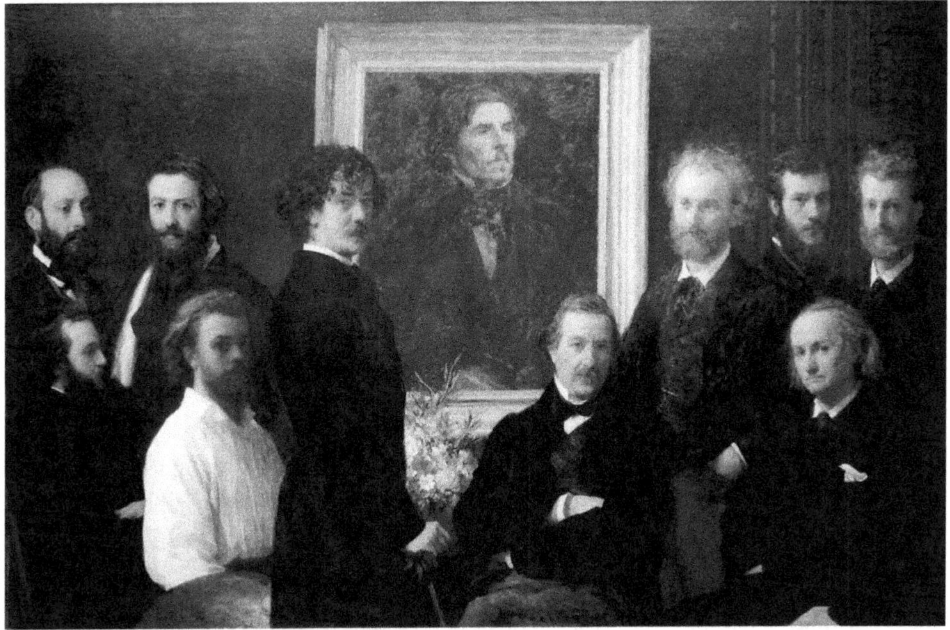

Fig. I.2. Henri Fantin-Latour, *Hommage à Delacroix* (1864), oil on canvas, 160 × 250 cm. Musée d'Orsay, Paris.

It may not, however, be quite that simple. Begun in October 1869, the painting was subject to significant revisions prior to completion. At some stage, Degas was eliminated and his place directly behind Manet taken by Fantin-Latour's old friend and equally dedicated admirer of Courbet, the German painter Otto Scholderer (1834–1902). And originally, to take a more pertinent example as far as Zola is concerned, another prominent art critic (and the one, moreover, credited with publicly christening the group as 'L'École des Batignolles'), Edmond Duranty (1833–1880), was to figure in it, as he had done in the *Hommage à Delacroix*. But he was subsequently replaced with Renoir on account of a lukewarm review of its members' submissions to the Salon of 1869 and, above all, an altercation with Manet so bitter that it provoked, in February 1870, a duel between the two men in which Zola acted as a second to the painter.[5] Of those who survived these revisions, much the most interesting, in the context of the present study, is the poet and critic Zacharie Astruc (1835–1907). For it is his portrait on which Manet, brush in hand, is seen to be at work, testimony to Astruc's personal and professional importance for the artist; and this overshadows Zola's importance, not least in qualifying the writer's oft-rehearsed claim that he was the very first to recognize Manet's greatness.[6] In spite of the inclusion, next to Zola, of Edmond Maître (1840–1898), the musician in the background of proceedings, the spatial distribution of the figures hints at an ambivalence undermining the representation of artistic harmony, as Bridget Alsdorf has suggested.[7] What is certain is that Zola's own positioning is not arbitrary, angled as he is away from adjacent faces to his right looking at, it must be assumed, Fantin-Latour himself. The latter had doubtless not forgotten that his *Hommage à Delacroix* had provoked the criticism that its subject's admirers had their backs to the portrait of him at its centre.[8] For whereas Bertall's caricatural version of *Un atelier aux Batignolles* (Fig. I. 3) realigns Zola within the six worshipping figures behind Manet at his easel, in the painting itself there is something not quite right about his participation in this 'celebration': turned away from the act of painting, staring into space, not integrated into the picture's compositional planes, Zola seems awkwardly misplaced. Analogous ambiguities, as will be seen in Chapter 4, inform Manet's 1868 portrait of the writer, equally symptomatic of the questions explored in this book and posed by Zola's relationship with the painters of his time.

This study of that relationship, the first to analyse the writer's art criticism as a whole, draws on evidence from a variety of sources: Zola's biography, correspondence, interviews and reported conversations; the modern works of art in his personal collection, many of them given to him as gestures of friendship or, and often *and*, tokens of gratitude by painters he had championed or merely publicly encouraged in his journalism;[9] book reviews of illustrated editions and art history monographs; essays and articles on a range of political and literary topics at some distance from the passing references to artists within them; and, most obviously, his art criticism itself. Over more than thirty years, from 1863 onwards, Zola's engagement with the visual arts results in some 150 texts, originally appearing in newspapers and periodicals both in France and abroad. Not least because almost two thirds of these have only recently become available to scholars, this corpus has never

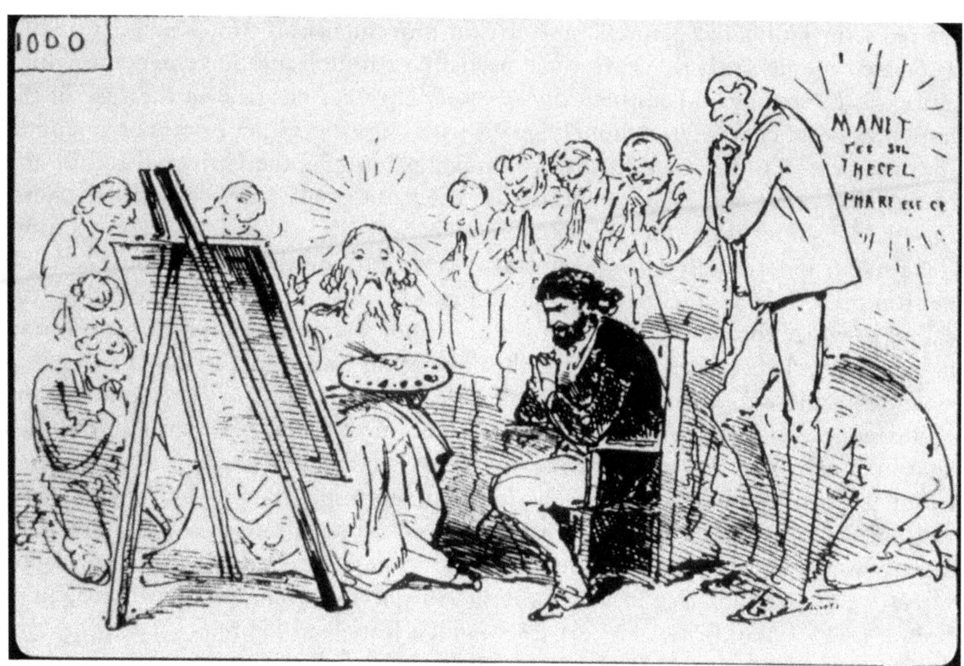

FIG. I.3. Bertall (pseud. of Charles-Albert d'Arnoux), *Jésus peignant au milieu de ses disciples, ou La Divine École de Manet, tableau religieux par Fantin-Latour* (*Le Journal amusant*, 21 May 1870).

been analysed in its own right as opposed to illuminating aspects of his fiction. But, as Henri Mitterand has stressed in relation to *Les Rougon-Macquart*, 'rares sont les romans du cycle où ne se montre pas le point de vue du critique d'art'.[10] This claim can be extended to novels and short stories both before and after the twenty-volume series which accounts for Zola's reputation as one of the greatest European writers of his generation. As, or indeed often more, instructive are the preparatory *dossiers* of his novels. *Rome* (1896) is unique in that an additional metatextual discourse is provided by the journal Zola kept while working on the novel, which is part of his late series, *Les Trois Villes*. (This will be exploited in Chapter 6.) But, especially in the case of *Les Rougon-Macquart*, Zola's preliminary notes, in the form of an authorial monologue, give us direct access to reflections on artists and their work prior to a fictional transposition shaped by the needs of narrative coherence, descriptive modulation and character portrayal.

The title of this book, *Zola's Painters*, signals its scope as well as, implicitly, its limits. The possessive underlines the assertive subjectivity of a critical perspective which privileges a highly personal canon. His first series of articles, on works shown at the 1866 Salon, are published in volume form under the self-consciously declarative title of *Mon Salon*, a break with protocol seized upon by hostile critics heading their own surveys with the professed neutrality of a definite article. Elective affinities are also increasingly proprietary to the extent that particular artists are, as it were, recruited under the banner of his own militant Naturalism. And this book's chapters on individual painters and artistic movements are inseparable from the associated premise that these were the particular painters and movements in which Zola was personally and aesthetically *invested*. This was not true in the case of the hundreds of other artists to whom he refers in his writing, either briefly or at length. In his review of the section devoted to French painting at the Universal Exhibition of 1867, for example, Zola concentrates on the painters officially consecrated there: Ernest Meissonier (1815–1891), Alexandre Cabanel (1823–1889), Jean-Léon Gérôme (1824–1904) and Théodore Rousseau (1812–1867). But this detailed response to what he ironically calls 'les quatre génies de la France' (*EsA*, p. 528) is motivated by the extent to which they exemplified conventions and criteria he *dis*owns. This was not, however, by chance. For (and perfectly illustrating the overlaid factors inflecting Zola's art criticism) this immediately followed the 1867 Salon jury's rejection of the submissions of Cézanne, Sisley, Bazille, Renoir and Monet, 'the worst across-the-board rejection that this group of artists was ever to experience'.[11] At the next such national glorification of artistic orthodoxy, the corresponding Exhibition of 1878, Zola adds to the list another set of painters who had been intermittently subject to his provocatively negative assessment, either absolute or relative, over the previous fifteen years: Carolus-Duran (1837–1917), Jean-Jacques Henner (1829–1905), Jules Breton (1827–1906), Ernest Hébert (1817–1908), Jean-Paul Laurens (1838–1921) and Gustave Moreau (1826–1898). And these are merely the best-known painters of the period, some of them enjoying enviable contemporary reputations and commercial success. In his art criticism more generally, Zola also refers to innumerable figures now completely erased from even the most comprehensive art-historical accounts of nineteenth-century culture. But this panoply of references is neither superfluous nor self-indulgently aggressive, serving Zola's purpose over and above the professional or contractual necessity of surveying the entirety of an exhibition or the evolutionary trends of French art. For they are often either contrastively positioned to Zola's preferences or allow him to develop the principles underlying them. His discussion of Manet's *Olympia*, compared by Zola to the profusion of traditional nudes at the annual Salon, is only the most famous example of such a discursive strategy. Nuanced views of Léon Bonnat (1833–1922), Henri Gervex (1852–1929) and Jules Bastien-Lepage (1848–1884) are just as inevitably exploited to articulate an ideal insufficiently attained by technical expertise alone. And this is also true of Zola's far less sustained writing on sculpture and the graphic arts.

It would be misleading, however, to suggest that the painters who are the focus of this book are the only ones Zola deemed worthy of serious attention — just as it would be misleading to suppose that all the others are victims of his excoriating prose and ubiquitously uncompromising judgements. He cannot fault, for example, the quasi-documentary exactitude of pictures of the Franco-Prussian War by Alphonse de Neuville (1836–1885) and Édouard Detaille (1848–1912), even though, in the case of the latter, Zola is unable to resist inserting an objection to the miniaturist dimension of paintings so clearly identifying him as a pupil of Meissonier, reviled by virtue of his invidious hostility to Manet (repeatedly assuring his rejection by the Salon jury) and Courbet (excluding him on political grounds from the Salon of 1872). The meticulous *natures mortes* of Antoine Vollon (1833–1900), 'qui a poussé la représentation des objets inanimés jusqu'à une rare perfection' (*EsA*, p. 281), are genuinely admired as masterpieces of the genre. The 'epic' magnificence of his *Armures* (1875) is echoed in Zola's agreeable surprise, shared by other reviewers faced with Vollon's change of manner in his next submission, *Femme du Pollet, à Dieppe (Seine-Inférieure)* (1876): 'L'intention réaliste est évidente; seulement c'est un réalisme à large envergure, s'envolant dans l'épopée' (*EsA*, p. 319). It hardly seems a coincidence that those very terms prefigure Zola's conception of his own fictional achievement. And while he has many unfavourable things to say about the art of portraiture as practised by artists such as William Bouguereau (1825–1905), making a fortune from flattering depictions of high-society ladies, there are notable exceptions: Fantin-Latour's *Portrait de M. et Mme Edwin Edwards* is perceived as one of the best paintings on display at the Salon of 1875, evidence of 'un peintre naturaliste qui a une grande science de la couleur' (*EsA*, p. 260); at that same Salon, Alexei Harlamoff (1840–1925), the close friend of Turgenev who had brought him to Zola's notice, is considered 'un peintre des plus remarquables' (*EsA*, p. 288) in the light of his joint portrait of Pauline Viardot and her husband; the following year, Zola is struck by that of the press baron, Émile de Girardin, 'une page très vivante, très juste, comme on en rencontre rarement chez Carolus-Duran' (*EsA*, p. 320), double-edged as such praise may be. Reservations about one of the many portraits of Sarah Bernhardt by Georges Clairin (1843–1919) (both of whom Zola knew well) on the grounds that it did not exactly catch the intelligence of her facial features, did not preclude him owning one.[12] He also owned a work by Jean-François Raffaëlli (1850–1924), cited alongside Ulysse Butin (1838–1883) and Jean Béraud (1849–1935), 'dont les mérites se font remarquer d'année en année' by virtue of 'le souffle moderne' they exemplify. But that last phrase underlines the extent to which Zola's enthusiasm for certain works, whether unexpected or not, is inseparable from a definition of modernism synonymous with the verisimilitude demanded by the novelist of both pictorial and literary representation.

It seems hardly by chance that Zola's earliest elaboration of the principles of literary representation should have recourse to visual metaphors, however traditional their provenance in that respect: his 'Théorie des écrans', elaborated in his letter to Antony Valabrègue (1844–1900) of 18 August 1864 has long been considered the foundational text of his aesthetic.[13] It concludes that 'je préfère l'Écran qui, serrant de plus près la réalité, se contente de mentir assez juste pour me faire sentir un homme dans une image de la création', in other words, as a filter though which the individual *tempérament* could be discerned. Although primarily concerned with realist *literary* practice, even the vocabulary is picked up in Zola's writing on the visual arts, with that individuation conceived as a perceptual filter differentiated from a pane of glass. What is more, the notion of the screen has a specific pictorial resonance in the habitual screening out of excessive light by generations of artists, as well as in exhibition spaces. As Zola well knew: 'tendu' from the ceiling of the gallery, in *L'Œuvre*, is 'un écran de toile blanche', resulting in 'une clarté égale' (*RM*, IV, 131). To Valabrègue, he admits that the screen between observer and object, 'entre notre œil et la création' is inevitably distorting. Anticipating his later thinking about the Impressionists' landscapes, he develops this 'phénomène optique' in precisely the terms of contemporary thinking about visuality: 'De même, des verres de différentes couleurs donnent aux objets des couleurs différentes; de même des lentilles, concaves ou convexes, déforment les objets chacune dans un sens.' Nor is this last opthalmic analogy arbitrary, given Zola's short-sightedness and reliance on his monocle to bring things into focus. The limits of this acknowledgement of the subjectivity of representation are discernible, however, in the conviction that what remains invariable is external reality itself, based on Zola's premise that 'la création étant la même pour nous tous', it is the accuracy of representation which should be the sole concern of artistic endeavour and critical judgement. If his early writing on Manet, in particular, is characterized by precisely these kinds of contradiction, it will also be argued that they point to Zola's increasingly unconcealed dismay with the directions taken in the *fin de siècle* by painters and writers alike, apparently at odds with his own mimetic imperatives.

The imbricated frames of reference of the verbal and the visual are explored in the opening chapter of this book, 'The Novelist as Art Critic'. It provides a summary of the overlapping contexts in which Zola's art criticism has to be set: that of his own career; the link between such writing and the development of his own aesthetic; the cultural background, one consequence of which is the exponential expansion of art criticism itself, resulting in tension between so-called 'professional' critics and the 'littérateurs' whose incursions into the genre were deemed unwelcome; the questioning of the competence of such 'amateurs', charges levelled at Zola too, and which were responsible for the vicissitudes of his journalistic commentary on the visual arts; the contrary evidence that he was uniquely qualified to engage in art criticism on account of his formative contacts with contemporary painters; and the ways in which his art criticism, even in its oppositional rhetoric, reflects the newly-acute antagonism between, on the one hand, convention and tradition, and, on the other, pictorial innovation and originality.

That the second chapter of this book should be devoted to Zola's relationship with Cézanne is justified by the latter's *personal* importance for the novelist. It explores anew the narrative of their thirty-year friendship in the light of the recent discovery of a letter which demolishes the legend, sustained for the best part of a century, that the publication of *L'Œuvre* in 1886 brought it to a dramatic end. While suggesting alternative reasons for their gradual parting of ways, the principal aim of this chapter is to underline Cézanne's seminal role in Zola's artistic education. Another is to rethink the virtual absence in Zola's art criticism of the painter he actually knew best.

The significance for Zola of Courbet is of another kind. For, apart from an early review-article on Gustave Doré, Courbet provided the novelist with the first opportunity, in 1865, to write at length about a major artist. As Chapter 3 demonstrates, however, this initial encounter with Courbet's work served mainly as a pretext for defining Zola's own aesthetic criteria. Subsequently his assessment of the painter had to overcome distrust, not least in respect of Courbet's personality and ambiguous attitude towards popular success. It is only once Courbet had been scapegoated, and forced into exile, as a direct consequence of his association with the Commune, that Zola's reflections on his pictorial achievements are liberated from prejudice. For Courbet then begins to take his place in Zola's 'pantheon' as one of the greatest painters of the age, a judgement finally confirmed in aligning him with the Old Masters, as will be argued in my final chapter.

The focus of Chapter 4 is Zola's championing of Manet. This occupies a heroic space in both art history and studies of the novelist. But it also requires another look. Without disputing the sincerity of Zola's views, it is also self-evident that his essays in support of Manet are motivated by an identification inseparable from the latter's controversial status, allowing the young writer to make his own name as a critic. The chapter argues that Zola's varying assessments of the painter's works correlate with the degree of hostility they provoked. And this is consistent with a reminder that his admiration for Manet is not absolute, or at least not in the 1870s: his less than fulsome remarks about his submissions to the Salon in that decade coincide with the painter's increasingly Impressionist phase; and, in a longer perspective, he is viewed by Zola not as the long-awaited modernist 'genius' but as merely a transitional figure in the history of art.

Zola was more comfortable with landscape than figure painting, the genre itself being less vulnerable to the 'category confusion' of literary, or narrative, superimpositions — of which, as a 'littérateur', he was acutely aware of the risks. As Chapter 5 argues, the landscapes of the Impressionists initially seemed to him to capture the reality of the natural world, thereby corresponding to Naturalist intentions. But the experimental directions of these painters, anticipating neo-Impressionist and *pointilliste* modalities, placed a gigantic question-mark over such presumed affinities. This is brought into sharper relief by comparing his gradual disenchantment with the Impressionists to his appreciation of the painters of the Barbizon School. Zola's writing about the likes of Corot and Daubigny has seldom been analysed, let alone positioned as exemplifying a picturing of the landscape against which that of the Impressionists could be measured and ultimately found wanting.

The final chapter of this book accommodates a review of the entirety of Zola's art criticism in explaining what is, at first sight, his surprising admiration for the Old Masters at the expense of the work of the artists he had known and written about. Such an inversion of his modernist credentials is an area which has received little attention to date.[14] Zola's visit to Rome in 1894 was a revelation in bringing him up close to the painters of the High Renaissance. In retrospect, however, it can be argued that this preference is the logical extension of his gradual disenchantment with the Impressionists, reinforced by what he termed the 'aberrations' of their successors. For the Old Masters offered him a compelling example of 'genius' as well as a mirror of his own literary ambitions and achievements.

Notes to the Introduction

1. In a letter of 19 February 1867 to Antony Valabrègue, explaining that 'je n'ai pas ici un seul littérateur avec qui causer' (*Corr.*, I, p. 473).
2. Bazille was one of the most talented of the emerging Impressionists. But he was killed during the Franco-Prussian War (at the battle of Beaune-la-Rolande on 28 November 1870, a week short of his twenty-ninth birthday). Zola had known him since 1863. He had singled out for praise his *Réunion de famille* at the Salon of 1868, 'qui témoigne d'un vif amour de la vérité' (*EsA*, p. 191), and likened it to a Monet. Bazille would be one of the models for Félicien d'Hautecœur in the novelist's *Le Rêve* (1888). Recent research has corrected the long-held view that Zola also figures amongst the painters assembled in Bazille's *L'Atelier de la rue Condamine* (1870). See *Frédéric Bazille (1841–1870): la jeunesse de l'impressionnisme,* ed. by Michel Hilaire and Paul Perrin (Paris: Fayard, 2016), p. 165.
3. In a preliminary drawing for the painting, however, Fantin-Latour had a caption aimed at the traditionalism of Gérôme and Cabanel, the two academic painters consistently attacked throughout Zola's art criticism.
4. John House, *Impressionism: Paint and Politics* (New Haven and London: Yale University Press, 2004), p. 6.
5. Zola would, many years later, characterize the episode as 'fort ridicule'; in *L'Écho de Paris*, 3 March 1895, reprinted in *Entretiens avec Zola*, ed. by Dorothy E. Speirs and Dolorès A. Signori (Ottawa: Les Presses universitaires d'Ottawa, 1990), p. 148. During the preparation of *L'Œuvre*, however, he had at one stage thought of inserting in its plot 'le duel de Manet', 'le duel peut-être (je voudrais un fait dramatique)' (Ms 10316, fols 316 and 2).
6. Manet's 1866 portrait of Astruc (see Fig. 4.9) alludes explicitly to *Olympia*, his sitter having inserted in the catalogue of the Salon of 1865 an explanatory quatrain which had provoked added hilarity at the painting's expense; see David Alston, 'What's in a Name? *Olympia* and a Minor Parnassian', *GBA*, 91 (1978), 148–54. Astruc had also been involved in planning Manet's visit to Spain in 1865 and, unlike Zola, had insisted, as early as in an article of 20 May 1863, on the crucial influence of the Spanish School on the painter's development: 'l'école espagnole l'attire invinciblement par ses colorations'; adding that 'l'injustice à son égard est si flagrante qu'elle confond' (*Le Salon de 1863*, no. 16). His championing of Manet was sustained throughout the 1860s.
7. Bridget Alsdorf, *Fellow Men: Fantin-Latour and the Problem of the Group in Nineteenth-Century French Painting* (Princeton, NJ: Princeton University Press, 2012), p. 130.
8. That painting is perhaps recalled in the central framing of Renoir, Delacroix's avowed 'disciple'.
9. A complete inventory of this collection is to be found in *EsA*, pp. 705–39: 'Œuvres d'art modernes appartenant à Zola'. The circumstances in which many of the works were acquired adds a level of irony to his low opinion of Gautier's art criticism, against which many of his own preferences are implicitly directed (notably Zola's positive view of Daubigny, Courbet and Manet). For in the context of the posthumous sale of Gautier's own collection in January 1873, Zola wrote: 'Sa critique bienveillante, son admiration un peu facile lui valaient des cadeaux de tous les peintres dont il s'occupait dans ses *Salons*. Ce sont ces cadeaux qu'on va vendre' (*EsA*, p. 649). During the preparation of *L'Œuvre*, he noted this habit of painters seeking a favourable mention: 'les rapports avec les critiques. On leur donne quelquefois un tableau, vieux jeu' (Ms 10316, fol. 364).
10. This important insight appears in Mitterand's critical apparatus for the Pléiade edition of *L'Assommoir* (*RM*, II, 1580). It is even true of a novel such as *Son Excellence Rougon* (1876), in which there is inserted into its political scenarios a parody of the traditional nude. Clorinde, 'dans sa pose de déesse' as Diana or Venus, with her 'taille de statue géante', 'le buste renversé à demi, haussant les pointes des seins', 'les cuisses nues, les bras nus, la gorge nue, toute nue' (*RM*, II, 61–63) is described in the novel's work-notes as 'une très mauvaise peinture' (Ms 10292, fol. 17), reflecting Zola's view of the nudes popularized by the likes of Cabanel. See Patricia Carles and Béatrice Desgranges, '*Son Excellence Rougon* ou la métaire des beaux-arts', *NCFS*, 21.1–2 (1992–93), 114–29.

11. Patricia Mainardi, *Art and Politics of the Second Empire: The Universal Exhibitions of 1855 and 1867* (New Haven and London: Yale University Press, 1987), p. 135. Zola immodestly blamed himself for these rejections, writing to Valabrègue on 4 April 1867 that 'le jury, irrité de mon *Salon*, a mis à la porte tous ceux qui marchent dans la nouvelle voie' (*Corr.*, I, 486).
12. On Zola's relationship with its creator, see Joy Newton and Claude Schumacher, 'Zola et le peintre Georges Clairin', *CN*, 61 (1987), 194–203.
13. *Corr.*, I, 373–82, from which all subsequent quotations here are drawn.
14. One exception is William Kloss, 'Zola and the Old Masters', in *Émile Zola and the Arts*, ed. by Jean-Max Guieu and Alison Hilton (Washington DC: Georgetown University Press, 1988), pp. 35–45, primarily concerned with the relation between a Titian portrait and the description of Irma Bécot in *L'Œuvre*, but adding that Zola's art criticism 'is of even less interest in the matter of old masters' (p. 36) and that, even in *Rome*, Zola reads the artistic past through a modernist perspective. Equally limited is Alain Mérot, 'Autour de *La Derelitta*: Zola et les maîtres anciens', in *Du romantisme à l'art déco: lectures croisées*, ed. by Rosella Froissart, Laurent Houssais and Jean-François Luneau (Rennes: Presses universitaires de Rennes, 2011), pp. 125–36; this is focused on the way in which Botticelli's painting functions as Pierre Froment's 'double' in *Rome*.

CHAPTER 1

The Novelist as Art Critic

'What Zola has in common with Balzac', Van Gogh wrote in 1883, 'is that he knows little about painting'.[1] Some aspects of the writer's incursion into the pictorial domain, he added, were 'interesting', but only 'in the same way as, for instance, a landscape by a figure painter: it isn't his genre'. Given Van Gogh's longstanding admiration for the novelist, such remarks are less surprising than they might seem at first sight. They were occasioned by a belated reading of *Mes haines* and *Mon Salon*, newly available in a second edition (1879) bringing these two sets of early essays together. The painter was in any case doubtless only familiar with a very small number of the texts published by Zola in the French press between his 1863 article devoted to Doré and those collected in *Le Naturalisme au Salon* (1880). Even more certain is that he had not seen Zola's extended studies of contemporary painting which appeared, in translation, in the Russian periodical *Viestnik Evropy* (*Le Messager de l'Europe*) between 1875 and 1880, let alone more than one hundred unsigned articles wholly or partly concerned with the visual arts which he had sent to *Le Sémaphore de Marseille* during the years 1871–77. But, above all, Van Gogh's comments are symptomatic of a response to Zola's writing on the visual arts often shared by contemporary painters, established critics of the period, and art historians. This chapter will explore the context of such reservations as well as evidence to be set against them.

Questions of Competence

Zola's unrelenting hostility to the celebrated painters of the day, initially voiced in his first full-length review of the annual Salon, in *L'Événement* in the spring of 1866, was reciprocated by both the artists concerned and their defenders, though usually in patronizing tones regretting the young critic's intemperance. Twenty years later, a number of the Impressionists were so dismayed by their apparently negative portrayal in *L'Œuvre* (1886) that a dinner party was held at which it was determined — so legend has it — that Zola's misunderstanding of their achievements made it imperative that, instead, only Joris-Karl Huysmans (1848–1907) should be entrusted to write on their behalf.[2] That is not to deny that Zola maintained lifelong friendships with some members of the group, such as Antoine Guillemet (1843–1918). But, in a more general sense, Degas's acerbity is telling: 'En un trait, nous en disons plus long qu'un littérateur en un volume'; and he argued that Zola had written *L'Œuvre* 'pour prouver la grande supériorité de l'homme de lettres sur l'artiste'.[3] That Degas claimed, four years after its appearance, not to have actually read the novel merely underlines the extent to which deeply held prejudices contaminated the cliché of the 'sister arts'. Merely by posing the question, Guillemet revealed doubts about its momentum, asking him in a letter (from Brittany, thus accounting for his metaphor) of 31 July 1867 whether 'la littérature et la peinture, ces deux belles sœurs naviguent-elles vent arrière?'[4] In an 1897 interview looking back on his art criticism, Zola seems to cling to the notion of *la fraternité des arts*: 'Les courants en littérature et en peinture me semblaient parallèles, — car ce sont des arts frères' (*EsA*, p. 702). But in *Les Romanciers naturalistes* (1880) he had written of a '*lutte avec les peintres*, pour montrer la souplesse et l'éclat de la phrase' (*OC*, XI, 75; my emphasis). There are numerous instances in *Les Rougon-Macquart* where a descriptive segment transposing a particular painting seems to demonstrate the 'superiority' of the verbal, in its capacity to accommodate narrative, modulations of point of view, and temporality.[5] And, without of course sharing Degas's malicious intent, *L'Œuvre* can indeed be read from within his perspective, but enlarged beyond a simplistic juxposition of its successful writer and failed painter. For the traditional solidarity of *ut pictura poesis* has been displaced, in persuasive recent research, by the recognition of a 'tendance fratricide'[6] informing the more or less explicit rivalry between literature and painting, most acutely registered at the permeable boundaries of competing cultural fields.

This latent antagonism, which has a long history,[7] leaving aside the perennial tensions between painters and their verbal commentators exemplified in Rembrandt's *Satire on Art Criticism* of 1644, is reinforced by contemporary critics denigrating Zola's writing on the visual arts on the grounds of his being unqualified to do so, much as Van Gogh would later suggest in his remarks about the novelist's generic transgression. It remains true, of course, that his art criticism is so substantial that it can be inserted in a lineage through Baudelaire and Gautier stretching all the way back to Diderot.[8] But it also coincides with the specific moment when commentators of every kind, journalists or men of letters by profession, take advantage of the proliferation of journals and periodicals, as well as newspaper columns and supplements, catering for the new-found importance of the Salon as both the must-see exhibition of the year and a major occasion in the Parisian social calendar (Fig. 1.1).[9]

In his own articles devoted to the annual Salon, Zola never fails to express his astonishment at its drawing power: in that of 1876, for example, he notes 104,775 admissions in its opening week alone and over 50,000 on its final day, a Sunday, when there was no entry fee. Over the previous decade, attendances during the six weeks of the exhibition had tripled. As well as the fashionable *Tout-Paris*, as he also regularly noted, the Salon drew to it collectors and dealers whose presence testified to a booming art market which was only one sign of the middle-class prosperity and speculative opportunities unleashed by the Second Empire's liberal economic policies. As Zola remembered, when preparing *L'Œuvre* some fifteen years after the régime's demise, 'les spéculations de l'empire arrive [*sic*]', while the rich 'n'aiment pas l'œuvre, ils ne voient que sa valeur' (Ms 10316, fol. 359). The

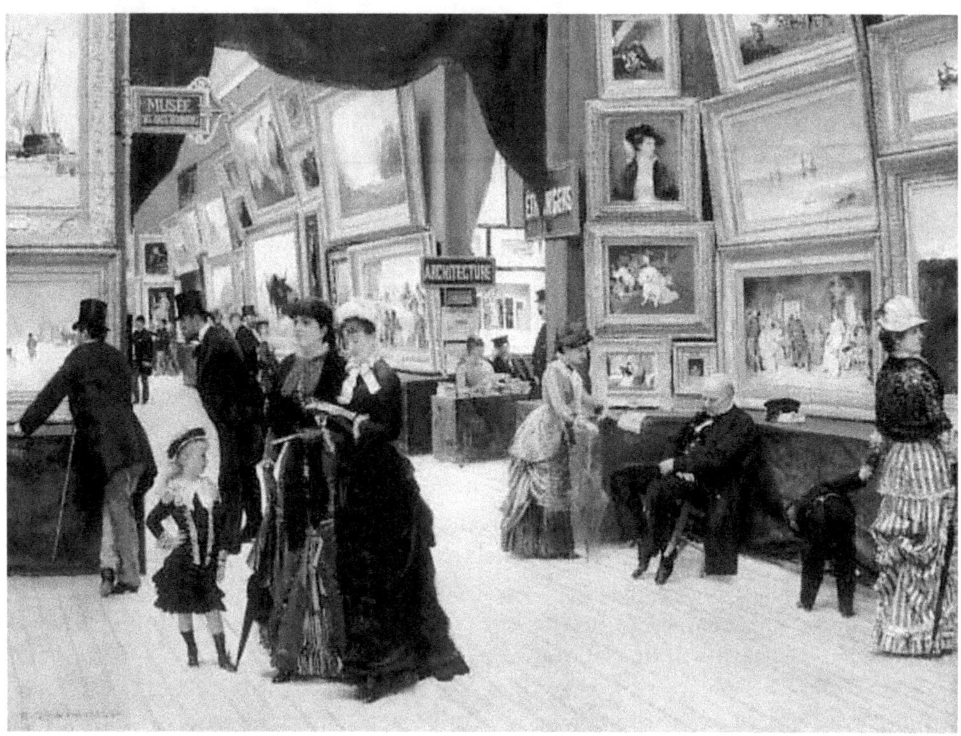

Fig. 1.1. Édouard Dantan, *Un coin du Salon, en 1880* (1880), oil on canvas, 97.2 × 130.2 cm. Private collection.

associated exponential expansion of art criticism could make or break reputations (what he calls, in the work notes for *L'Œuvre*, 'l'action du journal sur l'art') as well as influence the prices which artists could obtain, inflating the wealth of some while condemning others to penury. 'J'ai une telle peur de la presse', Renoir wrote to the art-dealer Paul Durand-Ruel (1831–1922) in 1885, that it was creatively paralyzing.[10] For the Salon was virtually the only showcase in which to display their work in the hope of securing buyers, commissions and awards. Zola's repeated use of the term 'bazaar' to describe it is neither gratuitously pejorative nor exclusive to him. Many of the painters he supports depend on this marketplace in order to survive. And it also explains why he encouraged those denied access to it to mount 'independent' exhibitions, as those of the Impressionists were known, outside the state-sanctioned institutional framework.

The scale of this symbiotic transformation of the Salon and art criticism devoted to it can be measured, substantiating Zola's 1875 remark that 'à aucune époque, les peintres n'ont été si nombreux en France', adding that he was only referring to those 'dont les toiles ont une valeur courante sur le marché' (*EsA*, pp. 268–69): in the period during which Diderot was penning his famous *Salons*, the Académie royale de peinture et de sculpture exhibited in the Louvre some 250 works by sixty or so painters; a century later, in the year in which Zola first reviews the Salon, held now (instead of in the Salon Carré) in the spacious galleries of the Palais de l'industrie, otherwise known as the Palais des Champs-Elysées (constructed to house the Universal Exhibition of 1855), visitors were faced with 3,398 works by 2,237 artists. In order to guide them, the vast majority of daily newspapers, from the beginning of the Second Empire onwards, included reviews of the exhibition: 134 in 1866, 84 in 1867, 66 in 1868 and no fewer than 262 in 1869.[11] And these statistics only cover the Parisian press. What is more, such surveys usually comprised a sequence of articles dealing in turn with the different categories of works on display: history painting, landscape, portraiture, drawing, sculpture, etc. They were signed by a variety of writers: on the one hand, art critics of such repute, like Gautier and Paul de Saint-Victor (1827–81), that they were invited to sit on the Salon jury of admission; on the other, members of an editorial team with the required expertise to write knowledgeably about art or even just those thought to have a modicum of good taste. As a consequence, art criticism as a genre was itself transformed,[12] for Zola was far from the only journalist to extend its remit beyond its traditional focus on factual elucidation and compositional technique. Liberated from such constraints, as well as from the genre's rhetorical conventions, such writing allowed itself a new discursive reach — from the major intellectual and cultural issues of the time to the political and ideological structures underlying them. These are fundamental to an understanding of Zola's art criticism, both in terms of the context in which it was produced and in terms of its elaboration.

It was wholly unsurprising that these developments were greeted with high-minded resistance from those whom Guillemet called 'les normaliens de la critique',[13] committed, so they claimed, to scholarly objectivity and quasi-scientific exactitude. One of the most eminent of them was Charles Blanc (1813–1882), whose name recurs throughout Zola's writing on the visual arts, either explicitly or by implication. For Blanc, who had authored a series of highly influential books prior to a brilliant career in arts administration,[14] articulated a more general concern in this respect. In the prestigious and conservative *Gazette des beaux-arts*, which he had founded in 1859, we find the most uncompromising rejection of the new direction of Salon reviewing. Without pointing a finger at Zola in particular, it was in the very year that the novelist first wrote about the exhibition that Blanc, in the introduction to his own review of the Salon of 1866, lamented the pretensions of those 'jeunes écrivains' trying their hand at art criticism and making up for their art-historical ignorance by expressing their personal and ephemeral opinions:

> Chacun s'est contenté d'avoir des impressions personnelles, et comme ces impressions changent constamment quand rien ne les guide, les lois de l'art sont devenues une pure affaire de caprice, une dépendance de la mode. Il en résulte [...] que la critique fait une besogne absurde et parfaitement inutile.[15]

This perspective is a constant theme of the period,[16] as well as in those histories of art criticism as a genre which single out Zola's lack of qualifications to engage in it.[17] In retrospect, even Diderot was not immune, reproached for the gall 'de parler peinture en littérateur qu'il est' and whose *Salons* had thereby 'jeté la critique d'art dans une voie dangereuse'.[18] Zola's art criticism stands in radical opposition to such mutually exclusive categories of 'littérateurs' and 'professional' art critics, in a context in which Théodore Duret (1838–1927) still felt it necessary in 1878, by way of a double negative, to differentiate between the former and those 'qui n'ont jamais passé dans le monde des arts pour des mauvais juges', namely Duranty, Philippe Burty (1830–1890), Jules Castagnary (1830–1888) and Ernest Chesneau (1833–1890). Zola himself was all too aware of the perceived distinction: 'je parle en poète', he wrote in *L'Événement* of 15 May 1866, 'et les peintres, je le sais, n'aiment pas cela'; he would make a conscious effort in his reviews, he promised, to 'parler métier' (*EsA*, p. 164). As a consequence of the proliferation of commentators on the visual arts, most of them less punctilious than a Flaubert readily admitting an insufficient technical expertise to be able to dabble in art criticism,[19] such a distinction hardly disguised the contemporary redefinition of the very notion of what François Fosca anachronistically terms 'les professionnels de la critique d'art'.[20] The latter notion remained pertinent enough, however, that Zola repeatedly found himself confronted by invidious doubts in respect of his competence. For when his first projected series of articles, devoted to the Salon of 1866, was brought to a premature end by the management of *L'Événement*, who were worried by its subscribers' objections to Zola's highly personal reviews, he was replaced by a critic with supposed art-historical credentials.[21] Even before Zola's valedictory 'Adieux d'un critique d'art' (20 May 1866, this very heading resisting his disqualification), his successor, in *L'Événement* of 16 May (casting a self-justifying eye on the newspaper's account of the Salon prior to his appointment), dismissed the novelist's expressed admiration for Manet as having been warped by 'des éloges sans discernement et sans compétence de quelques littérateurs fantaisistes'. And he sustained this perspective in more general terms, arguing that 'les littérateurs français sont des médiocres critiques d'art. La plupart d'entre eux n'ont fait, en aucune façon, l'apprentissage nécessaire à quiconque veut tenter d'apprécier, soit un tableau, soit une statue, dans un journal ou dans un livre'. Nor was it simply fellow critics espousing Blanc's dogmatic rejection of commentary not anchored by scholarship. As will be seen in the case of Manet's 1868 portrait of Zola, reservations of a more oblique kind could be expressed by the painters themselves. And it is not a little ironic that Zola himself virtually acknowledges the risks involved in writing about art without such a grounding. In his brief 1869 reference to Baudelaire's *Curiosités esthétiques*, for example, he admits that its author 'voit la peinture en littérateur' and that therefore 'ses critiques d'art ne resteront pas comme des jugements solides et justes' (*OC*, x, 777). Which begs the question of the durability of Zola's own assessment of the artists of his time.

Zola's Artistic Education

Zola's competence as an art critic was certainly acquired at one remove from the pedagogic training advocated and professed by his detractors, based as it was in a lifelong interest and immersion in the visual arts. His 1896 remark that, over time, 'je me suis un peu désintéressé de la peinture', referring to 'un silence d'un tiers de siècle bientôt' (*EsA*, p. 403) since he had last written on the subject in the French press, is so misleading that it can only be explained by the specific context of the nostalgic evocation of his militant campaigns on behalf of Manet and 'la nouvelle peinture' in the 1860s, overlaid by his revulsion at the directions taken by modern painting in the *fin de siècle*. In fact, Zola's 'apprenticeship', in the strict sense of the term, is one not only served in the company of the painters of his circle, especially before 1870 and thus at the beginning of his career as a writer, but through a familiarity prolonged and enriched over the following decades.

From his correspondence, one can track Zola's presence at the annual Salon, even in years when he was not reviewing the exhibition. In 1859, shortly after moving from Aix-en-Provence to the capital, he was already distinguishing himself from 'des personnes qui se piquent de se connaître en peinture et que je vois au Salon prendre des ânes pour des vaches'.[22] He immodestly alerted friends stuck in Aix to this new-found cultural expertise, as in a letter written immediately after visiting the Salon of 1861 in the company of Cézanne, in which Zola restrained himself from conveying his impressions of the exhibition on the grounds that they would be meaningless to the uninformed: 'Quoique j'aime les arts', he wrote to Jean-Baptistin Baille (1841–1918), 'je ne pourrais guère te parler de cette dernière manifestation de nos artistes. Tu ignores leurs noms, les différences d'école qui les séparent, leurs œuvres précédentes, et ainsi le moindre compte rendu serait sans intérêt pour toi.'[23] His frequent visits to the Louvre and the Musée du Luxembourg were an equally unbroken habit. During his stay in London in 1893, he would go to the National Gallery to see the Turners. The next year, in Rome, the historian of Italian art Adolpho Venturi gave him a guided tour of the Villa Borghese's collections. And in the Sistine Chapel, Zola would be subject to a visual experience with profound consequences, it will be argued in this book's concluding chapter, for any account of his art criticism.

It is also in his correspondence that we find evidence of the continually enlarged network of Zola's artistic contacts. In March 1877, for example, he dines at the home of the great collector Ernest Hoschedé (1837–1890), all too aware of the dire consequences for the Impressionists of the latter's financial troubles and imminent bankruptcy.[24] He collaborates with Raffaëlli on an edition of the artist's *Types de Paris* (1889) and received from the artist, as a token of thanks, a pencil and pastel drawing representing a scene in *L'Assommoir*.[25] Although by this point no longer 'surrounded' by painters, Zola had five years earlier written to Huysmans ('J'ai besoin d'art, dans mon trou'[26]) to secure a copy of his *Croquis parisiens*, illustrated by Raffaëlli and Jean-Louis Forain (1852–1931), added to a personal library which bears further witness to his sustained interest in the visual arts.[27] He also gets to know a new generation of art critics, among them Gustave Geffroy (1855–1926), who would in due course pay homage to their shared concerns by giving the title *Germinal* to an 1899 luxury album of lithographs by the most prominent artists of the period (Zola receiving the first copy of this limited edition). It was probably in 1885 that Zola initially made contact with Rodin; six years later, he commissioned him, on behalf of the Société des gens de lettres, to create a statue of Balzac, which he followed up with a forensic attention to detail hardly justified by the formalities of his presidential instigation of the project. His growing fame made it inevitable that other artists came into his orbit, notably those seeking to paint or sculpt his portrait: Ernest Boetzel (1830–1912); Armand Bloch (1866–1933); and, more significantly in 1901–1902, Félix Vallotton (1865–1925), who included Zola in his series of busts of seven writers. And in the public realm, he appears deliberately adjacent to Manet in a composition revealing the fractures in contemporary art criticism, namely Gervex's mural for the mairie of the 19th arrondissement, *Le Mariage civil* (1881),[28] as well as alongside former adversaries such as Meissonier (in *Un entr'acte à la Comédie française une soirée de première en 1885* (Salon of 1886) by Édouard Dantan (1848–1897)) or Gérôme (in *Le Déjeuner du Salon au café 'La Cascade'* (1889) by André Rixens (1846–1925)). In 1894, there is a record of an animated discussion *chez* Daudet during which Zola vigorously defended the recently exhibited 350 watercolours, under the collective heading of *Vie de Notre-Seigneur Jésus-Christ*, by James Tissot (1836–1902), never mentioned in his art criticism but about whom 'je déclare ce que je dois à Tissot, à ce qu'il a mis d'humanité et de vie dans la légende, d'avoir compris le Christ. Ne me parlez pas de technique: je vous répondrai par la vie'.[29] By contrast, an artist whose talents he signals belatedly, in 1896, was the Belgian painter, Alfred Stevens (1823–1906), 'qui a [...] conquis la maîtrise par sa sincérité si fine et si juste' (*EsA*, p. 407).[30] In January 1895, Zola had been one of the sponsors organizing the banquet to celebrate the seventieth birthday of Puvis de Chavannes (1824–1898), a painter to whom he first drew attention in an article of 1872 and to whose work he would return, with grudging admiration, on numerous occasions thereafter. He also lent his support to various other initiatives: in *L'Art libre, tribune des artistes*, the journal directed by his friend, the painter Numa Coste (1843–1907),[31] he republished in January 1881 his 1865 study of Courbet; ten years later, the 29 November 1890 issue of the short-lived *L'Art dans les deux mondes*, recently launched by Durand-Ruel, promised its readers a piece on Manet by Zola. And he is named as a member of its editorial committee alongside some of the most prominent art critics of the day: Roger Marx (1859–1913), Paul Mantz (1821–1895), Octave Mirbeau (1848–1917), Téodor de Wyzewa (1862–1917) and Geffroy. In 1897, in an interview published in the *Revue populaire des beaux-arts*, he rehearsed the retrospective account of the evolution of French painting which had appeared in *Le Figaro* the year before, while adding to it the personal dimension of the origins of *L'Œuvre* (*EsA*, pp. 700–04).

Such incidental evidence belying Zola's claim to have gradually lost interest in the visual arts can be supplemented by reference to the material context of his private life. His country house at Médan, purchased after the commercial success of *L'Assommoir* in 1876–77, has been aptly described as a work of art of his own: from its stained-glass windows to its interior decoration, delegated to master craftsmen such as Henri Baboneau (1845–1925) but overseen and altered by Zola at great expense, over nearly ten years, with what must have been a maddening focus on aesthetic minutiae, the end result is recognizable as an example of Art Nouveau.[32] It is also noteworthy that his collection of paintings was not limited to those given to him between 1868 and 1872, during the period he was in constant touch with the artists concerned. Many of those decorating his walls were acquired after 1880, often testifying to renewed interests, exemplified by the Japanese engravings of Gaston Latouche (1854–1913). As far back as 1868, contemplating a Degas picture, 'je songeais à ces gravures japonaises, si artistiques, dans la simplicité de leurs tons' (*EsA*, p. 201); this indicates Zola's familiarity with the vogue for *japonisme*, whether in relation to Manet's portrait of him, Monet's *Japonnerie* (1876) or in remarking that the Impressionists were 'accusés avec raison de s'être inspirés des gravures japonaises, si intéressantes, qui sont aujourd'hui entre toutes les mains' (*EsA*, p. 375).[33] And his own tastes continue to evolve, as may be seen in accounts of his domestic interiors by journalists granted access to Médan, with its panelled study resembling the so-called 'Peacock Room' in hues of gold and blue, created by James McNeill Whistler (1834–1903) for the London residence of a patron (whom he was simultaneously cuckolding!) in 1876–77.[34]

Nor should we forget, in substantiating Zola's abiding interest in pictorial representation, the intensity of his involvement in the process of illustrating his own texts. Unlike Flaubert,[35] not only does he encourage it, but he also takes a hands-on approach to the tasks contracted to painters and graphic artists by his publishers. He is bowled over ('stupéfait'), for example, by the frontispiece and thirty engravings produced by Edmond Rudaux (1840–1898) for the 1886 illustrated edition of his *Nouveaux Contes à Ninon*. In his letter of November 1885 to Léon Conquet (1848–1898), which would serve as a preface to the edition, he confided to this publisher known for his luxury publications that he was 'très sensible aux belles choses' and congratulated him on having made 'de la littérature un musée'.[36] For the Marpon-Flammarion edition of *L'Assommoir* (1878), twenty-two artists (including André Gill (1840–1885), Clairin, Butin, Renoir,[37] Gervex and Norbert Gœneutte (1854–1894), to name only those more or less remembered by posterity) produced no fewer than seventy full-page engravings. In *Le Petit Journal* of 29 April 1878, a sympathetic journalist enthused that Zola's text had thereby been transformed into an artistic manifesto. For the Cadart edition of the same novel a year later, Latouche provided fifteen such images. Clairin also contributed to the illustrated edition of *Nana* (1882). In the case of that of *Germinal*, Zola had mixed views: 'la plupart des illustrations sont très bien, bien que le sujet des gravures ne me paraisse pas toujours heureusement choisi.'[38] In a letter of 1888, Pierre-Georges Jeanniot (1848–1934) sought from Zola the reassurance that he was not too disappointed by his illustrations for the serialized text of *Le Rêve*, explaining that 'beaucoup sont éreintées à la gravure'. This painter, who was also one of the best-known book illustrators of the period, had previously collaborated with Zola on the illustrated edition of his *Contes à Ninon* (1883), as he would do again for *La Débâcle* (1893) and *La Curée* (1894), producing for the latter some seventy drawings. For that of *La Terre* (1897), Henri-Gabriel Ibels (1867–1936) created eighteen lithographs, one of the originals of which (*Triptique: La Grande; Le Père Fouan et Rose; Bécu*) Zola felt obliged to buy from him for 300 francs, in response to the artist's pleading in a moment of acute financial need.

The most systematic renewed involvement in painting during these years of 'silence' was occasioned by the preparation of *L'Œuvre* in 1885–86, with Zola finding himself besieged by journalists seeking to identify the real-life models for the novel's characters. To elaborate a fictional version of the artistic world of the 1860s, he inevitably had recourse to both personal memories and the historical context he had lived through. His work notes are enriched not only by this autobiographical material but also by a 'refresher course' in art history, institutional structures and the very practice of painting. He thus visited the Salon of 1885 with notebook in hand, documenting aspects of its organization and gallery spaces which he had barely registered before. And the substantial section of the preparatory dossier recording his conversations with Guillemet precisely accommodates a range of relevant subjects from the determining influence of art dealers and critics to the prosaic technicalities of a painter's craft: brushes and palette knives, pigments, paint tubes, outdoor easels, stretching a canvas, framing, etc. Already, in 1867–68, he had referred to the 'préparatifs minutieux', prior to 'le travail des pinceaux' (*OC*, I, 544) of the fictional painter of *Thérèse Raquin*. The sheer level of detail in notes almost fifteen years later suggests, on the novelist's part, an interest inadequately accounted for merely by the imperatives of authenticity.

It remains true that, however much that interest would be sustained over the decades, the most formative phase of Zola's 'apprenticeship' was the period before 1870, when he was indeed 'surrounded' by painters. Cézanne's role in this is so fundamental that it needs to be inserted in the chapter of this book entirely devoted to Zola's relationship with him. For it was through Cézanne that Zola got to know personally many of the young painters about whom he would write. He spent time with them, notably Monet, at the riverside hamlet of Bennecourt, watching them working *en plein air*.[39] He also joined them at Pontoise, where Pissarro lived on and off between 1866 and January 1869. And it was during this same period that Zola started to organize the Sunday evening gatherings of writers and painters transposed in *L'Œuvre*, 'tous révolutionnaires, animés de la même passion de l'art' (*RM*, IV, 52). That spirit had been catalyzed by the mounting of the Salon des Refusés in 1863, which Zola himself had visited and which would also be evoked in *L'Œuvre*, its impact, both personal and cultural, suggestively alluded to in the preparatory notes for the novel (Ms 10316): 'le salon des refusés. Grandes discussions avec moi' (fol. 2); 'L'école encore sourde n'éclate qu'après le Salon des Refusés' (fol. 37). Unsurprisingly, this turning point in the history of French art functions as a key reference point in much of Zola's art criticism in the years ahead. And he would often lend his support to attempts to repeat what had originally been simply a politically motivated experiment. But it had immediate consequences too: on the one hand, Napoleon III's apparently liberalizing decision to mount such an exhibition, allowing the general public to judge for themselves the works rejected by the Salon jury (in the hope, of course, that they would concur with its decisions), had the paradoxical effect of creating a community of artists newly energized in their determination to dismantle the institutional structures constraining their originality; and, on the other, the inclusion there of Manet's *Déjeuner sur l'herbe*, followed by the comparable hostility provoked by his *Olympia* at the Salon of 1865, resulted in his being perceived as the leader of a 'school' of a new generation of painters, united in fact only by their collective opposition to the traditional criteria against which their work was officially found wanting.

Zola's understanding of these artistic issues was undoubtedly shaped by his presence at the meetings, from January 1866 onwards, of Manet and his friends at the Café Guérbois, at no. 11, Grande-Rue des Batignolles, in the very heart of the quarter where the majority of them lived and worked. Initially informal and intermittent, these rapidly became a regular and ritualized Friday evening occasion. In a side room, described by a contemporary as having 'l'aspect d'une crypte', where noisy companionship did not preclude serious aesthetic debates, there would assemble an astonishing range of artists and critics, ever-expanding over time. These included Bazille, Fantin-Latour, Guillemet, Béraud, Marcellin Desboutin (1823–1902) and Alphonse Legros (1837–1911), as well as those who would figure at the first Impressionist exhibition in 1874: Astruc, Édouard Béliard (1832–1912), Monet, Degas, Renoir, Pissarro, Armand Guillaumin (1841–1927) and Félix Bracquemond (1833–1914). It was hardly a coincidence that it should be mounted in the studio, on the Boulevard des Capucines, recently vacated by Nadar (as Félix Tournachon (1820–1910)) was known). For the photographer was also part of this brilliant gathering of artists. Whistler and Stevens sometimes joined them, as did Antonin Proust (1832–1905), in due course one of Manet's most influential commentators as well as a future Minister of Fine Arts in Gambetta's cabinet. Other Manet champions there included Hippolyte Babou (1823–1878), the critic sharing Astruc's distinction of being one of the very first to defend the painter's achievement, in an article in the *Revue libérale* of June 1867 entitled 'Les Dissidents de l'Exposition: M. Édouard Manet'. Manet himself, with his discursive vigour, invariably dominated proceedings, as Zola remembered in preparing *L'Œuvre* in the notes for which Claude Lantier assumes the role of 'chef de la bande' (fols 44, 53 and 111). But the art critic Armand Silvestre (1837–1901) recalled that Zola also occupied a special place in the midst of heated discussions: 'Il parlait toujours, avec le calme des gens sûrs d'eux-mêmes [...] formulant une pensée toujours claire dans une forme pittoresque sans être désordonnément imagée.'[40] It was at the same moment that Zola put his own *soirées* on a more systematic footing, now on a Thursday,[41] inviting Cézanne and other *aixois* friends as well as some of the habitués of the Café Guerbois, becoming in the process what has been called the 'fédérateur' of the newly established 'école des Batignolles'.[42] His articles in *L'Événement* in 1866 served to strengthen his links with its members, as is evident from two paintings of that year: the witty expression of solidarity in Cézanne's portrait of his father (Fig. 1.2) reading this newspaper, its title itself punningly making of his friend's articles in it an 'event', with Zola's contrary perspective, upending conventional criteria, reflected in that title appearing upside-down; and Renoir's *Cabaret de la mère Antony*, in which it is spread by Sisley across a table.

At one level, as was suggested at the very beginning of this book, Fantin-Latour's *Un atelier aux Batignolles* confirms the unique relationship with the pictorial avant-garde which Zola enjoyed during this crucial period of his own development as a writer, providing him with an 'education' of a kind sufficient to invalidate

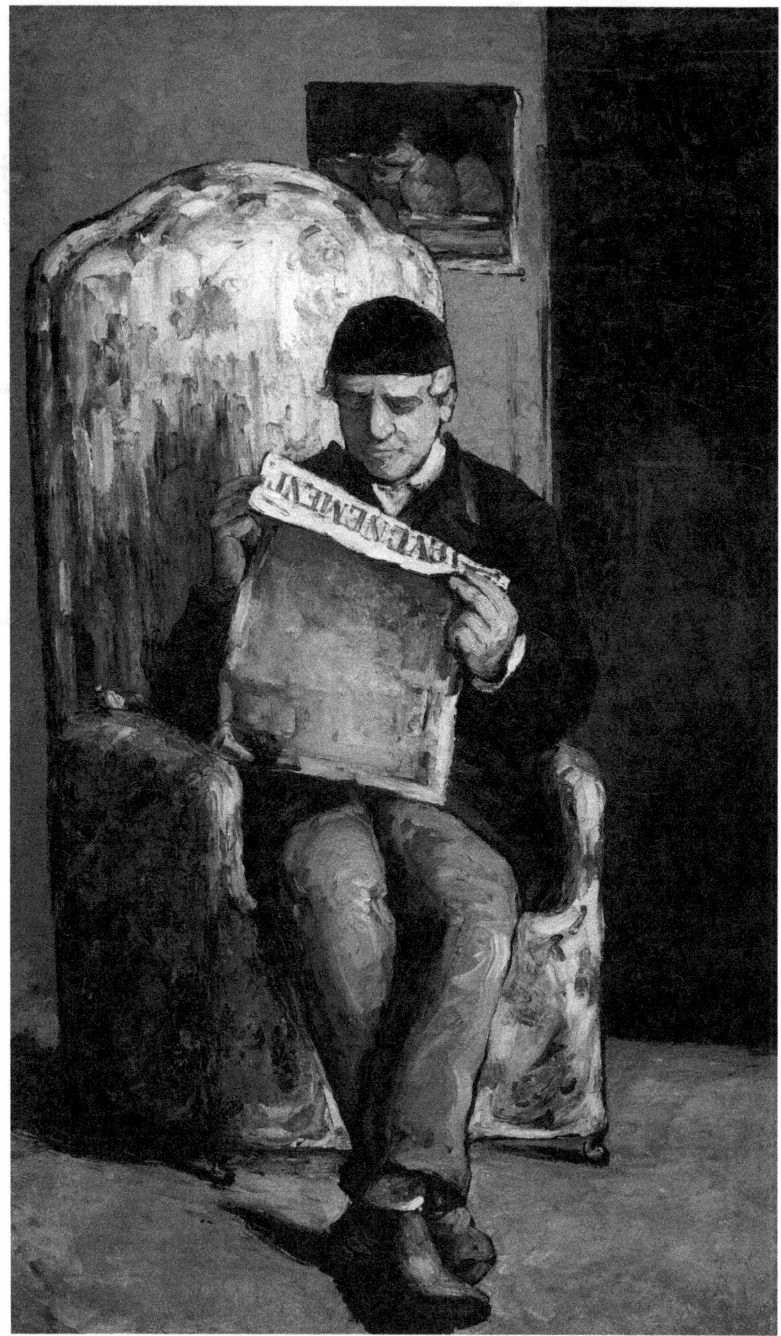

Fig. 1.2. Paul Cézanne, *Portrait de Louis-Auguste Cézanne, père de l'artiste, lisant 'L'Événement'* (1866), oil on canvas, 198.5 × 119.3 cm. National Gallery of Art, Washington D.C. Collection of Mr and Mrs Paul Mellon.

charges that he lacked the 'competence' to engage in art criticism. Nor is it beside the point to stress that alongside his painter friends Zola got to know some of the most influential art critics of the time. Their commentary is discernible in his own texts, either in shared perspectives or in an antithetical positioning against which to elaborate his own. Among those cited by Duret in 1878 as being acceptable in artistic circles, both Burty and Duranty were very much present at the Café Guerbois. To the latter, Zola wrote that 'on me parle beaucoup de votre *Salon*, dont on dit grand bien'.[43] As will be seen in due course, Duranty's *La Nouvelle Peinture* (1876) is a key text in Zola's understanding of, and ultimately disenchantment with, Impressionism. But it was Duret himself who was a major influence on Zola's thinking about painting. For while it may have been Duranty who first introduced him to Manet, Duret's own relationship with the latter was much closer, grounded in the good fortune of having met the painter during his visit to Spain in 1865. Duret would be the essential point of contact between the novelist and Manet, often arranging to meet Zola at the painter's studio.[44] That triangular set of links would endure even beyond Manet's death in 1883: Duret would be at Zola's side as one of the pallbearers at his funeral; and he would revise, correcting the occasional error in, the draft of Zola's preface to the catalogue of the 1884 retrospective of his work. They shared political as well as aesthetic views, Duret having given Zola access to the columns of *La Tribune*, the opposition newspaper he had founded in 1868. In his review of the Salon of 1870, Duret went out of his way to focus on Zola's presence in Fantin-Latour's collective portrait. It was not until after this that Duret really concentrated on art criticism. By the time of his death in 1927, however, he had established such a reputation in the field that obituary notices referred to him as 'le doyen de la critique d'art'.[45] For his early book, *Les Peintres français en 1867* (1867) was only the first of a series of studies of 'la nouvelle peinture', however limited at this stage to citing Manet as its principal exponent but alluding in its preface to Zola's insights in his writing on the painter in 1866–67. There is even a sense in which such influences were reciprocal: in a letter of 20 May 1868, Zola asked Duret what he had thought of his article of the day before, enthusing about Pissarro, an artist whom the critic had not even mentioned in his 1867 study, but on behalf of whom he would subsequently make amends, often and at length. The correspondence between Zola and Duret confirms the fact that the novelist did not enjoy such a stimulating relationship with any other contemporary critic.

But it would be a mistake to discount others, even those of a contrary persuasion. Confrontations with inimical views allowed Zola to define his own critical stance, writing in his 'Adieux d'un critique d'art' that one regret of his being sidelined was that a complete campaign would have 'plu à aiguiser mes armes pour les rendre plus tranchantes' (*EsA*, p. 167). Even a figure as eminent as Sainte-Beuve served such a purpose: while acknowledging his status as 'un des princes de la critique contemporaine' (*OC*, x, 631), Zola found his lauding of the history painter Horace Vernet (1789–1863) completely unacceptable: 'le peintre lui a echappé'. As a reader of *Le Figaro*, he was well aware of the art criticism of Albert Wolff (1833–1891) — so influential that, as Guillemet reminded him during the preparation of *L'Œuvre*, some painters lived in fear of his reviews. As a contributor to the same newspaper,

Zola was more circumspect than Wolff's implacable hostility to Manet might have warranted: in 1880, he excused himself from the necessity of a detailed account of that year's Salon on the grounds that 'mon collaborateur Albert Wolff s'en est occupé, avec sa grande compétence et son esprit habituel' (*EsA*, p. 396). Others equally disparaging of Manet were accorded less respect: the preferences articulated in the review of the 1866 Salon by Edmond About (1828–1885) are the target of Zola's disdain; as for Gautier, 'il parla peinture [...] avec une indifférence parfaite et une complaisance exemplaire' (*OC*, x, 230), like Paul de Saint-Victor, 'en appellant à leur aide tous les adjectifs éblouissants du dictionnaire' (*OC*, x, 722). At this same moment, in 1866–67, Zola was actively contemplating producing a study entitled *L'Œuvre d'art devant la critique*, and it is not hard to gauge what would have been the thrust of this aborted project.[46]

On the other hand, Zola's texts are sometimes indebted, and in one instance explicitly, to art critics in *Le Rappel*, such as Camille Pelletan (1846–1915) and Judith Gautier (1845–1917). In his review of the Salon of 1876, expressing his bewilderment in trying to fathom the meaning of Moreau's work, Zola was reduced to citing verbatim the entire paragraph which Gautier's daughter, 'un critique enthousiaste', had devoted, in *Le Rappel* of 6 May, to an interpretation of the painter's *Salomé*: 'car, franchement, je m'avoue incapable d'en écrire une semblable' (*EsA*, p. 329). In 1864, reading Castagnary's articles in *La Revue de Paris* devoted to that year's exhibition, he had carefully digested the views of the most authoritative of art critics, and one moreover who had introduced the term *naturalisme* in his reviews of the Salon in the period 1863–67. Zola did not know him personally and would never admit the conjunction, in their critical positioning, of certain aesthetic principles and values, 'sans que', as François-Marie Mourad has put it, 'l'auteur de *Mon Salon* ait pris la peine de signaler sa dette'.[47] This debt includes the emphasis on imaginative liberation from teaching and tradition; the recognition of modern landscape's subversion of conventional pictorial hierarchies allied to the necessity of effecting an analogous 'revolution' in portraiture; and the primacy of representing the real world at the expense of idealized conceptions of it. More problematic is Zola's awareness of a predecessor of Baudelaire's stature, an ambivalence reinforced by his knowledge of his friendship with Manet and that 'une vive sympathie a rapproché le poète et le peintre' (*EsA*, p. 479), but concluding nevertheless, in the same vein as his remarks about his *Curiosités esthétiques*, that Baudelaire, 'sans avoir la bienveillance de Théophile Gautier [...] est aussi singulièrement doux pour les artistes qu'il ne pouvait aimer'. As a self-declared 'réfractaire en art', as he provocatively asserted in 1868 (*OC*, x, 722), Zola's writing on painting is radically at odds with such benign indulgence, reflected in the unambiguous title of his collected essays: *Mes haines*. And not the least of his self-interested concerns was to stake out, in a burgeoning field, the originality of his own art criticism.

'Au contact des œuvres et des hommes', as Antoinette Ehrard has underlined, 'c'est une formation qui n'a rien de livresque.'[48] But she does point out that between 1863 and 1869 Zola put together some 650 book reviews, of which almost four dozen were devoted to treatises on aesthetics, scholarly studies by art historians, and illustrated editions. A number of these are no more than a few lines in length, advertising recent publications — integral to Zola's job as head of the publicity department at Hachette between December 1863 and 31 January 1866. That role put him in touch with writers who enjoyed a public profile, as well as having the additional benefit of enriching his personal library.[49] But his subsequent regular column in *L'Événement*, 'Livres d'aujourd'hui et de demain', from 1 February onwards, the day after he had left the publishing house, required a less superficial gloss, as did his reviews in other newspapers and journals to which he was starting to contribute. It is doubtful, to say the least, that he read the volumes involved from cover to cover. But, and without dissenting from the view that Zola's was not a 'bookish' education in the history of art, it is arguable that these reviews forced him to assimilate the broad outlines of related subjects. His reading of, or browsing through, Ferdinand de Lanoye's *Ramsès-le-Grand ou l'Égypte il y a mille trois cents ans* (1865) is a pertinent example: approaching it with his disingenuous 'curiosité d'homme ignorant', he learned enough, overlaid by his own critical perspectives, to include it in *Mes haines* the following year (*OC*, x, 93–98), cross-referencing its hypothesis of cultural determinism ('ce fut le peuple entier qui signa les œuvres') with insights in his essay on Pierre-Joseph Proudhon (1809–1865), also originally published in *Le Siècle*. There is a gentle irony at the expense of G. Clerk's *L'Imagination et les beaux-arts* (1869), with its 'excellents conseils aux artistes qui veulent toucher et émouvoir le public' (*OC*, x, 817). But in 1866, coinciding with Zola's growing reputation in the eyes of the painters of his social circle, his review of the *Tableau historique des beaux-arts*, compiled by Louis and René Ménard, damns without faint praise 'un ouvrage essentiellement académique, écrit selon les formules officielles', representing the very worst of 'l'art patenté, les opinions admises et réglées par le sacré collège de nos artistes'. For as he wrote in another review of the same book three days later: 'J'ai, en art, des croyances personnelles diamétralement opposées à celle des auteurs' (*OC*, x, 666). In the case of monographs on a single artist, Zola's developing critical criteria are equally manifest: for the drawings of Grandville (1803–1847), his appreciation is less than lukewarm ('une admiration assez froide'), the artist having in his view 'paru se servir d'une aiguille épointée [...] aux dépens de la vigueur et de la puissance' (*OC*, x, 691–92); the engravings of Hector Giacomelli (1822–1904), by contrast, are characterized by 'des finesses exquises' (*OC*, x, p. 705). Such a counterpoint, between sterility and imaginative dexterity, mere technical skill and sensory impact, feeds in directly to Zola's art criticism, both at the time and in the years ahead. And, it will be argued in the final chapter of this book, the familiarity with the Old Masters afforded by this reviewing activity would leave its distant mark in unsuspected ways.

The various dimensions of Zola's formative experience of the visual arts, from the personal to the professional, may not add up to the kind of 'competence' or expertise the absence of which has been so often lamented, both during and after his lifetime. But it is difficult to dispute the oft-made claim that, with the possible exception of Baudelaire, no other nineteenth-century writer enjoyed such a close relationship with the art of his time. Zola himself was in no doubt, of course, that he was uniquely qualified to write about it. This is implicit in one of the essays he wrote about Flaubert, soon after his death in 1880, in which the sole reservation concerns his single-minded focus on literature, 'à ce point qu'il en était injuste pour les autres arts, la peinture et la musique par exemple, qu'il appelait avec dédain les "arts inférieurs"'. And Zola extends this differentiation from his own wide-ranging tastes and interests by adding that 'en peinture, il n'avait pas la moindre idée critique; il ne parlait jamais tableaux, il avouait son ignorance' (*OC*, xi, 152). It is almost beside the point, notwithstanding a parenthetical nod to Flaubert's fascination with the work of Moreau, that Zola's sweeping generalization is patently false.[50] For it not only legitimizes the practice of art criticism in tandem with his career as a novelist; it also hints at the indissociable relation between them, both aesthetic and strategic. The imperatives dictated by the patterns of his career go some way towards explaining the rationale of his somewhat misleading 1896 remark that he had more or less distanced himself from contemporary painting. In 1878, Zola had already admitted that 'autrefois, ç'a été la peinture qui m'a servi de champ de manœuvres. Aujourd'hui, j'ai choisi le théâtre, parce qu'il est plus près' (*OC*, xi, 383). No assessment of his art criticism can be separated from that military metaphor and its polemical implications.

Writing on the Visual Arts: Formats, Polemical Strategies and Imaginative Elaboration

To that strategic end, Zola's writing on the visual arts exploits a panoply of journalistic formats dictated by circumstance and opportunity. 'Je ne suis pas ici critique d'art', Zola stressed in *Le Sémaphore de Marseille* of 4 May 1875, 'mais simplement chroniqueur' (*EsA*, p. 261). He would often repeat this distinction between the work of a contracted Salon reviewer and a correspondent's task of simply providing factual information for a paper's readers without evaluating the works on display at a particular exhibition. 'Je sais', he had written in 1865, 'que le mot chronique ne signifie autre chose que l'exposé des faits au fur et à mesure qu'ils se présentent' (*OC*, xi, 45). In practice, however, Zola generally fails to respect such constraints, admitting in this same piece that he was, in his own words, 'un chroniqueur indiscipliné', with an innate sympathy for a decidedly less neutral 'chroniqueur casseur de vitres'. In perusing his texts within this capacious genre ('Causerie', 'Lettres parisiennes', 'Lettres de Paris', etc.), one is left, indeed, with the impression that Zola was temperamentally incapable of referencing works of art without inserting his own opinion, judging them against his long-held criteria. While some pieces are conceived as free-standing essays, a number of his 'chroniques' have to be read as marginal additions to, or previews of, his commentary on the Salon in question. Such complementarity also applies to the Salon reviews themselves: his 1866 article on Manet, for example, forms the basis of his long study of the painter submitted for the January issue of *La Revue du XIXe siècle* the following year; and the one within his *Salon* of 1868 constitutes an epilogue to the revised version of that study published in May 1867. Another example of this kind of textual superimposition is his 'Lettre parisienne' in praise of Jongkind, published in *La Cloche* of 24 January 1872, amplifying his passing remarks in his 'Les Paysagistes' which had appeared in *L'Événement illustré* four years earlier.

Writing in several newspapers simultaneously, Zola clearly found it opportune to re-use such texts, either wholly or in part, but inflected by the specificity of their reading public.

More radical than the freedom from convention Zola allowed himself in penning his 'chroniques' is the unorthodox structure of his Salon reviews themselves. Journalists normally adhered to an established template, either proceeding by gallery, genre or the alphabetical sequence of the exhibition catalogue, in order to provide their readers with an exhaustive account of the works on display. Zola's *Salon* of 1866 does none of these things. As he admitted in 1876, 'je décrivais des expositions en ne citant que quelques peintres, ceux qui à mon avis donnaient le ton à l'époque' (*EsA*, p. 312). Consistent with the assertive subjectivity of the title of *Mon Salon*, his art criticism introduces a set of categories unmistakeably organized according to his own preferences and dislikes: 'Les Chutes' (15 May 1866); 'Quelques bonnes toiles' (9 June 1868). Far more egregious, as his fellow critics recognized, was to devote one of his 1866 articles to Manet, who did not even figure at the exhibition under review, his submissions having been rejected by the Salon jury. Zola would repeat this infraction in 1876 when once again the painter failed to gain admission. The oppositional tone had been evident from the very beginning of his writing on the visual arts: in his 'Confidences d'une curieuse', a set of anecdotal remarks prompted by preparations for the Salon of 1865, the imagined confrontation of two antithetical conceptions of artistic practice (the 'frères ennemis, un néo-classique et un réaliste') is marked by a caricatural violence ('cris, injures, discussions esthétiques à péroraison de coups de poing' (*EsA*, p. 120)). With altogether greater sobriety, Zola's account of the Salon of 1866 opens with one of the most disquieting of all prefaces to a sequence of reviews, in evoking the suicide of a painter rumoured to be the despairing victim of the admission jury's narrow-mindedness; and this is followed, the next week, by an *ad hominem* diatribe subjecting the majority of its members to undisguised contempt. It was little wonder that some responded publicly to Zola's impugning of their integrity, with one securing an apology for the defamatory ridiculing of their qualification to judge the works submitted to the Salon. Between his explanation of the title of *Mes haines* and the inscribed copy of *L'Assommoir* Zola would later send to Flaubert, 'en haine du goût', there is a continuity which his reaction to Duret's second article on the Salon of 1870 reinforces; it seemed, he suggested, echoing what he had said about Baudelaire's art criticism, 'un peu doux': 'Dire du bien de ceux qu'on aime n'est point assez; il faut dire du mal de ceux qu'on hait.'[51] This guiding principle, particularly in evidence in Zola's early writing on the visual arts, assured the novelist too of a satisfyingly rapid notoriety.

But this also carried risks. If his 'Adieux d'un critique d'art', bringing to a close his seven articles devoted to the Salon of 1866, allowed him a final pretext to castigate his adversaries, the fact that Zola had not been able to publish what he had over-optimistically planned (a sequence of at least sixteen texts) also had prosaic consequences. In an effort to find alternative means of earning a living, he admitted to Valabrègue in April 1867 that, having given up on the hope of finding a newspaper which, despite his notoriety, might accept his offer to write about that year's Salon, it remained possible 'que je lance quelque brochure sur mes amis peintres'.[52] That project ultimately came to nothing. But it was doubtless inspired by the imminent publication of his study of Manet, in which he alluded to 'le livre que je me propose d'écrire sur mes croyances artistiques' (*EsA*, p. 477), implicitly on a larger scale than the mere 'brochure' serving its purpose as an 'acte de présence', so Zola claimed in the study's preface, 'en attendant que je puisse faire un nouveau *Salon*' (*EsA*, p. 468). His frustration in this respect was not for want of trying. This included personally asking one of the editorial directors of *La Situation*, a recently founded paper about to bring out its first issue, whether there might be a slot for 'quelqu'un pour parler des deux expositions de peinture',[53] in other words both the Salon of 1867 and the art section of that year's Universal Exhibition mounted on the Champ-de-Mars. In the end, it was only in a single article devoted to the latter that his direct approach was rewarded. But in this, dated 1 July 1867, Zola was true to form. For rather than reviewing the exhibition as a whole, he limited himself, as mentioned in my Introduction, to demolishing the reputations of the four French artists hyperbolically celebrated at it.

In 1868 he tried again, outlining to Duret how he envisaged his responsibilities on the staff of *La Tribune*: 'Je serai chargé de tenir les lecteurs au courant du movement artistique dans le sens large de cette expression [...]: les arts, les expositions particulières et le Salon annuel seront aussi de mon domaine.'[54] Although there are in fact a number of his articles devoted to the fine arts in *La Tribune*, its editors were unwilling to give Zola such scope. Finally, however, his hopes of renewing his career as a Salon critic were rewarded: the director of *L'Événement illustré* was sympathetic to his proposal, almost certainly because Manet's submissions to the Salon of 1868, including his portrait of the novelist, had been accepted. This time, at least, Zola's account had a somewhat more conventional structure, beginning with a description of the formal opening of the exhibition and accommodating different genres — such as landscape and sculpture. But to no avail. Unable to resist expressing an admiration for his favourite painters, effectively offset by the scathing disparagement of most of the others, Zola was once again relieved of his commission, as he had been in the case of *L'Événement* in 1866. Taking over his column, a certain Paul Delmas deplored Zola's 'point de vue personnel' and promised to repair both the lacunae in his reviews and what he considered to be his predecessor's reckless damage to artists as 'brilliant' as Cabanel and Bouguereau. So that was that. And never again, in the years ahead, or at least not in France, would Zola be given the opportunity to put together a complete set of reviews of the annual Salon.[55]

Prior to being liberated from material concerns by the commercial success of *L'Assommoir*, Zola found two other platforms (neither within Van Gogh's purview, as mentioned at the beginning of this chapter) from which to comment on the visual arts: *Le Messager de l'Europe*, the Saint-Petersburg journal with liberal tendencies and a wide circulation; and *Le Sémaphore de Marseille*. In the case of the former, it was through Turgenev's good offices that Zola initially made contact with its director, as a result of which he published some sixty texts in translation between 1875 and 1880, subsequently re-translated into French for modern editions of his work. Five of these constitute his most extended essays on contemporary art, rehearsing and developing critical perspectives characteristic of his earlier writing. Zola's articles in *Le Sémaphore de Marseille*, published between 1871 and 1877, are of a different kind. A number are free-standing reviews, such as the brief account of the Salon of 1874 and a longer piece devoted to the Impressionists' inaugural exhibition. Most of his commentaries on the visual arts in this newspaper are appended to synoptic coverage, for a provincial readership, of Parisian events of note — whether literary, social or political. As he self-deprecatingly admitted to Flaubert, such a journalistic burden 'm'aide à faire bouillir ma marmite. C'est une de mes petites hontes cachées':[56] out of sight, because his pieces were published anonymously;[57] and 'shameful' to the extent that they often recycle (sometimes word for word) information lifted mainly from the daily digest put together by Ernest d'Hervilly (1839–1911) in *Le Rappel*.[58] That second-hand information, however, is seldom presented without Zola inserting his own point of view.

While Zola's texts in these two papers are characteristically combative, they are less polemical, bracketing out retorts and counter-arguments which would have been more or less incomprehensible for foreign or provincial readers far from the discursive threads of Parisian political and cultural debates.[59] The latter are inseparable from each other, particularly in the intensifying climate of the Second Empire's final years. In the coded language of oppositional journalism, 'sincerity' and 'personal' are implicitly at odds with 'officially approved'; 'original' is synonymous with not sanctioned by the state; 'purely artistic' or 'art for art's sake' had tried the patience of the censors during the whole of the period, since 1852, during which they had been implementing draconian constraints on freedom of expression. Zola himself had disingenuous recourse to the 'art for art's sake' argument in defending Manet's *Exécution de l'Empereur Maximilien* in 1869.[60] Nobody familiar with Zola's more explicit political journalism at this time imagined that the premature end of his review of the Salon of 1866 was a result of the offense to the purely artistic sensibilities of his readers. By the end of that year, *L'Événement* had been shut down. The arbiters of public taste challenged by Zola, including critics repeatedly likened to 'sergents de ville' (*EsA*, pp. 469–70, p. 497),[61] are merely the policing representatives of authoritarian power. Nor was this exclusive to the régime of Napoleon III. That, even as late as 1881, in the anti-republican columns of *La Gazette de France*, Manet is described as 'le Zola de la peinture', reinforces Pierre Vaisse's thesis that the language and tenor of art criticism during the Third Republic are no less ideologically resonant: the institutional structures of the Salon are subject to democratic campaigns for expanded suffrage 'comme si le jury avait été une Chambre de deputés et les artistes les citoyens d'une République des arts'.[62] This is the discourse which animates Zola's own art criticism, and its politicization is by no means limited to attacks on the machinations or membership of a Salon admissions jury more identifiably self-interested than can be inferred from Gervex's version of its boisterous deliberations (Fig. 1.3). For its other recurrent themes are as devastatingly elaborated: the unacceptable privileges of artists exempt from having to submit their work to the jury by virtue of having been awarded a medal at a previous exhibition; opposition to such a system of official rewards, including

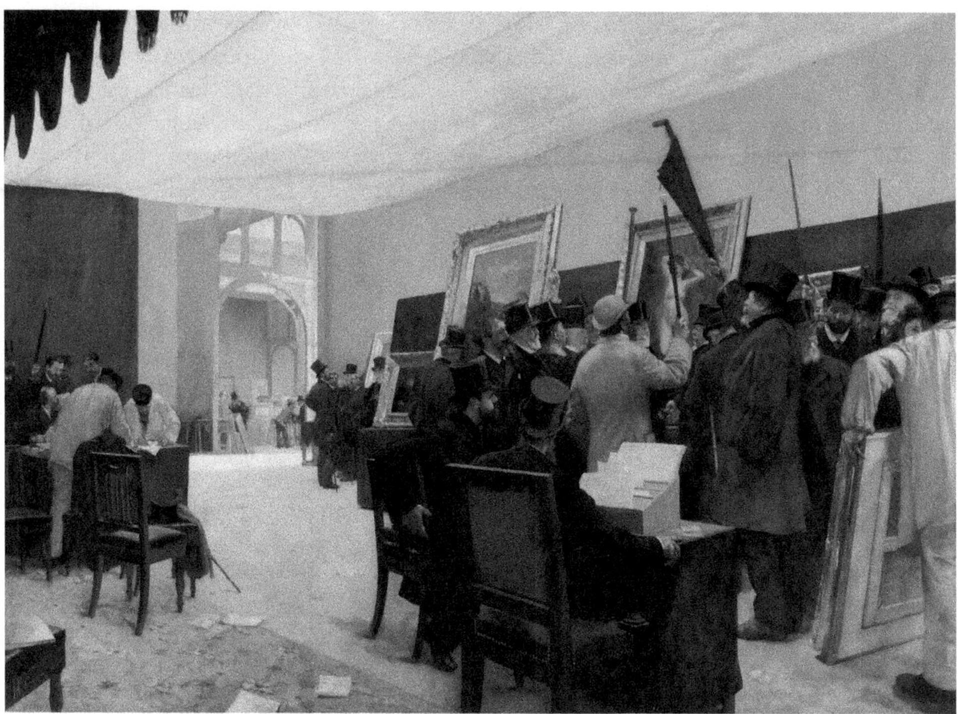

Fig. 1.3. Henri Gervex, *Une séance du jury de peinture* (1885), oil on canvas, 299 × 419 cm. Musée d'Orsay, Paris.

State purchases and commissions; the anachronism of the Prix de Rome; the administrative 'dictatorship' of the Ministère des Beaux-Arts. The consistent thrust of Zola's writing on the visual arts, whether overt or oblique, is the need for radical change. And his championing of particular painters has to be seen in the light of that imperative.

What is distinctive about his art criticism are some of the qualities we associate with Zola the novelist. Lexical analysis of it confirms the extent to which this writing draws from a fund of expressions equally discernible in his critical studies of various *literary* forms.[63] More germane is his use of the pictorial term *ébauche* to head the preliminary outline, or sketch indeed, of all his novels from *Le Ventre de Paris* (1873) onwards (the first of the *Rougon-Macquart*, not coincidentally perhaps, to introduce the fictional painter Claude Lantier). Beyond a rhetoric of antithesis which accommodates his oppositional stance, his art criticism is also marked by a verbal aggressivity which goes a long way to explaining the hostility it provoked. But Zola's language also transforms the factual into imaginative evocation: the buzz of the Salon's opening day: the atmosphere, dictated by rain or shine, of the crowds emerging from the galleries and shaking off the layers of dust filling the air from thousands of elegant feet trampling through them; the ribald laughter of spectators contemplating pictures at odds with convention. More problematic, notably in the case of the representation of human figures — as contrasted with *natures mortes* — is a tendency to focus on subject rather than compositional technique, tempting him to construct its hypothetical narrative, or novelistic, extension. In this respect, the irony in *L'Œuvre* is self-directed: the quasi-autobiographical writer Sandoz is 'malgré lui [...] parfois tenté d'introduire de la littérature dans la peinture' (*RM*, IV, 47); and Jory, the art critic whose pioneering journalism on behalf of the *école du plein air* in some ways resembles Zola's own early engagement with it, does not escape a similar retrospective distancing, with the Café Guerbois (renamed in the novel as the Café Baudequin[64]) transparently identified as the 'berceau d'une révolution' thanks to his 'fameux article' (*RM*, IV, 79). He would later confess that titles such as *Mes haines* and *Mon Salon* (Figs 1.4 and 1.5) were excessive, attributable to 'un orgueil provocant' (*EsA*, p. 402). But his writing on the visual arts, laced with comic effects, pejorative vocabulary, telling images, extended metaphors and memorable turns of phrase also exactly reflects the virulent energy of the period's cultural debates. The gaps, emphases and judgements in the novelist's critical 'transgressions' (as Van Gogh put it) are both an essential part of, and bear witness to, what Zola calls the 'bouleversement' (*EsA*, p.701) renewing French art in the second half of the nineteenth century.

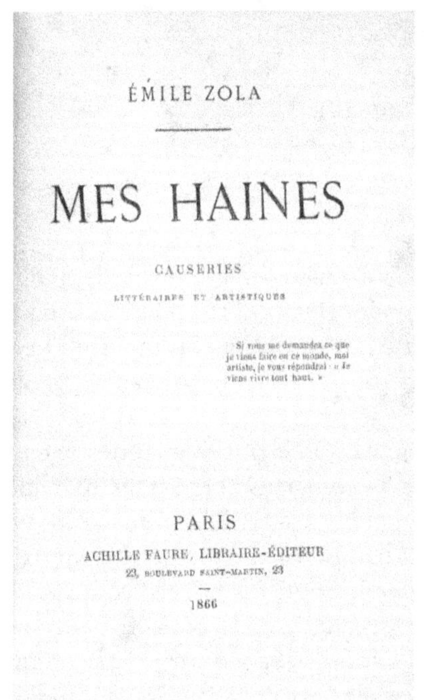

ÉMILE ZOLA

MES HAINES

CAUSERIES

LITTÉRAIRES ET ARTISTIQUES

Si vous me demandez ce que je viens faire en ce monde, moi artiste, je vous répondrai : « Je viens vivre tout haut. »

PARIS

ACHILLE FAURE, LIBRAIRE-ÉDITEUR

23, BOULEVARD SAINT-MARTIN, 23

1866

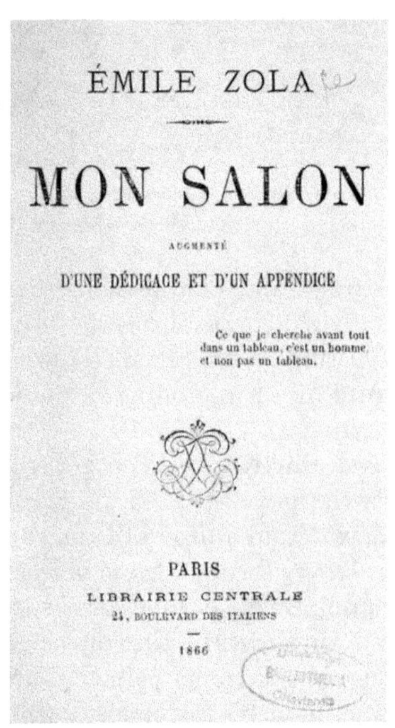

ÉMILE ZOLA

MON SALON

AUGMENTÉ

D'UNE DÉDICACE ET D'UN APPENDICE

Ce que je cherche avant tout dans un tableau, c'est un homme et non pas un tableau.

PARIS

LIBRAIRIE CENTRALE

24, BOULEVARD DES ITALIENS

1866

Fig. 1.4. Émile Zola, *Mes haines* (Paris: Achille Faure, 1866).

Fig. 1.5. Émile Zola, *Mon Salon* (Paris: Librairie centrale, 1866).

Notes to Chapter 1

1. In a letter to Anton van Rappard, on or about 3 July 1883. Translated from the Dutch, in Vincent van Gogh, *The Letters: The Complete Illustrated and Annotated Edition*, ed. by Leo Jansen and others, 6 vols (London: Thames & Hudson, 2009), II, 366–70. Van Gogh also described Zola's fictional painters in *Thérèse Raquin* (1867) and *Le Ventre de Paris* (1873) as 'pale ghosts' of Manet and the Impressionists. Somewhat curiously, given the pages devoted to Millet in *Mon Salon*, Van Gogh deplored the absence of that painter in Zola's essays (repeating what he had said to his brother, Theo, at exactly the same time (2 July, II, 364–66)) while acknowledging that, in the case of Manet at least, he was not 'utterly wrong'.
2. Lionello Venturi describes the 'banquet' as having been attended by Monet, Pissarro, Mallarmé, George Moore and a number of prominent art critics; in *Les Archives de l'impressionnisme*, 2 vols (Paris: Durand-Ruel, 1939), I, 80. In a letter to his son, Pissarro wrote: 'J'ai beaucoup parlé avec Huysmans. Il est très au courant de l'art nouveau, très désireux de rompre des lances en notre faveur' (cited in *RM*, IV,1388). But Pissarro was less convinced than Monet that *L'Œuvre* would damage public perception of the Impressionists, and remained an admirer of Zola's writing on Manet (see his December 1882 letter to Durand-Ruel, cited by Venturi (II, 11)).
3. In, respectively, Daniel Halévy, *Degas parle...* (Paris: La Palatine, 1960), pp. 47–48, and Berthe Morisot's recollections, as noted by Paul Valéry, *Œuvres*, ed. by Jean Hytier, 2 vols (Paris: Gallimard, 1960), II, 1226. Degas described Zola's totalizing ambitions for the *Rougon Macquart* as 'puerile', comparing him to 'un géant qui travaille le Bottin', cited by George Moore (*Impressions and Opinions* (London: David Nutt, 1891), p. 319) who also 'remembered' (pp. 288–89) that Zola had told him that no painter of his generation could be advantageously compared to the three or four greatest writers of the century. Degas was not unaware of reservations Zola had expressed about certain of his paintings, and was perhaps apprised of at least the drift of his letter to Huysmans of 10 May 1883: 'Je connais beaucoup Degas, et depuis longtemps. Ce n'est qu'un constipé du plus joli talent' (*Corr.*, IV, 388).
4. Cited by Renée Baligand, 'Lettres inédites d'Antoine Guillemet à Émile Zola (1866–1870)', *CN*, 52 (1978), 173–205 (p. 184). In her comments on this letter, Lucie Riou is overly circumspect in stating that 'l'écart qui disjoint désormais les deux sœurs semble admis par certains écrivains'; see her *Les Arts visuels dans les romans, l'œuvre critique et la correspondance d'Émile Zola* (Paris: Honoré Champion, 2020), p. 10. That 'écart' is évident in Fantin-Latour's *Un atelier aux Batignolles*, as suggested in my Introduction.
5. See my 'Zola's Transpositions', in *Translation and the Arts in Modern France*, ed. by Sonya Stephens (Bloomington: Indiana University Press, 2017), pp. 131–47. A further example explored there is the transposition in *Une Page d'amour* of Renoir's *La Balançoire* (1876).
6. Nicolas Valazza, *Crise de plume et souveraineté du pinceau: écrire la peinture de Diderot à Proust* (Paris: Classiques Garnier, 2013), p. 18.
7. See Joseph Jurt, *Les Arts rivaux: littérature et arts visuels d'Homère à Huysmans* (Paris: Classiques Garnier, 2018), pp. 291–316 of which are devoted to Zola.
8. It was the publication of *L'Œuvre*, however, which prompted contemporaries to engage in comparisons between Zola and Diderot: see the review of the novel cited in *RM*, IV, 1394–95; and Gita May, 'Zola, entre le texte et l'image: l'exemple de Diderot', *CN*, 67 (1993), 235–44.
9. As Zola would underline during the preparation of *L'Œuvre*, notably in 'Ma Visite' to the Salon of 1885 (Ms 10316, fols 326–40); elsewhere, he notes: 'La Mode du Salon, Paris au Salon. Les artistes emplissant les journaux — l'écrasement du dimanche — la foule de cinquante mille visiteurs. L'épanouissement de la publicité moderne. La rage de l'information. Le bruit exagéré autour de la plus petite œuvre annoncée, attendue, enrageant, et oubliée' (fol. 173).
10. Cited by Venturi, *Archives*, I, 134.
11. The figures are drawn from Christopher Parsons and Martha Ward, *A Bibliography of Salon Criticism in Second Empire Paris* (Cambridge: Cambridge University Press, 1986), pp. 165–217.
12. See Martha Ward, 'From Art Criticism to Art News: Journalistic Reviewing in Late Nineteenth-Century Paris', in *Art Criticism and its Institutions in Nineteenth-Century France*, ed. by Michael Orwicz (Manchester: Manchester University Press, 1994), pp. 162–81; and *L'Invention de*

la critique d'art en France, ed. by Pierre-Henry Frangne and Jean-Marc Poinsot (Rennes: Presses universitaires de Rennes, 2002).

13. Cited in *Corr.*, II, 373, n. 2.
14. His best-known publications were his *Histoire des peintres français au XIXe siècle* (1845), *Grammaire des arts du dessin* (1867) and a monumental *Histoire des peintres de toutes les écoles* (1849–76). Twice appointed Director of the École des Beaux-Arts (during the 1848 Revolution, and again in 1870 thanks to the presidential intervention of Adolphe Thiers), he was elected to the Académie française in 1876 and to the Chair of Aesthetics and the History of Art at the Collège de France two years later. These complementary aspects of his career gave him the opportunity to rehearse in the public domain a classical conception of Beauty and of generic hierarchy, precisely those principles which Zola rejected in advocating alternative criteria against which modern painting should be judged.
15. *GBA*, 20 June 1866, p. 498.
16. See, for example, Pierre Petroz echoing Blanc's strictures in his *L'Art et la critique en France depuis 1822* (Paris: Germer Baillière, 1875), arguing that, in the case of those penning reviews 'en littérateurs et en curieux', 'leurs *Salons*, signés souvent de noms illustres, démontrent, en général, une assez médiocre connaissance des conditions, des exigences de la peinture et de la sculpture' (p. iv), denouncing 'poètes, romanciers, fantaisistes de tout genre, égarés dans la critique' (p. 10), except those, as he insists in his preface, 'critiques qui n'ont été et n'ont voulu être que des critiques' (p. v). In his *Un Critique d'art au XIXe siècle* (Paris: Felix Alcan, 1884), the only such exception distinguished from 'des hommes, d'une compétence douteuse, qui ont émis sur les arts des opinions plus ou moins banales, plus au moins excentriques' (p. 5) was William Bürger (the pseudonym adopted by T. Thoré (1807–1869) after the *coup d'état* of December 1851).
17. As Anita Brookner wrote of Zola's art criticism, it has 'always had a bad press' (*The Genius of the Future: Studies in French Art Criticism* (London: Phaidon, 1971), p. 91. And nowhere more damning than in François Fosca's *De Diderot à Valéry: les écrivains et les arts visuels* (Paris: Albin Michel, 1960); his target are those 'nombreux littérateurs' who, in spite of their 'timides tentatives de marier le jargon d'atelier et une érudition bien rudimentaire [...] ne s'occupaient guère que du sujet', exemplified by the reputation as art critics of a Gautier or a Zola being 'complètement injustifiée' (pp. 235–36).
18. According to that most conservative of literary critics, Ferdinand Brunetière, in the ultra-conservative *Revue des deux mondes* of 15 May 1880, cited by Marcel Nicolle, 'Une anthologie de la critique d'art en France', *GBA*, 817 (1931), 45–63. The debate had been renewed by an 1876 study by Philippe Burty, praising Diderot as 'le vrai père de la critique moderne', on the occasion of the publication of the first complete edition of his writings on art.
19. To George Sand, in a letter of 27 March 1875, he explained why he had declined Paul Meurice's invitation to contribute a review of the Salon to *Le Rappel*: 'j'ai dénié l'honneur, car je n'admets pas que l'on fasse la critique d'art dont on ignore la technique!' (*Correspondance*, ed. by Jean Bruneau and Yvan Leclerc, 5 vols (Paris: Gallimard, 1973–2007), IV, 917).
20. Fosca, *De Diderot à Valéry*, p. 230. Only in the first supplement to the *Grand Larousse*, in 1878, is there an item devoted to art criticism as such.
21. Frédéric Bernard (1820–1868), writing as Théodore Pelloquet, had published an 1861 monograph on Henri Murger and had been editor in chief of *Beaux-Arts: revue de l'art ancien et moderne* (1863), as well as the author of a number of utilitarian guides to museum collections. In 1867, he would review the Salon in *Le Monde illustré*. His prominence in certain circles is testified to by Monet's pencil drawing, *Le Journaliste Théodore Pelloquet* (1858). Obituary notices in the press underlined his status as 'un de nos critiques d'art les plus *compétents*' and as 'un critique d'art singulièrement *érudit*' (respectively: *Le Figaro*, 31 December 1868; *L'Illustration*, 9 January 1869; my italics). His opposition to Zola's preferences goes beyond the case of Manet, celebrating Millet (in his *Salon* of 1863) at the expense of Courbet, and suggesting that the latter's landscapes were inferior to those of Léopold Robert.
22. Letter of June 1859 to Louis Marguery (*Corr.*, I, 112).
23. Letter of 1 June 1861 (*Corr.*, I, 288).
24. On a more intimate level, Monet's familiarity with the collector, including decorating the principal drawing room in his magnificent château, had the unintended consequence of

Hoschedé's wife and mother of his six children, Alice, leaving him to live with the painter (widowed in September 1879) and marrying him after her husband's death.

25. See Joy Newton, 'Zola et Raffaëlli', *CN*, 66 (1992), 47–58.
26. Letter of 13 November 1885 (*Corr.*, v, 333).
27. On Zola's art books, see my 'Zola et ses livres', *CN*, 65 (1991), 191–97.
28. As Jean-Pierre Sanchez has argued, no other work confronts more implicitly 'les contours et les divisions internes de la scène politique et idéologique à partir de laquelle s'exprime la critique d'art de 1881'; in *Henri Gervex, 1852–1929*, exh. cat., Galerie des Beaux-Arts de Bordeaux (Poitiers: Paris-Musées/SPADEM, 1992), p. 153.
29. According to Charles Morice, in *Le Journal* of 20 August 1894; reproduced in *Entretiens avec Zola*, ed. by Speirs and Signori, pp. 138–42 (p. 141).
30. It remains somewhat curious that Zola had never before referred to Stevens: a close friend of Manet's and (like the novelist, Monet and Duret) one of the pallbearers at his funeral in May 1883, as well as working with Zola in organizing the great retrospective exhibition on Manet the following year. With Gervex, Stevens had produced the monumental *Histoire du siècle, 1789–1889* (conceived for the centenary of the French Revolution celebrated at the Universal Exhibition) in which Zola himself figures. Stevens was often in financial trouble, however, and it may be that Zola's mention of him was designed to raise his profile, which is acknowledged in the painter's note of thanks: 'Je vous suis reconnaissant du mot charmant que vous avez bien voulu écrire sur mon art dans votre article' (cited by Henri Mitterand, *Zola*, 3 vols (Paris: Fayard, 1999–2002), iii, 206, n. 1).
31. Zola owned two 1862 paintings by Coste. Although described as a 'peintre amateur', Coste had one work exhibited at the Salon of 1865 and, retaining his Paris studio for at least the next fifteen years, two more at the Salon of 1880, which Zola searched for in vain on his visit to it on that occasion (letter to Coste of 4 May 1880, *Corr.*, iii, 459).
32. See Mitterand, *Zola*, ii, 493. Baboneau (a major artist in his own right, exhibiting at the annual Salon from this moment onwards) was also contracted to provide the stained-glass decoration for Zola's apartment at 21bis rue de Bruxelles, to which he moved on 10 September 1889, and where again he was subject to Zola's extraordinarily precise instructions, exemplified by his letter to Baboneau of 4 August; see Christophe Oberle, 'Onze lettres inédites d'Émile Zola (1862–1902)', *CN*, 95 (2021), 339–47 (p. 344).
33. While this particular remark dates from 1880, he had already subscribed to Duret's hypothesis, two years earlier, that 'avant l'apparition des albums japonais notre peintre mentait toujours' (*EsA*, p. 575). But he also qualified his enthusiasm in *Le Naturalisme au Salon*: 'J'ajouterai pourtant que, si l'influence du japonisme a été excellente pour nous tirer de la tradition du bitume et nous faire voir les gaietés blondes de la nature, une imitation voulue d'un art qui n'est ni de notre race ni de notre milieu, finirait par n'être plus qu'une mode insupportable' (*EsA*, p. 375).
34. It is difficult to know how it came to be that Zola was inspired by Whistler's example. The painter organized a private press viewing of the Peacock Room (dismantled in 1904 and now in the Freer Gallery of Art, Washington DC) on 9 February 1877; and in the *Chronique de l'art et de la curiosité* of 24 March, a detailed description of it by Lionel Robinson referred to 'un point de vue nouveau dans l'application des arts décoratifs à la vie journalière' (p. 112). As in the case of Tissot, Whistler is never mentioned in Zola's art criticism, in spite of his many submissions to the annual Salon and numerous exhibitions outside it. But he would have come across him as a member of Manet's circle and as an habitué of the café Guerbois. There is an allusion in *L'Œuvre* to his *Dame en blanc* (exhibited at the Salon des Refusés and, again, at the Universal Exhibition of 1867), as a 'très curieuse vision d'un œil de grand artiste' (*RM*, iv, p. 124). One of Whistler's biographers names both the painter and Zola as regular customers of La Porte Chinoise, situated in the arcades of the Rue de Rivoli; see G.H. Fleming, *James Abbott McNeill Whistler: A Life* (Moreton-in-Marsh: Windrush Press, 1991), p. 105.
35. In one of his posthumous essays on Flaubert, Zola recalled that 'quand on lui parlait de faire illustrer un de ses livres, il entrait dans une violente colère, disant qu'il ne faut pas respecter sa prose pour y laisser mettre des images qui salissent et détruisent le texte' (*Les Romanciers naturalistes*, *OC*, xi, p. 152).

36. *Corr.*, v, 340–41.
37. On Renoir's three compositions visualizing scenes from the novel, see Jean-François Thibault, 'Renoir illustrateur de *L'Assommoir*', *CN*, 66 (1992), 147–56.
38. Letter of 29 December 1885, in Oberle, 'Onze lettres inédites', p. 342.
39. These stays have been documented by Rodolphe Walter in two ground-breaking articles: 'Zola et ses amis à Bennecourt' and 'Émile Zola et Claude Monet'; in, respectively, *CN*, 17 (1961), 19–35, and 26 (1964), 51–61. In the preparatory notes for *L'Œuvre*, Zola refers to the Bennecourt house 'que nous avons louée' (Ms 10316, fol. 87).
40. Armand Silvestre, *Au pays des souvenirs: mes maîtres et mes maîtresses* (Paris: Librairie illustrée, 1892), p. 159.
41. On Zola's 'jeudis', see Anthony Glinoer and Vincent Laisney, *L'Âge des cénacles : confraternités littéraires et artistiques au XIXe siècle* (Paris: Fayard, 2013), pp. 158–60.
42. Mitterand, *Zola*, i, 610.
43. 'Même l'école des Batignolles', he added, in this letter of 17 May 1870 (*Corr.*, ii, 217); the year before, Duranty had written the somewhat lukewarm review of the group's latest paintings which had led to his exclusion from Fantin-Latour's collective portrait.
44. For a complete study of their relationship, see Joy Newton, 'Émile Zola and Théodore Duret: Portrait of an Art Critic', *Nottingham French Studies*, 27.1 (1988), 13–23, and 27.2 (1988), 13–24.
45. *Le Figaro littéraire*, 22 June 1927.
46. In a letter of 26 July 1866, he confided to Coste that he had 'commencé un livre de haut critique [...] que je publierai sans doute vers novembre' (*Corr.*, i, 453), a project doubtless overtaken by his essays on Manet in which hostile critics of the painter are sufficiently targeted, as in his 1867 study of him: 'Les critiques d'art sont des mélodistes qui tous, à la même heure, jouent leurs airs à la fois, n'entendant chacun que leur instrument dans l'effroyable charivari qu'ils produisent' (*EsA*, p. 496).
47. François-Marie Mourad, *Zola critique littéraire* (Paris: Honoré Champion, 2003), p. 349.
48. Antoinette Ehrard, 'Émile Zola: l'art de voir et la passion de dire', in *La Critique artistique: un genre littéraire* (Paris: Presses universitaires de France, 1983), pp. 101–22 (p. 103).
49. In 1898, Zola recalled having been given signed copies of some of the books he had advertised, including 'de très beaux volumes, ceux illustrés par Gustave Doré entre autres', but which, given his financial circumstances at the time, he had had to sell, 'les beaux surtout, ceux qui avaient une valeur' (*Corr.*, xi, 309).
50. As Adrienne Tooke has demonstrated in her magisterial *Flaubert and the Pictorial Arts: From Image to Text* (Oxford: Oxford University Press, 2000).
51. Letter of 30 May 1870 (*Corr.*, ii, 219).
52. Letter of 4 April 1867 (*Corr.*, i, 500).
53. Letter of 2 April 1867 to Jules Noriac (*Corr.*, xi, 46).
54. Letter to Duret of 8 May 1868 (*Corr.*, ii, 122)
55. This was despite his best efforts: in 1873, Zola thought he had just about secured a contract from Édouard Portalis, the owner of both *Le Corsaire* and *L'Avenir national*, to cover that year's Salon (see his letter to Duranty of 4 March 1873; *Corr.*, ii, 333); in the end it was instead Paul Alexis who devoted three articles to it in *L'Avenir national* of 19 May, 2 and 17 June.
56. Letter of 9 April 1874 (*Corr.*, ii, 353).
57. Identification of Zola's authorship relies on Roger Ripoll's indispensable *Émile Zola journaliste: bibliographie chronologique et analytique, II ('Le Sémaphore de Marseille', 1871–1877)* (Paris: Les Belles Lettres, 1972).
58. His column, headed 'Les On-Dit', appeared over the pseudonym of 'Le Passant'; d'Hervilly's presence in artistic circles is captured in Fantin-Latour's *Un coin de table* (1872) alongside Rimbaud and Verlaine. Zola's practice, encouraged by the director of *Le Sémaphore de Marseille*, was characteristic of Parisian journalists supplementing their income by retailing events in the French capital for provincial readers.
59. On how Zola's articles in these papers are angled towards their specific reading public, see: Juliet Simpson, 'Plenitude, Potential and Provence: Zola, Art Criticism and *Le Sémaphore de Marseille*', *AJFS*, 46 (2009), 111–25; and Rosalind Blakesley, 'Émile Zola's Art Criticism in Russia', in

Critical Exchange: Art Criticism of the Eighteenth and Nineteenth Centuries in Russia and Western Europe, ed. by Carol Adlam and Juliet Simpson (Bern: Peter Lang, 2009), pp. 263–84.

60. 'Manet et la censure', *La Tribune*, 4 February 1869 (*EsA*, pp. 513–16).
61. Such an analogy comparing the Second Empire to a police state is consistent with the repressive presence of 'sergents de ville' in his fiction: see, for example, in *Le Ventre de Paris* (*RM*, I, 610 and 629).
62. Vaisse, *La Troisième République et les peintres* (Paris: Flammarion, 1995), pp. 19–28. See also John Duffy, 'The Aesthetic and the Political in Zola's Writing on Art', *AJFS*, 38.3 (2001), 365–78. In the work-notes for *L'Œuvre*, the analogy is one used by Zola himself in relation to the election of the Salon jury: 'Aujourd'hui, un peintre pour entrer au jury est un peu comme un candidat à la députation. Mêmes intrigues électorales' (Ms 10316, fol. 377).
63. See Antoinette Ehrard, 'L'Esthétique de Zola: étude lexicologique de ses écrits sur l'art', *CN*, 58 (1984), 133–50.
64. As Zola repeated in the novel's preparatory notes: 'le café Guerbois de la chose, le café de l'école posé'; 'au café de l'école sur le boulevard des Batignolles' (Ms 10316, fols. 51, 152 and 193).

CHAPTER 2

❖

Cézanne

Zola owned more works by Cézanne than by any other artist. Thirteen of them were sold at auction in March 1903,[1] almost six months after the writer's death. Confirmed by his habitual claim that, on principle, he never purchased a painting,[2] these were evidently gifts from Cézanne himself. That Zola retained these works, all from the 1860s, throughout his life suggests at least a sentimental attachment to their shared past: a childhood friendship extended over more than thirty years. Whether he actually liked Cézanne's paintings is another question. The art dealer and Cézanne's first biographer, Ambroise Vollard (1866–1939), recalled that when he visited the novelist at his Parisian address, he refused to show him his collection of Cézannes: 'Je les ai cachés à la campagne. Sur les instances de Mirbeau, qui voulait les voir, je les ai fait rapporter ici. Mais je ne les mettrai jamais au mur. Ma maison, vous ne l'ignorez pas, est la maison des artistes.'[3] Although Vollard's memoirs are notoriously unreliable, this reported response would take hold, to the extent that Zola's daughter later repeated that the paintings were hidden away, precisely stressing 'dans son grenier à Médan'.[4] In 1880, on the other hand, the journalist Fernand Xau had reported on the Cézanne landscapes on the walls of Zola's apartment in the Rue de Boulogne, as did Saint-Georges de Bouhélier in 1896, in describing his *cabinet de travail* in the Rue de Bruxelles.[5]

Such contradictions are symptomatic of many accounts, whether by art historians or biographers, preoccupied by the relationship between a major writer and an equally famous painter which is unique in the annals of French culture. The focus on it has been intensified by Zola's apparent failure to recognize the painter's greatness, all the more striking in the light of the writer's prescience in relation to Manet, in particular, and his more general critical support for artists exemplifying the advent of pictorial modernism. The present chapter explores the various dimensions of this conundrum. It could have been headed 'Zola's Cézanne', as evidenced by their correspondence, partial fictional portraits and the novelist's art criticism. But this is less straightforward than simply negotiating differences of interpretation. For Zola's view of Cézanne is itself vitiated by alternative constructions of his perspective, aimed as much at the writer as at the painter.

Friendship and its Discontents

What has not been subject to doubt, at least until now, has been the long-held assertion that the publication of *L'Œuvre* brought their long friendship to a sudden end, Cézanne having been wounded by his fictional portrait in Zola's novel of 1886. While various personal reminiscences had suggested as much, it was in 1936 that John Rewald's doctoral thesis on Zola and Cézanne established its academic credibility; and the story was so authoritatively sustained by the distinguished art historian that even the most informed of scholars have simply repeated it, and continue to do so even today.[6] A few sceptics have occasionally offered alternative explanations for their parting of ways, ranging from the biographically plausible to the carelessly, or even maliciously, speculative.[7] They have made little headway against the 'human interest' of the prevailing legend. That was generated by Rewald's conclusion, rehearsed ever since, on the basis of Cézanne's letter to Zola on receipt of *L'Œuvre*, both on account of its apparent brusqueness and because there was no evidence of any further contact between the two men. That legend has been exploded by the belated (in 2013), and indeed sensational, discovery of an 1887 letter from Cézanne to Zola, more than a year after the supposedly definitive and dramatic *rupture* occasioned by the appearance of the novel, thereby vindicating those who had never quite subscribed to it, now justified in looking anew at the relationship between writer and painter.[8] But even before it surfaced, the most scrupulous of Cézanne's modern biographers had surmised that '*L'Œuvre* was not the cause of the break'.[9]

The postscript to that letter of 28 November 1887, on receipt of *La Terre*, is possibly more revealing than it might seem: 'Quand tu seras de retour, j'irai te voir pour te serrer la main' (*LC*, p. 419). Cézanne obviously knew that Zola had been away from Paris (with the exception of 10–24 October) for much of the time since the end of April, but not that he had in fact already returned more than a fortnight earlier. It suggests, it could be argued, that the two men were no longer in regular contact. On the other hand, this was not the first time Cézanne had shown himself to be unaware of Zola's exact whereabouts.[10] Whether or not Cézanne's intention was followed up, what we do know is that, from time to time after 1886–87, second-hand news of each other was exchanged.[11] There is no reason to doubt Cézanne's reported distress at the news of Zola's death in September 1902, nor his mawkish behaviour in Aix-en-Provence in 1906, shortly before his own death, when an initiative was launched by Zola's widow to publish her late husband's *Lettres de jeunesse* in which the painter's early correspondence with him would take pride of place. But, leaving aside whatever role *L'Œuvre* may have played, this was a friendship that was unravelling. Many of Cézanne's friendships did, often on pretexts so slight that they simply confirmed his volatile nature. Vollard cites Cézanne's barely concealed impatience with the self-regarding pomposity of competitive social intercourse around Zola's dining table, enhanced by his ever-expanding country house.[12] And, in this same account, the painter reproaches Zola for making no effort to get in touch with him, either in Paris ('logé rue Ballu, à côté de son hôtel [...] j'espérais que le hasard nous ferait nous rencontrer') or during the writer's visits to Aix in 1892 and 1896. Leaving aside the contention that he was increasingly uncomfortable in Zola's bourgeois homes, the distance between the then-unknown painter and the established novelist is registered in the mock obsequiousness of epistolary regards to 'Madame Zola' and in the third-person greeting to 'l'auteur des *Rougon-Macquart*', in thanking Zola for sending him a copy of *L'Œuvre*, the formality of which has preoccupied exegetes less minded to ponder what immediately follows it: Cézanne's appreciation of its remembrance of times past and his expressed hope that they might soon meet again.

But it is ultimately not by chance that the rift between lifelong friends widened around 1885–86, for reasons other than the coincidence of timing with the publication of *L'Œuvre*. As Cézanne's biographers have acknowledged, some with regret, Hortense Fiquet, his live-in companion since 1869, was viewed with disdain by the newly respectable Alexandrine Zola,[13] perhaps uncomfortably reminded of her own humble origins. Nor was the painter unaware that the members of Zola's social circle shared such a sense of superiority, referring to his partner as 'La Boule' (as her son, born out of wedlock in 1872, was known as 'Le Boulet').[14] For Alexandrine also had little affection for Cézanne's person or his paintings: in respect of the latter, Zola's daughter substantiated her claim that they were consigned to the attic by suggesting that, in putting them out of sight, 'il a peut-être cédé à sa femme qui n'aimait pas cette peinture'. On a more intimate level, Cézanne's visit to Médan in the summer of 1885 had involved Zola in the unwelcome complications of seeking to help his emotionally distraught friend disentangle himself from a brief affair,[15] prior to finally marrying his longtime mistress on 24 April 1886. At which point, it has been noted, Zola's wife seems to have put a stop to Cézanne's visits. While the painter himself could be just about tolerated, there was no question from now on of welcoming to any of Zola's homes a couple of such dubious provenance and with a secret family to boot.[16]

Political Distortions

Surely as important in explaining this parting of ways, however, is the fact that during the Dreyfus Affair, Zola and Cézanne were on opposite sides. It is arguable that this has far-reaching implications, not least for the very construction of the myths surrounding *L'Œuvre*, the lack of contact between Zola and Cézanne in the *fin de siècle* and, above all, for subsequent accounts of the vicissitudes of their relationship.[17] Cézanne's anti-Dreyfusard positioning has not exactly been hidden from view. But it has tended to be subordinated to his professed indifference to politics and his deliberate retreat from Paris to Provence in order, so he repeatedly stressed, to concentrate on his painting. Alex Danchev's fine biography is somewhat dismissive of claims that Cézanne held explicitly right-wing views, underlining instead an all-enveloping misanthropy at odds with particular allegiances. Those claims do not survive further scrutiny. For a start, Cézanne's much-cited self-imposed exile in the Midi cannot be taken at face value. It *seems* to fit with a refusal to be, as he apparently complained to Vollard about Zola, 'sous l'influence des événements'.[18] More problematic, if seldom noted (except by contemporaries who knew him as 'le perpétuel voyageur'),[19] are the painter's annual visits to Paris throughout the years of the Dreyfus Affair, sometimes for extended periods. In 1895, for instance, he was there from January, when Captain Dreyfus was subjected to his dishonourable discharge, right up until June. In 1896, the year in which the polemical debate intensified with the November publication of Bernard-Lazare's *Une erreur judiciaire. La vérité sur l'affaire Dreyfus*, Cézanne rented a studio in the Batignolles in August and subsequently returned to Paris in December. He was there again in January 1898, the very month in which *J'Accuse...!* appeared, on the 13th, with the resultant furore. Not even within the enclosure of the Villa des arts, in the 18th arrondissement, could Cézanne have been unaware of the hue and cry of the several hundred extra paper boys on the streets, selling 300,000 copies of *L'Aurore*. Zola's trial for libel opened on 7 February. On 23 February, he was found guilty and given the maximum sentence, including a year's imprisonment, only to have the verdict overturned on appeal (because of a legal technicality) before appearing once again in court, between 23 May and 18 July, on the evening of which he left for exile in England rather than face incarceration. Danchev asserts that Cézanne merely 'observed' these events 'as from a distance'; but he admits, without reference to a literal proximity, that 'it is possible that [he] attended to [Zola's] pronouncements on the *affaire* rather more carefully than is often supposed'.[20]

What is certain is that Cézanne's *parti-pris* was never in doubt. For many artists, Zola's *J'Accuse...!* was the moment in the Dreyfus Affair when they were forced to take sides. If Cézanne was one of them, it was clear which he would choose. Vollard, wrote that 'on comprend que l'amour de sa chère armée l'ait rendu antidreyfusard',[21] without mentioning, of course, that Cézanne had twice escaped the draft to serve in it! Another factor in his distancing from Zola was his related adherence to militant Catholicism. Louis Aurenche, who met the painter in 1900, traced its origins to his schooling at the Collège Bourbon 'dirigé par des religieux dont Cézanne parlait toujours avec respect et qui avaient su impregner son âme de l'idéal divin qui ne le quitta jamais'.[22] This may be coloured by the wisdom of hindsight, Cézanne's return to orthodoxy being generally dated to 1891, as their mutual friend Paul Alexis felt bound to report to Zola that year: 'converti, il croit et pratique.'[23] Cézanne's religious beliefs, indeed piety, seldom figure within critical accounts of his heroic modernism. Most of his friends, associates and acolytes, during the 1890s and beyond, were fervent Catholics. As Philip Nord has remarked, Cézanne's milieu was so steeped in Catholic reaction that it is 'a miracle that his anti-Dreyfusism is so muted'.[24] If his letter to Zola of 28 September 1887 is the last record we have of his familiarity with Zola's fiction, it is unlikely that *La Terre* itself would have served to repair these multiple cracks in the relationship between painter and novelist. Although belatedly finding Zola's complimentary copy of it on returning to Aix, Cézanne could not have failed to notice 'Le Manifeste des Cinq', published in Paris on 18 August, which was only the most newsworthy early marker of a debate focused on the novel's representation of a brutal and rapacious peasantry. This debate would extend into the Dreyfus Affair. The sculptor Jean

Baffier recalled in 1898 that '*La Terre* de M. Zola était non seulement un mauvais livre, mais aussi une mauvaise action', precisely because it undermined 'le culte de notre terre natale',[25] at odds as it was with the mythology of 'la France profonde' to which Cézanne also subscribed. His series of *Joueurs de carte* (1890–96) is in part, it has been argued by John House, a repudiation of *La Terre*'s savage demystification of rural life.[26] It has even been suggested that its pipe-smoker is possibly Zola himself. More certain, given the writer's antipathy to religion, is that the painter would not have been displeased by the violent denunciation, in the Catholic press, of both *Lourdes* (1894), immediately placed on the papal Index, and *Rome* (1896).

The significance of these political and ideological differences between Zola and Cézanne lies in their exploitation by right-wing commentators in order to separate writer and painter in the public mind. In the case of the militant anti-Dreyfusard Joachim Gasquet, for example, there is no mistaking the pleasure he derived from 'quoting' Cézanne's suspicion of literary highjacking ('le mal que Proudhon a fait à Courbet, Zola me l'aurait fait'),[27] and from widening the rift between painter and writer by drawing Cézanne's attention to Zola's 1896 *Figaro* article in which the former is labelled as a 'grand peintre avorté' (*EsA*, p. 402) — more painful, one might imagine, than his reading of *L'Œuvre*. That is not to deny the unreliability common to many of the testimonies of Cézanne's view of Zola. It goes beyond Gasquet's flowery rewriting of the painter's sentences, many of them taken from the earlier 'recollections' of the painter Émile Bernard (1868–1941), or the accuracy of Vollard's somehow verbatim transcription of his conversations and what even his admiring biographer calls his talent for the 'reconstitution embellificatrice de la mémoire'.[28] Scholarly scepticism is insufficient to dismiss them out of hand. For what needs to be stressed is that if they are self-serving, it is because they are driven by the need to *disassociate* Zola and Cézanne, thereby creating a break with a well-known childhood friendship to better champion the painter at the writer's expense. Ironically instructive of the risk of a failure to do so is Henri Rochefort's article, entitled 'L'Amour du laid', in *L'Intransigeant* of 9 March 1903, provoked by the opening of the posthumous Drouot sale of Zola's effects, including his Cézannes, in which the polemicist elides Dreyfusard and aesthetic criteria, even to the extent of using the painter's early work owned by Zola as evidence that 'il y avait des dreyfusards longtemps avant l'affaire Dreyfus'. It is ludicrous that he should have placed Cézanne in the same ideological frame as the author of *J'Accuse...!*, but a sign of the times. As was the fact that, as the painter wrote to his son: 'inutile de me l'envoyer, chaque jour j'en trouve sous ma porte, sans compter les numéros de *L'Intransigeant* qu'on m'adresse par la poste'.[29] For those concerned with the value (in every sense) of a painter revealed to the world in Vollard's inaugural exhibition of November 1895, it may not have been helpful that one of the most extensive reviews of it was by a prominent Dreyfusard, Arsène Alexandre. His 'Émile Zola et les arts', in *Le Figaro* of 1 October 1902, immediately after the novelist's sudden death, was a tribute which evoked his links with Cézanne and may have reinforced Rochefort's misapprehension. By heading his 1895 article 'Claude Lantier', and being at pains to point out that Cézanne 'n'était aucunement le lamentable bonhomme que l'on s'est representé sur la foi du roman de Zola', Alexandre had paradoxically assured the indexing of *L'Œuvre* within future assessments of the painter's achievements, both for contemporaries and for posterity.

What was imperative, according to Bernard, was to discriminate between Cézanne and 'la déplorable école inaugurée par M. Zola'.[30] As a young acolyte, Bernard had got to know Cézanne in 1904–05. Abroad for most of the decade after 1893, that in no way constrained this dedicated admirer of Maurice Barrès (1862–1923) from attacking the 'Jewish conspiracy', anticlerical politicians and Naturalist writers, convinced that the salvation of France lay in a return to Faith. Consistent with what has been called his 'reactionary idealism', and as 'an uncompromising enemy of the Republic and its egalitarian pretensions',[31] he espoused (like Gasquet and Cézanne himself), the values and aesthetic of 'la Vieille France'. His recollections of Cézanne are patently distorted, nowhere more so than in 'remembering' Cézanne saying that *L'Œuvre* had been sent to him out of the blue ('un beau jour'), not having seen Zola, the 'ami détestable', for 'de longues années'.[32] In fact, in 1885 (only the year before) he had spent the evening of 14 June *chez* Zola in Paris and several days at Médan in the second half of July, as mentioned above, undoubtedly aware that the writing of *L'Œuvre*, started on 12 May 1885, was underway. Brought together in volume form in 1912, as *Souvenirs sur Paul Cézanne*, the more durable interest of these anecdotal pieces (originally published in 1904 and 1907) lies in their further recycling by Vollard in his seminal biography, two years later, and in subsequent 'recollections' of his own.[33]

Vollard is a crucially important figure in the narrative of the Zola-Cézanne relationship, its inflection determined by his self-interested 'agenda'. That he was one of the greatest art-dealers of the *fin de siècle*, both in his prescient tastes and commercial acumen, is beyond doubt. In this respect, his investment in Cézanne is unique, launching the unknown painter's career, and indeed his own (aged barely 29), and having a virtual monopoly of his paintings, so that by 1900, two thirds of all of them — at least 678 works — had passed through his hands. All his writing, for the rest of his life, not least the template 1914 biography which is, as Michael Doran terms it, a 'luxueuse entreprise publicitaire d'un marchand de tableaux plutôt que d'une monographie très précise',[34] is angled towards a booming market in Cézannes, catalysed by the late 'discovery' of 'le Maître d'Aix' and given further impetus by the artist's death. Vollard's 1895 exhibition, which Zola would reference in his final assessment of the painter, was followed by another 'retrospective' in May–June 1898, a few months after *J'Accuse...!*. He would remain particularly concerned to counter those attacking Cézanne *through* Zola, even posthumously. Rochefort's singularly vile 1903 commentary (in *L'Intransigeant* of 9 March) starts by expressing his disgust at 'tous les snobs du dreyfusisme' crowded into the Hotel Drouot, before focusing on the hilarity provoked by 'un ultra-impressionniste nommé Cézanne [...] dont Zola a ainsi récolté la production [...] qui poussait à la propagation de pareilles inanités picturales'. It is significant that Vollard himself quotes from the penultimate paragraph of Rochefort's article: 'Quand on voit la nature comme l'interprétaient Zola et ses peintres ordinaires, il est tout naturel que le patriotisme et l'honneur vous apparaissent sous la forme d'un officier livrant à l'ennemi les plans de la défense du pays'. To prove that Rochefort was 'mal renseigné', Vollard goes to some lengths to distance Cézanne from Zola. He 'cites' the painter's view that his old friend's public stance was merely another example of his endless capacity for self-promotion, compensating for his repeated failure (19 attempts from 1888 onwards) to be elected to the Académie française: 'Et si l'on aurait voulu de lui, il aurait trouvé là son contentement, et n'aurait pas eu besoin, pour épater le pauvre monde, d'entrer dans cette affaire Dreyfus, où il n'était pas de force! Seulement, quand on est un peu mince d'étoffe, on cherche toujours à péter plus haut que le nez.'[35] It was thus the necessary separation of writer and painter, from Vollard's point of view, that could be abetted by indicating, as was suggested at the beginning of this chapter, that Zola did not even like Cézanne's paintings. Prefaced by a professed concern, at the start of their meeting, with Zola's victimization by anti-Dreyfusard crowds in the streets below his apartment, Vollard sought to reinforce that disjunction between writer and painter by implying that Zola himself was no longer close to Cézanne: 'Dans ma crainte d'éveiller les susceptibilités de Zola, je me gardais de mettre la conversation sur les "Cézanne".' While there may have been ulterior, and predatory, motives for the dealer's visit,[36] the oblique inclusion of *L'Œuvre* amongst Cézanne's reported complaints about Zola contributed to a critical consensus which has had a long history.[37]

L'Œuvre: The Legend and the Text

That Vollard saw *L'Œuvre* as damaging to Cézanne's reputation is evident from his public reply to Frantz Jourdain, refuting the latter's claim that his paintings were *not* hidden away and attributing to Zola 'des sentiments beaucoup plus pareils à ceux que nous révèle son roman *L'Œuvre* qu'à ceux que s'est plu à découvrir chez lui l'affection conciliante de M. Frantz Jourdain'.[38] If 'the legend of *L'Œuvre* stoked the legend of Cézanne', as Danchev neatly puts it,[39] it is inseparable from contrary attempts to dismiss the novel as a travesty. Gasquet is exceptional, and all the more notable in light of his lack of sympathy for Zola, in insisting that the painter 'm'affirma toujours, et il ne mentait jamais, que ce livre n'était pour rien dans cette brouille avec son vieux compagnon', but his testimony was not published in full until 1921.[40] Bernard earlier 'remembered' Cézanne referring to Zola as 'une intelligence fort médiocre' and the novel itself as 'un fort mauvais livre complètement faux', outraged by his portrayal in *L'Œuvre*, 'une épouvantable déformation, un mensonge tout à sa gloire',[41] grist to the mill of those confronting the retrospective reading of it in light of Alexandre's 1895 'Claude Lantier'. In this, the critic had claimed that the potential link between Cézanne and Zola's fictional painter had already been made by others. At the time of the novel's appearance, however, reviewers only highlighted the autobiographical dimension of the figure of Sandoz. The sole painter singled out was Manet. As Monet wrote to Zola: 'Vous avez pris soin, avec intention, que pas un seul de vos personnages ne ressemble à aucun de nous, mais [...] j'ai peur que [...] nos ennemis ne prononcent les noms de

Manet ou tout au moins les nôtres' (cited in *RM*, IV, 1387), writing on behalf of those who had recently met to discuss the novel's negative impact, at that dinner (mentioned in the previous chapter) at which Cézanne was not present. In *Le Figaro* of 5 April 1886, Philippe Gill wrote that 'dans Claude Lantier, je trouve un peu de Manet, de Pissarro, de Cézanne, de Monet'. Which is hardly surprising given the amalgams effected in Zola's composite portrait, more layered than the novelist's over-simplified 1897 equation suggests: 'Claude, à vrai dire, est un mélange d'Édouard Manet et de Paul Cézanne' (*EsA*, p. 702).[42]

While it may be true, as Wayne Anderson puts it, that the novel's protagonist has been 'recklessly interpreted by many art historians as a portrait of Cézanne',[43] it has long been recognized by literary scholars, at least, that *L'Œuvre* does inevitably reflect *certain* aspects of Cézanne's personality and career. With recourse to the intermittently explicit preparatory notes for the novel, Robert Niess (more than half a century ago) identified within *L'Œuvre* what adds up to Zola's summative assessment of the painter.[44] This includes, on a personal level, Cézanne's mood-swings, propensity to discouragement and morbid self-doubt, his attitude towards women and a perceived emotional insecurity which his mental state during his visit to Médan in 1885 could have done nothing to dispel. In relation to his art, what is clear is that a residual Romanticism, inseparable from the temptations of allegory,[45] was at odds with Zola's thinking about both literary and pictorial representation. Claude's last painting, in *L'Œuvre*, has defeated every scholarly detective looking for its possible model. What remains interesting about its gigantic nude ('la Femme au sexe fleuri d'une rose mystique' (*RM*, IV, 353) emerging from the Seine, set against the backdrop of the Île de la Cité, is the extent to which it exemplifies what Zola terms (in the novel's work notes) Claude's 'pointe romantique, inavouée' (Ms 10316, fol. 28). And even more significant is Zola's prefiguring of the critical reaction to it, voiced by Sandoz, the novel's authorial surrogate: 'Pas logique, pas vraisemblable, pas moderne' (fol. 443). Together with a reference to Claude being 'un monstre d'art' (fol. 15), it is possible to identify here Zola's contemplation of Cézanne's work up until 1885, alternating between realist pictures and an admixture of imaginary landscapes and larger-than-life symbolic figures. To which both stylistic experimentation and Cézanne's frustration bear witness, not least in destroying unfinished canvasses as he had done in the case of portraits of Zola himself.[46]

By contrast, in his brief expression of thanks to Zola for his copy of the novel, in the legendary 'last letter' of 4 April 1886, Cézanne refers only to 'ce bon témoignage de souvenir' evoked in the novel's opening chapters. Indeed, his specific reference to 'l'impression des temps écoulés',[47] rather than to other parts of the text, only makes sense if we remember that in July 1885, when he visited Médan and would almost certainly have been, however distracted by his amorous travails, privy to progress on *L'Œuvre*, Zola had not got much further than the pages devoted to its protagonist's formative years in the Midi and subsequent stays in Paris in, as the novel's internal chronology indicates, the 1860s (*RM*, IV, 35–49).[48] Nostalgia, on Cézanne's part, is justified by both the joyous tone and biographical origins of these passages, whether read to him by Zola in 1885 or re-read in due course.[49]

Even as late as 1897, Zola would recall with similar emotion this period of their lives: 'J'avais pour ami le peintre Paul Cézanne que je considérais comme mon frère et que je ne quittais presque jamais' (*EsA*, pp. 701–02). The work notes for *L'Œuvre* include a 'Liste de mes souvenirs' in which Cézanne figures prominently.[50] Transposed recollections in the novel itself start with those of a shared childhood in Aix, 'où le peintre et [Sandoz] s'étaient connus, en huitième, dès leur première culotte usée des bancs du collège'.[51] This evocation of the Collège Bourbon, where Zola and Cézanne had both been pupils between 1852 and 1856, is followed by memories of 'les trois inséparables',[52] the two of them plus their fellow schoolmate Jean-Baptistin Baille (1841–1918), and their adolescent escapades in the Provençal countryside, reading poetry and courting local lasses under the summer sun. However creatively indifferent a picture, Zola would retain until his death some five decades later Baille's watercolour of Mont Saint-Victoire.[53] What Danchev calls Cézanne's 'incorrigible versifying' of 'Zola nageur'[54] in the river Arc, south of Aix, is possibly reflected in the androgynous *Femme piquant une tête dans l'eau* (1867–70), in which not even an anatomical close-up is sufficient to deny a latent homoerotic tension figured in the naked body diving into a pool.[55] Less speculative are the reasons Zola owned *L'Estaque* (*c.* 1867), one of many of Cézanne's pictures of this once-picturesque fishing village outside Marseilles where they spent time together and which Zola described as 'un des plus beaux endroits que je connaisse' (a view with which nobody would concur today!).[56] In this geographical context, Cézanne's early drawings are not unlike those of Claude Lantier, in 'un album où il crayonnait des bouts d'horizon', as are his landscapes with their rocky motifs, for which authorial appreciation, guiding the reader of the novel around his studio, is manifest and consistent with his intention that he would describe 'quelques beaux morceaux sur les murs' as evidence that his fictional painter was 'pas un raté' (Ms 10316, fols 28, 36 and 38): 'l'ardent ciel bleu sur la campagne rousse'; 'une plaine s'étendait, avec le moutonnement des petits oliviers grisâtres, jusqu'aux dentelures roses des collines lointaines'; 'un désert farouche, roulant à l'infini ses vagues de pierre'; 'une fraîcheur de bouquet parmi les champs calcinés'; 'le Jas de Bouffan, d'une blancheur de mosquée, au centre de ses vastes terres, pareilles à des mares de sang'. The Jas de Bouffan, purchased by his father in 1859, was one of Cézanne's favourite sites, confirmed by his repeated paintings of it from 1865–66 onwards. The period in question is characterized by fictional writer and painter, surrogates both, being 'ravagés d'une fièvre de littérature et d'art'.

If the very conception of *L'Œuvre* is retrospective in intent, Zola's withdrawal from journalistic criticism allowing him a more distanced *summa* of the artistic debates in which he had been involved, this particular autobiographical section of the novel in some ways represents Zola's acknowledgement of his debt to Cézanne, in having introduced him to the visual arts and the challenges involved in writing about them. Initially separated by Zola's move to Paris in 1858, the correspondence between the two reads like a transcript of the enthusiastic discussions described in the novel.[57] Cézanne's letters from this period are especially prolix, if wonderfully enhanced by their marginal sketches. But from these often wildly uncontrolled musings batted back and forth there emerge fundamental principles, both common to, as well as differentiating, literary and pictorial representation. In this respect, as in the case of so many painters (as stressed in the previous chapter), according to Gasquet, 'Cézanne se méfiait en Zola du littérateur'.[58] On 26 April 1860,[59] Zola prefaced a letter to his friend still in Provence with the self-deprecating claim that 'lorsque je vois un tableau, moi qui sais tout au plus distinguer le blanc du noir, il est évident que je ne puis me permettre de juger des coups de pinceau'. Émile Bernard would later have the bright idea of citing this extract from the correspondence (published in the Fasquelle edition of 1907–08) as evidence of Zola's inability to understand Cézanne's achievements.[60] But Bernard of course failed to put this expression of false modesty in context, suppressing the following long paragraph in which Zola developed his argument: for in grappling 'plus hardiment' with 'le sujet de peinture', he returned to the question of the tension between commenting on the formal qualities of a painting and the temptation of recuperating artistic intentionality: 'en un mot, sans m'occuper du métier, je parle sur l'art, sur la pensée qui a présidé à l'œuvre.' 'Je me borne à dire', he admitted, 'si le sujet me plaît', while engaging in an analysis of colour-values to reassure Cézanne ('loin de moi la pensée de mépriser la forme') of the indivisibility of form and content: 'plus l'idée est grande, plus la forme doit être grande aussi. C'est par elle que le peintre est compris, apprécié'. To that end, he even offered some advice, cautioning that 'un tableau ne doit être seulement pour toi des couleurs broyées sur une toile', which can be compared in hindsight with his admiration for Manet's practice. But this letter is only one example of interchanges between Zola and Cézanne which begin to advance, however hesitantly, the novelist's thinking about painting. It was above all during his returns to Provence on vacation that he enjoyed the extraordinary privilege of watching the painter at his easel. That it was not until 1860 that Zola could address the pigmentation of Cézanne's 'coups de brosse' can be explained by the fact that it was only then that he began to paint in oils, having been forced by the dictates of the École municipale de dessin in Aix to work only with pencil and ink. Cézanne's impatience to be liberated from such constraints was further proof for Zola of what would be one of the major themes of his art criticism: the absolute incompatibility of pictorial originality and the pedagogically enforced conventions of artistic expression.

L'Œuvre also registers (*RM*, IV, 35) Cézanne's own move to Paris in the spring of 1861. It was through him that Zola renewed contact at that point with the so-called 'école d'Aix', the group of painters now in the capital whom he had got to know in their native city.[61] Although a short-lived experiment, lasting only until September, it was during this initial visit to Paris that Cézanne took one stage further Zola's growing familiarity with the art of his times. Only a year before, Zola was still countering realist practice by naively affirming that 'Greuze a toujours été mon favori' and that Ary Scheffer (1795–1858) was a 'peintre de génie'.[62] He was rapidly disabused of an idealist sentimentality perfectly attuned to the work of those two artists. Whether or not he was as dazzled as the painter himself claimed to be by *everything* they had seen together at the Salon of 1861,[63] Cézanne's euphoric reaction to Doré's 'tableau mirobolant' shown there may be indirectly linked to Zola's writing in praise of the artist two years later, in his first-ever such critical piece. But it was during Cézanne's more extended stay in the capital, between November 1862 and the summer of 1864, that their joint exploration of the city, excitedly evoked in *L'Œuvre*, left its mark. For it was through Cézanne that its author came to be 'entouré de peintres', the former taking him to artists' studios: 'y traînait Zola, dont il fit ainsi', as Gasquet recorded from his conversations with the painter, 'l'éducation artistique'.[64] It was at the Académie suisse, where Cézanne worked in the mornings,[65] that Zola came into contact with a widening circle: Pissarro, Guillaumin and the Spanish painter Francisco Oller (1833–1917). Cézanne's own new acquaintances included Guillemet — through whom Zola met Bazille, who then extended this network by introducing him to Renoir, so close a friend that he would share a studio with him after 1866. It is impossible to know either whether these introductions consisted of no more than a handshake or which of these painters were subsequently invited on a regular basis to Zola's *soirées* in 1863. But what is not in doubt is that this expanded social circle, for which Cézanne was primarily responsible, is retrospectively, and unambiguously, *celebrated* in Zola's novel of 1886, from its initially happy dinner parties to the chapter in *L'Œuvre* recalling Zola, Cézanne and their friends, 'la bande peu à peu accrue des camarades racolés en chemin, la marche libre d'une horde partie en guerre' (*RM*, IV,72), united in their renegade 'passion de l'art' culminating in the Salon des Refusés': 'On se sentait là dans une bataille gaie, livrée de verve, quand le petit jour naît, que les clairons sonnent, que l'on marche à l'ennemi, avec la certitude de le battre avant le coucher du soleil' (*RM*, IV,124). Amplifying the reminder in Zola's 'Liste de mes souvenirs' ('Paris, conquérir, promenades, dédain' (fol. 316)), it is no wonder that Cézanne was genuinely grateful to him for the 'impression des temps écoulés' he found in *L'Œuvre*.

But by the time has was talking to Gasquet, in the spring of 1896, Cézanne seems to be part of the new consensus that its fictional portrait of him went much further than the one silhouetted in the first half of the novel: 'Mais Zola m'a très bien empoigné, quand même, dans *L'Œuvre*, vous ne vous en souvenez peut-être pas, lorsqu'il beugle: "Ah! la vie! la vie! la sentir et la rendre dans sa réalité"',[66] even if this too is cited from an early chapter (*RM*, IV, 83). As for the novel as a whole, he would tell Gasquet that he was perfectly relaxed about a tragic plot determined by the imperatives of the *Rougon-Macquart* cycle. In any case, he had read Alexis's 1882 biography of the writer and was perfectly aware that, in the planned novel about 'le monde artistique', 'naturellement, Zola [...] se verra forcé de mettre à contribution ses amis, de recueillir leurs traits les plus typiques'.[67] It was only subsequently, in the 1890s, that he would be identified by his detractors as the neurotic model for Zola's doomed protagonist. His champions' *ex post facto* assertions of his dismay in having recognized himself in *L'Œuvre* are often as specious as they are strategic, as well as being unreliable and post-dated transcriptions of what Cézanne is supposed to have told them.[68] What remains true is that they are indeed *conversations* and, even if not wholly accurately recorded, their *thrust* alone (as well as echoes in others *not* recorded) would have been sufficient to poison the relationship between Zola and the painter, at the time, as well as colouring both our own reading of *L'Œuvre* and its place in our cultural histories.

Real Pictures and Fictional Portraits

The inordinate space and weight given to *L'Œuvre* in inferring Zola's view of Cézanne has tended to blot out other dimensions of their relationship. Although the painter's more regular presence in Paris results in a far less sustained correspondence with Zola after 1862, the rest of that last decade before the Franco-Prussian War bears witness to a continuing closeness between them. Before leaving Paris in August 1870, Cézanne completed a picture of a clock belonging to Zola, *La Pendule noire* (Fig. 2.1), the most enigmatic detail of which is that it has no hands. If it is risky to interpret this as indexing, shortly before the painter's departure, a *timeless* friendship, it is in any case a reminder of Cézanne's easy access to Zola's domestic interior and increasingly bourgeois comforts. This is equally true of the companionship registered in two other paintings, both dating from 1869–70, which Zola also retained: *Une Lecture de Paul Alexis chez Zola* and *Paul Alexis lisant à Émile Zola*. The same could be said of his *Tête de Femme* (1864), presumed to be of Zola's wife, and his gift to her in 1869 of the sombre watercolour *Usines à L'Estaque* which, in spite of her reservations about the painter, she kept until her death in 1925.[69] On the occasions, exceptionally, when Cézanne was away from Paris (back in Aix in the summer and autumn of 1865, and again in October 1866, or at Bennecourt earlier that year), he continued to keep Zola abreast of works in progress,[70] parenthetically mentioning financial difficulties which did not fall on deaf ears in the years ahead (at least until 1878) any more than they had in the past. 'Sightings' of Zola have been pinpointed in a number of Cézanne's early paintings, notably *Pastorale [Idylle]* (1870), *La Tentation de St Antoine* (1870) and *Le Déjeuner sur l'herbe* (*c.* 1870–71).[71] More certainly, several pictures of the village of Médan, including pencil sketches, a watercolour and two oil paintings, executed by Cézanne from across the other side of the river from Zola's house, testify to specific visits there between 1879 and 1881.[72] And from his letters over the next four years, we know of other visits to what he called 'ta résidence des champs'.

Given their closeness, particularly during the 1860s, much has also been made of the thematic continuities between the work of Zola and Cézanne during that period, though it is not obvious which of them inspired the other. 'Perhaps it is no coincidence', suggests Richard Verdi, that *L'Enlèvement* was painted for Zola in his house in the rue La Condamine 'in the very year in which *Thérèse Raquin* was published, 1867'.[73] There are 'clear parallels', according to Mary Louise Krumrine, between Zola's early novels and the erotic violence and dark landscapes of Cézanne paintings such as *Le Meurtre* (*c.* 1867–68).[74] 'Cézanne is never far from Zola's imagery', she writes, extending 'fascinating' comparisons between the morgue episode in *Thérèse Raquin* and *La Toilette funéraire ou L'Autopsie*, painted at exactly the same time. An entire subfield of Cézanne scholarship has indeed been devoted

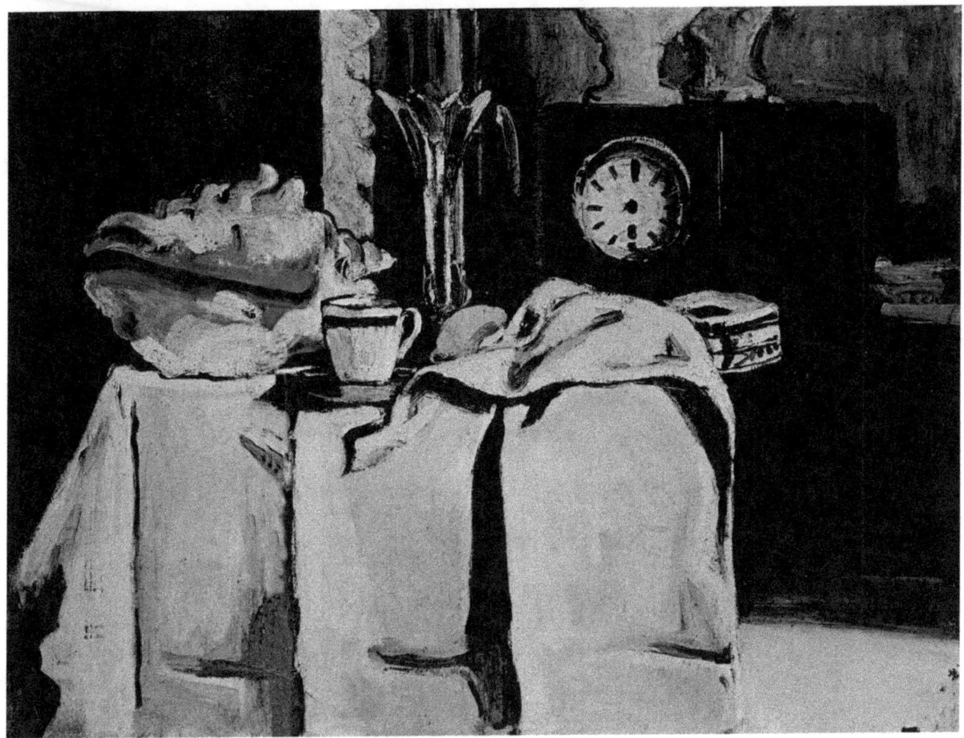

FIG. 2.1. Paul Cézanne, *La Pendule noire* (1869–70), oil on canvas, 55.2 × 74.3 cm. Private collection.

to literary influences on his work, starting with precise details which seem to be 'clearly drawn' from the Zola texts with which he was familiar. More significant in adducing Zola's view of Cézanne is the extent to which his own novels reveal what struck him about the painter's subjects and their treatment. The interest of *Thérèse Raquin* in this respect is less its murderous scenario and sinister backdrops than what Zola writes about its fictional painter Laurent. There is widespread agreement,[75] in this case, that he is, as the prototype of Claude Lantier in *L'Œuvre* almost twenty years later, with his 'peinture brutale', 'esquisses terrifiantes' and 'tons violents, des grands traits de pastel sabrant les ombres' (*RM*, IV, p 27), partly modelled on Cézanne: struggling with his demons; slashing his canvasses in frustration; and dejected to the point of creative impotence. But this is not evidence of what Krumrine calls the psychological 'affinities' between Cézanne and the homicidal protagonist of *Thérèse Raquin*. It is rather a practical demonstration of how, consistent with the foundational principle of the novelist's art criticism, pictorial representation is 'un coin de la création vu à travers un tempérament'. This principle's application, however, is riven with the same contradictions as Zola's 'Théorie des écrans': the ideal of an exactitude afforded by transparency is uneasily set against a necessarily distorting subjectivity. On the one hand, we are told that all Laurent's paintings somehow resemble each other by virtue of the individual personality of which they are the product — notwithstanding the fact that his attempts to paint an exact portrait of Camille are a disaster, as are Laurent's grotesque results in conforming to the rigorously mimetic approach Zola would advocate in his *Salon* of 1868: 'ces premiers essais étaient restés au-dessous de la médiocrité; son œil de paysan voyait gauchement et salement la nature; ses toiles, boueuses, mal bâties, grimaçantes, défiaient toute critique' (*OC*, I, 542). That could leave us unsure about whether such a condemnation parodies the critical reception of Cézanne's work in the 1860s, during which every one of his submissions to the Salon was rejected in those terms. But it is only, paradoxically, when 'il résolut de peindre au gré de sa fantaisie, sans se soucier de la nature' that Zola describes 'la naissance de cet artiste'. And there is no mistaking the power of his achievement:

> sa pensée délirait et montait jusqu'à l'extase du génie; [...] la névrose dont tout son être était secoué, développait en lui un sens artistique d'une lucidité étrange; [...] son cerveau éperdu lui semblait immense, et, dans ce brusque agrandissement de sa pensée, il voyait passer des créations exquises, des rêveries de poète. Et c'est ainsi que ses œuvres étaient belles, rendues tout d'un coup personnelles et vivantes. (*OC*, I, 629)

But whether this accommodates merely wishful thinking on Zola's part is another matter. For if Laurent's compositions are certainly as individuated as Cézanne's seemed to Zola, there remains, immediately following this euphoric account of imaginative liberation, an ambivalence about a disconcertingly heterogeneous range of subjects, in a passage which again overrides (as do my ellipses) incidental cross-references to the novel's plot (*OC*, I, 630):

> L'artiste esquissa successivement les têtes les plus diverses, des têtes d'anges, de vierges avec des auréoles, de guerriers romains coiffés de leur casque, d'enfants blancs et roses, de vieux bandits couturés de cicatrices [...]. Alors Laurent se jeta dans la caricature, il exagéra les traits, il fit des profils monstrueux. Il inventa des têtes grotesques, et il ne réussit qu'à rendre plus horribles les portraits [...]. Il finit par dessiner des animaux, des chiens et des chats.

The novel more explicitly anticipating *L'Œuvre* is *Le Ventre de Paris* (1873), in which the character of Claude Lantier makes his first appearance in Zola's series. In preparing *L'Œuvre*, in order to establish a degree of continuity between the two novels, he reminded himself to re-use his earlier portrait of the fictional painter[76] which bears an uncanny resemblance to the Cézanne of his self-portrait of 1872 or as depicted by Pissarro in 1874 (Fig. 2.2):

> C'était un garçon maigre, avec de gros os, une grosse tête, barbu, le nez très fin, les yeux minces et clairs. Il portait un chapeau de feutre noir, roussi, déformé, et se boutonnait au fond d'un immense paletot, jadis marron tendre, que les pluies avaient déteint en larges traînées verdâtres. Un peu courbé, agité d'un frisson d'inquiétude nerveuse qui devait lui être habituel. (*RM*, I, 617)

Zola's work notes for *Le Ventre de Paris* are easily decipherable in this respect: 'Claude figure longue, front accentué, *visage arabe* (C.)' (Ms 10338, fol. 105); 'Le poser pour le type futur, selon le portrait de C...' (fol. 112). And, as in *Thérèse Raquin* and *L'Œuvre*, one can extract from its plot a number of aspects which transpose,

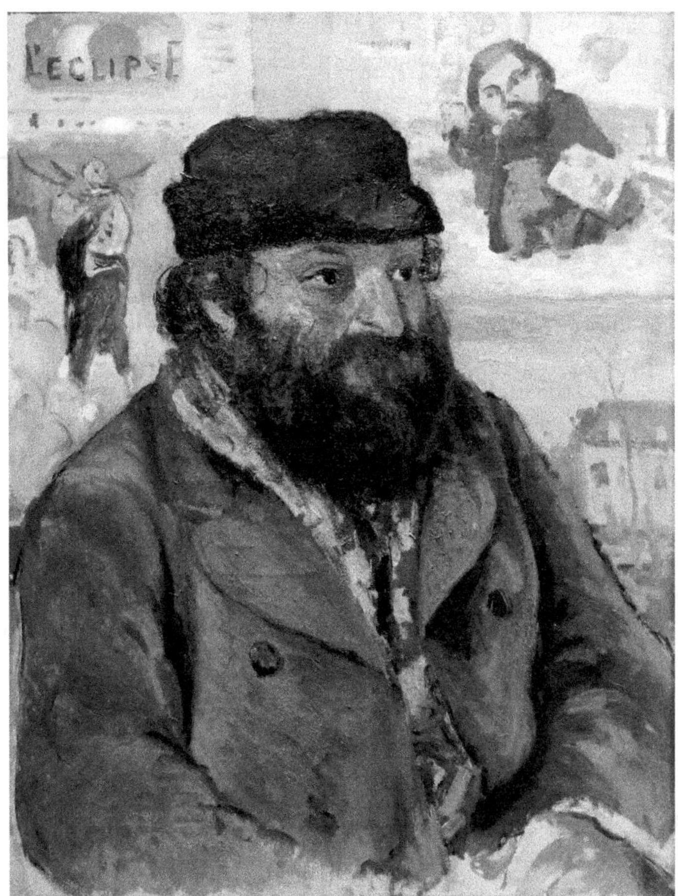

Fig. 2.2. Camille Pissarro, *Portrait de Paul Cézanne* (1874), oil on canvas, 73 × 59.7 cm. Private collection.

through the grid of Zola's memories and perceptions, those of Cézanne's career up until that point, all the clearer in 1872–73 than they would be more than a decade later. Zola's preparatory jottings are as revealing of his view of Cézanne as the finished text, traceable back to remarks and information in their correspondence, and going well beyond the original intention that Claude's role in the novel should be 'purement épisodique' (fol. 95). One example is the stress on his painting of 'superbes natures mortes': 'Je donnerai surtout une place au jeune homme, dont je ferai mon peintre plus tard [...] avec l'amour des natures mortes qu'il crayonnera'; 'Claude a rêvé un tableau superbe [...] au milieu d'une nature morte colossale'.[77] His early works are 'des études étranges' and his inconsistent pictorial styles are the result of his being 'très oscillant dans ses théories' (fols 95 and 62). In terms of his character, the reference to sexual inhibitions is noted not just in the same sentence as, but immediately before, 'le portrait de C...': responding to a teasing question about being attracted to the young Cadine, Claude's negative '"Moi! ah! non, il ne faut pas de femme"' is followed by Zola's note 'Il est timide', amplified in this novel and similarly prefiguring *L'Œuvre* in this respect.[78] But *Le Ventre de Paris* is so close to Zola's first-hand knowledge of Cézanne that many dimensions of the fictional painter needed no aide-mémoire: because his 'ébauches épouvantent tout le monde', 'font une peur atroce aux bourgeois', he was quite content to turn his back on society. As he confesses: 'Je suis un égoïste. [...] [L]orsque je peins, je songe uniquement à mon plaisir personnel.' This is consistent with a scepticism about socialist ideals which explains his prioritizing painting over politics: 'un tableau splendide auquel je songeais pendant que vous discutiez la question'. His associated delusions that this one would be 'le succès du Salon [...] un succès à tout caser, un vrai tableau moderne celui-là' (*RM*, I, 848–49), ultimately incorporated Zola's note that 'mon peintre, sombre déjà, ayant des parentés avec Florent, mais en art', but are ironized in the ineffectual slogans of the latter and his motley crew of would-be revolutionaries and, by extension, the painter: 'vous m'avez l'air de faire de la politique absolument comme je fais de la peinture' (*RM*, I, 849). In Claude's case, 'cet enthousiasme d'artiste' (*RM*, I, 623), conjuring up pictures described as 'extravagants, fous, sublimes' (*RM*, I, 627), is confronted by the prosaic business of working at his easel: 'Il s'emporta contre la peinture, dit que c'était un métier de chien, jura qu'il ne toucherait de sa vie à un pinceau [...], sujet à ces emportements d'artiste impuissant en face des œuvres solides et vivantes qu'il rêvait' (*RM*, I, 680). As he would do in *L'Œuvre*, he kicks through canvasses and, as Zola remembered from his letters admonishing Cézanne, hurls his paint-brushes at the ceiling.[79]

The Cézanne discernible in *Le Ventre de Paris* is an artist in the throes of confusion. On the one hand, Claude espouses Cézanne's avowed intention, as he wrote to Zola 'à ne faire que des choses en plein air',[80] with the fictional painter having the vague idea that a friend might pose for him in the countryside: 'je l'ai vu nu, et s'il voulait me poser des académies, en plein air...' (*RM*, I, 621), a suggestion which is undercut by the conventional genre proposed. He is as enchanted as any Impressionist by 'un effet de lumière' (*RM*, I, 622). But he is never satisfied: his watercolour of the rue Pirouette is considered 'pas trop mauvaise' (*RM*, I, 618), before being dismissed as a 'faiblesse' by virtue of its faulty perspectival structure (*RM*, I, 624), or, as it was even more negatively imagined in Zola's notes, 'dont il s'accuse comme un crime' (Ms 10338, fol. 221). Every day is 'un long effort désespéré' and sleepless nights are racked by 'toutes ces sacrées études que je ne peux achever' and a raging self-doubt corroding his sense of self: 'Il jurait, cherchait des mots orduriers, s'abîmait en pleine boue, avec la rage froide d'un esprit tendre et exquis qui doute de lui et qui rêve de se salir' (*RM*, I, 680–81).

Countering such self-abasement with a residual assertion of his unique talent, the above is perhaps Zola's most authentic appraisal of Cézanne, as both man and painter. It is further illuminated by chapter 4 of *Le Ventre de Paris*: for this is so detached from the text's narrative development that it reads like an awkwardly inserted digression which culminates in the stirring proclamation of 'un manifeste artistique, le positivisme de l'art, l'art moderne et tout matérialiste' (*RM*, I, 776). This obviously articulates the critical positioning of Zola himself faced with Cézanne's pictorial instability. His preparatory notes for the chapter refer to 'une sorte d'idylle dans la Halle', opposing 'le nain romantique' (of Hugo's *Les Misérables*) and the figure of Marjolin as the 'jeune garçon réaliste' (fol. 71). The absolute incompatibility of these two aesthetics is underlined by two deliberately incongruous analogies in the novel's work notes: 'L'idylle, Paul et Virginie aux Halles' and 'Théocrite aux Halles'.[81] The significance of the latter is reinforced by Danchev's insights into the 'strong Theocritan flavor' of 'Cézanne's beloved *Eclogues*' and the 'shadow identity' of Virgil's master which Zola once suggested for him.[82] Set against the painter's strange but bucolic *Idylle* (*c.* 1870), created only two years before work on *Le Ventre de Paris* got under way and invariably described as 'the peak of Cézanne's Romantic imagining', referencing pastoral tradition and including a dreaming figure akin to a self-portrait,[83] Zola's antithetical demonstration is unambiguous: 'Il me faut l'idylle parisienne très pimentée.'[84] Which, in the light of what that idea becomes in the novel itself ('l'idylle effrontée') is something of an understatement. Far from shepherds and unrequited platonic love, or the Michelet nostrums he and Cézanne had rehearsed in their youth, Zola's version of the 'courtship' of Marjolin and Cadine moves from innocence to experience in graphic detail. Liberated from social norms, the two adolescents lead an increasingly feral existence characterized by unrestrained sexual appetites, 'libres et sans honte, comme les moineaux qui s'accouplent au bord d'un toit' (*RM*, I, 771); and the associated casual promiscuity climaxes in Marjolin's attempted rape of another woman: 'il la culbuta [...]. Et il allait la prendre à la taille, ainsi qu'il prenait Cadine, d'une brutalité d'animal qui vole et qui s'emplit' (*RM*, I, 795).

Claude's reaction to simulations of the kind staged in both *Thérèse Raquin* and some of Cézanne's paintings parodies their hostile reception: revolted 'devant cette ordure, "cette fille crevée, ramassée à la Morgue". Il s'emportait contre cette nudité de cadavre, cette laideur du joli' (*RM*, I, 781). But faced with realities in due course encoded in the very title of Zola's *La Bête humaine* (1890), a term already used by him as early as 1866,[85] Claude is so incapable of distinguishing between materiality and the picturesque[86] that his ambitions come to nothing: 'Il rêva longtemps un tableau colossal, Cadine et Marjolin s'aimant au milieu des Halles [...] échangeant le baiser idyllique'; 'Mais pendant près de deux ans, il recommença les esquisses, sans pouvoir trouver la note juste. Il creva une quinzaine de toiles' (*RM*, I, 776). Zola charts his fictional painter's aspirations to leave behind an outdated aesthetic ('Claude déblatéra contre le romantisme [...]. On devait [...] faire du moderne' (*RM*, I, 624)), seeing in the representation of modern life 'une satire de la peinture à idées, un soufflet donné aux vieilles écoles' (*RM*, I, 776), exemplified by painting, in the shadow of the medieval church of St Eustache, the differently beautiful Les Halles.[87] And these are self-evidently the criteria against which Zola judges Cézanne, intermittently subscribed to by the painter but not always put into practice. The Claude Lantier of *Le Ventre de Paris* is by no means a total failure: he produces 'une nature morte étonnante', 'barbare et superbe', 'une véritable œuvre d'art' (*RM*, I, 800–01), akin to three of Cézanne's (together with the landscapes evoked in *L'Œuvre*) which Zola had on his walls and which he doubtless found less disconcerting than his human figures. The novel as a whole engages in an indirect series of critical exchanges with Cézanne, encouraging him to definitively adopt the writer's now-established aesthetic values, by liquidating their previously shared, but immaturely 'poetic', enthusiasm for the likes of Musset, Hugo and Lamartine. But its own brilliantly elaborated verbal *natures mortes*, for which *Le Ventre de Paris* is justly famous, could also be seen as an early demonstration of, as Zola would be accused by Degas of doing in *L'Œuvre*, 'la supériorité de l'homme de lettres sur l'artiste'.

Cézanne and Zola's Art Criticism

Conversely, the relative absence of Cézanne in Zola's published art-critical writing remains a source of controversy. That absence has been seen as proof of the limitations of his art criticism more generally. Accusations to that effect were initiated in the shadow of the Dreyfus Affair, reinforcing the antithetical positioning of the former friends by devaluing Zola's understanding of the visual arts. Bernard's malicious traducing of an 1860 letter as further evidence of this is anticipated, unsurprisingly, by Vollard who went rather further. There are instances, in his writing on contemporary painters, when Vollard's hostility to Zola seems almost gratuitous, as in his report that Renoir loathed his fiction; or in 'recalling' that Cézanne 'vitupérait feu Zola qui avait osé reprocher à Corot de n'avoir pas, dans ses paysages, mis des paysannes au lieu des nymphes'.[88] But, in relation to Zola's art criticism, Vollard's motivation is clear. For, from 1919 onwards, in all the subsequent editions of his 1914 biography, as well as in *En écoutant Cézanne*, he appended extracts from reviews of the biography. This included, for example, Joseph Péladan's 'J'y ai trouvé un portrait de Zola qui m'a expliqué bien des choses et que cet homme d'un talent indiscutable était, au fond, un imbécile'; and also an objection, from Frantz Jourdain, that 'M. Vollard présente l'auteur de *Mes Haines* (Zola) comme un doux gâteux débitant toutes les âneries possibles sur la peinture'.[89] Even the interests of a balanced assessment could serve the thesis of Zola's incompetence as an art critic.

Less clear is how Cézanne himself responded to his art criticism. Gasquet's reference to Zola's writing on Proudhon makes it clear that Cézanne was familiar with *Mes haines*, the second edition of which he had been sent in June 1879. And he was apparently thrilled to have Zola's 1866 articles in *L'Événement* dedicated to him, in the shape of a long prefatory letter ('À mon ami Paul Cézanne'), when they were republished in volume form as *Mon Salon* the next year. His portrait of his father reading that newspaper (see Fig. 1.3) (which he never did, only familiar with the more conservative *Le Siècle*[90]) underlined the critical authority of a Zola of whom Louis-Auguste Cézanne disapproved as a bad influence on his son in encouraging him to pursue an artistic career rather than a legal one.[91] A few months earlier, Zola had also dedicated *La Confession de Claude* (1865) to Cézanne as well as to Baille, not least because this largely autobiographical text draws on the experiences of 'les trois inséparables'. But the painter was mistaken if he saw either *dédicace* as a gesture of militant solidarity grounded in Zola's expectations that both his art criticism and this first novel would provoke the kind of hostility exemplified by critical responses to Cézanne's own early work.[92] For Zola's open letter prefacing *Mon*

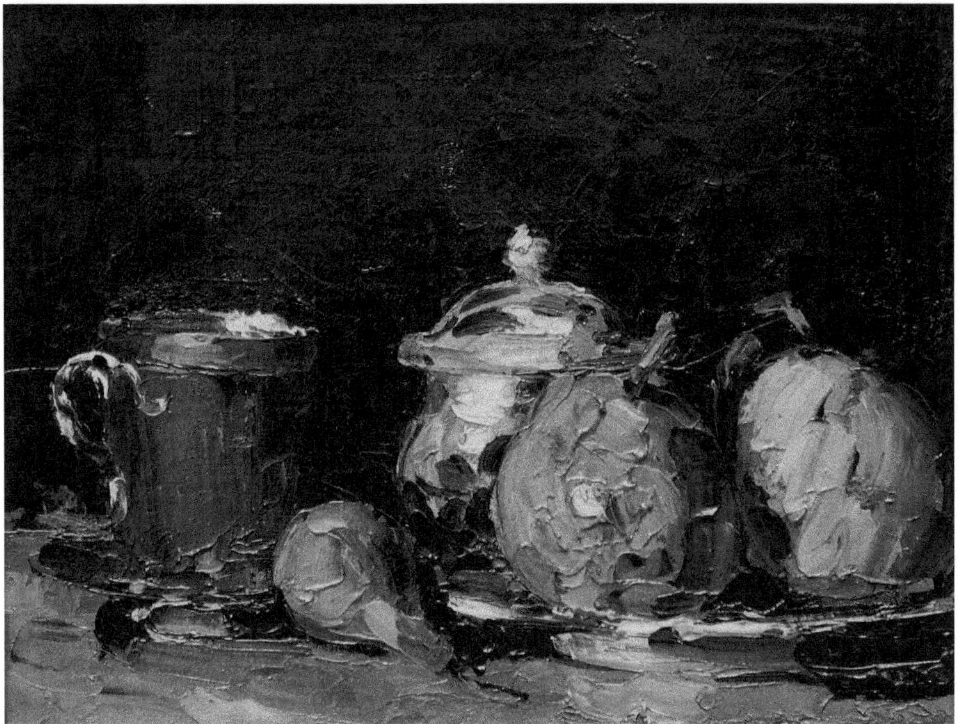

FIG. 2.3. Paul Cézanne, *Sucrier, poires et tasse bleue* (1865–66), oil on canvas, 30 × 41 cm. Musée Granet, Aix-en-Provence.

Salon so effusively evokes their undying friendship that it could be read as a pre-emptive apology for not actually having mentioned him in the articles collected in the volume. Whether or not Cézanne understood that Zola was thereby reserving judgement on him *as a painter*, there is an intriguing detail in his 1867 portrait of his father: for behind the sitter's head hangs an unframed image of his *Sucrier, poires et tasse bleue* (*c.* 1866) (Fig. 2.3) which has been seen as an assertion of his own painterly identity. What has not been pointed out by art historians, however, is that Cézanne gave this still life to Zola,[93] obliquely reminding him perhaps of a pictorial presence omitted from his writing in *L'Événement*.

Beyond that, however, things become more problematic, not least because there are only six mentions of Cézanne in Zola's writing between 1866 and 1896, and not a single analysis of any of his paintings. To Manet, by contrast, there are over one hundred references, leaving aside his major 1867 study and detailed appreciation of individual canvasses. It is precisely because of this gap that Zola's view of Cézanne, unlike his judgements of other artists, can only be inferred. The longest intervention in the press on Cézanne's behalf was Zola's open letter to *Le Figaro*, published on 12 April 1867, correcting the spelling of the name 'd'un de mes amis d'enfance, d'un jeune peintre dont j'estime singulièrement le talent vigoureux et personnel' and expressing his solidarity with the painter who had, 'en belle et nombreuse compagnie' (*EsA*, p. 499) had two works rejected by that year's Salon jury. That Cézanne considered Zola to be an influential critic is clear from his request, in his letter of 10 May 1880, to reprint in *Le Voltaire* the letter being sent to the authorities by Monet and Renoir about the disadvantageous hanging of their pictures, asking that the Impressionists be included in the following year's Salon 'dans des conditions convenables'. It would be helpful, Cézanne added, if Zola were to add to this 'quelques mots [qui] tendraient à démontrer l'importance des impressionnistes et le mouvement de curiosité réel qu'ils ont provoqué'.[94] He responded by publishing a series of four articles, between 18 and 22 June, later collected as *Le Naturalisme au Salon*, certainly more than a 'few words' but somewhat less unequivocally supportive than Cézanne might have hoped. But he nevertheless thanked Zola on 19 June, having seen the one in *Le Voltaire* on that day, and notwithstanding the brief mention of himself as 'un tempérament de grand peintre qui se débat encore dans des recherches de facture' (*EsA*, p. 376). Rewald suggests that, together with the remark that Cézanne 'reste plus près de Courbet et de Delacroix', Zola's comment may not have been taken amiss by the painter, given his gradual detachment from Impressionist practice allied to the rethinking of his own. Although not as fervent as their youthful correspondence, other letters between them up until 1885 testify to their continuing shared focus on both the pictorial ups and downs of individual artists and, more generally, critical debates on the directions of modern painting.

It seems not by chance, however, that Bernard's remark about Zola's critical incompetence should be framed by reference to Zola's contrasting privileging of Manet, whose overt Republicanism had been aligned with that of the novelist. For nobody could be in any doubt that, whatever reservations he might bring to a final judgement on Manet, from 1866 onwards Zola's championing of him was common knowledge. Here again, Cézanne and Zola diverge. The painter could hardly have failed to notice that, contrasting with his own omission, an entire essay in *Mon Salon* had been devoted to Manet, notwithstanding both their 1866 submissions having been rejected. The copy of the volume Zola personally sent to Manet bore the inscription of its 'témoignage de sympathie'. In 1860, he had conveyed to Cézanne his 'beau rêve' of a book written by himself, 'que tu avais illustré de belles, de sublimes gravures. Nos deux noms en lettres d'or brillaient, unis sur le premier feuillet', evidence of a 'fraternité du génie'. If that was comprehensively deflated by his 'Ce n'est encore qu'un rêve malheureusement',[95] Zola's instinctive sense of Cézanne being unlikely to realize his share of such a project would find its pragmatic substitute in seeking, seven years later, to persuade his publisher to bring out an illustrated edition of his *Contes à Ninon* and thereby to 'mettre le nom de Manet sur une de mes œuvres'.[96] As early as 1866, Zola had referred to Manet as 'un des maîtres de demain' (*EsA*, p. 151). And his next novel, *Madeleine Férat*, was dedicated, on 1 September 1868, not to childhood friends but to Manet, and in fulsome terms linking their names in an association as 'entière et durable' as in Manet's portrait of the writer earlier in the year. To look again at Cézanne's *La Pendule noire* (see Fig. 2.1) is to wonder whether the porcelain inkwell to the

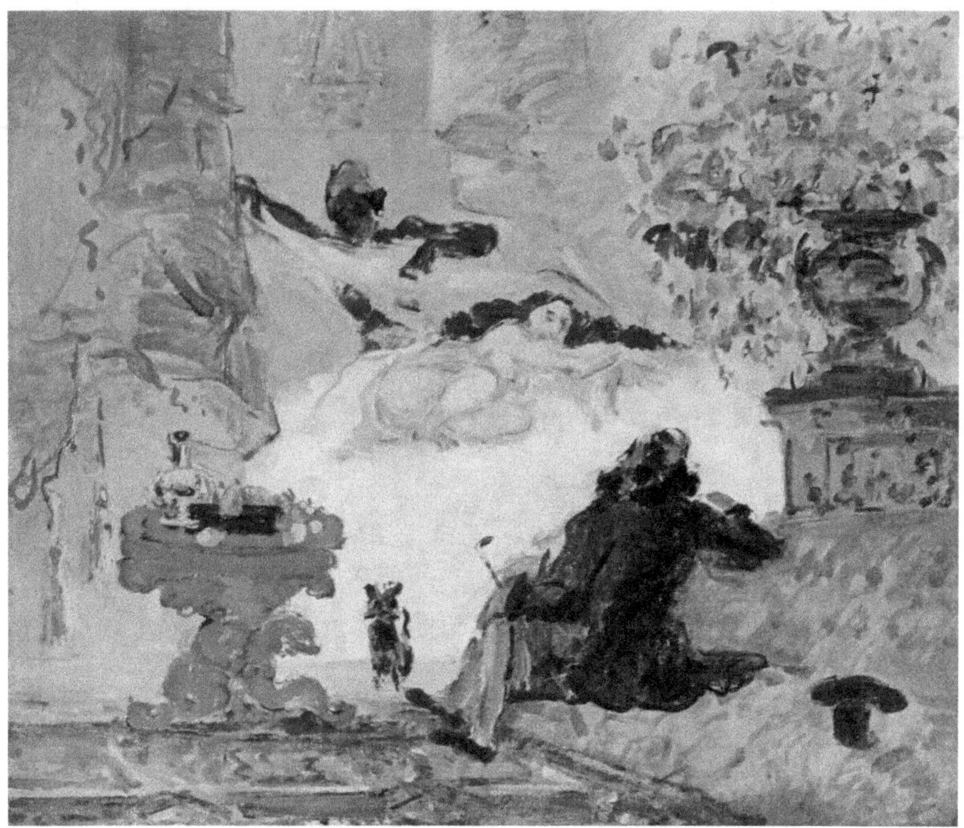

FIG. 2.4. Paul Cézanne, *Une moderne Olympia* (1869–70), oil on canvas, 46 × 55 cm. Musée d'Orsay, gift of Paul Gachet.

right of the clock-face is an iconographic reminder of the one in that portrait (see Fig. 4.1); or a discreet reproach juxtaposing the timelessness of their friendship and Zola's possibly more ephemeral association with Manet. Shy and awkward as he was, Cézanne spoke of his initial veneration for the worldly Manet.[97] But he ultimately viewed him as petty and overly concerned to secure public honours and social recognition. His self-portraits in the 1870s and 1880s are a savage rejection of the sartorially elegant Manet projected by Fantin-Latour (see Fig. 4.5).[98] Cézanne's renderings of Zola himself, it has been argued, are a critique of Manet's style, turned as it was towards issues of surface and retinal sensation.[99] That he refuses the latter his avant-garde status is evident from his 1869–70 and 1873 reworking, in *Une moderne Olympia* (Fig. 2.4), of the very painting Zola had praised as Manet's masterpiece.[100] The adjectival inversion is as emphatic as his sketch of it being included in the first Impressionist exhibition of 1874 in which Manet, as he would on all subsequent occasions, refused to participate. Cézanne's *L'Après-midi à Naples [avec servante noire]* (*c.* 1866–67) grotesquely elaborates the narrative which *Olympia* (Fig. 2.5) holds in check. In his own *Déjeuner sur l'herbe* (1870–71), he produces

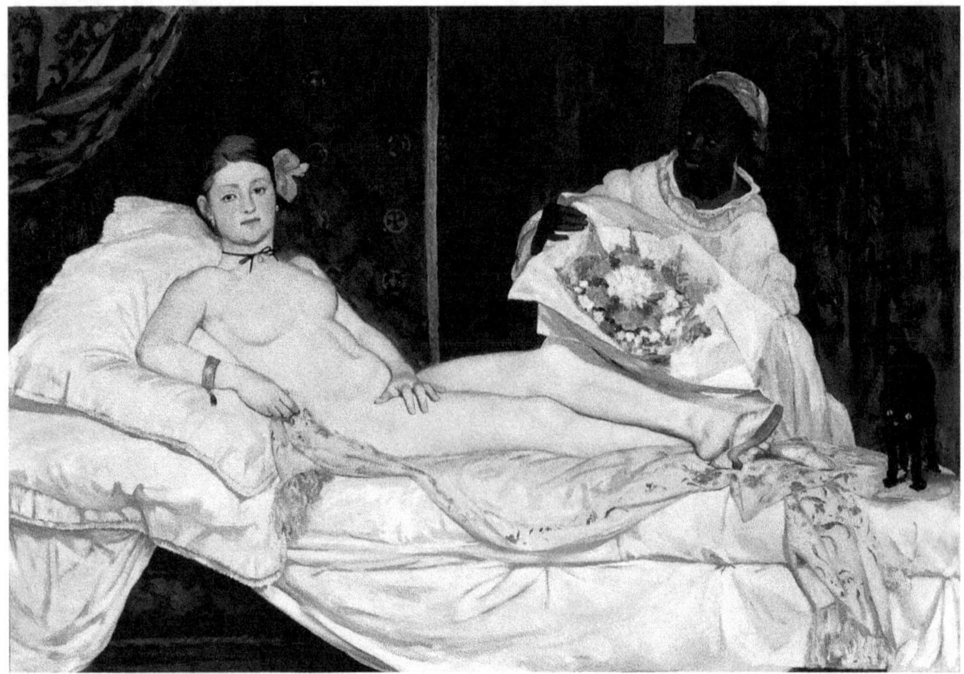

FIG. 2.5. Édouard Manet, *Olympia* (1865), oil on canvas, 130.5 × 190 cm. Musée d'Orsay, Paris.

a similarly ludic version of the Manet which he and Zola had seen together at the Salon des Refusés. Vollard, of course, was keen to stress Cézanne's superior originality: 'Il fut tout de suite pris par la force de réalisation de Manet. "Il crache le ton!" s'exclamait-il; seulement, à la réflexion, il ajoutait: "Oui, mais il manque d'harmonie, et aussi de tempérament".'[101]

The virtual absence of Cézanne in Zola's art criticism was certainly more than a matter of personal taste. Expanding on the writer telling him that Cézanne's paintings were hidden away, Vollard cites Zola's view of the painter's unfulfilled talent, which is a constant refrain in the few published references to him: 'Ne me demandez pas de les sortir, cela me fait trop de peine, quand je pense à ce que mon ami aurait pu être, s'il avait voulu diriger son imagination et aussi travailler sa forme'; 'Mon cher grand Cézanne avait l'étincelle. Mais s'il eut le génie d'un grand peintre, il n'eut pas la volonté de le devenir. Il se laissait trop aller à ses rêves.'[102] This particular recollection does seem genuine. No less than forty years earlier, Zola had written to Cézanne in precisely these terms: 'dans l'artiste il y a deux hommes, le poète et l'ouvrier. Et toi qui a l'étincelle, qui possède ce qui ne s'acquiert pas [...] tu n'as pour réussir qu'à exercer tes doigts, qu'à devenir ouvrier.'[103] There is also a distinct echo in such a lament of the unbridled pictorial inventiveness ascribed to Laurent in *Thérèse Raquin*, consistent with the 'haine intransigeante' Cézanne retained, so Gasquet reported,[104] for the very notion of *la ligne droite* predicated by the likes of Flaubert[105] and Zola. At one stage, Zola had misplaced hopes that

'Cézanne travaille; il s'affirme de plus en plus dans la voie originale où sa nature l'a poussé. J'espère beaucoup en lui'.[106] In his mention of the painter in 1877, Zola shares Manet's once-held view of him as 'le plus grand coloriste du groupe' (i.e. of the Impressionists), but ends once again with a declaration of judgement deferred: 'le jour où M. Paul Cézanne se possédera tout entier, il produira des œuvres tout à fait supérieures' (*EsA*, p. 589. It contrasts painfully with his confident prediction that 'le destin avait sans doute marqué au musée du Louvre la place future de *l'Olympia* et du *Déjeuner sur l'herbe*' (*EsA*, p. 497).

Zola's Cézannes

It is somewhat ironic, in the final analysis, that so much attention has been paid to an estrangement which has multiple threads, stitched across biographical intersections and resentments, and opposing religious and political beliefs which became magnified in the associated critical discourse strategically forcing Zola and Cézanne apart. A contrary argument would insist that Zola was too close to the intensity and vicissitudes of the painter's life, preventing him from distinguishing between the man and his work. Any assessment of their relationship cannot avoid returning to the premise that all Zola's writing on contemporary art is inseparable from viewing painters in the mirror of his own self-definition as a novelist and a critic. Nothing could be further from the truth in that respect than his assuring Cézanne that 'sous bien des rapports, nos caractères sont semblables [...]. Ne suis-je pas dans le même cas que toi?'.[107] His awareness that they were in fact utterly different more usually seeps through in even his earliest letters to his friend. In writing to him in July 1860, with a frankness born of exasperation as a result of Cézanne's vacillation as to whether his painting was a vocation or a displacement activity, Zola could hardly contain himself: 'tu deviens pour moi une énigme, un sphinx, un je ne sais quoi d'impossible et de ténébreux' (*Corr.*, I, 212). In a letter from Baille to Zola, there was a similar but even less reassuring description of their 'ami poétique, fantastique, bachique, érotique, antique, physique, géométrique'.[108] The serial indeterminacy of the painter's own self-portraits, in only one of which he is holding a palette (and then only in 1886), perhaps testify to those disparate identities and the difficulty of *being* Cézanne, underlying Zola's difficulty too in bringing these images into a coherent focus.

His letters of the 1860s to other friends rush from the excitement of Cézanne's imminent arrival in Paris to the despairing and soon-to-be confirmed expectation that the painter would shortly be packing his bags and returning to Provence. Zola was not alone in his impatience with Cézanne's procrastination, still shared by an equally concerned Guillemet a decade later: 'Il est temps qu'il produise selon son idée et il me tarde de lui voir prendre la place qu'il doit avoir.'[109] But Zola, having seen Cézanne's outrageous and uncompromisingly provocative submissions to the Salon, such as his *Le Punch au rhum* in 1867 (Fig. 2.6), had never shown the slightest surprise, let alone been wont to protest as he would in the case of Manet, at the painter's year-on-year rejection. 'Toujours refusé', as Zola wrote of Claude Lantier in his work notes for *L'Œuvre* (fol. 147). In Cézanne's case the only exception was

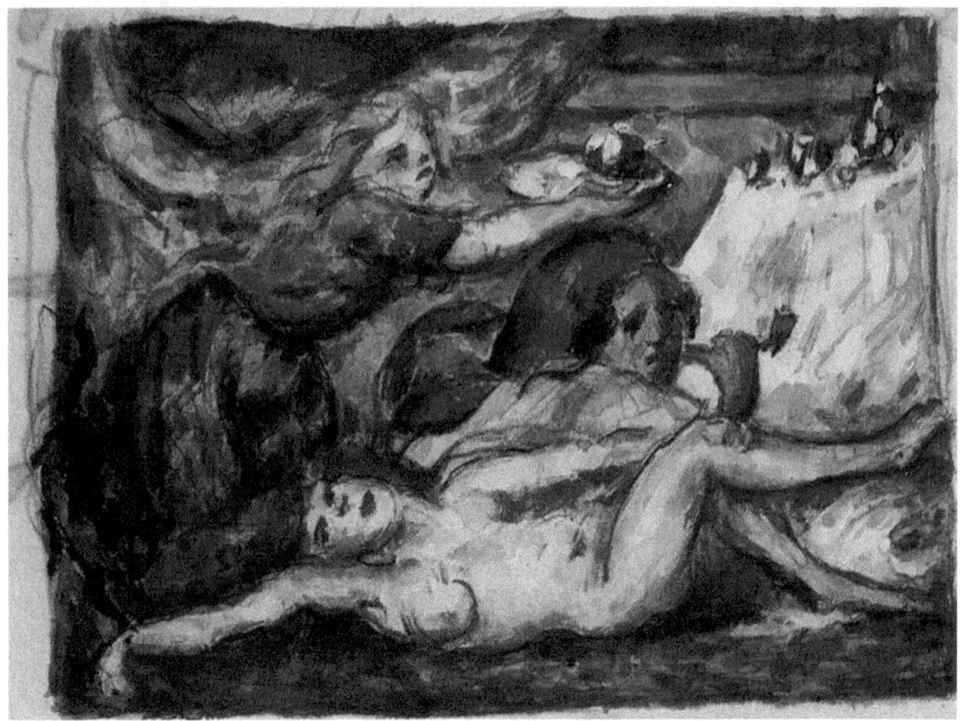

FIG. 2.6. Paul Cézanne, *Le Punch au rhum* (rejected by the Salon of 1867), pencil, pen, watercolour and gouache on cardboard, 11 × 14.8 cm. Private collection.

in 1882 when, masquerading as a pupil of Guillemet, the latter worked behind the scenes to have one of his paintings accepted: his *Portrait de M. L. A....* That too would be incorporated into the novel, transposed as Claude's painting of his dead child, on the basis of Guillemet confiding to Zola the process whereby a member of the admissions jury was allowed a 'charitable' acceptance notwithstanding the collective cynicism (fol. 386):

> Pour Cézanne, les rires au chevalet. Guillemet demande. Henner vote seul avec lui. 'Ce n'est pas si mauvais que ça: on dirait une tapisserie — les jurés qui regardent la signature. Cabanel pour refuser: 'Ça! ça !'. Et il se baisse, voit le nom: 'le n° 1 messieurs'. Le mot de Gervex à Guillemet: 'Si tu soutiens ça, c'est pour qu'on mette ton nom dans les journaux'.

It was one thing for Zola, in 1860, to address Cézanne as 'monsieur mon ami, monsieur le grand peintre futur';[110] far from such joshing, his prediction to Baille was quite another: 'Paul peut avoir le génie d'un grand peintre, il n'aura jamais le génie de le devenir.'[111] But there would remain a genuine sympathy for Cézanne, a quarter of a century later, characterizing the relationship in *L'Œuvre* between authorial surrogate and his painter friend as the 'fraternité douloureuse de celui qui produit devant celui qui ne peut produire' (fol. 134).

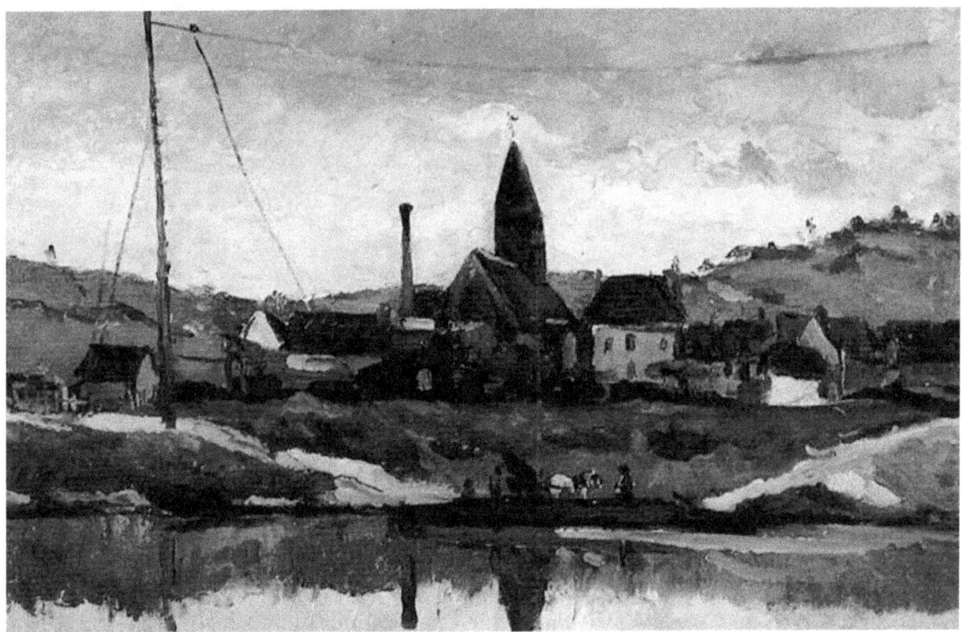

FIG. 2.7. Paul Cézanne, *Vue de Bonnières* (1866), oil on canvas, 38 × 61 cm. Musée Faure, Aix-les-Bains.

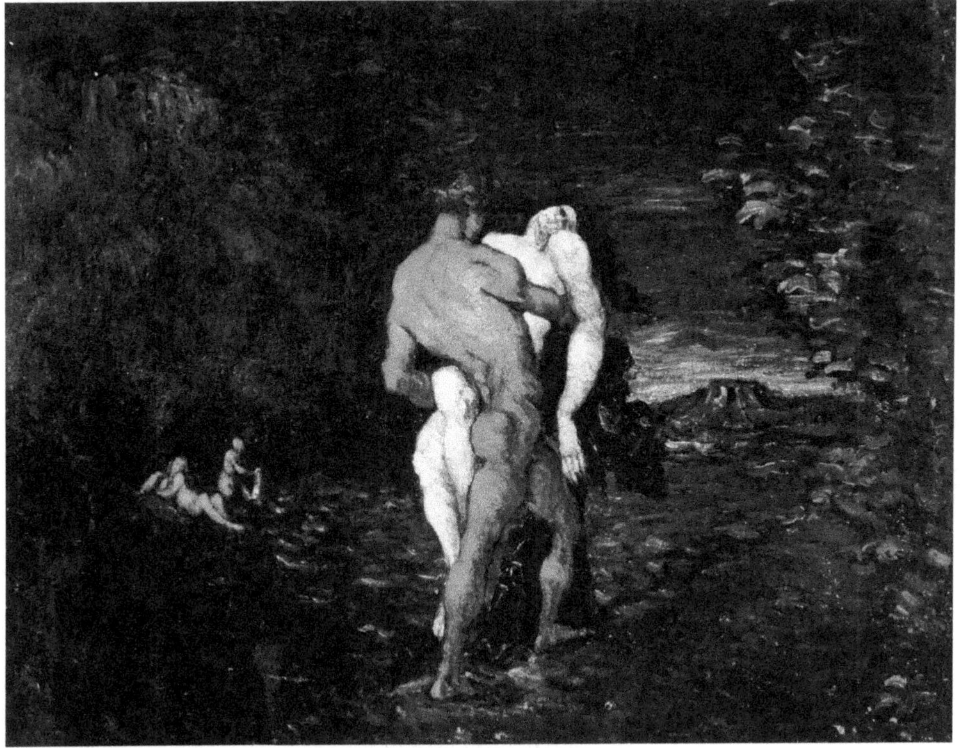

FIG. 2.8. Paul Cézanne, *L'Enlèvement* (1867), oil on canvas, 90.5 × 117 cm. King's College, Cambridge; on loan to the Fitzwilliam Museum, Cambridge.

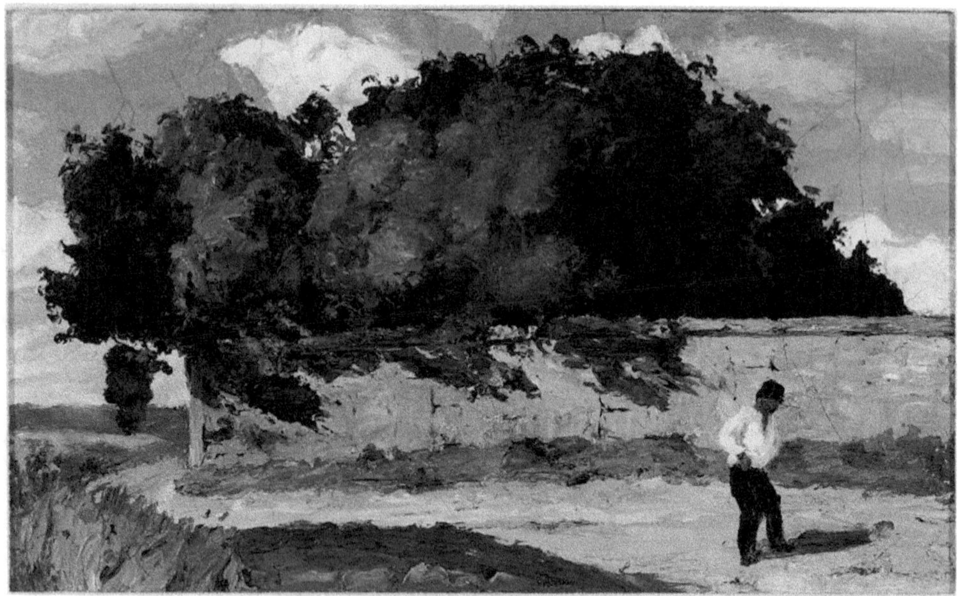

Fig. 2.9. Paul Cézanne, *Mur de jardin* (1867–68), oil on canvas, 23 × 38 cm. Private collection.

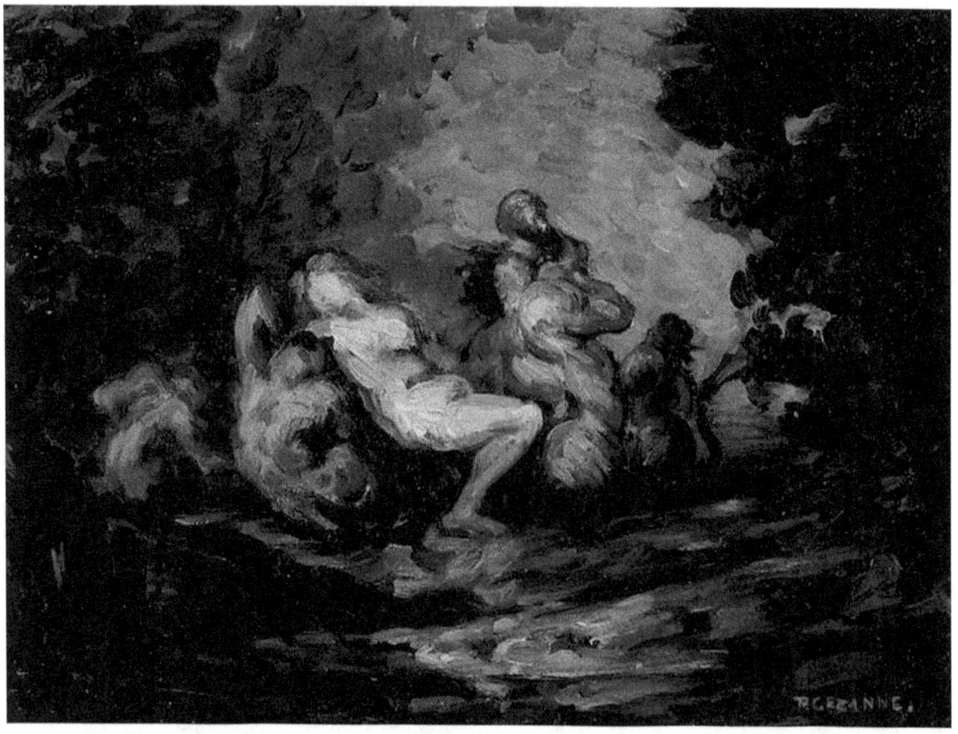

Fig. 2.10. Paul Cézanne, *Néréides et Tritons* (c. 1867), oil on canvas, 23.5 × 31 cm. Private collection.

To encourage Cézanne's efforts to realize his talent and raise his profile, Zola's solicitous but unsolicited and repeated advice was wide-ranging: greater self-discipline; efficient timetabling; weekly budget; better daily habits; greater consistency; not to continually re-work canvasses; choose subjects which might appeal to a wider public; don't use exclusively dark pigments; be more stoical; avoid being so infuriatingly illogical. The thrust of each of these was 'be more like me'. It may well be that Zola's art criticism could not accommodate the implied reservations generating such advice without causing offense. The novelist himself was of the view that all publicity, however hostile, was good publicity. But in the open letter to Cézanne prefacing *Mon Salon*, he had referred to an over-sensitivity to criticism which certainly applied to its recipient: 'Vous autres peintres, vous êtes bien plus irritables que nous autres écrivains [...]. Mais les artistes ont la peau plus tendre' (*EsA*, p. 124). In a letter to Baille in the summer of 1861, Zola had said as much: 'Paul, excellente nature et plein de dons naturels, ne peut cependant pas souffrir une remontrance, quelque douce qu'elle soit.'[112] But, over and above these footnotes to an awareness of Cézanne's vulnerability in this respect, it is clear that Zola's art criticism is the testing-ground for the development of his own theoretical positioning. At a purely rhetorical level, much of it works by analogy, comparison and conflation, by equivalents, metaphorical substitutions and superimpositions eroding the distinction between different artistic practices in the service of his own literary projects. By contrast, in the creative re-invention of his styles, never fixed within an identifiable school or movement, a development or an evolution or even a tendency, Cézanne does not stand still. There is no more graphic illustration of this than the comparative juxtaposition of two sets of paintings he gave Zola in the space of a couple of years: *Vue de Bonnières* and *L'Enlèvement* (Figs 2.7 and 2.8); and *Mur de Jardin* and *Néréides et Tritons* (Figs 2.9 and 2.10). He is thus impossible to *place*, in Zola's terms and lexicon, to situate or classify, to explain or define, to include or leave out, other than in the interstices and silent margins of transition. In Zola's looking glass, as it were, Cézanne can never be more than an inverted image of himself.

Notes to Chapter 2

1. For details, see *EsA*, pp. 716–18. One further work was sold at his wife's death in 1925, an 1869 watercolour which Cézanne had created to decorate her sewing table. Another, *Paul Alexis lisant à Émile Zola* (*c.* 1869–70), was supposedly found in 1927 in the attic of Zola's country house at Médan, vacated by his widow in 1905.
2. See his letter of 21 October 1897, in Émile Zola, *Lettres à Alexandrine, 1876–1901*, ed. by Brigitte Émile-Zola and Alain Pagès (Paris: Gallimard, 2014), p. 191.
3. Ambroise Vollard, *En écoutant Cézanne, Degas, Renoir* (Paris: Grasset, 2003), p. 111. Zola's reference to Octave Mirbeau's interest in seeing them allows one to calculate that this visit took place at the turn of the century.
4. Denise Le-Blond Zola, *Émile Zola raconté par sa fille* (Paris: Grasset, 1931), p. 156.
5. Both cited in *Guide Émile Zola*, ed. by Alain Pagès and Owen Morgan (Paris: Ellipses, 2002), p. 118.
6. See chapter 20 ('La Rupture avec Zola') of Rewald's *Cézanne, sa vie, son œuvre, son amitié pour Zola* (Paris: Grasset, 1939): 'le roman [...] qui sépara définitivement les deux camarades de

collège' (p. 6); 'la cause déterminante de leur rupture' (p. 323). Of the response itself, included in Rewald's edition of the painter's *Correspondance* (Paris: Grasset, 1995), he is categoric that it was 'la dernière [lettre] que Cézanne lui ait adressée' (p. 282, n. 1).

7. Symptomatic of speculative excess is Catherine Dean's suggestion that Cézanne's marriage, in the same month as he received a copy of *L'Œuvre*, 'was perhaps provoked by Zola's rejection'; in her *Cézanne* (London: Phaidon, 1991), p. 66. Equally far-fetched is Joaquim Gasquet's 1921 version, in his *Cézanne*, ed. by François Solesnes (Paris: Les Belles Lettres, 2012) of Cézanne recalling that a 'smile' between Zola and a maid, in 1886, had driven him away for ever (p. 95). This hypothesis is not enhanced by the fact that the painter had not visited Zola in 1886.
8. This is the thrust of Henri Mitterand's forceful 'Mise au point: Cézanne et Zola', in his *Zola tel qu'en lui-même* (Paris: Gallimard, 2009), pp. 171–204.
9. Alex Danchev, *Cézanne: A Life* (London: Profile Books, 2012), p. 260.
10. For example, his letter from Estaque of 4 November 1878 to Zola at his Parisian address 'pensant que tu as effectué ton retour en ville' (Cézanne, *Correspondance*, p. 221), when in fact Zola did not return from Médan until 3 January 1879.
11. As in Alexis's letter to Zola of 13 February 1891, reporting from Aix that Cézanne 'est expansif et vivant', busy painting at the Jas de Bouffan (Paul Alexis, *'Naturalisme pas mort': lettres inédites de Paul Alexis à Émile Zola, 1871–1900*, ed. by B.H. Bakker (Toronto: University of Toronto Press, 1971), p. 400); or in those from Numa Coste the same early spring and again in 1896, both cited in Cézanne, *Correspondance*, pp. 295–96.
12. 'Je n'étais plus à mon aise chez lui, avec ses tapis par terre, les domestiques [...]. Cela avait fini par me donner l'impression que je rendais visite à un ministre. Il était devenu [...] un sale bourgeois [...]. J'espaçais encore davantage mes visites' (Vollard, *En écoutant Cézanne*, pp. 115–16).
13. As Zola puts it in the work notes for *L'Œuvre*, referring to his authorial surrogate's wife: 'Madame Sandoz devenue naturellement très élégante avec la fortune' (Ms 10316, fol. 193).
14. That Alexis, in his letter of 13 February 1891, felt able to refer to this 'rejeton' as 'son crapeau de fils' suggests that Zola himself would not have had a less condescending view of Cézanne's son (*'Naturalisme pas mort'*, p. 400). 'La Boule' alludes to her Maupassantian plumpness; the heroine of *Boule de suif* does not have the other qualities ascribed, however unfairly, to Hortense by Zola's social circle: her coarseness, extravagance and a hen-pecking disposition which explains Alexis's reporting to Zola in this same letter that Cézanne had gone to live with his mother at Jas de Bouffan instead of with Hortense.
15. Throughout the summer of 1885, Cézanne confided in Zola about his 'folly' ('j'implore ton absolution'), seeking the novelist's services as a go-between in the hoped-for exchange of passionate missives (Cézanne, *Correspondance*, pp. 271–78). It is not clear whether this remained strictly *entre hommes* or whether 'Madame Zola' was in the know, prompting Zola to demur, at first, when the nomadic painter thought of inviting himself to stay.
16. See my 'The End of the Affair: Zola and Cézanne', *French Studies Bulletin*, 133 (2014), 95–99; and Evelyne Bloch-Dano, *Madame Zola* (Paris: Grasset, 1997), pp. 141–42. As Zola noted of his fictional painter during the preparation of *L'Œuvre*, 'Comme Claude n'est pas marié, on ne reçoit pas encore sa femme' (Ms 10316, fol. 114).
17. I have explored this at greater length, notably in relation to evidence of Cézanne's anti-Dreyfusard prejudices, in 'Rethinking Zola and Cézanne: Biography, Politics and Art Criticism', *Journal of European Studies*, 46.2 (2016), 126–42.
18. Vollard, *En écoutant Cézanne*, p. 118.
19. 'Le perpétuel voyageur d'appartement en appartement, d'Aix à Paris, de Paris à Aix, et encore, et toujours' (Arsène Alexandre, 'Claude Lantier', *Le Figaro*, 9 December 1895). So frequent were his train journeys to and from the capital that it is not surprising that, at his death in 1906, Cézanne's estate revealed ownership of an enormous number of shares in the Paris-Lyon-Mediterranean railroad company, worth some 236,000 francs (more than the sum secured by the posthumous sale of his own paintings). So much for the self-styled country bumpkin refusing to have anything to do with modern industrial society or its materialist values!
20. Danchev, *Cézanne*, p. 134.
21. Vollard, *En écoutant Cézanne*, p. 104.

22. Cited by John Rewald, *Cézanne, Geffroy et Gasquet, suivi des souvenirs sur Cézanne de Louis Aurenche et de lettres inédites* (Paris: Quatre Chemins, 1959), p. 62.
23. See Alexis's letter of 13 February 1891, in *'Naturalisme pas mort'*, p. 400.
24. Philip Nord, 'The New Painting and the Dreyfus Affair', *Historical Reflections/Réflexions historiques*, 24 (1998), 115–36 (p. 121).
25. Cited by Bertrand Tillier, *Les Artistes et l'Affaire Dreyfus* (Seysell: Champ Vallon, 2009), pp. 34–35.
26. 'A riposte and a critique of Zola's vision of the peasantry in *La Terre'*, John House argues in 'Cézanne's Card Players: Art without Anecdote', in *Cézanne's 'Card Players'*, ed. by N. Ireson and B. Wright (London: Courtauld Gallery, 2010), pp. 55–71 (p. 69).
27. Gasquet, *Cézanne*, p. 179.
28. Jean-Paul Morel, *C'était Ambroise Vollard* (Paris: Fayard, 2007), p. 280.
29. Cézanne, *Correspondance*, p. 368
30. Bernard, cited in *Conversations avec Cézanne*, ed. by Michael Doran (Paris: Macula, 2011), p. 80.
31. Neil McWilliam, 'Émile Bernard's Reactionary Idealism', in *Academics, Pompiers, Official Artists and the Arrière-Garde: Defining Modern and Tradition in France, 1900–1960*, ed. by Natalie Adamson and Toby Norris (Newcastle: Cambridge Scholars, 2009), pp. 25–50 (p. 47).
32. *Conversations avec Cézanne*, ed. by Doran, p. 108.
33. Vollard's *En écoutant Cézanne* was originally published in 1938. It brings together various pieces by Vollard since his original, and much republished September 1914 biography, but also reprints exactly the chapter therein entitled 'Cézanne et Zola', characterized by J. Pellerin as a 'chef-d'œuvre' in its own right — immodestly recalled by Vollard himself in his *Souvenirs d'un marchand de tableaux* (Paris: Albin Michel, 2007), p. 298. This had first appeared in *L'Occident* in April and May 1914. Vollard had met Gasquet in 1896, during his first face-to-face meeting with Cézanne; and he was close to Bernard throughout the first decade of the twentieth century.
34. *Conversations avec Cézanne*, ed. by Doran, p. 27.
35. Vollard, *En écoutant Cézanne*, p. 118.
36. On an earlier visit to Alexis, Zola's closest friend, he had successfully tempted the latter to sell the Cézanne paintings he owned, probably given to him by the painter during his stay in Aix in 1891: see the letter of 5 May 1899 which may have forewarned Zola of Vollard's motives for seeking a meeting (Alexis, *'Naturalisme pas mort'*, pp. 448–49). At the 1903 Zola sale, the dealer finally got his hands on three of the writer's Cézannes up for auction: *L'Enlèvement* (1867); *Mur de Jardin* (1867–68) and an unidentified landscape not in the Drouot catalogue.
37. Cézanne's reported discomfort in Zola's bourgeois milieu tails off: '... Et ensuite, Zola fit paraître *L'Œuvre*'; and Vollard stressed that the painter would have forgiven him the novel had he made an effort to stay in touch: 'Comprenez un peu, monsieur Vollard, mon cher Zola était à Aix! J'oubliais tout, *L'Œuvre* et bien d'autres choses aussi' (Vollard, *En écoutant Cézanne*, pp. 115–16).
38. *Le Bonnet Rouge*, 7 June 1914, reprinted in Morel, *C'était Ambroise Vollard*, pp. 403–04.
39. Danchev, *Cézanne*, p. 249.
40. Gasquet, *Cézanne*, p. 95.
41. Cited in *Conversations avec Cézanne*, ed. by Doran, pp. 107–08. Not the least irony of this is that Bernard had recommended the novel to his parents, having re-read it '3 ou 4 fois', as he confessed in a letter of 11 July 1886; and even in March 1899, he admitted to his mother that 'il y a dans ce livre des choses que j'aimerais à revoir: elles sont crânes et courageuses et elles sont d'un autre Zola que celui de *Paris* ou de *Rome*'. In Émile Bernard, *Lettres d'un artiste (1884–1941)*, ed. by Neil McWilliam (Dijon: Presses du reel, 2012), p. 47 and pp. 554–55.
42. On the different elements of the composite portrait, see Sara Pappas, 'The View from the Bridge: Zola's *L'Œuvre* and its Many Composites', *Word & Image*, 27 (2011), 234–45, and my 'Against Recuperation: The Fictions of Art in *L'Œuvre*', *Romanic Review*, 102 (2011), 449–63.
43. Wayne Anderson, *Cézanne and the Eternal Feminine* (Cambridge: Cambridge University Press, 2004), p. 82. Heather McPherson, for example, is categoric in asserting that Zola's fictional painter was 'modelled on Cézanne'; in *The Modern Portrait in Nineteenth-Century France* (Cambridge: Cambridge University Press, 2001), p. 123.

44. See Robert J. Niess, *Zola, Cézanne, and Manet: A Study of 'L'Œuvre'* (Ann Arbor: University of Michigan Press, 1968), especially 'Lantier-Cézanne' (pp. 78–86) and 'Cézanne: the Novel and the Biography' (pp. 87–112). Barely had Zola started the novel's *ébauche* than he writes of Claude: 'un Manet, un Cézanne dramatisé; plus près de Cézanne' (Ms 10316, fol. 265); this follows on from the note relating to the Salon des Refusés, in which the parallel is less hesitant: 'Claude avec un ami au retour, Cézanne et moi à nos retours' (fol. 264).
45. In the preparatory notes for *L'Œuvre*, Zola stresses that Claude is 'contre la peinture à idées' (Ms 10316, fol. 80); but, with his 'symbolisme inavouée' (fol. 443), he fatally succumbs to its temptations in 'le symbolisme de la femme nue' (fols 157 and 295).
46. In a letter of 1 June 1861, Zola writes excitedly to Baille that 'Paul va faire mon portrait' (*Corr.*, I, 288). The only such portrait (exclusively representing Zola) presumed to survive is the one (*c.* 1862–64) reproduced in *Cézanne: The Early Years 1859–1872*, ed. by Lawrence Gowing, exh. cat. (London: Weidenfeld and Nicolson, 1988), p. 23 (fig. 16).
47. In Rewald's original transcription of the letter, this phrase read 'sous l'impulsion des temps écoulés' (Cézanne, *Correspondance*, p. 282); Henri Mitterand deciphered it as 'sous l'inspiration des temps écoulés' (*RM*, IV, p. 386). It has been definitely corrected by Jean-Claude Lebensztejn in his *Paul Cézanne, cinquante-trois lettres* (Tusson: L'Echoppe, 2011), and cited here from *LC* (p. 418). Perhaps even more significant in respect of the timeframe to which Cézanne refers is his manuscript correction substituting 'temps' for 'jours'.
48. In a letter to Jacques van Santen Kolff of 6 July, Zola wrote that 'c'est toute ma jeunesse que je raconte, j'ai mis là tous mes amis' (*Corr.*, V, 279), adding, on 26 July, that he had now abbreviated this section 'pour des raisons de composition' (*Corr.*, V, 289).
49. The novel had been serialized in *Gil Blas* between 23 December 1885 and 27 March 1886, before its appearance in volume form on 2 April. Even assuming he received an advance copy, whether Cézanne had read the whole of it before his letter to Zola two days after its publication must remain a matter of doubt. Mitterand is categoric: having received a copy on 3 April, 'il ne l'a pas encore lu' when he wrote to Zola; but he admits that there remains the possibility that he might have read some of the novel during its serialization (*LC*, p. 418, n. 2).
50. 'Ma jeunesse au collège et dans les champs — Baille, Cézanne [...]. À Paris. Nouveaux amis. Collège. Arrivée de Baille et de Cézanne — Nos réunions du jeudi [...]. Les ateliers de Cézanne. Tous les traits de son caractère. Les poses chez lui [...]. Je voudrais des personnages gais' (Ms 10316, fol. 316).
51. A conflation of facts: Zola, 15 months younger than Cézanne, was in the class below the painter.
52. Regularly evoked both in their correspondence and in the preparatory dossier of *L'Œuvre*: Ms 10316, fols 26, 35, 227, 231 and 298.
53. *EsA*, p. 713. On Baille, see Colette Becker, 'Jean-Baptistin Baille', *CN*, 36 (1982), 147–58.
54. Danchev, *Cézanne*, p. 21, citing the poem included in the painter's letter to Zola of 9 July 1858: 'Zola nageur/Fend sans frayeur/L'onde limpide./Son bras nerveux/S'étend joyeux/Sur le doux fluide.' In his own versified response, on 20 July, Zola writes of his 'bien fendant tout nu le flot limpide' (*LC*, p. 81). On the back of a letter of 20 June 1859, Cézanne sent 'le dessin d'une baignade' (*Correspondance*, respectively, p. 37 and p. 62). In a letter to Cézanne of 5 May 1860, Zola refers to 'nos parties de nage' (*Corr.*, I, 161), those 'baignades sans fin' evoked at length in part III of 'Souvenirs', originally published in *La Cloche* of 20 June 1872 and included in his *Nouveaux Contes à Ninon* (1874): 'Nous ne mettions pas même de caleçons' (*OC*, IX, 415–16).
55. Félix Fénéon gave this tiny work (15.6 x 16.2 cm; graphite, watercolour and gouache) such a title only in 1919. But it has been persuasively suggested that the figure has much in common with the male aggressor in the watercolour version of *L'Enlèvement* (1867) (*Cézanne: The Early Years*, ed. by Gowing, p. 100–03), the definitive painting being given to Zola by Cézanne for reasons which remain unclear.
56. In a letter of 17 May 1877 to Catulle Mendès (*Corr.*, XI, 97).
57. See Lucie Riou, 'La Correspondance avec les artistes: laboratoire d'esthétique et genèse de la création romanesque', in *Éditer et relire la correspondance de Zola*, ed. by Sophie Guermès (Rennes: Presses universitaires de Rennes, 2018), pp. 169–84.
58. Gasquet, *Cézanne*, p. 55.

59. *Corr.*, I, 148–52, from which the following quotations are drawn.
60. Bernard, 'Cézanne et Zola', cited by R. Rapetti, 'L'Inquiétude cézannienne: Émile Bernard et Paul Cézanne au début du XXe siècle', *Revue de l'art*, 144 (2004), 35–50 (p. 48).
61. Zola's contacts with these painters deserve further research. It was as a result of Cézanne's working with the portraitist and history painter Joseph Villevieille (1829–1916) that the novelist too got to know other artists in the group under the latter's tutelage. In a letter of 25 March 1860, Zola reminded Cézanne of 'ces baigneuses [...] que je dessinais si maladroitement un jour chez Villevielle', in Aix the year before (*Corr.*, I, 140). The group included Victor Combes (1837–1876), Auguste Truphème (1836–1898) and Achille Emperaire (1829–1898), best remembered by Cézanne's three portraits of him in 1869–70. Cézanne and Zola were not overly impressed by their work, even though they occasionally had paintings accepted at the annual Salon (Truphème in 1865 and 1866, Combes in 1866). Another of these Provençal artists who had gravitated to Paris and to whom Zola alludes was Joseph Chautard (born in Avignon in 1821), who had first exhibited at the Salon of 1845 and who, like Villevieille, took it upon himself to 'correct' some of Cézanne's early studies. The painter Zola saw most of was Jean-Baptiste Chaillan (born in 1831), a fellow student of Cézanne's in Aix, with whom he often went to the Louvre to watch him copy the Old Masters and who would be the model for the near-homonym Chaîne in *L'Œuvre*: 'Fort mediocre copiste,' he wrote to Cézanne, 'dès qu'il faut inventer il est complètement mauvais' (*Corr.*, I, p. 151). Perhaps the most important, however, was Paul Guigou (1834–1871), who was included in the Salon des Refusés of 1863; Duret would refer to him in *L'Électeur libre*, in the context of the Salon of 1870, as would Zola in his review of the Salon of 1872. On the links between Cézanne and the 'école d'Aix', see the exh. cat. *L'Estaque: naissance du paysage moderne* (Musée Cantini, Marseille, 25 June–25 September 1994) and Nina Athanassoglou-Kallmyer, *Cézanne and Provence: The Painter and his Culture* (Chicago: University of Chicago Press, 2003).
62. In 1860 letters to Cézanne of 16 January and 25 March 1860 (*Corr.*, I, 131, 141). In the latter, he urged him to 'travailler le dessin fort et ferme [...] pour devenir [...] un Ary Scheffer, pour ne pas être un réaliste'.
63. As Cézanne wrote in a letter to his friend Joseph Huot on 4 June (having visited the Salon with Zola on 26 May): 'Pour un cœur jeune, pour un enfant qui naît à l'art, qui dit ce qu'il pense, je crois que c'est là ce qu'il y a vraiment de mieux parce que là tous les genres s'y rencontrent et s'y heurtent' (Cézanne, *Correspondance*, p. 122). Based on the laconic verses included in this letter, but without knowing whether he and Zola had viewed exactly the same pictures among the more than 4,000 on display, the artists identified by Cézanne are Courbet, Cabanel, Léon Glaize (1842–1932), Jean-Louis Hamon (1821–1874), Adolphe Yvon (1817–1893) and Théodore Gudin (1802–1880), all of whom had at least two paintings exhibited at the Salon of 1861: Courbet, Hamon and Gudin each had five, Cabanel six.
64. Gasquet, *Cézanne*, p. 54.
65. In his letter to Huot of 4 June 1861, Cézanne refers to working there 'de six heures du matin jusqu'à onze' (Cézanne, *Correspondance*, p. 121 and n. 3), thereby, according to Rewald's annotation of it, following Zola's advice, the latter having written to him on 3 March recommending that 'de six à onze tu iras dans un atelier peindre d'après le modèle' (*Corr.*, I, 272). In the work notes for *L'Œuvre*, Zola recalls Cézanne's 'éducation artistique, au musée de Plassans [the fictional version of Aix-en-Provence in all the *Rougon-Macquart*], et maintenant dans une académie libre, et au Louvre' (Ms 10316, fol. 33), more precisely the 'atelier Suisse libre' (fols. 27 and 36).
66. Gasquet, *Cézanne*, pp. 159–60.
67. Paul Alexis, *Émile Zola: notes d'un ami* [1882], ed. by René-Pierre Colin (Paris: Maisonneuve & Larose, 2001), pp. 121–22. In 1881–82, Zola had involved himself in correcting the proofs of this first authorized biography. It is interesting that mentions of Cézanne in it are few and far between, restricted to the friendship of 'les trois inséparables' during their schooldays. 'Son projet', Alexis wrote of the future *L'Œuvre*, 'est de raconter dans ce roman ses années de Provence' (p. 122). Little space is given to Zola's contact with artists before 1870. He did not correct Alexis's characterization of Cézanne as 'le peintre impressionniste que l'on sait' (p. 30).

68. Mitterand refers to 'les ragots de Vollard' (*Zola*, II, 789). Danchev views Bernard's 'fantastic talk' as 'surely garbled or invented', as Gasquet 'plundered *L'Œuvre* to produce a confection of his own lurid imagining' (*Cézanne*, p. 80).
69. Lawrence Gowing remarks that, designed for her 'elegant work-box', 'one cannot imagine a more incongruous purpose for an image that gloried in industrial squalor' (to which one might counter that it was indeed an image of *work*), adding that 'this was the single moment at which Cézanne's brand of realism [...] coincided with Zola's' (*Cézanne: The Early Years*, ed. by Gowing, pp. 11–12).
70. Zola may well have seen, as well as being apprised of, Cézanne's earliest known work, the decorative panels for the Jas de Bouffan. In a letter of 13 June 1860, he reports having spotted in a café outside Paris 'de grands panneaux comme tu veux en peindre chez toi' (*Corr.*, I, 175). The panels (*Les Quatre Saisons*) are reproduced in colour in *Cézanne: The Early Years*, ed. by Gowing, pp. 68–69 (figs 1a–1d). He reported on both successes and failures: in a letter of 2 November 1866, for example, he writes that his *Marion et Valabrègue partant pour le motif* 'ne s'est pas fait et que, ayant tenté une *soirée de famille*, ça n'est point venu du tout' (Cézanne, *Correspondance*, p. 164).
71. See Mary Louise Krumrine, 'Parisian Writers and the Early Work of Cézanne', in *Cézanne: The Early Years*, ed. by Gowing, pp. 20–31.
72. See Geoff Woollen, 'Zola, Cézanne and *Le Château de Médan*', *Bulletin of the Émile Zola Society*, 20 (1999), 3–12. On 19 June 1880, Cézanne confirmed that it would be a pleasure to come to Médan, at the same time asking Zola whether 'si tu n'es pas effrayé par le long temps que je risque d'y mettre, je me permettrai de porter une petite toile et d'y faire un motif, le tout si tu n'y vois pas d'inconvénients' (Cézanne, *Correspondance*, p. 242); receiving no response, he reminded Zola a fortnight later that 'je te demandais si je pouvais aller chez toi, pour y peindre, il est vrai' (p. 243). So extended was his stay that, on 22 August, Zola wrote to Guillemet, who had seen Cézanne at Médan on 14 July, to say that 'Paul est toujours ici avec moi. Il travaille beaucoup' (*Corr.*, IV, 93–94). There has been much scholarly debate about whether or not (and, if not, why) Cézanne's Médan pictures exclude Zola's house, concluding that this was determined by compositional and picturesque priorities.
73. Richard Verdi, *Cézanne* (London: Thames & Hudson, 1992), p. 35.
74. Krumrine, 'Parisian Writers', p. 22.
75. Ever since John Lapp's insights in this respect, in his *Zola before the 'Rougon-Macquart'* (Toronto: University of Toronto Press, 1964), pp. 101–02.
76. 'Prendre le portrait physique [du Ven] qui se trouve dans le *Ventre de Paris'* (Ms 10316, fol. 218). In *L'Œuvre*, this is abbreviated (*RM*, IV, p. 15). Of the one in *Le Ventre de Paris*, Mitterand notes that 'on sait que Claude est dessiné, au physique, sur le modèle de Paul Cézanne' (*RM*, IV, 1405, n. 1). The notes Zola made in 1885, during his rereading of the earlier novel, are instructive in many other respects too: 'Emportement d'artiste impuissant en face des œuvres solides et vivantes qu'il rêvait' (fol. 221).
77. Ms 10338: respectively fols 276, 112 and 61. In the novel this becomes: 'rêvant des natures mortes colossales, des tableaux extraordinaires' (*RM*, I, 623). Zola had written to Numa Coste on 26 July 1866 reporting that Cézanne was engaged on 'de grandes œuvres, des toiles de quatre à cinq mètres' (*Corr.*, I, 453).
78. Ms 10338, fol. 112; cf. his 'peur d'essayer': 'Il ne me faut pas de femmes à moi, ça me dérangerait trop' (*RM*, I, 850), copied directly from his synopsis of *Le Ventre de Paris* and underlined by Zola as 'Très important' (Ms 10316, fol. 224). As his 'double', Florent 'dépensait en rêve trop de sa virilité' (*RM*, I, 738).
79. In his letter to Cézanne of 25 June 1860, Zola's impatience is clear: 'tu ne parles rien moins que de jeter tes pinceaux au plafond' (*Corr*, I, 191); as it is in that of the end of July: 'Tu jettes, me dis-tu, parfois tes pinceaux au plafond, lorsque la forme ne suit pas ton idée' (*Corr.*, I, 213).
80. Letter of 19 October 1866: 'tous les tableaux faits à l'intérieur, dans l'atelier, ne vaudront jamais les choses faites en plein air. En représentant des scènes du dehors, les oppositions des figures sur les terrains sont étonnantes, et le paysage est magnifique. Je vois des choses magnifiques, et il faut que je me résolve à ne faire que des choses en plein air' (Cézanne, *Correspondance*, p. 157).

81. Ms 10338, fols 34 and 71–72. Virtually coinciding with the penning of the latter, Zola wrote ironically of Napoléon Bonaparte surrounded by works of art, forgetting his penury, 'rêv[ant] les campagnes de Théocrite, fai[sant] le songe d'une île chimérique et charmante' (in *La Cloche* of 21 June 1872; *OC*, XIV, 91).
82. Danchev, *Cézanne*, p. 201.
83. *Cézanne: The Early Years*, ed. by Gowing, p. 174.
84. Ms 10338, fol. 71. In the same note, Zola reminds himself to differentiate it from 'celle de Silvère et de Miette' in *La Fortune des Rougon*. Planning that opening novel of his series, he had written of that relationship that, as an 'idylle jetée dans le sombre drame de l'insurrection', it would depict 'un amour charnel qui s'ignore', while Miette, on the threshold of womanhood, offered him a 'moment charmant et délicat à peindre. Ses ardeurs et ses virginités' (Ms 10303, fols 4–6). It was to Cézanne that Zola turned in April 1869 to secure from his sister details of the peasant clothes Miette would be wearing. The carnality of the reworked episode in *Le Ventre de Paris* is further testimony to Zola's liquidation of a Hugolian legacy.
85. In his article in *L'Événement* of 26 February 1866 (*OC*, X, 379); and in *Le Vœu d'une morte* (*OC*, I, 208).
86. In his work notes, Zola writes of Claude's 'poésie de la nourriture' (Ms 10338, fol. 34); in the novel, contemplating the market-stalls, Claude 'ne songeait même pas que ces belles choses se mangeaient. Il les aimait pour leur couleur' (*RM*, I, 623).
87. As Zola's preparatory notes indicate: 'Le côté artistique est les Halles modernes, les gigantesques natures mortes des huit pavillons' (Ms 10338, fol. 48).
88. Vollard, *Souvenirs*, p. 196. Whether or not this was the painter's opinion of it, Zola had indeed expressed precisely this objection in 1866: 'Si M. Corot consentait à tuer une fois pour toutes les nymphes dont il peuple ses bois, et à les remplacer par des paysannes, je l'aimerais outre mesure (*EsA*, p. 168), suggesting Cézanne's familiarity with the novelist's early art criticism.
89. Vollard, *En écoutant Cézanne*, p. 413. In an unconvincing 1921 rebuttal, he rejects Jourdain's view que 'je faisais démolir Zola par lui-même' (cited by Morel, *C'était Ambroise Vollard*, p. 409).
90. In the second version of his *Ouverture de Tannhaüser*, as reported to Zola by Guillemet in a letter of 2 November 1866 (Baligand, 'Lettres inédites', p. 180), Cézanne had included a portrait of his father, looking like 'un pape sur son trône' and reading *Le Siècle* — for which *L'Événement* was, in a similar homage to Zola, subsequently substituted. In the final 1869 version of the painting, its cast of characters is exclusively feminine.
91. As Zola was aware, acknowledging in his letter to Cézanne at the end of July 1860 that 'je ne dois pas être au mieux avec ta famille. Je suis sans doute pour eux la liaison dangereuse, le pavé jeté sur ton chemin pour te faire trébucher' (*Corr.*, I, 213).
92. In reviews of the novel, only their mutual friend Marius Roux, in *Le Mémorial d'Aix* of 3 December 1865, drew attention to the prefatory mention of Cézanne making of the text 'une proclamation', thereby acceding to Zola's request in his letter of 14 November: 'Tâche de faire une réclame à Baille, surtout à Cézanne, ce qui fera plaisir à leurs familles' (*Corr.*, I, 420). On 4 December, Zola thanked him for his review as 'le meilleur qui ait paru sur ce livre. [...] Merci aussi pour Cézanne et pour Baille' (*Corr.*, I, 425–26).
93. In a letter of 28 March 1878, Cézanne asked Zola whether he could borrow back for a forthcoming Impressionist exhibition 'la nature morte que tu as dans ta salle à manger'; in fact, the 1878 exhibition never took place and Cézanne did not figure in either of those of 1879 or 1880; Rewald assumes Cézanne was referring to *La Pendule noire*, commenting on the strangeness of including this rather than a more recent work (Cézanne, *Correspondance*, p. 205 and n.1), as does Mitterand (*LC*, p. 345, n. 1). Zola owned two paintings by Cézanne, more properly *natures mortes* than the picture of his clock: the *Sucrier, Poires et Tasse Bleue*, possibly the one in mind given its quasi-manifesto status, and *Le Poêle de l'atelier* (*c.* 1865).
94. Cézanne, *Correspondance*, p. 240, and pp. 241–42, n. 1.
95. Letter of 25 March 1860 (*Corr.*, I, 141).
96. Letter to Albert Lacroix of 8 May 1867 (*Corr.*, I, 497).
97. Vollard, *Souvenirs*, p. 62.
98. A possibly apocryphal anecdote has Cézanne, on the grounds that he had not washed for a week,

refusing to shake Manet's hand and responding 'Un pot de merde!' to the latter's enquiry about what he was intending to submit to the Salon of 1866.

99. See André Dombrowski, 'Cézanne, Manet and the Portraits of Zola', in *Interior Portraiture and Masculine Identity in France, 1789–1914*, ed. by Temma Balducci, Heather Belnap and Pamela Warner (Farnham: Ashgate, 2011), pp. 101–20.
100. See Figure 2.5. Much later, from a historical perspective unclouded by rivalry, Cézanne would admit of Manet that 'il faut toujours avoir ça devant les yeux. C'est un état nouveau de la peinture. Notre Renaissance date de là' (cited by Mitterand, *LC*, p. 239).
101. Vollard, *En écoutant Cézanne*, p. 36.
102. Vollard, *En écoutant Cézanne*, p. 111.
103. Letter of 16 April 1860 (*Corr.*, I, 146). Zola repeats the phrase in his letter of 26 April: 'l'idée, l'étincelle est en toi' (*Corr.*, I, p. 149).
104. Gasquet, *Cézanne*, p. 36.
105. As in his letter to Louise Colet of 31 January 1852: 'je tâche d'être boutonné et de suivre une ligne droite. Nul lyrisme, pas de réflexions, personnalité de l'auteur absente'; or in that of 19 September 1855 to Louis Bouillet: 'Il faut entasser œuvres sur œuvres, travailler comme des machines et ne pas sortir de la ligne droite'; in Flaubert, *Correspondance*, II, 40 and 594.
106. Letter to Numa Coste of 26 July 1866 (*Corr.*, I, 453).
107. Letter of July 1860 (*Corr.*, I, 212–13).
108. Letter of 26 July 1858 (cited in *LC*, p. 85).
109. Baligand, 'Lettres inédites', p. 193.
110. Letter of 25 March 1860 (*Corr.*, I, 141).
111. Letter of June/July 1861 (*Corr.*, I, 301)
112. *Corr.*, I, 301.

CHAPTER 3

Courbet

'Il m'est donné de voir, rue Hautefeuille, dans l'atelier du maître', Zola wrote in *Le Salut public* of 31 August 1865, 'certains de ses premiers tableaux' (*EsA*, p. 425). Nothing in the novelist's biography allows us to confirm with any precision when, or even whether, such a visit to Courbet's studio, which he had occupied since the winter of 1848–49, actually took place.[1] Zola subsequently added that it was during one of the painter's absences. It is equally plausible that this assertion of familiarity served merely to reinforce a critical authority positioned against the ideological interpretations of Courbet's paintings in the book which served as a pretext for his essay on the painter: Pierre-Joseph Proudhon's *Du principe de l'art et de sa destination sociale*, considered as 'l'œuvre d'un homme profondément incompétent' (*EsA*, p. 429), thereby displacing precisely the charges in due course levelled at his own art criticism. Although Zola insists that 'Proudhon a vu comme moi les tableaux dont je parle' (*EsA*, p. 425), there remains a question mark. For amongst these early works, what both Zola and Proudhon refer to as *La Baigneuse* was clearly no longer in Courbet's studio at 32, rue Hautefeuille, having been bought by Alfred Bruyas, the painter's friend and patron, after it had been exhibited at the Salon of 1853.[2] Nor does Zola's supposed viewing square with Champfleury's 1860 description of the artist's studio being cluttered with unsold rolled-up canvases.[3] On the other hand, we do know that, in the company of Cézanne, Zola had seen the Courbets at the Salon of 1861.[4] And, given his regular visits to the annual Salon, he probably also saw those in the exhibitions of 1863 and 1865.[5] But, in any case, Proudhon was certainly not able to respond to Zola's long essay of 1865, entitled 'Proudhon et Courbet' and published in two instalments (the first on 26 July) in *Le Salut public*, nominally a Lyon newspaper but with a national readership. For he had died in mid-January at the age of 56, his unfinished book appearing in June, as part of the *Œuvres posthumes* being published by Garnier since his death. It therefore seems almost perverse that Zola should urge Proudhon to look anew at the painter's work, and in particular his *Le Retour de la foire* (*c.* 1855), *Les Casseurs de pierres* (1849), *La Baigneuse* (1853) and *Les Demoiselles près de la Seine* (1857).[6] But it is a measure of the rhetorical design of Zola's essay that he was not one of those hostile critics feeling slightly guilty that the author of the book under review 'n'est plus là pour en répondre' to the charges that 'ce livre est un tissu d'affirmations, de négations, de contradictions'.[7] For the opportunity to publish a first extended reflection on the visual arts took priority over such sentiments, offering Zola a platform from which to expound his own aesthetic criteria. And, as this chapter will also explore, this initial thinking about Courbet's work is significant in its own right, developed as it would be over the next two decades.

Texts and Pretexts

Zola's essay aggressively dismantles the application to Courbet's paintings of Proudhon's premise: that artistic value was synonymous with a work's social or moral utility. As Proudhon put it himself, with his own italics: '*L'Art est une représentation idéaliste de la nature et de nous-mêmes, en vue du perfectionnement physique et moral de notre espèce*', a definition which Zola quoted back at him in contrarily spelling out his own: 'Ma définition d'une œuvre d'art serait, si je la formulais: "Une œuvre d'art est un coin de la création vu à travers un tempérament"' (*EsA*, p. 419). Such an interchange perfectly illustrates the dialectical relationship fashioning his own critical stance. Ironically enough, but probably unbeknown to Zola, not only had Courbet collaborated with Proudhon on the book but also claimed to be delighted that it exactly mapped, whether *ex post facto* or not, his satirical intentions.[8] Zola's essay takes the form of a set of present-tense altercations, interpolating (in the vocative) objections to Proudhon's commentary, cited verbatim, on individual pictures ('Je crois pouvoir vous répondre...', etc.), in a dialogue not of the proverbial deaf but with the dead. And that this could be sustained nevertheless is hardly by chance.

For the topicality of *Du principe de l'art* was reinforced by the completion of Courbet's posthumous portrait of Proudhon, with his two children in the background and on which he had been working for many years, which he submitted to the Salon of 1865 and which Zola could have seen there. Even if he didn't, he could hardly have failed to be apprised of the enormous publicity it generated. Courbet's submission was preceded by open letters in the press, in which the painter kept readers abreast of his progress in finalizing the canvas. *Pierre-Joseph Proudhon et ses enfants en 1853*, alas, was not judged a success from an artistic point of view. But it was also thought of as unintentionally conveying 'all that was weakest, confused and most distracted in Proudhon and his thought'.[9] Some references to the portrait respectfully stuck to the facts: 'Sans rien préjuger du mérite de l'exécution de cette œuvre, on peut prédire à cette toile, hommage rendu par Courbet à la mémoire de son célèbre compatriote Proudhon, un succès d'intérêt et de sympathie' (*La Presse*, 23 April). But that was in short supply: 'Ce n'est pas un portrait', wrote Jules Claretie, 'c'est une caricature.'[10] In *Le Figaro* of 25 June, he judges it as 'cet éloge de Courbet un peu bien énorme'. For Proudhon's incursion into art history was an easy target, even if Zola himself professed to resist it ('Je voudrais être juste, ne pas me laisser tenter par une raillerie vraiment trop aisée', (*EsA*, p. 424)): nobody could be as publicly rude as Flaubert, in his private letter to the Goncourt brothers, describing the book's 'pignouferie socialiste' as having had the effect on him of 'une de ces fortes latrines, où l'on marche à chaque pas sur un étron. Chaque phrase est une ordure. Le tout à la gloire de Courbet!'[11] The most double-edged contemporary assessment was that his intellectual energy had resulted in 'ce livre curieux' (*La Presse*, 2 July); a self-confessed ignorance about painting made it 'la condamnation de Proudhon critique d'art'. For Ernest Chesneau, the eminent art critic, the book was an opportunity to dismiss Courbet as 'un peintre dépourvu de talent' (*Le Constitutionnel*, 16 May). But for Léon Lagrange, obviously *au fait* with Courbet's contribution to it, ridicule was the mode of choice in reviewing 'ce livre incohérent' with its 'candeur enfantine à l'endroit du maître-peintre d'Ornans': 'Mais Proudhon guidé par M. Courbet dans les sentiers de l'esthétique, vous figurez-vous un groupe plus étrange, après celui de don Quichotte et de Sancho Pança.'[12]

Such a polemical context serves to explain the timing and, indeed, the heading of Zola's essay. In one sense, this first extended engagement with painting found in Proudhon's book a pretext to develop a critical perspective and vocabulary fundamentally at odds with it, thereby elaborating aesthetic 'principles' of his own. Zola considered the essay sufficiently foundational to be included in the texts collected in *Mes haines* in June of the following year. The preface to the latter, pre-published in *Le Figaro* of 27 May 1866, does not name names. But, reading between the lines of this explanation of its title, Proudhon (along with Barbey d'Aurevilly) fits perfectly into the category of the narrow-minded targets of Zola's invective. It is a measure of his more general concerns that, in the first instalment of his essay, Courbet is afforded not a single mention. Even fifteen years later, Proudhon would remain for Zola the pernicious example of a critic who 'n'a pourtant pu se défendre de vouloir traiter l'art comme un point de l'économie politique' (*OC*, x, 1391). In 1868, he refers to himself as 'pas assez proudhonien' to succumb to the pathos of Courbet's *L'Aumône d'un mendiant à Ornans* (*EsA*, p. 198), still deploring the way Proudhon had exploited him 'pour son usage' (*EsA*, p. 414). Writing to Béliard in 1875, he cautioned this painter sometimes known as 'le Proudhonien' against 'les bêtises qu'il a dites': 'Voyez quelle chute que celle de Proudhon, dès qu'il a abordé l'art.'[13] Here, in 1865, Proudhon offers Zola the opportunity to assert the primacy of individuated artistic expression at the expense of a *peinture à idées*. Consistent with the polemical tenor of his essay, he skates over, or traduces, numerous judgements voiced by Proudhon to which he subscribes. These invoke a range of artists from the Renaissance to Romanticism. But Zola's own focus on Courbet, in particular, is inseparable from a number of related factors: the renewed public association at this moment between the politically subversive painter and his equally left-wing commentator;[14] the wider debate about realism orchestrated by Champfleury;[15] and the view that chapter 10 of Proudhon's book was 'semblable à une charretée de condamnés', with Courbet the only survivor of 'la hâche du critique-bourreau' which had mercilessly 'dispatched' David, Delacroix, Ingres, David d'Angers, François Rude, Léopold Robert and Horace Vernet. Or, as Zola himself wrote of the book as a whole, 'c'est une seconde création, un meurtre et un enfantement' (*EsA*, p. 418).

In order to prove that Proudhon gives to Courbet's paintings 'un sens politique, religieux, ou de simple police des mœurs' (*EsA*, p. 426), the middle section of Zola's essay comprises a series of refutations which implicitly cite, out of context,

Proudhon's more notorious remarks about the four paintings Zola had urged him to revisit: *Le Retour de la foire* was a statement of rural values invulnerable to 'la démagogie'; *La Baigneuse* pictured a 'bourgeoise charnue et cossue, déformée par la graisse et le luxe'; and *Les Demoiselles de la Seine* (with its connotations of 'l'orgeuil, l'adultère, le divorce et le suicide') was contrasted with *Les Casseurs de pierres* (swearing 'par leurs haillons vengeance contre la société et l'art'). Such remarks exemplify, Zola argues contemptuously, 'la bouffonerie' of 'le nouveau critique d'art, celui qui se vante de jeter les bases d'une science nouvelle'. Zola himself makes no attempt to engage with them. His own position can only be inferred from the oblique acknowledgement that 'il y a même des observations fortes et justes dans ce que pense Proudhon mis en face des tableaux de Courbet'. Of these, although left unsaid, Zola would surely have endorsed the following: the distance between Courbet's *Paysans de Flagey* (i.e. *Le Retour de la foire*) and the 'paysans adonisés de L. Robert'; 'une profondeur de l'observation qui est, selon moi, le vrai point de l'art'; 'les tableaux du peintre d'Ornans sont des miroirs de vérité', on the basis that 'le réel n'est pas la même chose que le vrai'; indignation that the painter's work 'souleva contre l'école prétendue *réaliste* une réprobation générale dont la clameur poursuit encore M. Courbet'; the contrast between his nudes and 'une odalisque de M. Ingres, ou tout autre miroir aphrodisiaque'; outrage that Courbet's submission (*Vénus et Psyché*) to the Salon of 1864 should have been rejected, as had his *Le Retour de la conférence* the year before, whereas Cabanel's *Naissance de Vénus* ('avec sa figure provocante, sourire voluptueux' likened to '[des] trotteuses du boulevard') had not only been exhibited there but also purchased by Napoleon III ('comment se fait-il que la police des mœurs, qui refuse les tableaux de Courbet, ait admis cette immoralité?'); and such official hypocrisy being only matched by that surrounding *La Séduction de Léda*, by a pupil of Ingres, at the Universal Exhibition of 1855 ('M. de Nieuwerkerke a fait acheter à l'Empereur une *Léda* tenant un cygne entre les cuisses').[16]

Zola's only remarks about the specific qualities of Courbet's work are those following on from his claimed visit to the painter's studio (*EsA*, pp. 423–25). These are not only generalized but also, in many respects, not very different from those of Proudhon on the painter's distinctive rendering. Admiration for 'le maître puissant qui nous a donné quelques pages larges et vraies' is common to them both. To single out 'les chairs, fermes et souples' of 'les femmes grasses et les hommes puissants' echoes Proudhon's highlighting of the fleshy contours of the naked woman seen from behind in *La Baigneuse* and the muscular bodies of the two figures in *Les Casseurs de pierres*.[17] Unlike Proudhon, however, Zola stresses 'la façon énergique dont il a saisi et rendu la nature', and the way in which, in Courbet's paintings, 'les fonds s'emplissaient d'air, donnaient aux figures une vigueur étonnante' (p. 425).[18] And nowhere in Proudhon's study is there an equivalent to Zola's emphasis on structure and compositional perfection ('d'une seule masse'; 'l'ampleur du métier établissant les plans'; 'chaque détail a un relief étrange'; 'une peinture serrée, large, d'un fini et d'une franchise extrêmes'), 'la coloration, un peu sourde' or the harmonious 'justesse de tons'. As Zola underlines, as a result of Proudhon's exclusive concern with the subject-matter and social meaning of Courbet's paintings, 'il les a vus autrement, en dehors de toute facture'. And Zola found in Proudhon's book a panoply of successors which he would often repeat in the future in plotting Courbet's pictorial lineage: Théodore Rousseau, Corot, Daubigny and Millet, among others, as evidence that 'l'école française va dans la même direction que Courbet'.[19] In spite of his selectively damning quotations from the text of *Du Principe de l'art*, it can be argued that Zola's reading of Proudhon added a dimension to an appreciation of Courbet already prepared by his conversations with Cézanne, not least in the declaration oft-repeated by the latter (though not by Proudhon) that, as 'le seul peintre de notre époque', Courbet 'a pour frères, qu'il le veuille ou non, Véronèse, Rembrandt, Titien' (*EsA*, p. 425).[20] Although himself not entirely innocent of the charge of distorting Proudhon's commentary, the starting-point of the second instalment of Zola's essay is that 'le philosophe a tellement travesti Courbet' that it necessitated a return to masterpieces which he insisted should be considered not as ironizing discourse aimed at the bourgeoisie but as paintings in their own right.

In the interests of confirming a radical antithesis ('en un mot, je suis diamétralement opposé à Proudhon', *EsA*, p. 422), Zola goes so far as to conclude that 'j'aime Courbet absolument, tandis que Proudhon ne l'aime que relativement' (*EsA*, p. 427). This refers not to the latter admitting that 'Courbet a ses défauts',[21] but rather to the fact that, according to Zola, the only paintings held up for inspection by Proudhon were those pictures of modern life whose artistic value was relative to the effectiveness of their social critique. Just as notable, however, is that far from Zola's admiration being as unqualified as he claims, there is a discernible ambivalence in his writing about Courbet. And it is not just in 1865 that both the man and the painter are subject to his reservations.

That ambivalence, however, cannot be properly understood without reference to the wider debate about Realism (most publicly ignited by the prosecutions of *Les Fleurs du mal* and *Madame Bovary*), in which Courbet had figured so largely between his private exhibition outside the Universal Exhibition of 1855 and his so-called *Pavillon du Réalisme* at that of 1867. In particular, the critical perspective hovering out of sight in Zola's essay is that of Champfleury (the pseudonym of Jules-Antoine-Félix Husson, 1821–89), the most influential of the painter's early spokesmen in associating Courbet, to the latter's supposed discomfiture, with the aesthetic principles articulated in his *Le Réalisme* (1857). This was not accepted as unambiguously positive. Duret, sharing many of Zola's modernist enthusiasms, categorized Courbet (in his chapter on the painter in *Les Peintres français en 1867*) as 'un réaliste' only to deplore the lack of emotional resonance in his work's optical exactitude. To Champfleury's criteria, and although caught in the crossfire of the critical hostility of the moment,[22] Zola himself refused to subscribe, subjecting his novels to the charge that their prosaic details were simply tedious and calling, in 1866, for 'moins d'exactitude' (*OC*, x, 686). A more devastating critique of Champfleury as 'le chef de l'école réaliste' would be included in *Les Romanciers naturalistes* (*OC*, xi, 224–25); and in *Le Roman experimental*, Courbet merits a passing mention as Zola's anecdotally recalls that the painter and Champfleury were both fearful of the 'zèle de ce jeunes gens qui immolaient tous les puissants sur l'autel du réalisme' (*OC*, x, 1344). Fifteen years earlier, the section of his review of the Salon of 1866 headed 'Les Réalistes' takes indirect issue with Champfleury in asserting that, by contrast, he himself was *not* 'le porte-drapeau d'une école' and that 'je me moque du réalisme' if this label implied a uniformity of mimetic representation at the expense of the freedom of each and every artist to view the external world differently.[23] Zola rebuts Proudhon's claim that Courbet was merely exemplary: 'Je ne crois pas que le peintre d'Ornans fasse école' (*EsA*, p. 428). What is more, 'le mot "réaliste" ne signifie rien pour moi, qui déclare subordonner le réel au tempérament' (*EsA*, p. 149). Insisting once again on the synonymity of originality and 'l'expression vivante d'un tempérament', Zola concludes: 'J'admire les mondes de Delacroix et de Courbet. Devant cette déclaration, on ne saurait, je crois, me parquer dans aucune école' (*EsA*, p. 156). In his 'Proudhon et Courbet' the year before, Zola's own lexicon of subjectivity, at odds with Proudhon's, gestures towards an individuality suppressed by claims on the painter's behalf of his objective realism: 'ma chair', 'mon sang', 'mon cœur', 'ma pensée', 'personnel'. As Gisèle Sésinger has pointed out, it is not always noticed that here Zola defines 'l'art comme une "expression" et non comme une imitation du réel'.[24] Zola underlines this in his rejection of any work, however famous, 'si elle n'est pas du sang et des nerfs, si elle n'est pas l'expression entière et poignante d'une créature' (*EsA*, p. 422). This would be central to his writing on Manet, which privileges the consistency of the *tempérament* through which reality is pictured and registers disappointment when it appears to be compromised. So too, Courbet would be charged in 1866 with precisely such a deviance from his true nature identifiable in his earlier paintings. But it remains important to distinguish between that artistic *tempérament* and character, between Zola's claim that 'mon Courbet, à moi, est simplement une personnalité' (*EsA*, p. 424) and the person.

Looking at the Painter through the Man

As far as the person is concerned, and notwithstanding the above theoretical distinction, one cannot but feel that Zola's affection for, and affinity with, Manet is not irrelevant in looking by contrast at his writing on Courbet. The remark that 'il n'y a pas la moindre ressemblance entre Courbet et M. Manet' (*EsA*, p. 155), reinforcing the justification of differentiated visions, could be read more personally. For it was a constant of contemporary criticism on Courbet that the man himself was politically suspect as well as intolerably arrogant. Even Proudhon devotes a whole chapter of *Du principe de l'art* to what he calls 'Mes réserves' about the artist's character: 'Il se fait l'apologiste de l'orgueil; en cela, il se montre tout à fait artiste, mais artiste de second ordre'; 'Il s'est trop souvent occupé de lui-même et quelque peu fanfaron de vanité.'[25] The painter's almost consciously cultivated lack of modesty made him an easy target, not least in respect of his regular announcements that his next painting would be a masterpiece even more brilliant than the last.

As Claretie wrote ironically in *Le Figaro* of 17 September 1865: 'le portrait de Proudhon lui-même a été *son chef-d'œuvre* pendant un mois ... avant l'Exposition.' Neither its reception nor the reviews of Proudhon's study in any way undermined his irresistible self-confidence: these were simply evidence of Parisian envy that he should have occupied so special a place in the great philosopher's thinking. In responding to Proudhon's view of Courbet's character, Zola only alludes to it in further undermining the hypothesis that the painter knew exactly what he was doing in educating the public about the social ills of his time: 'Si Courbet, que l'on prétend très orgueilleux, tire son orgueil des leçons qu'il prétend nous donner, je suis tenté de le renvoyer à l'école' (*EsA*, p. 425). Twenty years later, in the preparatory notes for *L'Œuvre*, Zola would return to this commonly held view of the man in imagining 'dans le fond, l'artiste de génie immobile': 'le monstre enflé de sa personnalité, sans critique, et qui est devenu Dieu: Courbet, Hugo'. But earlier, in this preliminary sketch of Bongrand within the novel's *ébauche*, he had attenuated, if only slightly, the portrait of the older fictional painter by contrasting him with these two examples: 'il faut que ce vieux n'ait pas l'orgeuil d'un Hugo ou d'un Courbet. Mettre dans le fond, un vaniteux énorme, toujours content, convaincu de ses chefs-d'œuvre, vivant dans une placidité de dieu.'[26] As Zola had admitted of Proudhon's pen-portrait in 1865, 'il se peut que le Courbet en chair et on os ressemble par quelques traits à celui du publiciste' (*EsA*, pp. 423–24).

Further evidence of Zola's ambivalence is to be found in his review article in *L'Événement* of 5 May 1868, headed '*Le Camp des bourgeois*, illustré par Gustave Courbet' (*EsA*, pp. 413–15). The artist had provided eleven engravings for Étienne Baudry's collection of aphorisms and comic scenarios targeting bourgeois values. While pointing out that Courbet had only once before collaborated on an illustrated edition,[27] Zola did not hide the fact that 'son talent, rude et solide, s'accommode assez mal des délicatesses de la gravure'. But he could not resist taking a swipe at Baudry's championing of the peasantry, consistent with a political agenda akin to that of Proudhon: 'Courbet ne pouvait guère trouver un texte dont l'esprit convînt mieux à son genre de talent.' Zola's support was reinforced in the remark about Courbet's reputed contempt for 'la peinture académique'. But what really grabbed his attention was 'le chapitre où Courbet expose lui-même ses théories sur les destinées de l'art', elaborated in the form of an imagined dialogue between the painter and an art collector, in which Courbet, in condemning the commercialization of art, recommends that paintings be hung in the waiting rooms of stations transformed into 'les temples de l'Art'. The intratextual reference ('les destinées de l'art') to Proudhon is hardly subtle. Nor is Zola's irony at the expense of Courbet's self-important pronouncements: 'Le maître y déclare carrément qu'il faut fermer les musées et les remplacer par les gares de chemin de fer. Personne ne va plus au Louvre, tandis que tout le monde voyage de temps à autre.' Such a logic was inseparable from the painter's advocacy of an anti-élitist and properly 'democratic' public art. And there is no ambiguity about Zola's view of his suggestions: 'c'est donc dans les salles d'attente qu'il faut maintenant accrocher les tableaux'; that the masterpieces of the past should be destroyed; and that the only legitimate artistic subjects of the future would be the representation of the world of manual labour.

Courbet's involvement in the Commune simply confirmed, but with a sharper edge, Zola's reservations about him as an individual. 'Le grand Courbet' assuming the presidency of the Commune's Fédération des artistes was, for Zola, one of those 'spectacles qui sont d'un comique irrésistible', testifying to a 'rusé personnage' with 'toute la finesse du Franc-Comtois' suspected of engineering 'une réclame colossale'. Between 1871 and 1876, he would keep readers of *Le Sémaphore de Marseille* abreast of the painter's legal tribulations (*EsA*, pp. 430–35). 'Courbet était un gros homme, vaniteux et bête', Zola wrote on 31 May 1871, whose gullibility had been exploited by the Commune with the result that 'un des artistes les plus étonnants des temps modernes' had obviously, he joked, gone mad. It was Proudhon, Zola still insisted, who was responsible for the contamination of his mind and art, having committed 'l'énorme plaisanterie de déclarer philosophique et humanitaire sa belle peinture grasse de paysan!': 'ce sont ses amis, avec leur prétendu art social, qui l'ont jeté dans cette épouvantable catastrophe.' Zola was sympathetic to the efforts of those pleading on the painter's behalf: 'On veut sauver Courbet, et l'on a raison', he wrote in *Le Sémaphore de Marseille* of 17 August 1871. 'Un jour l'histoire nous demandera compte de ce grand artiste, qui n'a pas fait le moindre mal, et dans lequel on ne condamnerait que le principe insurrectionnel.' But when, in 1873, he was found guilty of instigating the destruction of the Colonne Vendôme, Zola (unlike Daumier, Corot and Daubigny) was not one of those calling for leniency prior to his sentence, which included his being ordered to pay for its restoration. Nor did he protest at Courbet's exclusion, on political grounds, from the Salon of 1872. Although he would later overcome his initial reaction to 'sa sottise d'un moment', Zola would never quite forget, as he put it in his *Salon* of 1875, Courbet's 'bêtise impardonnable de se compromettre dans une révolte où il n'avait aucune raison de se fourrer' (*EsA*, p. 267). Even in 1880, by which time the painter's greatness in the eyes of posterity (and certainly in Zola's version of it) is almost assured, his suggestion, in *Le Figaro* of 6 December, that he should be one of those creative artists honoured by a statue ('Courbet, le dernier de nos maîtres, le plus sain et le plus fort'), has appended to it 'celui qui eut un jour l'idée bête de vouloir renverser la colonne' (*OC*, xiv, 486). This notorious episode in the painter's life also left its mark on *Le Ventre de Paris* (1873), on which Zola was actively working at the same time as he was commenting on Courbet's arrest and indictment.[28] The novel's fictional painter, it has been argued, 'est un Courbet fourvoyé dans l'idéalisme esthétique'.[29]

Ambivalence

Nor, in respect of the painter's work, does Zola's declaration that 'j'aime Courbet absolument' survive closer scrutiny. As in the case of Cézanne, a knowledge of the man interposes itself between critical purchase and pictorial achievement. Even in his 1865 essay on 'Proudhon et Courbet', there is an uneasy feeling that Proudhon might be partly right: 'J'accorde que certaines toiles du peintre peuvent paraître avoir des intentions satiriques' (*EsA*, p. 424). This was assuaged only with a certain

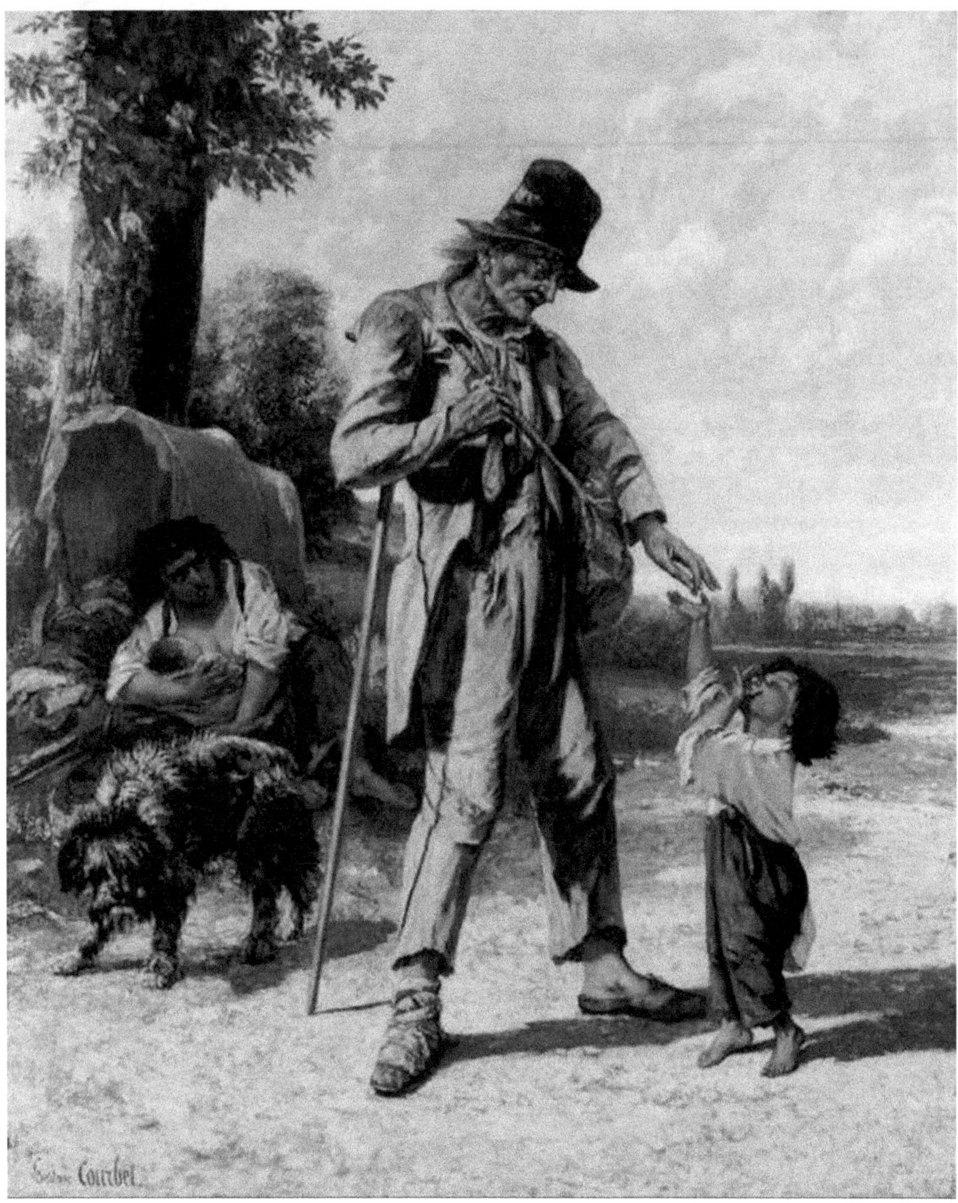

FIG. 3.1. Gustave Courbet, *L'Aumône d'un mendiant à Ornans* (1868), oil on canvas, 210 × 175 cm. The Burrell Collection, Glasgow.

degree of awkwardness when looking at the painter's *Aumône d'un mendiant à Ornans* (Fig. 3.1) at the Salon of 1868, as is suggested by the lengths to which Zola goes in order to distance himself from what Proudhon would have seen as yet another example of 'la philosophie doucement humanitaire de Courbet' (*EsA*, p. 198). He could not have been unaware that, almost unanimously indeed, the painting was seen, mainly by detractors but also by the odd champion, as socialist propaganda.[30] In admitting that 'Courbet n'a pas été heureux avec la critique', Zola restricted himself, however, to reporting that it had been 'quelque peu traîné dans la boue par les idéalistes en question' (implicitly pointing to Gautier having underlined the sheer ugliness of the painting, in the *Journal officiel* of 11 May). But even in refuting such criteria, Zola offers very little by way of appreciation of the picture in its own right. He does not mention its human figures at all. He regrets that 'il n'est pas d'une peinture aussi solide que les anciennes toiles de l'artiste', while reverting to the formulaic 'bâties à chaux et à sable' (*EsA*, p. 425) of his 1865 essay: 'il est encore bâti à chaux et à sable comparé aux toiles encensées par la critique' (*EsA*, p. 198), consistent with Cézanne's metaphorical characterization of Courbet as 'un rude gâcheur de plâtre'.[31]

L'Aumône d'un mendiant sits rather precariously in Zola's category of 'Quelques Bonnes Toiles' singled out in his review of the Salon of 1868. But his remark that it was less 'solide' than Courbet's earlier works fits into a pattern. In his 1865 essay, he clearly revealed a preference for those of the 1850s, unhesitatingly dismissing his more recent ones as 'très inférieures' (*EsA*, p. 425). The painter's submissions to the Salon of 1866 found him relegated to what Zola calls 'Les Chutes', artists considered to be in decline, though he was careful to add that 'lorsque Courbet faiblit, il reste encore un des premiers peintres de l'époque' (*EsA*, p. 197). It may be that he was conflicted, 1866 being the year when a number of his friends were rejected by a Salon jury whose members he took individually to task. Monet's *Camille* (also known as *La Femme à la robe verte*) and his *Route dans la forêt de Fontainebleau* figured among the 3,000 or so works accepted, as did one of Bazille's, both of Sisley's and Berthe Morisot's, a single Pissarro landscape and a Degas steeplechase scene. On the other hand, and most provocatively for Zola, Manet's two pictures were excluded, as were the submissions of Guillemet, Renoir and Cézanne. It is perhaps unsurprising that the latter, too, was of the opinion that the Courbet paintings exhibited at the Salon of 1866, *La Femme au perroquet* (Fig. 3.2) and *La Remise des chevreuils* (Fig. 3.3), were symptomatic of the decline of his artistic talent. For Zola, they were not merely that: they signalled that 'Courbet, paraît-il, a passé à l'ennemi' (*EsA*, p. 135). In alluding to official efforts to bribe the 'terrible tapageur' with medals in return for curing himself of the 'indigestion de démocratie' fed to him by Proudhon, Zola was simply rehearsing rumours in the press. The suspicion that these had some substance was not allayed by Courbet being congratulated for his evident change of subject-matter, no longer of a political or didactic potential, by the likes of Cabanel. Zola knew that, following the rejection of his own submissions, Cézanne's letters of protest addressed in April to the Surintendant des Beaux-Arts, the comte de Nieuwerkerke, had been given short shrift. It must have been galling to learn from the newspapers during that very same month that, by contrast, their recipient had been so enchanted by Courbet's two 'masterpieces' — to the extent of wanting to purchase *La Femme au perroquet* — that the painter himself did not deny that he was expecting to be awarded the Salon's 'médaille d'honneur'. Zola's hostility to any such recognition by the state runs through everything he ever wrote on the visual

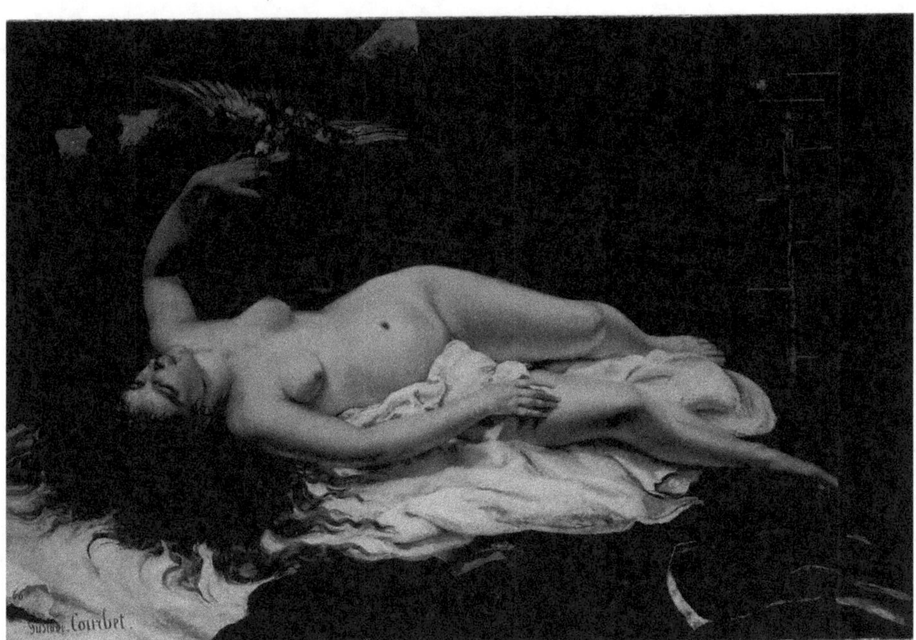

FIG. 3.2. Gustave Courbet, *La Femme au perroquet* (1866), oil on canvas, 129.5 × 195.6 cm. Metropolitan Museum of Art, New York. H. O. Havermeyer Collection. Gift of Mrs H. O. Havermeyer.

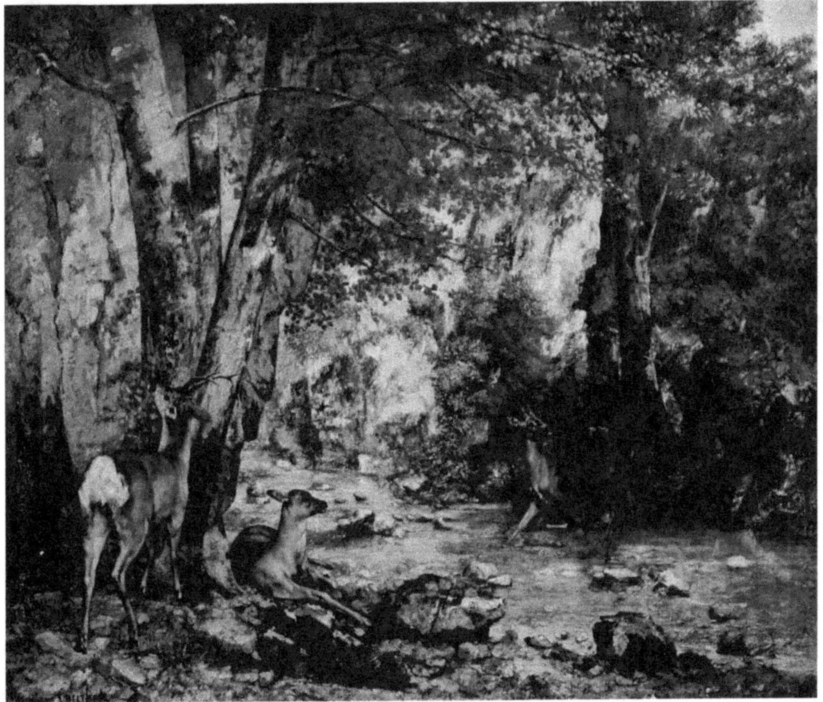

FIG. 3.3. Gustave Courbet, *La Remise des chevreuils au ruisseau de Plaisir-Fontaine* (1866), oil on canvas, 174 × 209 cm. Musée d'Orsay, Paris.

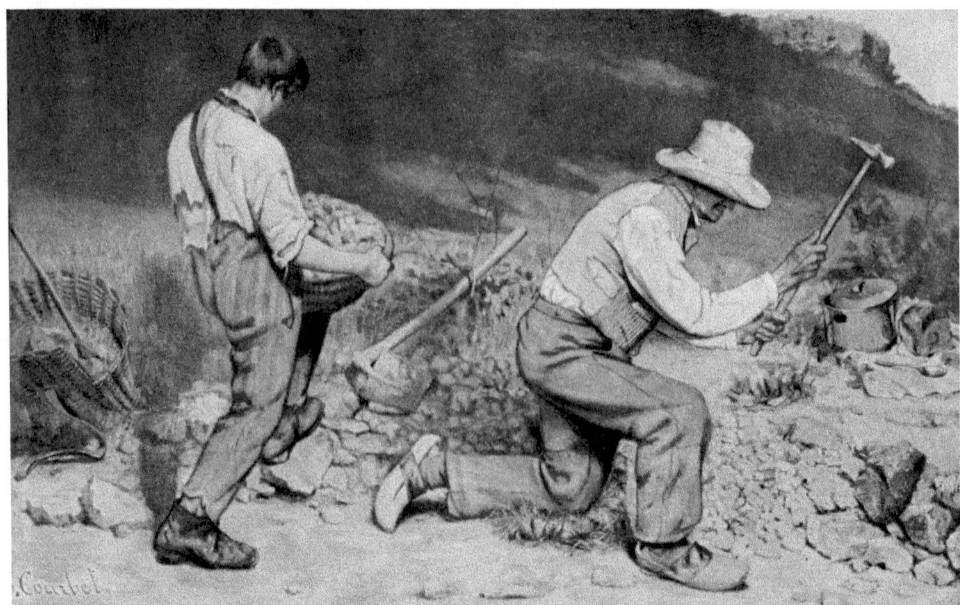

FIG. 3.4. Gustave Courbet, *Les Casseurs de pierre* (1849), oil on canvas, 165 × 257 cm. Formerly in Dresden but destroyed during World War II.

arts. In the event, no such reward was forthcoming in Courbet's case. And Zola may have underestimated the painter's sense of humour in playing along with flattering solicitation of his adherence to a less controversial pictorial mode.[32] But an art critic as informed as Castagnary reflected a widespread view: that to exhibit his paintings for the first time in the prestigious 'salon d'honneur' at the entrance of the Palais de l'Industrie would be justified because 'Courbet, revenu de ce qu'on a appelé ses défaillances, obtient un universel succès'. In the same week as this celebration of Courbet's return to the fold, Zola struck an altogether different note in respect of the two paintings which testified to this apparent conversion: 'il manque à ces toiles le je ne sais quoi de puissant et de voulu qui est Courbet tout entier' (*EsA*, p. 164).[33]

To track Courbet's decline, alongside that of Théodore Rousseau and Millet, was therefore to adopt a perspective, differentiated from Champfleury's, totally at odds with official approval (in the shape of both the positive outcome of the Salon jury's deliberations and the associated commentary). This perspective was also radicalized by the polemical virulence of Zola's first contracted review of the annual exhibition, marking the advent of a personally dissident art criticism. These overlapping contexts serve to explain, at least in part, the contradictions within Zola's assessment of Courbet in 1866. For he starts off by repeating almost word for word the introductory paragraph to the second instalment of his 'Proudhon et Courbet' the year before, though only clarifying here that his visit to the painter's studio had taken place during one of the latter's absences. In repeating his surprise that the pictures seen bore no resemblance to the caricatural versions of them peddled by unsympathetic critics, Zola was obviously distancing himself from such philistinism. This is consistent with a perspective which runs through *Mon Salon* in its championing of Manet and the artists of his circle at the expense of the orthodoxies of the day. On the other hand, to lament that Courbet's submissions to the Salon of 1866 were inferior to his earlier work was to reflect a consensus grounded in a reiterated admiration for precisely those paintings created in the shadow of the 1848 Revolution whose political dimension Zola had refused to acknowledge.

The justification for consigning Courbet to the 'dustbin' of 'Les Chutes' lies in Zola's perception that the official *imprimatur* signalled by his two paintings on display itself testified to a change of style motivated by courting popular success and thus betraying his originality (*EsA*, pp. 161–64): 'Courbet, cette année, a arrondi les angles trop rudes de son génie.' To make his point, it is here that, for the first time, Zola invokes *Un Enterrement à Ornans*,[34] but simply in order to contrast its hostile critical reception in 1850–51 with the collective enthusiasm for *La Femme au perroquet* and *La Remise des chevreuils*. These 'deux délicieuses choses de cette année' are also compared to *La Baigneuse* and *La Curée* (1857), the second of which Zola may possibly have seen for himself at the Salon of 1863,[35] as well as to *Les Casseurs de pierres* (Fig. 3.4), but again less in relation to their pictorial qualities than to their contemporary devaluation. It was these works rather than his 1866 submissions, Zola argues, for which the painter should have been rewarded. For 'cette année, il est admis que les toiles de Courbet sont charmantes. On trouve son paysage exquis et son étude de femme très convenable' (*EsA*, p. 161). This was not entirely true.[36] But to content himself with such a generalization was to substantiate once again an equation measuring artistic value in inverse relation to public enthusiasm or disgust: 'une règle qui s'impose forcément à moi: c'est que l'admiration de la foule est toujours en raison indirecte du génie individuel' (*EsA*, p. 162). As for the paintings themselves, Zola's minimal comments verge on the platitudinous: *La Remise des chevreuils* is 'charming'; *La Femme au perroquet* is 'une solide peinture, très travaillée et très nette', the stress on such formal qualities almost wilfully eschewing interpretative possibilities offered by this erotic nude at some remove from the notion of the 'convenable'.

Such a relative lack of interest may also account for the otherwise surprising omission of any mention, in Zola's writing about Courbet, of the painter's major exhibition, in his constructed pavilion on the Place de l'Alma, which opened on 30 May 1867. It was this exhibition which inspired Duret's remarks on Courbet mentioned above. Although overtaken by his involvement in Manet's own private show,[37] also mounted in the margins of that year's Universal Exhibition and literally adjacent to Courbet's, at one stage Zola seems to have planned to devote to the latter's 'une courte étude'.[38] Of the 115 works on display there (to which subsequently were added another twenty), the only work to which he refers is *La Curée*, but merely aligned with Delacroix's *Massacre de Scio* (1824) and Manet's *Déjeuner sur l'herbe* as yet another example of a painting left unappreciated by a philistine viewing public.[39] As such, this mention further illustrates the extent to which Courbet is often invoked simply as a foil to the prize-winning orthodoxies of

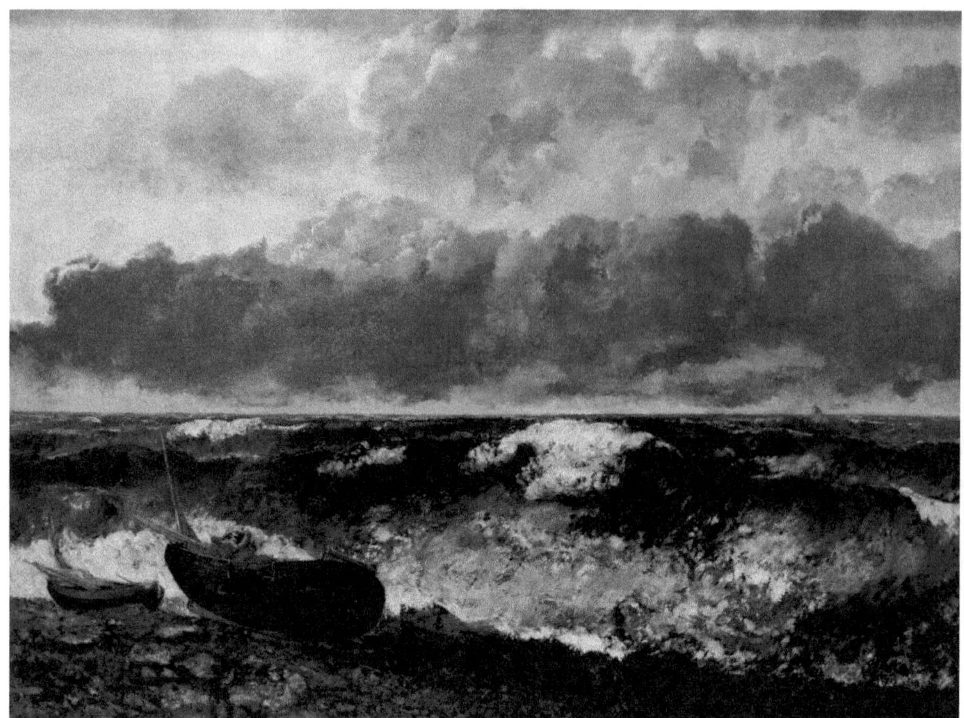

FIG. 3.5. Gustave Courbet, *La Mer orageuse (La Vague)* (Salon of 1870), oil on canvas, 116 × 160 cm. Musée d'Orsay, Paris.

the day. The celebrated Second Empire portrait artist Édouard Dubufe (1819–1883), for instance, is only invoked in order to underline his oppositional stance: 'J'ai commis l'énormité de ne pas admirer M. Dubufe après avoir admiré Courbet' (*EsA*, p.170). Reviewing the Salon of 1880, 'M. Jules Breton, qui est un peintre creux, me fait toujours regretter Courbet' (*EsA*, p. 385). Cabanel and Gérôme's popular success is contrasted with Courbet's lack of it (*EsA*, p. 550). Even artists whose real qualities he admits, like Bonnat, suffer from this kind of juxtaposition: 'on en viendra à le traiter de simple esclave de Courbet, qui ne rachète pas la lourdeur de sa brosse par la délicatesse de ses tons' (*EsA*, p. 360). Whatever their putative adherence to 'le mouvement naturaliste', 'aucun d'eux', Zola writes of Bonnat, Henner, Vollon and Laurens, 'n'a résumé la formule avec la facture magistrale d'un Courbet' (*EsA*, p. 387). Courbet's solo exhibition of 1867 offered no such comparative perspective. Nor did his three innocuous pictures at that year's Universal Exhibition,[40]

Zola's more general failure to engage with Courbet's landscapes needs to be inserted within the same polemical frame. At one level, it is clear that he did not much like them: 'Son talent a une ampleur et une sévérité qui s'accommodent mal des gaietés blondes de la nature'; and, in this same 1868 article, Zola compared him unfavourably with Boudin, 'j'avoue n'aimer que médiocrement ses dernières marines, très fines, il est vrai, mais un peu minces pour sa rude main magistrale' (*EsA*, p. 199). By contrast, Zola's enthusiasm for *La Vague* (Fig. 3.5), included in the Universal Exhibition of 1878, almost seems extravagant, comparing its wonderful sea and sky to the artifice and symbolic import of their rendering by the likes of Cabanel and Paul Baudry: 'une vraie vague déferlant sur le rivage [...] superbe du point de vue technique' (*EsA*, p. 544). But it needs to be remembered that, to the outrage of avant-garde critics and in an almost insulting repudiation of the traditional commemoration of the recent death of a major artist, this was the *only* Courbet painting on display, initially shown at the Salon of 1870, its unique status enhanced by having been recently bought by the state and hung in the Musée du Luxembourg.[41] Or as Zola put it, 'cette œuvre n'est pas d'une grande portée' and, above all, 'n'est pas compromettante' (*EsA*, p. 544). In cheekily advising the painter, in 1866, 'de revenir à sa première façon de voir' (*EsA*, p. 199), Zola reveals the real reason behind his preference for Courbet's early pictures. As in the case of Manet's, it is the degree of hostility they provoked, whether in the guise of hilarity or repugnance, which underlines their convention-breaking originality. Rejection by the Salon jury is its formal expression, as Zola explains to his Russian readers in 1876, advocating its abolition to ensure that artists like Courbet could no longer be excluded (*EsA*, p. 308). It can be suggested, indeed, that Zola was often more interested in the painter's critical reception than in the particular qualities of his work. Before proceeding to make the somewhat unconvincing case that *L'Aumône d'un mendiant* qualified as one of the 'Quelques Bonnes Toiles' at the Salon of 1868, Zola admitted that 'rien n'est amusant comme l'attitude de la critique à l'égard de Courbet' (*EsA*, p. 197). When he wrote to Burty, asking for a meeting to discuss Courbet, it is probable that this related to a project to write, as mentioned in Chapter 1, 'un livre de haute critique: "L'Œuvre d'art devant la critique"'.[42] Without specifying which of his ten works shown there he had in mind, Zola is alluding to Courbet in recalling the Salon of 1848, genuinely revolutionary in admitting every submission ('la démocratie [...] qui entrait dans le temple'), including 'un tableau brutal traité avec les rudesses du génie' (*EsA*, p. 511).[43] In the section of his 1867 study of Manet dealing with his critical reception, he asserts that 'l'histoire artistique de notre temps est là pour dire que ce groupe de badauds et de rieurs aveugles s'est formé devant les premières toiles de Decamps, de Delacroix, de Courbet' (*EsA*, p. 493). In his Salon of 1875, again citing these three 'victims' of public incomprehension, he repeats that this is the fate of 'tous les talents originaux' (*EsA*, p. 277). It is a general truth, according to Zola in 1880, that 'tous les maîtres ont commencé par être lapidés, ils n'ont grandi que dans la lutte' (*EsA*, p. 383), this time including even Ingres alongside Courbet.

It would be going too far, however, to conclude that Zola's referencing of Courbet was merely strategic. Some of his polemical juxtapositions are extended to define the painter's distinctiveness. The comparative dismissal of Breton's stylized rural scenes is backed up by explaining his preference for 'les paysannes de Courbet, non seulement parce qu'elles sont mieux dessinées du point de vue technique, mais aussi parce qu'elles sont plus proches de la réalité' (*EsA*, p. 362). In contrasting him with Carolus-Duran, to take another example, Zola's rubbishing of this fashionable society painter leads him to counter that 'chez Courbet domine un sens du réel et du vrai, une transcription puissante et fidèle de la nature telle que la création humaine ne pourra sans doute jamais la dépasser' (*EsA*, p. 559). There is no doubt that Zola considered him one of the great painters of the nineteenth century. In 1865, prior to discovering Manet, Zola had declared that Courbet was 'le *seul* peintre de notre époque' (*EsA*, p. 425; my emphasis). There could be no higher accolade than the subsequent elevation of Manet to such a rank amongst the living artists of the period. Alluding, while self-deprecatingly ironizing his use of the jargon, to 'ce qu'on appelle, je crois, la loi des valeurs', he proclaims that 'je ne connais guère, dans l'école moderne, que Corot, Courbet et Édouard Manet qui aient constamment obéi à cette loi en peignant des figures' (*EsA*, p. 478). It was primarily in the interests of the latter, obviously, that this remark of 1867 was justified. So too was the prediction that Manet had only to be patient in the face of public scorn to overcome the similar 'destinée des maîtres, de Delacroix et de Courbet, par exemple' (*EsA*, p. 494). 'Nos pères ont ri de Courbet', he wrote in 1866, 'et voilà que nous nous extasions devant lui' (*EsA*, p. 149). The struggle to overcome public prejudice is continually rehearsed in Zola's art criticism. But that is not to deny his sincerity. To cite in 1868 'les œuvres remarquables de Manet et de Courbet' as the only ones worthy of consideration was bold. To bracket them would not be without its risks in the political climate of L'Ordre Moral: Louis Enault, writing in the ultra-conservative *Constitutionnel* of 5 May 1873 about Manet's *Le Bon Bock*, established a comparison of a more invidious kind in declaring that the painter 'a le tort de ressembler au grotesque déboulonneur de la colonne'. Zola was less partisan. In tracking the consequences of Courbet's involvement with the Commune, initial mockery gives way to genuine concern and increasing sympathy (*EsA*, pp. 432–35): in June 1871, he is advised to get back to his paintings 'qui seront une gloire de nos musées'; two years later, Zola is aghast that the punitive measures of the authorities should include seizing the contents of his studio; by 1874, he refers to 'ce pauvre grand Courbet'; in 1876, he talks about his 'gloire immortelle de peintre', while deploring the fact that his exile meant he had sent nothing to the annual Salon for the three years previously;[44] and more than a decade after the painter's death, Zola still laments that 'Courbet a perdu son talent et sa vie dans la crise imbécile de la Commune' (*EsA*, p. 396). In 1878, the not-long deceased Courbet is described as a pariah hounded by bailiffs, to the eternal shame of France 'dont il aura été l'une des gloires'. To gesture towards his 'martyrdom' ('les sept dernières années de sa vie ont été de ce fait un long martyre' (*EsA*, pp. 543–45)) was part of the national process of rehabilitation, of what Linda Nochlin has called the 'de-politicization' of Courbet,[45] given posthumous impetus from 1878 onwards. Ephemeral governments and politicians would soon be forgotten, Zola predicted, while 'Courbet revivra et fleurira de l'éternelle jeunesse de son talent. On lui ouvrira les portes du Louvre, l'heure de son apothéose sonnera' (*EsA*, p. 545). What is more remarkable is that he had said as much back in 1866: 'la place de Manet est marquée au Louvre comme celle de Courbet' (*EsA*, p. 155).

Courbet Reconsidered

It was Courbet's enforced absence from the artistic stage, even before his death, which also allowed Zola to position him in a longer historical narrative stretching to posterity. In the 'grandes ombres' of the departed, Delacroix and Ingres, the painter's disappearance, 'vieilli, chassé comme un lépreux', meant that 'Courbet [...] s'en va déjà à leur suite dans l'histoire. Lui aussi appartient dès aujourd'hui aux morts, aux artistes dont les tableaux seront éternels par leur force et leur vérité' (*EsA*, p. 314). Over and beyond parallels between the critical reception of Courbet and others like Delacroix and Manet, there emerges a retrospective account of a lineage of predecessors and successors which would form a stable set of reference points within Zola's art criticism from the mid-1870s onwards. This account was reinforced by reading Duranty's *La Nouvelle Peinture* in 1876. At a sufficient distance from Duranty's more dogmatic theorization of the mid-1850s, Zola was struck by his argument that the development of realism in painting was inseparable from Courbet who had, 'comme Balzac, tracé le sillon d'une façon si vigoureuse'.[46] Zola would in due course rehearse such an analogy between literary and pictorial representation, positioning the Impressionists 'à la suite de Courbet et de nos grands paysagistes', stressing that 'Courbet était un maître qui a laissé des œuvres impérissables', while 'derrière lui, le mouvement a continué, comme il continue en littérature, derrière Stendhal, Balzac et Flaubert' (*EsA*, p. 373). In 1875, Zola had already identified the painter's pioneering role: in a struggle sustained after them by Manet, but with definitive victory postponed, 'Delacroix et Courbet ont porté les premiers coups' (*EsA*, p. 293); in the 'recherche des vérités naturelles' characteristic of artistic endeavour, 'après les œuvres éblouissantes d'Eugène Delacroix, Courbet fut le premier à pousser dans cette direction' (*EsA*, p. 354); Manet had continued 'le mouvement réaliste, déclenché par Courbet' (*EsA*, p. 356). In spite of the above apparent distinction between Courbet and 'nos grands paysagistes',[47] Zola gradually, in a conscious slippage or not, also incorporates as his successors the major landscape artists of the period prior to Impressionism — ironically enough, given both that this had been precisely the lineage sketched by the much-maligned Proudhon and that Zola had seldom paid attention to Courbet's landscapes, arguably central to his artistic achievement as well as his commercial success. After Courbet, Zola writes in 1878, 'venait toute une grande école de paysagistes: Théodore Rousseau, Daubigny, Corot, sans parler de Diaz et de Millet' (*EsA*, p. 342). The following year, he recognizes in Bastien-Lepage's *Saison d'octobre* 'le petit-fils de Courbet et de Millet' (*EsA*, p. 357). All of them, including Courbet, are recruited into the Naturalist hegemony declared towards the end of the 1870s. Much more problematic is the premise rehearsed in Zola's conception of art history, whether in relation to the nineteenth century or the Italian Renaissance, that the gigantic stature of certain artists condemned their immediate successors to creative impotence or indirection: 'Ingres, Delacroix, Courbet ont laissé derrière eux un champ qui a l'air épuisé parce qu'eux et leurs disciples l'ont labouré dans tous les sens' (*EsA*, p. 574). This would have far-reaching implications for Zola's ultimate assessment of Manet and the Impressionists.

The preparation of *L'Œuvre*, in 1885–86, afforded Zola the opportunity to accommodate the modulations of his assessment of Courbet over the previous two decades. But this also posed problems of chronology, for the novel supposedly takes place in the 1860s, consistent with the precise historical limits declared in the subtitle of *Les Rougon-Macquart*: 'Histoire naturelle et sociale d'une famille sous le second Empire'. 'Il me faudra tricher', Zola admitted to himself: 'je suis décidé à dépasser 1870' (Ms 10316, fol. 219). And the date of the novel's composition also explains the frequent references in its preparatory *dossier* to the *fin de siècle* and to the anticipated 'débat du 20ème siècle' (fol. 278). One of the consequences of this retrospective stance is that the insertion of what Zola repeatedly calls 'une historique de la peinture' positions Courbet in a lineage defined by him only in the 1870s, particularly after his death, rather than reflecting his status as it was during the time-frame of the novel. 'Le moment artistique posé' is accordingly 'Après Ingres, Delacroix romantique, Courbet grand ouvrier classique' (fol. 28) — both in the writer's work notes and as adumbrated by his fictional characters.

At the same time as the view of Courbet in the eyes of posterity, also visible in the notes for *L'Œuvre* are traces of a number of remarks aimed at Courbet in the 1860s either by Zola or other critics. Identifying them is complicated by the lengths to which the novelist went to ensure that it would not be too easily read as a *roman à clef*. Over and above explicit allusions to Courbet's character, as mentioned earlier, an analogous process operates in the distribution of aspects of his work across authorial comments and invented conversations. Having taken extensive notes from Guillemet on what he called 'le côté matériel de la fabrication', including learning that 'Courbet peignait au couteau, puis blaireautait' (fol. 370). Zola at one stage lends this method to Claude Lantier, his fictional painter, in order to demonstrate a mastery of such technicalities virtually absent from his art criticism: 'la grosse affaire était le couteau à palette, car il l'employait pour les fonds, comme Courbet' (*RM*, IV, 247). That is not, on its own, in any way sufficient to align Claude and Courbet. In detailing some of the minor characters, however, partial superimpositions are more instructive. It is not only Chambouvard's personality, for example, which is a reminder of how Courbet is perceived by Zola, for the very subjects of his compositions (*Le Semeur, Le Lutteur, Eve, Baigneuse*, etc.') are integral to 'un ouvrier de génie, d'une pratique grandiose' (fol. 248). As Zola put it in his work notes: 'colossal, baissé d'un cran dans la production' (fol. 113). Mahoudeau's *Vendangeuse* is conceived as 'la Bachante énorme avec des délicatesses' (fols 41–42), as Zola had described Courbet's human figures. The association between painter and fictional sculptor is explicit: 'Je ferai alors de mon Dieu, de mon Courbet, un sculpteur' (fol. 293). Zola had highlighted Courbet's being drawn 'par toute sa chair' to 'le monde matériel qui l'entourait' (*EsA*, p. 425). The qualities characteristic of Mahoudeau are compared to a more modern art: 'ce gobage de soi, avec la matérialité des statues. L'épaisseur de la forme, la chair sentie' (fol. 294). Zola had written of Courbet in both 1865 and 1866 in such terms: 'il voulait peindre en pleine viande et en plein terreau' (*EsA*, p. 163, p. 425). And the attenuation of Mahoudeau's work, 'moins gros' and 'de plus en plus gracieux' (fols. 41–42, 48, 108, 183 and 238 ('la grâce qui surnage')) is exactly what had been condemned in Courbet's paintings of 1866. Or, to cite another example, Courajod, 'le vieux peintre oublié' to the point of generating rumours that he might be dead,[48] is reminiscent of Zola's 1876 remark that Courbet's exile meant that, in effect,'[il]appartient dès aujourd'hui aux morts' (*EsA*, p. 314).

The most significant set of overlaid remarks is to be found in Zola's elaboration of Bongrand's presence in the novel, initially planned as being a merely intermittent one. Although divested of the arrogance which had originally motivated the comparison between an imagined older painter and Courbet, and even without the subsequent parallel of the latter's *Enterrement à Ornans* and Bongrand's *Enterrement au village*, Zola's first attempt at a detailed character sketch is illuminating (fols 244–46). More important than his provincial origins in the Auvergne and 'le sang paysan',[49] is Bongrand's having 'trouvé une formule après Delacroix', 'avec plus de perfection dans le métier, plus de serré et de logique, une couleur moins intense, mais plus vraie'. These are the very terms which are ubiquitous in Zola's articles on Courbet. Repeated throughout the preparatory notes for *L'Œuvre* is the emphasis, as has been seen in Zola's writing on the painter, on a decline which nevertheless fails to undermine 'son immortalité assurée' (fol. 247). It is also noted that 'il aime la jeunesse et vient parfois fumer là une pipe' (fol. 45) and, in moments of discouragement, Claude is 'ravi, soulevé par l'éloge de Bongrand' (fols 49, 72). Courbet had similarly supported Monet ever since seeing his work in 1865–66, and even to the extent of helping him out personally when the younger painter was in dire financial straits.[50] Above all, however, Zola stresses that Bongrand 'a ramené l'art à une vue plus exacte de la nature, *sans en venir à l'impressionnisme*' (fol. 244). My italics here relate to what Zola wrote about Courbet in 1868 and 1879, pointing out that his 'coloration un peu sourde' (*EsA*, p. 425, p. 163), made him unsuited to engage in landscape painting. In preparing *L'Œuvre*, he wrote of Delacroix and Courbet that they were 'tous deux noirs, cuisinés' (fol. 28). Noting that *L'Aumône du mendiant* was 'lumineux', Zola put this down to Courbet's efforts 'à faire blond depuis quelque temps', adding that 'la jeune école, qui voit la nature par taches claires, lui a fait abandonner, sans doute à son insu, sa manière noire' (*EsA*, p. 199), to which he is advised to return. In 1879, at the moment that Zola's disappointment with the Impressionists is at its most acute, he wrote that 'on considère parmi eux que les beaux procédés techniques de Courbet ne peuvent donner que des tableaux magnifiques peints en atelier' (*EsA*, p. 355). This segment of his art criticism, picked up in the reference in the work notes to 'l'atelier vieux jeu' (fol. 106) goes directly into *L'Œuvre* in a scene in which Zola distances himself from such juvenile certainties. Claude Lantier proclaims that 'la peinture noire de Courbet empoisonne déjà le renfermé, le moisi de l'atelier où le soleil n'entre pas', but he is greeted by silence and ends up stumbling towards a logical conclusion deferred : '[Il] n'arrivait pas à formuler la sourde éclosion d'avenir qui montait en lui' (*RM*, IV, 45). For between 1868 and 1879, Courbet's place in Zola's thinking had undergone as radical a transformation as that of the Impressionists. The latter, in their 'travail hâtif' are charged with producing work lacking in compositional structure as well as verisimilitude while Courbet 'c'est l'artiste acharné au travail, asseyant sur une base solide la nouvelle formule naturaliste' (*EsA*, p. 542). It will be argued in the concluding chapter of this book that Zola's art criticism comes full circle in his admiration for the Old Masters at the expense of the avant-garde painters he had championed in the 1860s. That Courbet's pictorial qualities, notably his 'facture magistrale' (*EsA*, p. 387), should be assimilated to those of the great artists of the Italian Renaissance reinforces that paradox: as Zola had expressed his admiration for Courbet to more effectively devalue pictorial convention, so the painter provides the benchmark for Zola's ultimate devaluing of 'la nouvelle peinture'.

Notes to Chapter 3

1. It is nevertheless possible that it may have been included in the rounds of artists' studios organized by, and in the company of, Cézanne in the early 1860s. Cézanne remained a great admirer of Courbet and in close contact with one of his pupils, Francisco Oller. This was such common knowledge among his fellow painters that it is not by chance that there is an image of Courbet in the top right-hand corner of Pissarro's 1874 portrait of Cézanne (see Fig. 2.2). There is no evidence to support Antoinette Ehrard's claim that the visit took place in 1865 ('Zola et Courbet', *Europe*, 468–69 (April–May 1968), 241–51 (p. 242). In his *Journal* entry for 14 April 1879 (*Mémoires de la vie littéraire*, ed. by Robert Ricatte, 3 vols (Paris: Laffont, 1956), II, 775), Edmond de Goncourt records Zola's memory of seeing the painter (although unclear whether it was at his easel or during an exhibition) 'planté devant un de ses tableaux, se caressant la barbe', uttering 'C'est comique, cette peinture', a disingenuous phrase put into the mouth of Chambouvard, partly modelled on Courbet, in *L'Œuvre* (*RM*, IV, 133). Writing in 1882, Paul Alexis, the proofs of whose early biography had been checked by Zola himself, also cited the Courbet reference, though without mentioning any context for Courbet 'en extase devant une de ses toiles' (*Émile Zola: notes d'un ami*, p. 205).
2. Its title in the Salon catalogue is *Les Baigneuses*, but Proudhon explicitly refers to it in the context of the 1853 exhibition. Another painting exhibited at this Salon, and again at that of 1855, *La Fileuse endormie*, was also immediately purchased by Bruyas, who would go on, in the next four years, to buy eight more Courbets (including *Chasse au chevreuil dans les forêts du grand Jura; la curée* (1857)), subsequently lending back to the painter, for his private and public exhibitions, those of his works in his own collection — given in 1868 to the Musée Fabre in his native Montpellier.
3. Champfleury, 'Courbet en 1860', in his *Grandes figures d'hier et d'aujourdhui* [1861] (Geneva: Slatkine Reprints, 1968), pp. 245–63, noting 'que ses tableaux se vendaient mal, que son œuvre considérable s'accumulait dans son atelier en immenses toiles roulées dans un coin' (p. 248).
4. Their visit took place on Sunday 26 May 1861 (*Corr.*, I, 288–89, n. 1); for Cézanne, see his reference to Courbet in his letter of 4 June to Joseph Huot (Cézanne, *Correspondance*, p. 122). At this Salon, Courbet exhibited: *Le Renard dans la neige*; *Le Piqueur*; *Le Rut du printemps (combats de cerfs)*; *Le Cerf à l'eau (chasse à course)*; and *La Roche Oragon, vallon de Mezières (Doubs)*.
5. At the Salon of 1863: *Chasse au renard* and *Portrait de Mme L.*; in 1865: *Entrée de la vallée du Puits-Noir (Doubs); effet de crépuscule* and his portrait of Proudhon.
6. These are the only paintings which Zola mentions. Proudhon himself refers in addition to many other Courbet paintings: *L'Atelier du peintre (Allégorie réelle)* (1854–55); *Vénus et Psyché* (rejected by the Salon of 1864); *Le Retour de la conférence* (1862), also known as *Les Curés*; *Combat de cerfs* (1861); *Enterrement à Ornans* (1849–50); *L'Homme blessé* (1844[?]); and *Les Filles de Loth* (rejected by the Salon of 1844). He may have seen some of these in Bruyas's collection.
7. B. Jouvin, in his long review, pejoratively headed 'Les Hasards de la plume', *Le Figaro*, 11 June 1865.
8. Although Proudhon himself underlined his own interpretative licence: 'Courbet, plus artiste que philosophe, n'a pas pensé tout ce que je trouve', asserting his freedom 'à l'interpréter à ma manière' (*Du principe de l'art et de sa destination sociale* (Paris: Garnier Frères, 1865), p. 280).

9. Jack Lindsay, *Gustave Courbet: His Life and Art* (London: Jupiter, 1977), p. 199. The painting was altered after 1865, substituting a chair for Proudhon's wife!
10. Jules Claretie, 'Deux heures au Salon', *L'Artiste*, 15 May 1865, pp. 224–29 (p. 225).
11. Letter of 12 August 1865 (Flaubert, *Correspondance*, III, 454).
12. 'Bulletin mensuel: juillet 1865', in *GBA*, 19 (1 August 1865), 185–92 (p. 188).
13. Letter of 5 April 1875 (*Corr.*, II, 387–88).
14. As long ago as 1851, on account of their friendship and common Franche-Comté origins, a critic could declare that 'M. Courbet est le *Proudhon* de la peinture'; L. Enault, 'Le Salon de 1851', *Chronique de Paris*, 16 February 1851, cited by T. J. Clark, *Image of the People: Gustave Courbet and the 1848 Revolution* [1973] (London: Thames & Hudson, 1982), p. 170.
15. As Champfleury summarized it in 1861, 'l'histoire de Courbet [...], c'est l'histoire du "réalisme"' (*Grandes figures d'hier*, p. 263), cross-referencing his own *Le Réalisme* (Paris: Michel Lévy, 1857).
16. Proudhon, *Du Principe de l'art*, respectively: p. 187, p. 188, pp. 227–28, p. 212, p. 213, p. 257–58, p. 262. Cabanel's artificial *Naissance de Vénus* is a constant negative point of reference in Zola's art criticism; and in 'Madame Neigon' (a text written in 1879 and included in *Naïs Micoulin* (1884)), Zola invented a visit to the Salon in which a duchess and her two daughters 'regardaient sans sourciller une *Léda*, tandis que, derrière elles, un atelier de jeunes peintres s'égayaient du tableau en termes très libres' (*OC*, IX, 773).
17. His study of *Les Casseurs de pierres* focuses on corporeal signs and broken bodies. Courbet 'excelle', Proudhon writes, 'à rendre la beauté physiologique': in *La Fileuse endormie*, 'la taille puissante, les bras robustes, les doigts nourris'; in the *Enterrement à Ornans*, the 'fossoyeur au visage épaté, à la face de brute'; the woman in *La Baigneuse*, 'grasse et dodue, large de croupe et fournie d'encolure, brune et luisante' (*Du Principe de l'art*, pp. 206–07, p. 209, p. 213).
18. There are only two references by Proudhon to Courbet's depiction of the natural world: the claim that the river in *Les Demoiselles de la Seine* 'indique, par synecdoque, la civilisation parisienne', justifying the view that the canvas should have been called '*Deux jeunes personnes à la mode, sous le second Empire* (*Du principe de l'art*, p. 244); and 'la vulgarité de la scène contrastant avec la beauté du paysage' in *Le Retour de la conférence* (p. 276).
19. Proudhon, *Du principe de l'art*, p. 284.
20. See his comments on Courbet, as reported by Gasquet (*Cézanne*, pp. 200–02): 'un vrai peintre. Il n'y en a pas un autre dans ce siècle qui le dégote, [...] sa facture est celle d'un classique'; *La Vaneuse* compared to 'les plus beaux Véronèse'; the equal of Velázquez; and of *Les Demoiselles de la Seine*, 'on peut dire Titien'.
21. Proudhon, *Du principe de l'art*, p. 201.
22. In comparing his two early novels, *La Confession de Claude* (1865) and *Le Vœu d'une morte* (1866), in *La Revue du XIXe siècle* of 1 January 1867, Henry Houssaye (writing under the pseudonym of Georges Werner) saw in the idealized fabric of the second of these a contrast with 'le réalisme le plus sombre' of the earlier text, summed up as a transition from 'Courbet à l'Ange de Fiesole!'.
23. He would nevertheless find it a label difficult to resist: in 'Aux Champs' (a text of 1878), Zola evoked a rural inn frequented by 'une bande de peintres réalistes, vers 1845 [...]. Courbet y régna un moment' (*OC*, IX, 620). He not only refers to Courbet's 'realist' paintings, but in 1879 virtually echoes Champfleury in referring to 'le mouvement réaliste, déclenché par Courbet' (*EsA*, p. 356). In the work notes for *L'Œuvre*, Zola referred to the mounting of the Salon des Refusés of 1863 as evidence of 'les réalistes toujours expulsés' (Ms 10316, fol. 71).
24. Gisèle Sésinger, 'Le Lisible et l'invisible: Zola et les apories du naturalisme', in *Le Dialogue des arts, II: littérature et peinture aux XIXe et XXe siècles*, ed. by Laurence Richer (Lyon: Presses de l'université Jean Moulin, 2002), pp. 105–25 (p. 106).
25. Proudhon, *Du principe de l'art*, pp. 282–83.
26. Ms 10316, fol. 286 and fol. 274. Bongrand remains a composite character; he owes almost as much to Flaubert as to Courbet (see Afterword), notwithstanding his *Enterrement au village* evoking Courbet's *Enterrement à Ornans*. Through an associative move, the aspects of Courbet's personality noted by Zola are partly transferred to the self-satisfied fictional sculptor Victor Chambouvard, of whom Robert Niess writes that 'allowing for a good deal of exaggeration, we have a fairly exact portrait of Courbet, as the latter's contemporaries depicted him' (Niess,

Zola, Cézanne and Manet, p. 49). In the work notes, Zola writes: 'D'une vanité de dieu. Riant de complaisance devant ses œuvres. Trouvant ça épatant' (fol. 249); 'Chambouvard gagne très peu, et olympien tout de même' (fol. 85). On Courbet depicted as 'riant de complaisance', see above, n. 1. In the novel itself, Chambouvard is 'sans un doute, toujours solide et convaincu, il avait un orgueil de dieu' — blind to criticism, so certain is he of 'l'adoration où il était de lui-même' (*RM*, IV, 133).

27. He refers obliquely to 'un autre petit livre illustré par lui': authored by Courbet's lifelong friend Max Buchon (1818–69): *Essais poétiques par Max B...Vignettes par Gust. C...* (Besançon: Imp. Sainte-Agathe, 1839). Published in a limited edition, this contained four lithographs by the artist.

28. On 2 September 1871, Courbet had been sentenced to six months' imprisonment and fined 500 francs for his part in the Commune. Even before the subsequent trial specifically accusing him of instigating the destruction of the Colonne Vendôme (16 May 1871), the government ordered, on 19 June 1873, that all his possessions on French soil should be seized, at which point Courbet fled to Switzerland. That trial, opening on 19 June 1874, resulted in his being held personally responsible for the costs of rebuilding the monument. A convoluted series of appeals, however, postponed until 4 May 1877 the definitive confirmation that Courbet would have to pay 323,091 francs, in annual instalments of 10,000 francs. To meet this debt, the contents of his studio were forcibly auctioned at the Hôtel Drouot on 26 November 1877, just over a month before Courbet's death on 31 December.

29. David Charles, *Émile Zola et la Commune de Paris: aux origines des 'Rougon-Macquart'* (Paris: Classiques Garnier, 2017), p. 307. In the novel's *ébauche*, Zola likened him to Florent, his revolutionary protagonist, 'mais en art' (Ms 10338, fol. 95). Charles (p. 310) sees in Claude's 'On devait flanquer les vieilles cambuses par terre et faire du moderne' (*RM*, I, 624) a veiled allusion to the fate of the Colonne Vendôme. Also to be noted in any analogy with Courbet, but more specifically as a painter, is Claude's 'amour des belles brutes' (*RM*, I, 776). On rereading *Le Ventre de Paris*, during the preparation of *L'Œuvre*, Zola singled out in his notes this 'amour des belles brutes' (Ms 10316, fol. 222). Charles (p. 318) is the only scholar to have recalled, in the context of the genesis of *Le Ventre de Paris*, Zola's ironic addition (in his 1868 review of *Le Camp des bourgeois*) to Courbet's call for art to be publicly accessible: 'Courbet n'a peut-être pas songé que les Halles centrales offrent un développement de murs admirables et que la bonne peinture serait là au frais. Allons à l'œuvre, artistes de l'avenir! Peignez les différentes pêches, les milles espèces de poissons. [...] Nos bonnes et nos femmes, en allant au marché, ont besoin de voir un peu de vraie peinture' (*EsA*, p. 416). In some of the earliest notes for his novel, Zola wrote: 'Le côté artistique est les Halles modernes' (Ms 10338, fol. 48); and he lends to his fictional painter views ascribed to Courbet by Proudhon: 'Claude déblatéra contre le romantisme; il préférait ses tas de choux aux guenilles du Moyen Âge' (*RM*, IV, 624).

30. The detractors all blamed Proudhon for what was described as a 'tableau à sensation'; Ernest Chesneau, in *Le Constitutionnel* of 16 June 1868, wrote that *Du principe de l'art* had 'tourné la tête de M. Courbet' but that the work was so badly painted that 'j'ai peine à y voir un symbole de la France à venir'; for Francis Magnard, in *Le Figaro* of 6 July, 'le maître peintre, égaré par les louanges paradoxales de Proudhon, a cru évidemment soulever la question sociale dans cette comique composition'. Even the longest and most favourable review, signed by Castagnary, Courbet's champion, claimed that the painting prophetically figured the demise of capitalism, as yet another insight drawn from the artist's 'horoscope de la France à venir'. Jules-Antoine Castagnary, *Salons 1857–1879*, 2 vols (Paris: Hachette, 1892), I, 280–89 (p. 288).

31. Gasquet, *Cézanne*, p. 200.

32. It was in his letter of 6 April 1866 to Urbain Cuenot that Courbet reported on the comte de Nieuwerkerke's delight, endorsed by the Salon jury's unanimous verdict, so that he was in line to receive not just the 'médaille d'honneur' but also the Légion d'honneur (*Letters of Gustave Courbet*, ed. and trans. by Petra ten-Doesschatu Chu (Chicago and London: University of Chicago Press, 1992), p. 276). But correspondence with other friends equally hostile to the imperial régime suggests that Courbet much enjoyed unsettling both officials and critics by seeming to adopt a different pictorial mode. As Zola wrote in *L'Événement illustré* of 9 June 1868,

commentators were unsure whether to praise or condemn, because 'on semble toujours redouter une mauvaise plaisanterie de sa part' *(EsA*, p. 197).

33. Castagnary's encomium appeared in *La Liberté*, 5–13 May (*Salons*, I, 222–23). It hardly seems by chance that Zola's rebuttal (in *L'Événement*) is on 15 May.
34. It is one of the more curious aspects of Zola's references to this painting throughout his art criticism that he gives its title as *Le Convoi d'Ornans*. I have found no other critic using this nomenclature. Perhaps, by association, Zola was thinking of other such burial pictures entitled *Convoi funèbre*. In 1868 (*EsA*, p. 175) he refers to *Le Convoi du pauvre* (Salon of 1819) by Pierre-Roch Vigneron (1789–1872).
35. It is more likely that he was simply referencing a commonplace benchmark of Courbet's earlier work. *La Curée* had been purchased from the artist by an Anvers dealer in 1858, changing hands in 1862 but exhibited in 1863 at Alphonse Cadart's gallery and at that year's Salon, before being sold in April 1866 to the Allston Club in Boston for 25,000 francs.
36. While *La Remise des chevreuils* was almost universally praised, this was not the case with *La Femme au perroquet*: it was described in the *Journal des débats* of 16 June 1866 as 'mal posé, mal dessiné, mal peint'; and in *La Presse* of 10 June, Paul de Saint-Victor concluded that it 'n'a pas même la valeur d'un bon morceau de chair. La griffe du Réalisme s'étale ici dans toute sa laideur'.
37. And this was not only because Manet's exhibition opened on 24 May, a week earlier than Courbet's. To Albert Lacroix, in a letter of 8 May 1867, Zola's mention that 'M. Manet aura une exposition particulière de ses œuvres, à côté de l'exposition de Courbet' is designed to persuade his publisher that the huge publicity around the former, 'que Courbet a déjà eue en 1855', made it opportune to bring out an edition of his *Contes à Ninon* illustrated by Manet (*Corr.*, I, 496). Zola was keen to exploit the reputation he was already establishing as Manet's champion, which was not the case in relation to Courbet: as Claretie wrote in the preface to the first edition of *Peintres et sculpteurs contemporains* (Paris: Charpentier, 1873), in his survey of Salon criticism, 'M. Castagnary lutte pour M. Courbet, et M. Zola va plus loin et pousse jusqu'à Manet'. Courbet was, in any case, a less controversial figure than he had been when mounting his private exhibition in 1855. And in the context of a perceived rivalry between Courbet and Manet, there is no doubt that Zola felt a closer personal and aesthetic affinity with the younger painter.
38. 'Prochaine ouverture de l'exposition de Courbet', he wrote to Valabrègue on 29 May 1867, 'sur laquelle j'espère pouvoir faire une courte étude' (*Corr.*, I, 500).
39. Zola's only mention of Courbet's 1867 exhibition is to be found in a retrospective synopsis of the painter's career, penned in 1878, suggesting that this was the only way to have his work seen at the very moment the 'médiocrité académique de Cabanel' was universally hailed: 'Courbet a dû organiser une exposition particulière pour montrer ses œuvres au public' (*EsA*, p. 544).
40. *La Somnambule* (1865), a self-portrait of 1854 and a hunting scene of hounds and hare.
41. Comparing the inclusion of this single painting to ten by Gérôme and a dozen by Bouguereau, Zola's opinion is unambiguous: 'Voilà qui est honteux. Il aurait fallu assigner à l'Exposition universelle de 1878 toute une salle, comme on l'a fait pour Delacroix et Ingres à l'Exposition de 1855' (*EsA*, p. 543). 'Il est impossible', lamented Claretie, 'de se former une idée de Courbet d'après cette *Vague* payée trop cher' (*Les Artistes français à l'Exposition universelle de 1878* (Paris: Decaux, 1878), p. 64).
42. Burty was the author of the catalogue of the Delacroix sale (17–19 February 1864) and of Corot's 1875 retrospective, as well as of books on Millet (1861) and Théodore Rousseau (1868) and a study devoted to *Exposition de deux tableaux importants de Corot et Gustave Courbet* (Paris: A. Binet, 1876). In his letter to Burty of 20 May 1866 asking for a meeting to discuss a possible study of Courbet, Zola referred to having heard that 'vous avez collectionné tout ce qu'on a écrit sur l'art et les artistes depuis plusieurs années' (*Corr.*, I, 449). Burty granted him such a meeting, while telling Zola that he already seemed to know plenty about Courbet, having received second-hand reports that his 'Proudhon et Courbet' essay was 'juste et courageux' (*Corr.*, I, 450, n. 3).
43. To the Salon of 1848, Courbet submitted four drawings, three landscapes, a couple of portraits and *Jeune fille dormant* — the only painting which might conceivably have qualified as 'un tableau brutal' (by conventional standards). It is more likely that Zola has confused this with the Salon

of 1850 where Courbet astonished the viewing public with the starkness of his *Un Enterrement à Ornans* and *Les Casseurs de pierres*.

44. Although Zola writes that 'voilà trois ans qu'il ne donne rien de neuf' (*EsA*, p. 267), in fact, and for obvious reasons, Courbet's last-ever inclusion in the Salon had been in 1870.
45. Linda Nochlin, 'The De-Politicization of Gustave Courbet: Transformation and Rehabilitation under the Third Republic', *October*, 22 (1986), 76–86.
46. Cited from Duranty's text reproduced in *Les Écrivains devant l'impressionnisme*, ed. by Denys Riout (Paris, Macula, 1989), p. 116.
47. In his review of the Salon of 1875, Zola tells his Russian readers that 'Au siècle présent nous avons eu Delacroix, Ingres et Courbet, sans parler des créateurs du paysage moderne: Corot, Millet et Théodore Rousseau' (*EsA*, p. 270). The distinction remains in *Le Naturalisme au Salon* as late as 1880: 'Courbet et les paysagistes' (*EsA*, p. 379). Proudhon had named Rousseau, Fromentin, Daubigny, Corot and Millet as evidence that 'l'école française va dans la même direction que Courbet' (*Du principe de l'art*, p. 284).
48. Ms 10316, fol. 46: 'Il est mort — Mais non. Il vit.' Curiously, this also echoes Zola's reports about the painter's fate during the Commune, correcting rumours of his death, in *Le Sémaphore de Marseille* of 11–12 June 1871: 'Courbet était si peu mort, qu'on l'a retrouvé sous son lit' (*EsA*, p. 341).
49. Although Bongrand's origins are transferred to the Beauce, Zola imagines him having a 'père rentier' and being the grandson of 'un fermier qui a gagné beaucoup d'argent'. Courbet's father was, as a well-off landowner, somewhere between the two. Courbet *père*'s interest in agricultural theories may have contributed to Zola's note that Bongrand's father was 'passionné pour l'histoire naturelle'.
50. Courbet appears in the background of Monet's *Le Déjeuner sur l'herbe* (1865), testimony to his involvement with the next generation of painters. That Bongrand, in *L'Œuvre*, is similarly encouraging is another aspect of his characterization which may be modelled on Courbet.

CHAPTER 4

Manet

In addition to a series of lithographs,[1] Zola owned three works by Manet: the watercolour of *Le Christ mort et les anges* (1865–67);[2] the pastel *Portrait de Mme Émile Zola* (1879);[3] and the iconic 1868 portrait of himself (see Fig. 4.5). The last two of these Zola photographed, in 1900, in revealing compositions of his own. That of Manet's somewhat flattering portrait of Alexandrine Zola included a spray of roses and a photograph of himself.[4] It is consistent with a series he produced at this time (turning sixty and perhaps with intimations of mortality), designed to consecrate an authorized image of his personal life and professional career. More arresting in this respect is Zola's staging of Manet's portrait of him in its familiar setting of his home in the Rue de Bruxelles (Fig. 4.1). As in the case of his Cézannes, supposedly hidden from view, there have been many unsubstantiated indications of alternative domestic positionings of the painting as 'evidence' of his dislike of it.[5] That suggestion has sometimes been extended to confirm that 'Zola was not a man of visual needs', within an intermittent argument that he was fundamentally unresponsive to Manet's art.[6] Zola's remarkable photograph of the portrait does more than correct such oft-rehearsed assertions.[7]

In this photograph, Manet's portrait of Zola rests above a mantelpiece where its gilded centrality is enhanced by the cropped and less striking frames of other (indistinct) pictures. But an alternative central focus, nearer to the beholder, is the Alexandre Charpentier commemorative medallion of the defender of Dreyfus,[8] itself framed in a black case, distinct from the aligned *bibelots* echoing the floral patterns of the porcelain within Manet's painting and functioning as a caption to the portrait above it. In that sense (and at our own remove from the reproduction, as opposed to Zola's actual viewpoint), it is properly decipherable only in conjunction with the associated funereal compositions in which the image of a life's work is anticipated *in memoriam*, most notably the one in which that bronze medallion and its capitalized inscription are set against the monumental background of vertically stacked leather-bound volumes of *Les Rougon-Macquart* (not all of them, but with titles more readable than those of the books in the Manet portrait, the inaugurating *La Fortune des Rougon* at the base and the concluding *Le Docteur Pascal* at the apex) and juxtaposed with a small photograph of their author as a six year-old child: HOMMAGE À ÉMILE ZOLA, subsequently reproduced, after Zola's death, in *L'Illustration* (Fig. 4.2). And, in that light, the bouquet of flowers at the lower left of the photograph of his portrait seems to gesture towards the one in Fantin-

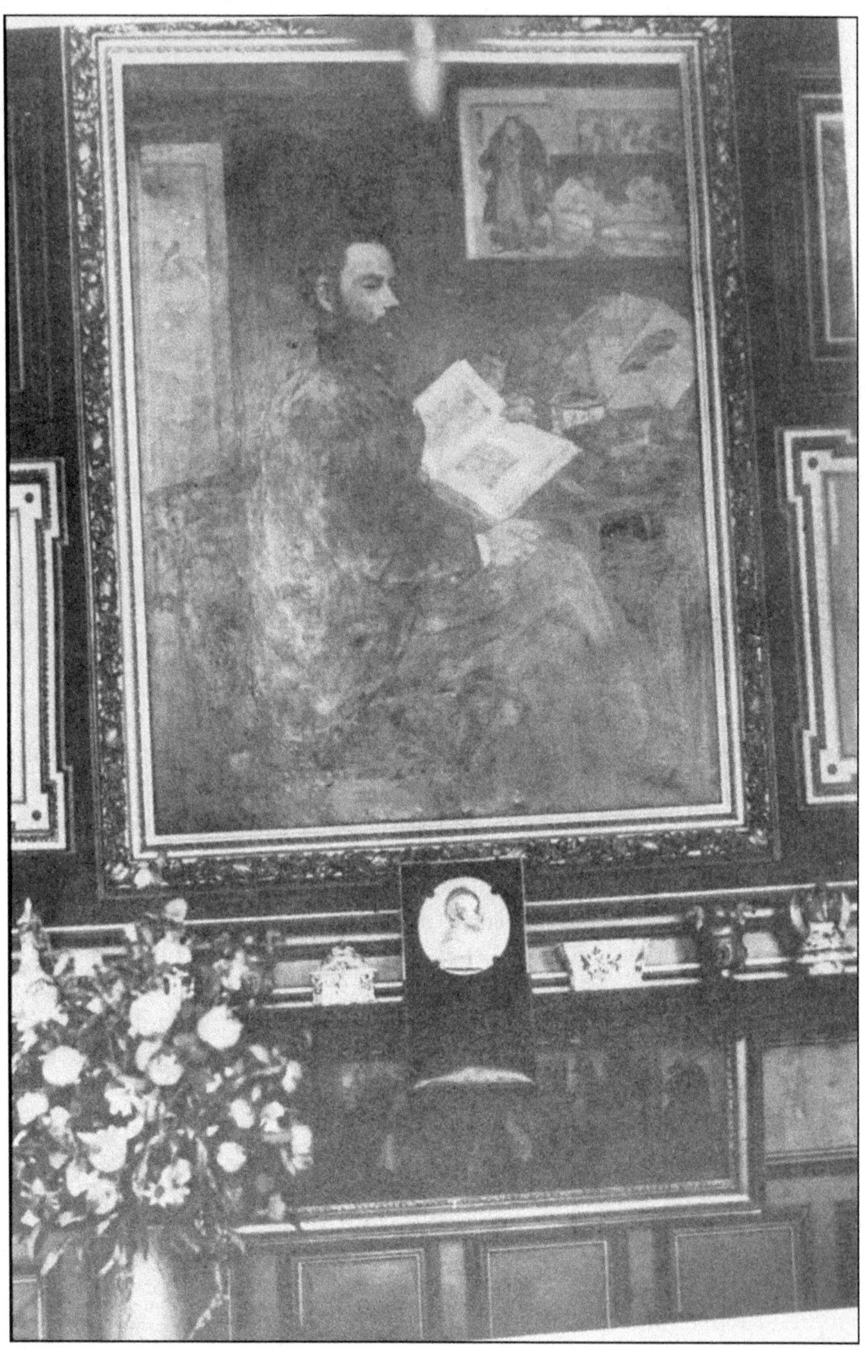

FIG. 4.1. Émile Zola, photograph of Manet's 1868 portrait of him (*c.* 1900).

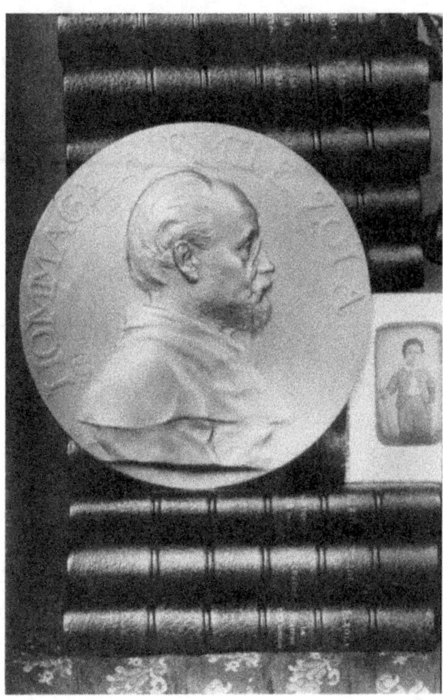

FIG. 4.2. *Apothéose de Zola par Zola* (*L'Illustration*, 11 October 1902).

Latour's *Hommage à Delacroix* (1864) (see Fig. I.2), also marked, of course, by Manet's presence. As such, the photograph both endorses the reality of the painting (and of the past it represents) and overlays on it a corrective distancing (of posterity).

It would be too easy to speculate further: to wonder, for example, whether looking at his portrait in black and white modified Zola's perception of it;[9] whether the composition can be compared to Berthe Morisot's last series of works, 'folding the past into the present', in which she reincorporated her favourite paintings of herself and photographs of her family;[10] about the extent to which the *mise en abyme*, picturing himself pictured, is deliberate (as in Degas's 1895 photographic image of Mallarmé and Renoir framed by a mirror) rather than fortuitous.[11] In any case, the *mise en abyme* is enriched by the artistic representations within Manet's painting, starting with the (photographed?)[12] etching of *Olympia* and the diversion of its subject's gaze towards Zola in possible recognition of how he had written about her in his art criticism. But a comparison with another early photograph allows us to see what he has effected in his own transposition of the painting.[13] For Zola not only flattens it; he also pushes it into the background of the composition, with his artificial lighting effacing its contours as surely as it highlights the foregrounded Charpentier medallion synonymous with his own identity. One of the senses of the very title of this book is the writer's *possessive* intent, inserting artists within his own perspective. In this image, Manet and his portrait are doubly possessed, located in Zola's space as one of his possessions and captured through his camera lens. The scope of the present chapter is not limited, however, to this photograph or indeed the Manets in his collection. Its aim is rather to explore the emblematic status of such a summative moment of self-contemplation in the mirror of Manet's achievement. For Zola's engagement with the painter, from his early championing to fictional transpositions, is grounded in this process of identification. And in the tensions between resemblance and differentiation, and between solidarity and rivalry, we can better account for the preferences in, and discern the contradictions of, Zola's versions of Manet and his work. As in the case of Cézanne, Manet's presence can be identified in his fiction, notably of course in *L'Œuvre*.[14] But whereas the absence of Cézanne in Zola's art criticism leaves us only with compensating recourse to other texts to infer his view of the painter, his writing on Manet is so extensive that his novels provide less a confirmation of his judgements than the testing-ground of their integrity.

In the Looking-Glass

If Zola's perspective on Manet is a mirroring one, it is brought into sharper relief by juxtaposing the image of Cézanne, in which Zola's contemplation of, or looking at, the man and his painting can be seen as what might be termed, by contrast, a process of negative self-definition. Which is not the case with Manet — or not at first sight. One can argue that Manet is for Zola the pre-eminent painter of his generation: partly, within the above dialectic, because he is *not* Cézanne. As Fantin-Latour's 1867 portrait of him (Fig. 4.3) also projects, this wordly, well-dressed and sophisticated gentleman was not at all, as Zola stressed, the 'rapin gouailleur' (*EsA*, p. 152) of sneering caricature and popular mythology: 'une sorte de bohème, de galopin, de croque-mitaine ridicule' (*EsA*, p. 473). If Carol Armstrong writes of Zola's definition of Manet's art as being 'intertwined with his own self-definition as a critic', making 'Manet in his own image',[15] that identification also extends to a desired social and sartorial persona, in absolute contradistinction to that of Cézanne with his dishevelled attire, as in Pissarro's 1874 portrait of him (see Fig. 2.2), and calculated bad manners: 'nous trouvons dans Édouard Manet un homme d'une amabilité et d'une politesse exquises, d'allures distinguées et d'apparence sympathique' (*EsA*, p. 473). In 1866, at the very moment he is once again entreating Cézanne to get down to work, Zola writes of Manet that 'il travaille d'ailleurs avec acharnement' (*EsA*, p. 152), as he was himself, most famously inscribed in the *Nulle dies sinea linea* overlooking his desk. There is almost an implicit reproach to Cézanne in his view of Manet's productivity and refusal to be discouraged: 'Il travaille avec âpreté, et le nombre de ses toiles est déjà considérable; il peint sans découragement, sans lassitude, marchant droit devant lui' (*EsA*, p. 473). Or, at least, that was the image of Manet projected for public consumption.[16]

As far as Manet's critical privileging is concerned, one of the reasons for it is the extent to which his development *structurally* conforms to Zola's, having left behind (in his view), by 1867, wayward beginnings, anxieties of influence and theoretical indirections. He skips over Manet's apprenticeship: six 'wasted' years ('perdant son temps' (*EsA*, p. 474)) as a pupil of Thomas Couture; and the proto-Spanish works of the early 1860s. He reserves his main analysis for a 'unity' synonymous with

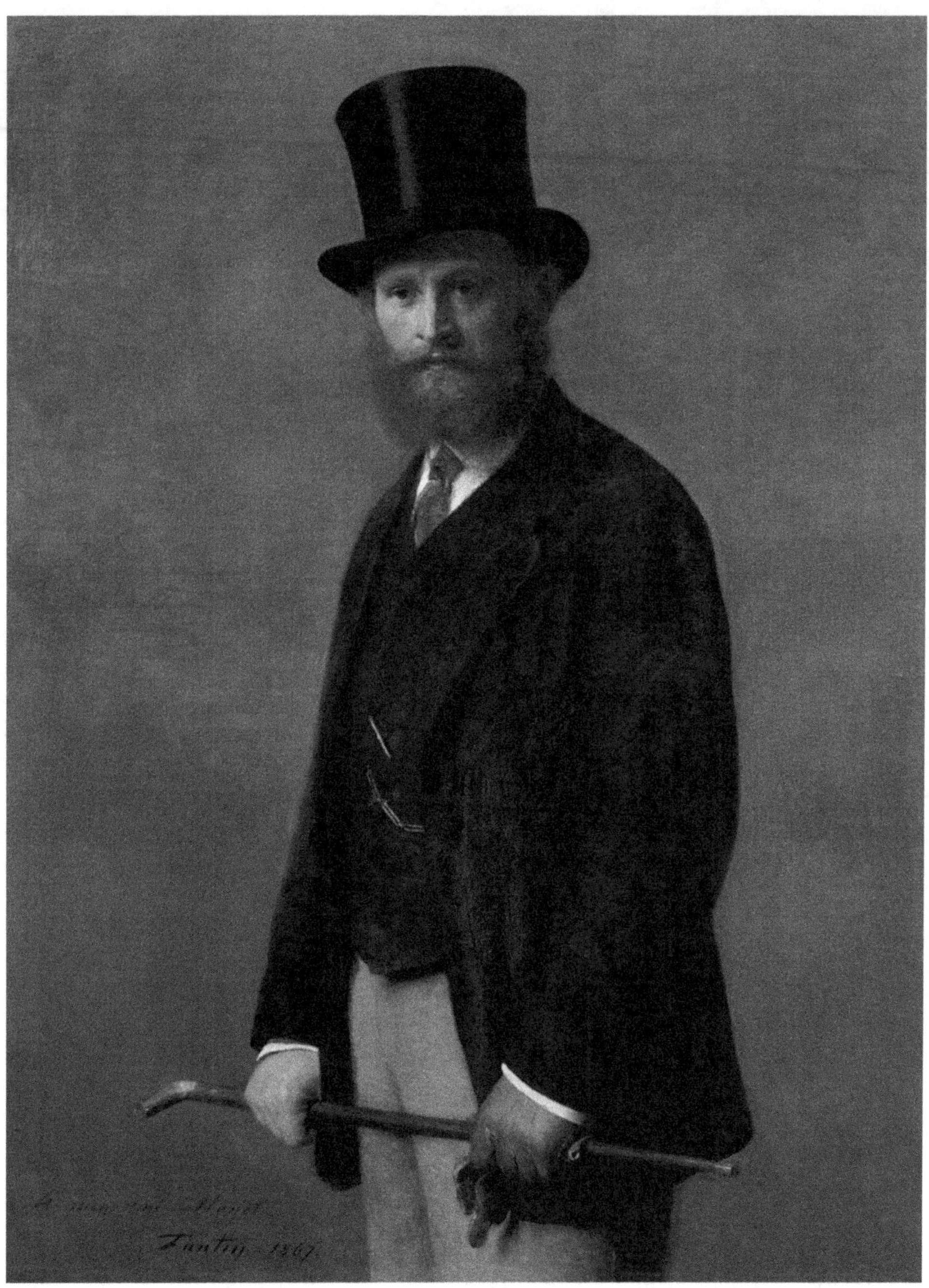

FIG. 4.3. Henri Fantin-Latour, *Portrait d'Édouard Manet* (1867), oil on canvas, 117.5 × 90 cm. Art Institute of Chicago. Stickney Fund.

originality, of which the unspoken model is Zola's own systematization and the obverse to be found in Cézanne's hesitations and unending stylistic experimentation. In the references to Manet still 'finding himself',[17] there are clearly echoes of the rationalization of his deferred judgement on Cézanne. But there is also a forward-looking optimism inseparable from his valuation of a 'solidity' equally applicable to the writer's compositional predilections and reflecting his strength of purpose, assuring both their future places in the pantheons of art. It is therefore no less ironic that his ensuing disappointment with Manet coincides with the painter's subsequent further development, in the 1870s (deviating from his earlier 'ligne droite'), which is apparently less incoherent than Cézanne's but still at odds with Zola's positivist assumptions and mimetic imperatives. It explains why ultimately Manet too, as he is viewed in Zola's preface to his 1884 retrospective, is considered a transitional figure in Zola's narrative of the modernist advance.

Paintings and Polemics

Zola's own seminal role in the positioning of Manet within that narrative occupies such a celebrated chapter in our histories of nineteenth-century French art that both the insights and weaknesses of his writing on individual paintings are too seldom situated in the polemical context which determines selectivity and interpretative purchase. His 1867 study, *Édouard Manet, étude biographique et critique*, is overtly generated by a visit to Manet's studio during which he saw between thirty and forty canvases originally being prepared for the Universal Exhibition, but the long footnote listing those necessarily beyond its scope is revealing.[18] For, in practice, Zola only considers in any detail fifteen of the fifty-six works ultimately shown instead at the painter's private exhibition at the Place d'Alma.[19] It reinforces the sense that the vast majority of Manets chosen for detailed commentary can be correlated, and even in the space allocated to each of them (unsurprisingly, the greatest is devoted to *Olympia* and *Le Déjeuner sur l'herbe*), to the hostility, either registered or anticipated (in the case of works not yet submitted or exhibited), of their reception, thereby justifying the culminating section of the study devoted to a diatribe against 'le public'. The paragraphs on *La Musique aux Tuileries* (1862) and *Le Christ mort et les anges* evoke negative reactions to them,[20] notwithstanding the latter's successful submission to the Salon of 1865; Zola claims to like *Le Joueur de fifre*, rejected by the Salon of 1866. Those accepted (*Le Chanteur espagnol* (1861), *Le Torero mort* (1864), *Jésus insulté par les soldats* (1865)) generally serve his purpose less well.

After 1870, however, Zola himself recognizes the diminished 'scandal' of Manet's pictures, and those highlighted by him are described with less energy. *Argenteuil* (1874), for example, prompts a rebuttal of critics accusing the painter of making the river too blue, but fades into a reiteration of Manet's freshness and charm. His response to his more Impressionist phase (*Le Linge* and the portrait of Marcellin Desboutin (both 1875)) is consistently framed by virtually automatic recourse to the tired refrain of Manet being the prime representative of Naturalist painting. By

1879, as 'le chef du groupe des peintres impressionnistes' (*EsA*, p. 356),[21] Manet's regression to the 'insuffisance technique' of an 'écolier enthousiaste' creates in Zola an ambivalence barely able to separate masterpiece and mediocrity, and thereby giving the lie to claims that 'le seul peintre de la nouvelle école sur lequel Zola n'a jamais avancé des réserves [...] c'est Manet'.[22] For that is far too reliant on the writer's historically resonant pronouncement, not quite true even in 1866 but echoing down the years, that 'je suis le premier à louer sans restrictions M. Manet' (*EsA*, p. 65). On the other hand, his essay which serves as the preface to the catalogue of the great Manet retrospective of 1884 at the École nationale des Beaux-Arts deserves to be re-read. It is often deemed to be half-hearted in its unwillingness to accord Manet the status of the great modern painter of the age. There is, however, not merely nostalgia for the battles of the past. Liberated from the latter, in this piece (exceptionally) not slanted for a newspaper, Zola introduces a slightly re-arranged set of Manets: *Olympia* and *Le Déjeuner sur l'herbe* remain the obligatory markers of struggle and strife; but, alongside them, we also find *Le Torero mort*, *La Chanteuse des rues*, *Le Déjeuner*, *Lola de Valence*, *L'Enfant à l'épée*, *Le Combat du Kearsarge et de l'Alabama*, *Le Bon Bock*, *Le Linge*, *Argenteuil* (here under the title of *Les Canotiers*), *Dans la serre*, *Le Café-concert*, *Le Bal à l'Opéra*, portraits of Eva Gonzalès, Antonin Proust, his parents, Duret and De Jouy, still lifes and even his 'interesting' copies of Titian, Tintoretto and Filipp Lippi. The commentary is condensed but not, as Armstrong claims,[23] identical to earlier remarks. Some of the works had never been mentioned before. And nor do they simply correspond to an inventory (let alone to the ordering of its catalogue) of the posthumous exhibition itself. Above all, Zola's genuine enjoyment of the pictures is not wholly reliant on either their critical fortunes or the ingenuity of their tonalities.

In the late 1860s, there was more at stake, both personally and politically. Zola's defence of Manet slides between self-advertisement and self-portraiture: the 'lutteur convaincu' determined to beat the crowd into submission hardly captures Manet's long-suffering resentment.[24] But his discursive manoeuvres activate inconsistencies with far-reaching consequences. As Beth Brombert has lamented, 'Zola's strictly formalist view would determine the critical optic on Manet's art for more than a century.'[25] Yet to divorce his advocacy of 'pure painting' from his simultaneously more radical contributions to *La Cloche* and *La Tribune* is to risk taking at face value a critical language freighted with, and inflected by, the politics of the day and which, moreover, is so vitiated by polemical pressures that it may not fully represent his experience of looking at Manet's paintings. We should ask ourselves, for example, to what extent his view of *Olympia* being 'without meaning' is a case in point. For this was adopted as a direct response to virulent hypotheses of Manet's intentions. Charges of immorality were met with the reply that critics had mistaken the object for the subject, that a Manet painting was 'un simple prétexte à l'analyse' (*EsA*, p. 489) in a translation of the world into an artistic reality. But, at the same time, Zola also replied to accusations that such an art was only a vulgar transcription of life by stressing that *Olympia* was indeed informed by a realism which challenged the idealized generalizations of tradition; and this argument ultimately dominates the polemical debate. As his opponents insisted that obscenity resulted from a perverse distortion of reality, Zola found himself denying that any such distortion had taken place, thereby entangling himself in the contradictions, as identified earlier, of his 'Théorie des écrans'. And as far as the painting being devoid of interpretative significance is concerned, I have tried to show elsewhere that Zola's imaginative reworking of its motifs, in *Thérèse Raquin*, suggests an understanding of it very different from *Olympia* being merely a structure of colours.[26]

Reflections and refractions

At the same time, no account of Zola's engagement with Manet is complete without interposing the competitive tensions of the period outlined in my Introduction. Lacking, as he saw it, the painter's enviable notoriety as a result of *Le Déjeuner sur l'herbe* and *Olympia*, an initially subordinate profile leads Zola to organize a vitriolic review of his own *Thérèse Raquin* explicitly associating painter and novelist.[27] In practice, the novel reverses this hierarchy of visibility. For, with (and against) its fictional artist whose neuroses, work habits, extravagant visions and 'ugly' pictures unmistakeably conjure up, in the first instance (as indicated in Chapter 2), Cézanne, *Thérèse Raquin* inserts the writer's own view of Manet in a number of ways. While the descriptive emphases of the riverside picnic of chapter 11 can be compared with both *Le Déjeuner sur l'herbe* and Courbet's *Demoiselles aux bords de la Seine*, most of the Manet-like segments in the text derive from *Olympia* (see Fig. 2.5), about which Zola was writing at exactly the time the novel was being prepared: the unsettling gaze and pose of its eponymous heroine, at one point likened to a courtesan; the suppression of intermediate semi-tones in her verbal portrait; the isolated splashes of colour set against the background to it. These effects only work by analogy, of course. More revealing are Zola's thematic reconfigurations: the connotations of Olympia's black slave in the otherwise curious African origins of Thérèse's latent sexuality; and, above all, in the role of François, the black cat. Reviewers of the novel, quite possibly prompted by Zola, leapt on the parallel: 'cette chambre à coucher renferme toutes les horreurs, jusqu'au chat de M. Manet qui jusqu'à ce jour n'avait figuré que dans la peinture.'[28] This is the place neither to explore (again) its pictorial function in *Olympia* nor to elaborate its textual equivalence. But Zola's exploitation of this most controversial detail of the painting certainly places a question mark over his dismissal of it, in his criticism, as no more than a non-signifying and counterbalancing black stain. And his own Baudelairean substitutions of the female and the feline point to a symbolic register at odds with Naturalist principles and his protesting denial of affinities between Manet and the author of *Les Fleurs du mal*. They may testify to a sensitivity to the painter for which Zola is seldom given credit, so prevalent are the orthodoxies of his public statements. Indeed, at the point that the text's fictional painter moves beyond his Cézanne phase, adopting a more Manet-like structuring of offsetting colours ('chaque morceau s'enlevait par taches magnifiques sur les fonds d'un gris clair' (*OC*, I, 628–29)), Zola refers to him as a 'poet', in a summary (straining to break out of its narrative context) which constructs a quite different Manet from the one hemmed in by polemics. But *Thérèse Raquin* is also the first example, in his work, of analogy transformed into demonstration. For the novel extends the psychological and moral possibilities of the image in complex directions unavailable, Zola felt, to visual representation. His virtuoso painterly performance, in other words, also asserts the capacities of the literary text.

This can be seen, to take another example, in his *Nana*, started in January 1879 and serialized in *Le Voltaire* between 16 October 1879 and 5 February 1880. There is a consensus, amongst art historians and Zola specialists alike, that the scene (in chapter 5) in which the character applying her make-up in her (un)dressing room, observed by *three* men, is inspired by Manet's *Nana* (Fig. 4.4), first shown in the window of Giroux's boutique in May 1877.[29] By then, Zola's reputation and self-assurance obviated the need for publicizing cross-references to the painter.[30] Later comparisons between text and image have fleshed out what they have in common, and the ideological implications of both. As Peter Brooks has argued, Zola's is a 'narrative response' to Manet's preoccupations.[31] If we shift the emphasis there to 'narrative' (and beyond what Brooks calls the 'preoccupation with representation of the woman's body in the painting of modern life'), it can be seen that it is not so much in the resemblances as in the differentiating refractions of the image that the novelist asserts the specificities of his own practice. Their scope is suggested by the relation between Manet's single painting and Zola's *two* mirror-scenes (i.e. also the one, in chapter 7, in which Muffat is transfixed by the sight of Nana contemplating, and pleasuring, herself narcissistically in the mirror), thereby temporally extending the 'narrative striptease'[32] originating in Zola's text (unlike the Manet painting) in the opening presentation of Nana at the theatre and the male spectators making their way backstage to find her virtually naked to the waist. The other differences are self-evident: in the movement, again (as opposed to the stasis of the painting), of the make-up ritual; in the changes of pose and expression; in the intercalated dialogue; in the sheer detail of brushes, rouges and creams; in the sensory dynamics of powder; in the perversity and variegation of male response (as opposed to the possibly grumpy, if enigmatic and disengaged, cropped figure in the Manet); and the fascinated revulsion which Zola constructs from a vision of unnatural vulgarity (indexing mere social standing), elaborated into the outward and symbolic signs of carnality and evil. Moreover, the movements of Nana's eyes allow Zola to replace authorial exposition with self-revelation, giving the reader the illusion of unmediated access to Nana's inner experience.[33] Rather than judge the comparative effectiveness of the pictorial and textual versions of *Nana*, it is sufficient to note that here again is a demonstration, on Zola's part, of the narrative, psychological, moral and allegorical possibilities open to the writer.

Nowhere, of course, are these competitive tensions more explicitly dramatized than in *L'Œuvre*, in 1886. It contains, in Claude's *Plein air*, what is too often assumed to be an unproblematic transposition of Manet's *Le Déjeuner sur l'herbe*.[34] But while it seems to invite such recuperation, it also frustrates the temptations of similitude. At one level, as one saw in the case of Cézanne, this is as tactical

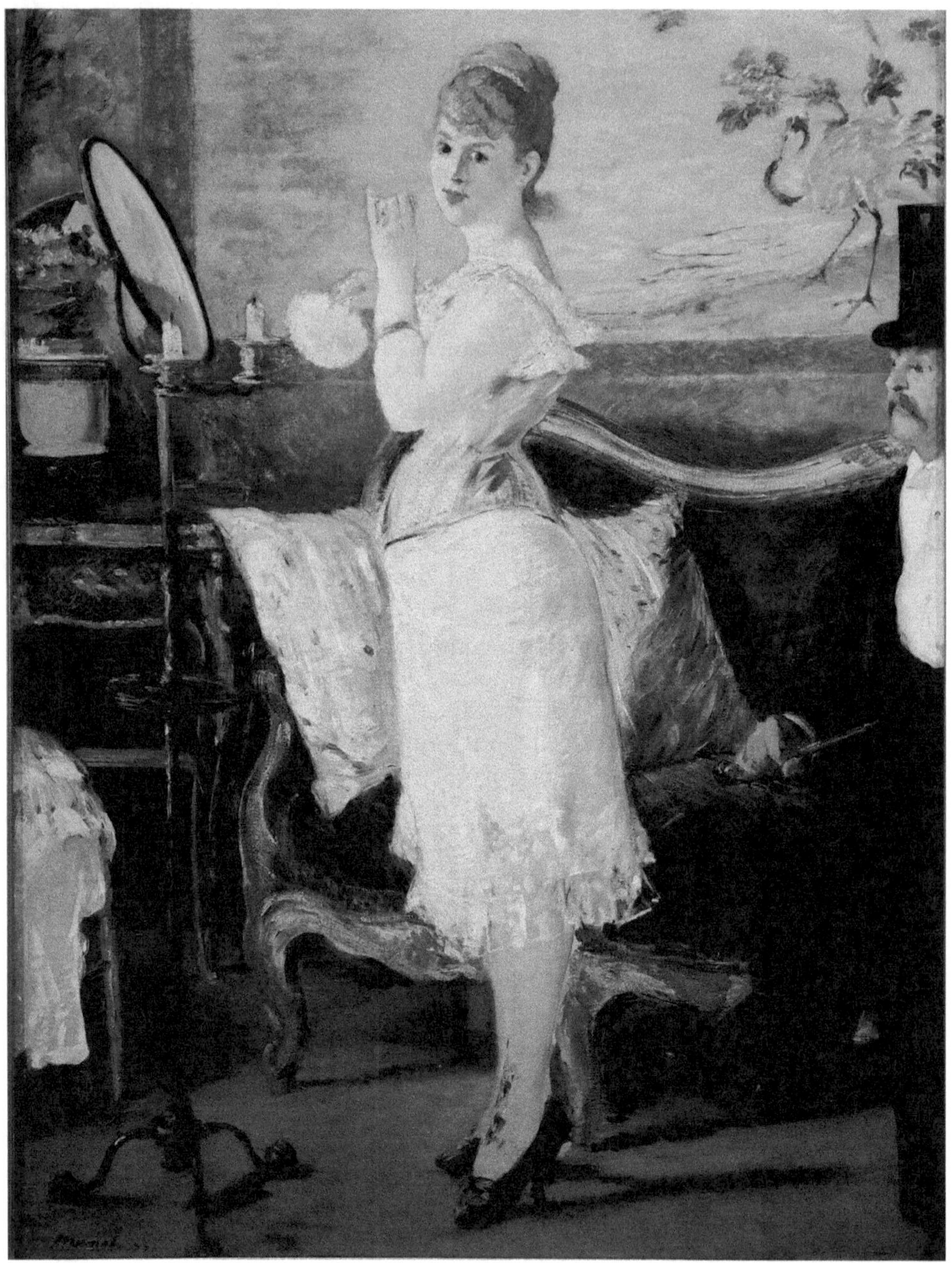

FIG. 4.4. Édouard Manet, *Nana* (1877), oil on canvas, 154 × 115 cm.
Kunsthalle, Hamburg.

as the impossibility of locating in a particular fictional character any one real-life painter. But if Manet's 1863 painting can be discerned, in both size and layout, as the prototype for Claude's painting, the differences are calculated. These start with the fact that Zola's invention *à la Manet* has only one male figure in it and that, in contradistinction to the 'original', the figure is turned away from the viewer rather than staring directly at us. What is more, Zola replaces that of the seated bather with that of a naked woman who lies back with her eyes *closed* and puts in the background *wrestling* women (which they are patently not doing in the Manet!). There remains a sense, however, in which *Plein air* and, behind it, *Le Déjeuner sur l'herbe*, are recomposed, later in the novel, in Fagerolles' significantly-entitled *Un Déjeuner*, in which the spectacle — much admired by the viewing public — of two men and three women under some trees, complete with the *nature morte* of the picnic, derives from Claude's earlier failure.[35] These transpositional amalgams and exercises in ekphrasis are emblematic of autobiographical and creative distortions of the kind valorized by Richard Schiff,[36] in so far as Sandoz (the novelist and quasi-anagrammatic Zola, 'mon portrait modifié' (Ms 10316, fol. 226)) poses for the male figure in *Plein air* with his face turned away from recognition: 'on ne voyait de lui que sa main gauche, sur lequel il s'appuyait' (*RM*, IV, 33). This idea seems to have its origin in an earlier conception of another (subsequently eliminated) fictional painting, a work note for which refers to 'dans le fond, tranquillement, un batelier [...], vu de dos, en bras de chemise, les bras nus' (Ms 10316, fol. 31). As Sandoz complains to the painter: '"elle n'est pas commode, ta pose!"' (*RM*, IV, 35); as well he might, given the dematerializing immobility to which it condemns him, thereby replicating the transformation into a *nature morte* which Zola remembered from having his own portrait painted by Manet.[37] There is a specific echo in the asides, in *L'Œuvre*, that 'la main, plus poussée que le reste, faisait dans l'herbe une note très intéressante, d'une jolie fraîcheur de ton' (*RM*, IV, 47) and that 'décidément [...] la main seule était belle' (*RM*, IV, 127); for in his Salon review of his own 1868 portrait, Zola had singled out for praise the hand placed on his knee, going on to say that had the portrait as a whole been so successful it would have been hailed as a masterpiece.[38] The imposed immobility results in the figure becoming at once unrecognizable and provisional: 'Au premier plan, le monsieur, recommencé trois fois, restait en détresse (*RM*, IV, 92). Ultimately this immobility, which is impossible to sustain, becomes a metaphor for the novel itself, in the preparatory notes for which Zola had written, referring to his original intention of positioning Sandoz as no more than a mouthpiece of the author: 'Moi, fatalement, je suis immobile.'[39]

To track back, from *L'Œuvre* and *Nana* to *Thérèse Raquin*, Zola's reflections on, and of, Manet is to measure an interlocking set of relativities: of progression and self-confidence; and of identification and rivalry. The above self-perception of his own 'immobility', faced with the increasingly unclassifiable indirections of French painting in the 1880s, points, however, to a level of irony in the summative novel of 1886 in respect of his own stance as an art critic. For if the fiction often re-transcribes almost verbatim, or dramatizes, his earlier commentary, there is also a distancing from it. His 'heroic' journalistic campaign on Manet's behalf, transferred to the self-serving Jory, designated in the novel's work notes as 'chroniqueur et critique d'art' (fol. 175), is uncomfortably mocked;[40] and there is ambivalence (at best) in his depiction of the surrogate novelist's engagement with, and understanding of, modern painting. Nowhere is this clearer than in the interchange between Sandoz and Claude about *Plein air* (*RM*, IV, 47): 'Décidément, comment appelles-tu ça', asks the former; but the latter's curt response (consisting only of the work's title) 'parut bien technique à l'écrivain qui, malgré lui, était parfois tenté d'introduire de la littérature dans la peinture'; and his '*Plein Air*, ça ne dit rien' is trumped by the painter's 'ça n'a besoin de rien dire'. Here, in a reworking of his remarks on *Olympia* ('Qu'est ce que tout cela veut dire? Vous ne le savez guère, ni moi non plus' (*EsA*, p. 489)) and on other Manets catalyzing uncomprehending hilarity, Zola both rehearses the necessity of the spatial distinction of literature and painting but also revealingly confesses his transgressions, the avoidance of which often leads him to deflect attention towards landscape and away from human figures and their possible stories, while reminding himself not to judge Manet 'en littérateur' (*EsA*, p. 480).

The innate limits, and limitations, of painting doubtless relate the urgency of distinctiveness to a newly heightened anxiety, in the 1880s, about the absence of hierarchy and authority which legitimizes the exclusivity of his own. They also seem to mark the definitive leaving-behind of the period of idealism when he had conveyed to Cézanne his youthful 'dream' of seeing both their names, in brilliant gold lettering, on the cover of a collaborative volume, or tried to persuade Manet to illustrate his *Contes à Ninon*. That was almost twenty years before. His now unequivocal understanding of cultural antagonism is filtered, in *L'Œuvre*, through the figure of Christine: her reservations about Claude's Impressionism are Zola's own; but, so too, in the conventional rivalry between Art and Woman,[41] there is the subtext of a more fundamental opposition: 'Cette peinture, elle ne la comprenait pas, elle la jugeait exécrable, elle se sentait contre elle une haine, la haine instinctive d'une ennemie' (*RM*, iv, 93). To Cézanne, Zola had once admitted that he assumed that any painting expressed some idea and that his sole focus was on its subject.[42] By the time of his 1865 essay on Courbet, Zola has moved, publicly at least, to an absolutely contrary position, caricaturing Proudhon's 'literary' interpretation of the artist and insisting that the object or person painted were only 'pretexts'. While this prefigures exactly the axiom in his study of Manet (the subject as a 'un prétexte à peindre' (*EsA*, p. 487), what his fiction implicitly demonstrates is that the pre-textual (to restore its etymological potential) is the preliminary, the anterior invitation to the writer to complete, in the richness of his own medium, the expressivity denied to the pictorial, in precisely the way which the narrator of *L'Œuvre* takes over Claude's necessarily unfinished urban landscapes, and as the author of *Le Ventre de Paris* had compensated for his fictional painter's earlier inability to capture the *natures mortes* of Les Halles. As the Romantics are condemned for their literary preoccupations, so Gustave Moreau's work is viewed as regressively cognate precisely because it is a 'painting of ideas'. Zola's apparently perverse disassociation of Manet and Baudelaire rests on the assertion that Manet had never been so foolish as to put ideas into his painting (*EsA*, p. 479). In the preparation of *L'Œuvre*, this principle is rehearsed: 'Contre la peinture à idées, littéraire' (fol. 80). It is in this context that Zola's otherwise enigmatic reflection, in the earliest notes for the novel, is illuminated: 'un art mangé par l'autre et ne produisant rien' (fol. 295). But in this quasi-Darwinian scheme, the subsequently encoded taboo on voracity applies mainly to pictorial encroachment, rather than the other way round; and, to extend the metaphor, one could almost describe *L'Œuvre* as a cannabilistic novel which, far from respecting the spatial autonomy of painting, appropriates the pictorial in so many ways, from its descriptive fabric to the heterogeneity of Claude's successive styles. As Alexandra Wettlaufer has so cogently argued, in the case of Zola's 1867 writing on Manet, it is metaphor itself which denies the painter's visual 'language' access to meaning (which is the preserve of the verbal).[43] And of those metaphors, in *L'Œuvre,* none is more appropriating than the one superimposed on the painter's ultimately inarticulate expression, translating back his proliferating pictorial visions into 'la série des grandes *pages* qu'il rêvait' (*RM*, IV, 203; my emphasis).

Manet's Portrait of Zola (1868)

These tensions and contradictions which inform Zola's engagement with the visual arts, and his dialogue with Manet in particular, find a response in the painter's *Portrait de M. Émile Zola* (Fig. 4.5), exhibited at the Salon of 1868. At the least problematic level, it represents the culmination of a series of exchanges between writer and painter initiated by Zola's pioneering defence of Manet in an article of 7 May 1866, included in his review of the Salon of that year. Only by reconstructing that dialogue is it possible to determine whether Manet was simply repaying a debt when he agreed to Zola's own suggestion to paint his portrait. For if the painting has been seen as evidence of Manet's 'penchant for calling attention to himself in concealed but insistent ways',[44] it constitutes a precise response to the less discreet self-reflection in Zola's earlier studies of the artist. In these, as Manet could hardly fail to note, Zola took the opportunity to write about himself, both directly and by implication. He underlined his own audacity and courage as a critic in daring to attack the arbiters of public taste, and referred to the hostility he would incur as a result of his admiration for the painter's work: 'on rira peut-être du panégyriste comme on a ri du peintre. Un jour, nous serons vengés tous deux' (*EsA*, p. 155). Much more specifically than Cézanne might have imagined on the basis of *La Confession de Claude*'s *dédicace* to him and Baille, it was in response to *Manet*'s critics, who had reproached the artist for his 'brutalités voulues' and his 'violences systématiques', that Zola was in effect also answering those who had criticized his first novel, compared by him to an 'eau-forte', for 'la crudité de tons' and its 'hideux réalisme'.[45] To trace Manet's development from his reliance on tradition to the free expression of 'cette langue originale qu'il venait de découvrir au fond de lui' (*EsA*, p. 475) was to outline his own career as a writer. As Zola wrote, 'je fais d'une question individuelle une question qui intéresse tous les véritables artistes', in calling for 'une saine critique, non pour Édouard Manet seulement, mais encore pour tous les tempéraments particuliers qui se présenteront' (*EsA*, p. 470). What is more, Zola

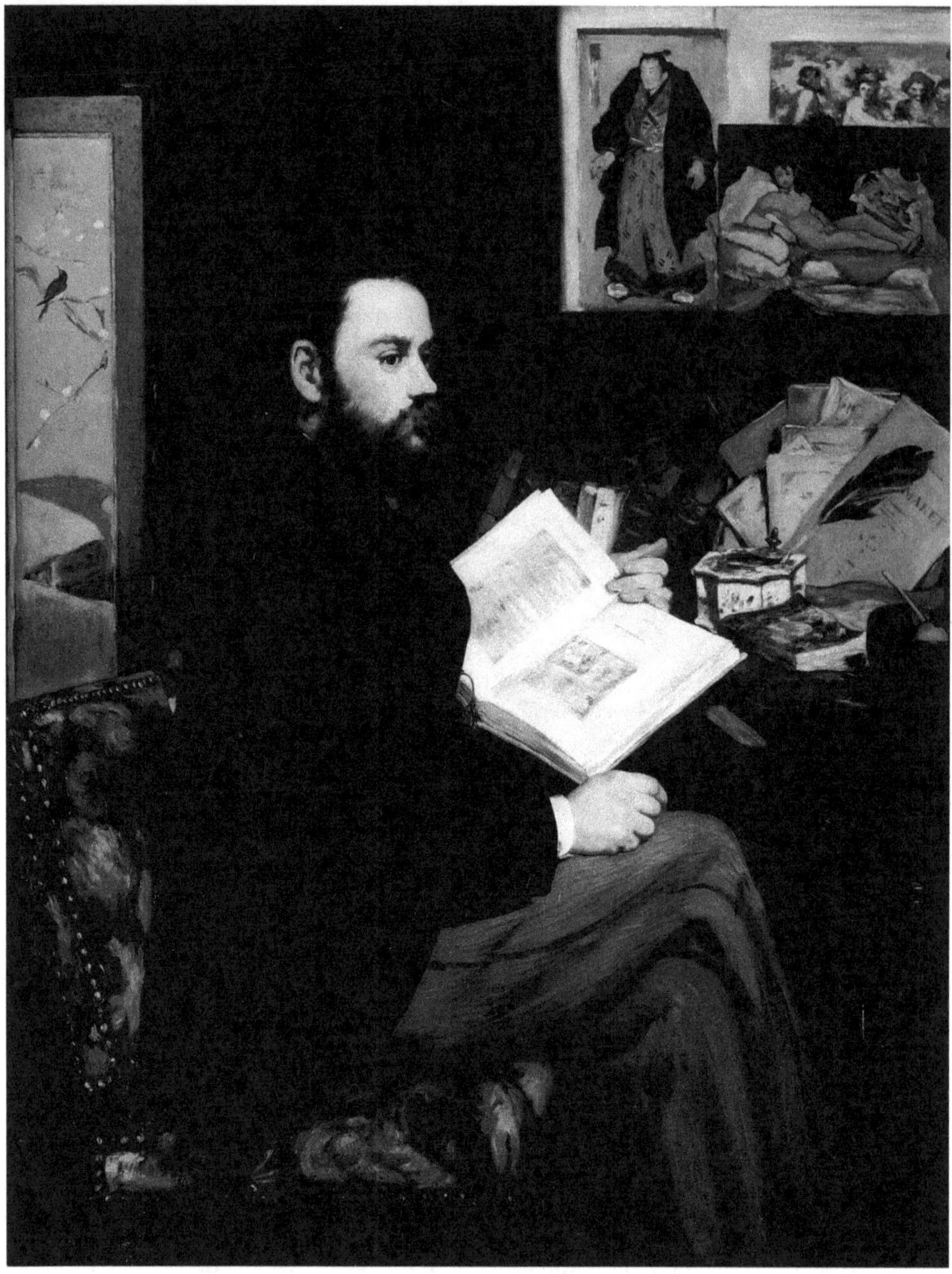

FIG. 4.5. Édouard Manet, *Portrait de M. Émile Zola* (1868), oil on canvas, 146 × 114 cm. Musée d'Orsay, Paris.

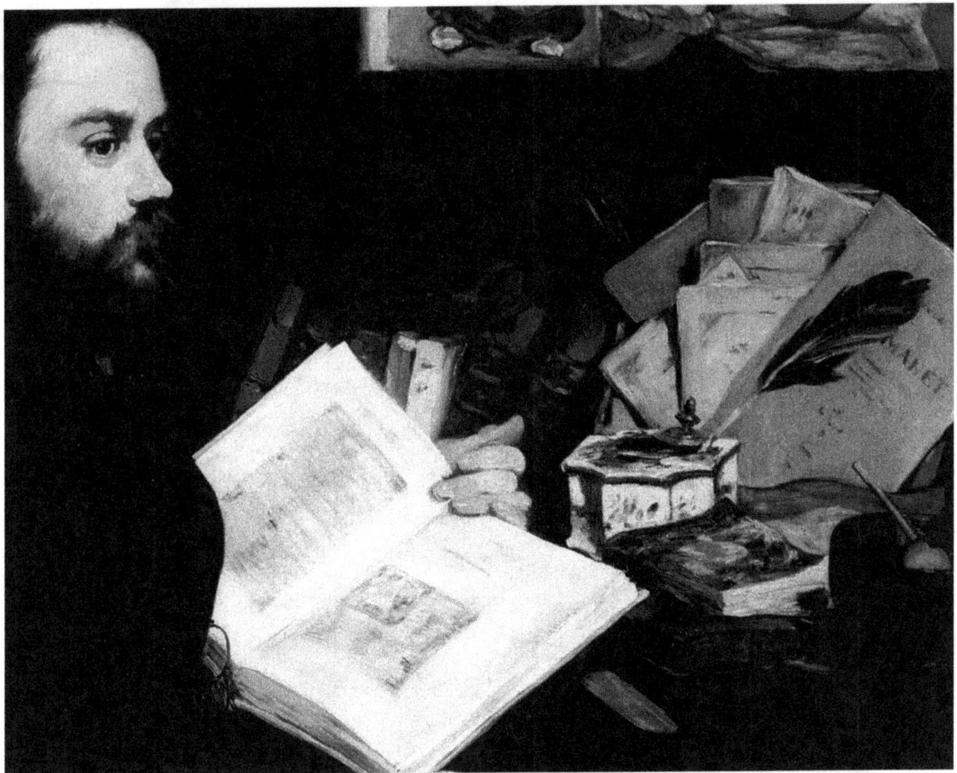

FIG. 4.6. *Portrait de M. Émile Zola* (detail).

offered his 1867 study of Manet as an example of his own critical method: 'Mon étude sur Édouard Manet est une simple application de ma façon de voir en matière artistique, et [...] je livre à l'appréciation de tous un essai où l'on jugera des mérites et des défauts de la méthode que j'emploie' (*EsA*, p. 468). This study is inevitably marked by the pseudo-medical jargon of two important texts contemporary to it, namely 'Un Roman d'analyse' (in *Le Figaro* of 16 December 1866) and his 'Deux définitions du roman' (prepared the same month) in praise of 'le roman analytique'. Zola's labelling of Manet as 'un peintre analyste', in January 1867, prefigures the notion of 'la peinture naturaliste' in his Salon articles of 1868. His own role as novelist and critic, and Manet's talent as an artist, would all be increasingly defined according to the criteria of a developing, if still inconsistent, Naturalist aesthetic.

Zola's efforts to link his name with Manet in the public mind had continued throughout 1867. And it may be significant that Manet hesitated before approving Zola's suggestion to republish his January study (which had appeared in the *Revue du XIXe siècle*) in brochure form to coincide with the opening, on 24 May, of his private exhibition in the Place de l'Alma. At the very least, it is clear that the painter was uneasy about such blatant exercises in publicity. Another such effort was Zola's attempt to persuade his publisher to bring out an illustrated edition of his *Contes à Ninon*. In a letter to Albert Lacroix of 8 May 1867,[46] he disclosed that Manet had

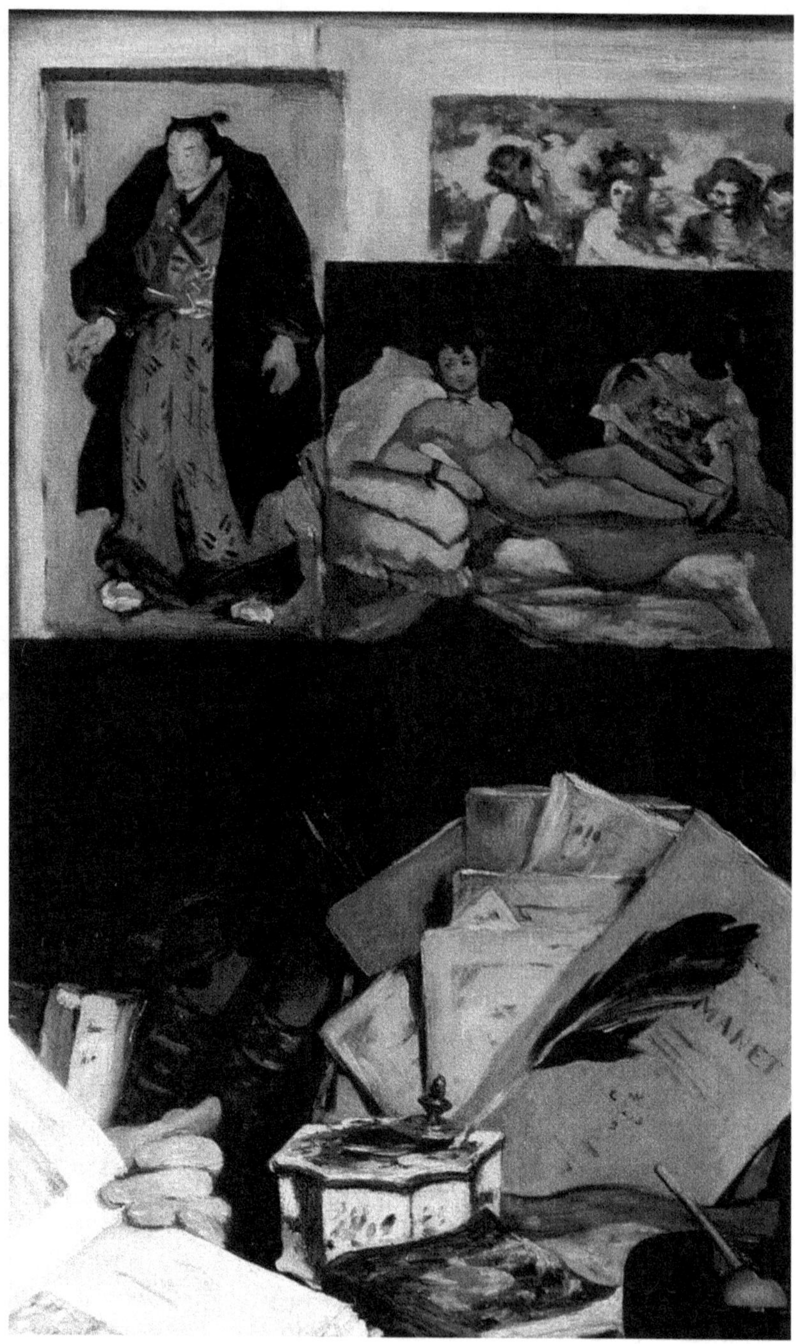

FIG. 4.7. *Portrait de M. Émile Zola* (detail).

agreed 'par reconnaissance, par sympathie' to provide the drawings for such a project; success was assured, Zola promised, owing to Manet's 'bruyante réputation' which could only be helped by the 'publicité énorme' expected to surround his exhibition. 'Nous désirons avant tout faire une œuvre *purement artistique*', he stressed; but, as the former head of Hachette's publicity department, went on: 'Si vous m'accordez quelque expérience en matière de réclame, croyez à mes assurances; mon nom et celui de Manet sur une même couverture doivent tirer l'œil des passants et les forcer à s'arrêter'; and Zola concluded, in what is a revealing admission: 'jamais je n'ai si habilement travaillé à ma réputation qu'en cherchant à mettre le nom de Manet sur une de mes œuvres.'[47]

It may indeed have been because the project for an illustrated *Contes à Ninon* finally came to nothing that Manet proceeded to paint Zola's portrait between November 1867 and February 1868. It could be argued that the painting had the same tactical function as Zola's earlier physical portrait of Manet, designed to counter popular misconceptions of the artist as a 'rapin débraillé'. It was now Manet's turn, in other words, to present Zola to the public. And gratitude for the writer's support, it is invariably claimed, is not just circumstantial. The uncomplicated view of the painting is that in its general conception and internal reference to Zola's 1867 study of Manet, the portrait testifies not only to their friendship but also to a common commitment to a new aesthetic programme. A more equivocal reading of the painting might start with Manet's own signature, indexed by the writer's quill-pen which threatens to obscure this symbolic marker of his achievement (Fig. 4.6). But it is very much to the point that the nature of Manet's response resists interpretative certainty, in the same way, as was suggested in my Introduction, as the subsequent conjunction of Zola and the painters of his time in Fantin-Latour's *Atelier aux Batignolles*. For the same could be said of the ambiguities of his 1868 portrait. Zola should perhaps have taken greater note of his impression of Manet's slightly 'mocking' mien.[48] Ever since Theodore Reff, in his classic study of the painting, alerted us to instances of Manet's 'visual wit',[49] and in the light of a fuller understanding of his personality, pictorial language and citational modes, it has no longer been possible to see this allusive work as a simple expression of gratitude for Zola's support and a celebration of shared artistic aims and values. But nor can a contrary, wholly negative reading be sustained.[50] For, without even trying to provide an exhaustive survey of recent thinking about the portrait, what might be stressed here, within the perspectives of the present chapter, is simply its indeterminacy. Lodged somewhere between documentary reportage and imaginative play, Manet's portrait of Zola poses a set of overlapping and unanswerable questions.

The most fundamental of these, in the drama of identification informing the relationship between Zola and Manet, is whether this is actually a portrait of the writer. It has often been suggested that the painter transferred to Zola a large measure of his own physical distinction and sartorial elegance. While this was Manet's turn to present Zola to the public as a respectable bourgeois, whether such a transference was 'unconscious' is another question. It is certainly worth noting,

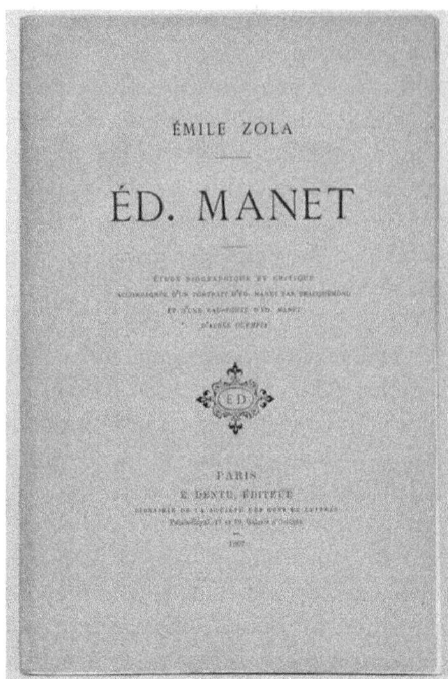

FIG. 4.8. Émile Zola, *Éd. Manet* (Paris: E. Dentu, 1867), cover.

however, that there is very little resemblance, least of all in his Manet-like beard and forehead, between the man represented here and other images of Zola between 1867 and 1870.

Nor is it clear whether the desired illusion of Zola in his own writing space is undercut by the pictorial context in which he sits, and literally 'sat' for the painting of his portrait. John House insists that he is surrounded by attributes which 'mostly belong generically to the world of the writer'.[51] The related claim, made by Françoise Cachin, that Manet's studio was 'carefully arranged to resemble a writer's study'[52] does not survive a comparison with Degas's portrait of Duranty (1879) or Caillebotte's *Portrait d'Henri Cordier* (1883). Or it might have been more convincing if the Manet too had a book-lined background and a desk on which there was rather more evidence of the act of writing. Zola's own, we know, was scrupulously organized, utterly different from the clutter from which Manet transforms an implausible medley of volumes into a decorative fan-like arrangement. If this allows just a glimpse of the only identifiable title (Zola's 1867 pamphlet (Fig. 4.8)), we might ask whether, like the other fans in Manet's work partially obscuring legibility, it is emblematic of the painting as a whole. Even the row of books, spacing leather-bound tomes with modern yellow editions, may be self-referential. Or is the decidedly ancient little book placed horizontally at the top of it simply a cross-reference to the same one which tops the pile in his portrait of Astruc in 1866 (Fig. 4.9)? And were it to be of sixteenth-century provenance, does it also refer to the 'Venetian mode' characteristic of the Zola?[53]

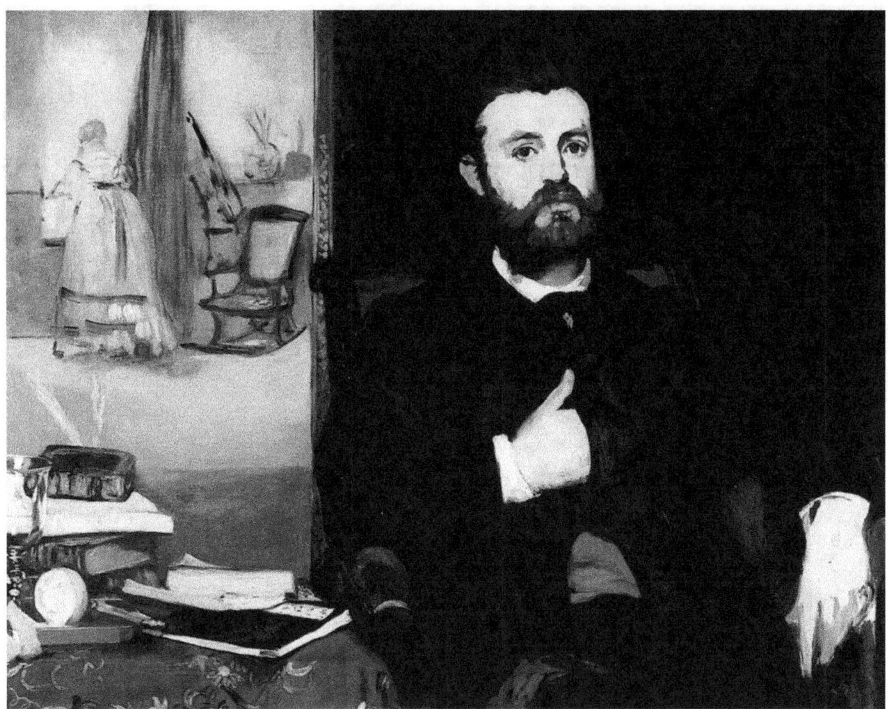

FIG. 4.9. Édouard Manet, *Portrait de Zacharie Astruc* (1866), oil on canvas, 90 × 116 cm. Kunsthalle, Bremen.

The painting's enigmas constantly tempt the viewer into such dead ends. The only book apparently open to our reading (unlike so many other books in nineteenth-century pictures of reading) is the one placed in Zola's hands. Although its text is veiled, or pictorially erased, by the blur, it was confidently identified long ago as part of Charles Blanc's encyclopaedic *Histoire des peintres de toutes les écoles* (1861–76), the seventh volume of which had appeared by 1867–68. That hypothesis, supported by the multiple ironies deriving from it, has now been discredited. For more recent research has established that it is in fact an issue of *La Gazette des beaux-arts* in which was to be found an article devoted to Goya and the latter's reworking of Velázquez.[54] But that does not in itself mitigate Manet's possible irony at Zola's expense. For the journal functions as a synecdoche of Blanc as its founder and is as certainly as his *Histoire des peintres* from Manet's library rather than Zola's.[55] All such reproductions were essential to the painter's working methods, and the fact that Zola is neither looking at the volume nor had properly acknowledged Manet's debt to the Old Masters could well be seen as testifying to the painter's reservations about what Zola had written about him, not least his relegation to the margins of the influence, indeed, of both Goya and Velázquez.[56] But that may be merely the beginning of a longer question rather than an answer. Is Zola visibly *not* taking account of Blanc's journal and his conservative criteria pointing to the depth of his (and, as far as the portrait is concerned, their joint) challenge to tradition? The

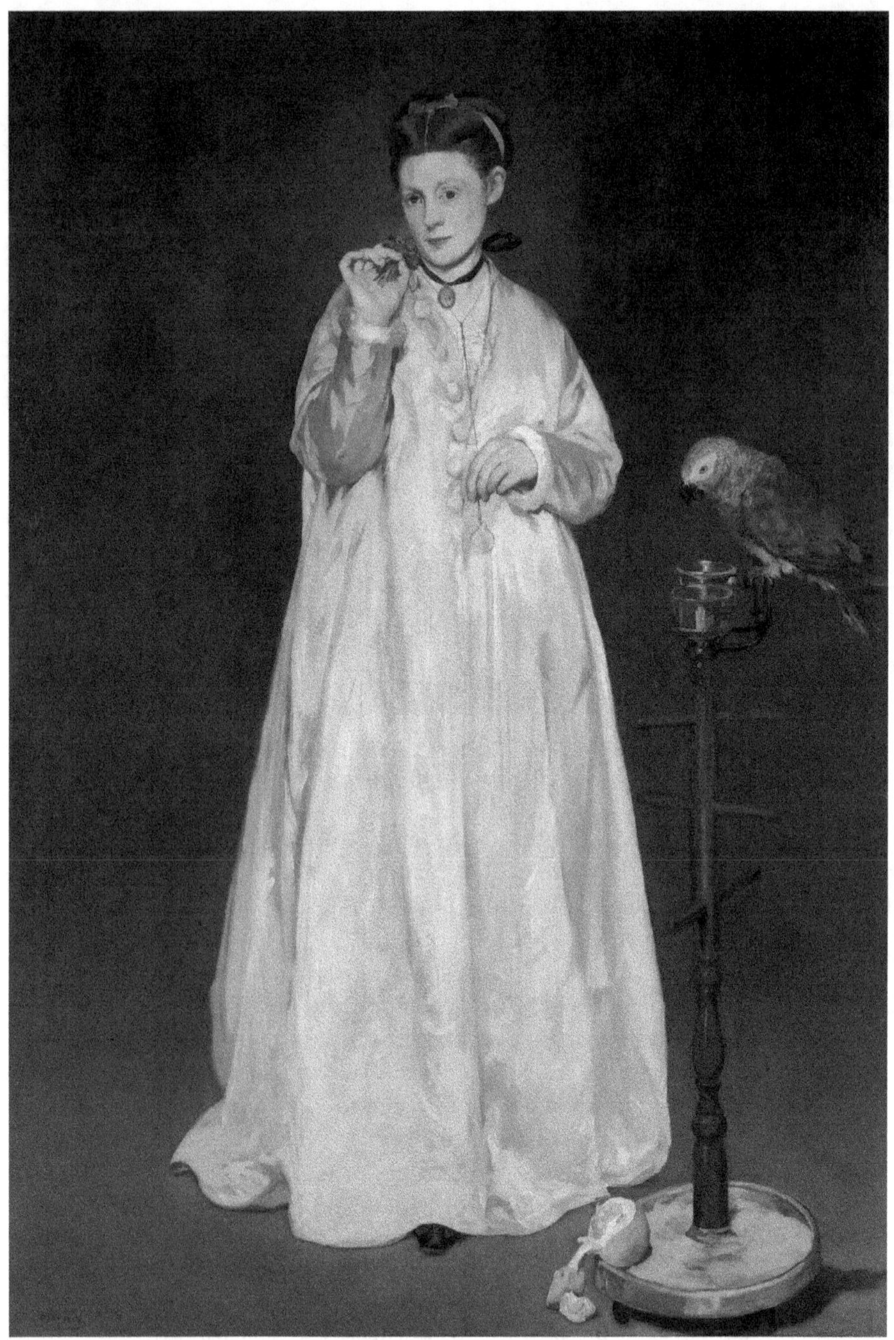

FIG. 4.10. Édouard Manet, *Jeune dame en 1866* (1866), oil on canvas, 185.1 × 128.6 cm. Metropolitan Museum of Art, New York. Gift of Erwin Davis.

volume is at the very centre of the canvas, highlighted by its whiteness set against Zola's jacket and the miscellany of colours behind it. But given Manet's predilection for visual and verbal punning (correcting his reputation as linguistically inept), we might also wonder whether the *white* volume, underwritten by Charles *Blanc*, also speaks of the *blank* of Zola's gaze.

That unreadable gaze poses one kind of problem, in that it is directed away from the painter and all the visual objects on display. It raises another in the detail of the dangling eye-glasses, at the fold of the volume, without which Zola could not see, and which is hardly ever mentioned in analyses of the painting. At sixteen, he had noticed he could not read posters; by the age of twenty he was wearing a *pince-nez*; in 1870 he was exempted from military service on account of his myopia. But before we conclude that the detail mocks his lack of pictorial insight, we may also have to refer across to the monocle hanging from the neck of the *Jeune dame en 1866* (also known as *La Femme au perroquet*) (Fig. 4.10) whose pink dress Zola had singled out for comment in his study of Manet and which the painter intended to send to the 1868 Salon as the complementary picture to the portrait of the writer. Unusual for a woman, rather than a lorgnette, Armstrong refers to it as signalling 'opacity converted into transparency and back again',[57] while failing to effect a fortuitous (or not) invocation of Zola's 'Théorie des écrans'. The citational link to the 1866 picture is reinforced by the Zola portrait's internal reference to *Olympia* and, by implication,Victorine Meurent who had posed for both. Whether this can be extended from the parrot of the former to the ornithological accessories of the Zola is yet another question. The fragile bird perched on a blossom-laden branch (echoed in the floral texture of the chair) within the Japanese screen, looking away from the writer but completing the pattern of dark cloaking (and lighter flesh) extending from Zola up to the assertive figure in the Kuniaki II print and down again to the delicate black and white quill, provides one set of counterpoints. The pair of peacock feathers above the sitter, also inscribed in this compositional indexing, may be traditionally referencing vanity (Manet's or Zola's, or both, or the portrait's). Fried prefers the perhaps equally valid sense of the feather's 'eye', substituted for those in the painting (Zola's, the wrestler's, those of Olympia and her slave, the drinkers above her) consistently turned away from the spectator.[58] Wettlaufer, on the other hand, wonders whether there is a play on the colloquialism of *se parer des plumes de paon*, such an 'adorning with peacock feathers' indicating an imposture and pretension applied to Zola's exploitation of Manet himself.[59]

Wettlaufer also takes this word-play as far as Zola's amputated feet, *perdre pied* suggesting being 'out of one's depth' and thereby consistent with an interpretation of the portrait as the painter's statement on the inadequacies of Zola's art criticism. It is certainly interesting that such cropping is exceptional in Manet's portraiture. But it may simply point to the painting's status as a pictorial representation rather than a quasi-photographic reproduction of Zola. In that respect, while the Japanese print may refer to that part of his artistic parentage (with *The Wrestler* possibly the 'lutteur convaincu' Zola had unjustifiably overlaid on Manet's persona), the lithograph after Velázquez, reflecting those in the *Gazette des beaux-arts* to which

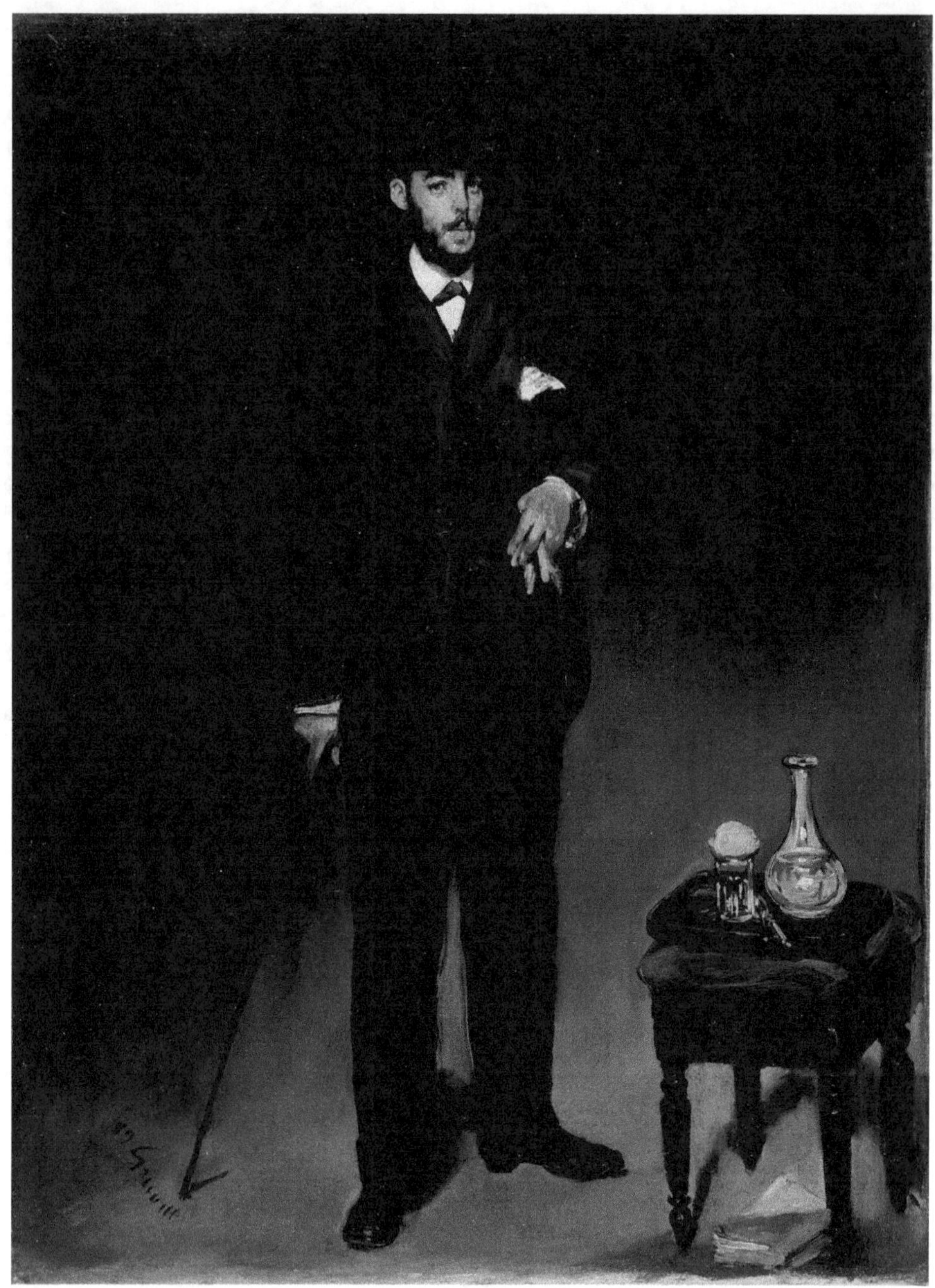

FIG. 4.11. Édouard Manet, *Portrait de Théodore Duret* (1868), oil on canvas, 43 × 35 cm. Petit Palais, Musée des Beaux-Arts de la Ville de Paris.

Zola seems oblivious, might reinforce a self-referentiality drawing attention to the artifice of this image filled with pictures (Fig. 4.7). If it also reworks Velázquez's uncomplimentary *The Dwarf Don Diego*,[60] Zola positively needs the grateful acknowledgement of Olympia's gaze being turned towards her defender. But the black cat in the etching, previously distinguishable only by its shining eyes, is now cropped so closely by the frame that the virtual occlusion of *Olympia*'s most controversial element may be Manet's way of sneaking her back, with her flowers wrapped in ephemeral newsprint, into the newly liberalized Salon of 1868.

What do we make of all this? Thoré thought the portrait devoid of human warmth. Odilon Redon praised it as a still-life. Gautier was rather confused, but probably less so than Zola. Was his portrait a manifesto of the self-sufficiency of painting, or, at Zola's expense, as surreptitious a laugh as Manet's portrait of Duret (Fig. 4.11) in the same year, with *his* book (of art criticism? Possibly Duret's own *Les Peintres français en 1867* in which he had intimated that Manet needed to work harder in order to fulfil his potential) thrown on the floor? Zola was certainly aware of what he calls its 'gamme savante' (*EsA*, p. 181), but more 'knowing' than perhaps he knew. Is it a picture of him in 1868, or a set of imbricated reflections of, and on, Manet's art, as quizzical as the sheen of lacquer on the lustrous frame of its ornamental screen, but as firmly behind the sitter as the unseen larger picture is above him? Is it too fanciful to detect within it, in the added curled lock of Olympia's fringe (not replicated in any other lithograph) an inverted question-mark? Whatever else its possible contradictions hide, the painting is certainly testimony to an irrepressibly witty Parisian intelligence.

That manifests itself, indeed, in the painting's overlaid allusions. The most visible is the apparent reference to Zola's writing on *Olympia*, characterized by him as Manet's outstanding work, 'son chef-d'oeuvre [...] la chair et le sang du peintre [...] l'expression complète de son tempérament' (*EsA*, p. 488). Across all of Zola's art criticism, no other painting is subjected to such extensive analysis. It was thus as appropriate for Manet to reproduce *Olympia* in a portrait of Zola in February 1868 as it had been for him to provide an etching of it for the latter's pamphlet nine months earlier. But recognition of the implied significance of Manet turning the courtesan's head (see Fig. 4.7) towards Zola remains profoundly double-edged. For it alerts the spectator to the multiple inscriptions which make of the painting as a whole the most *eloquent* refutation of the writer's unwillingness to grant Manet a degree of intentionality. It refers us back to Zola's attempt to deflect criticism from the painter's subject matter to his works' pictorial qualities; and to his refusal to allow Manet to be identified with the imaginative expression of an outdated Romanticism. If we are to believe that the painter experienced such difficulties with language that he had to enlist Zola's help to prepare the text of the preface to the catalogue of his private exhibition in 1867,[61] not the least of the ironies of this particular painting is that Zola's own texts are transformed into an arrangement as stylized as the cropped images above them. Even the highlighting of that cropping technique is *declarative* on Manet's part. It *speaks* of a complexity in his art which Zola had not really understood, registered in the collage of the upper right-hand corner of the portrait. Olympia is offset from, but inextricably related to, that composite design. The figure in the Kuniaki print pays the writer an equally qualified compliment. Broad shoulders enveloped in black are turned towards Zola in his frock-coat, and mirrored hands reinforce the allusion to the 'lutteur' the critic had characterized Manet himself as being. It is less clear whether the label returned is also one rejected as a definition of his own stance. But the print simultaneously completes Zola's commentary. Like the Japanese screen on the left, itself cropped, it points to a handling of perspective much vaunted by the painter but left unmentioned by Zola who fails even to spot the dividing screen in *Olympia*. The pictorial allusion to Velázquez, behind the copy of Manet's picture but not entirely out of sight, is another such reference to lacunae in Zola's texts. Most obviously it recalls Manet's admission that *Le Buveur d'absinthe* (1859) was a Parisian character painted with the technical simplicity he had discovered in Velázquez. Zola, by contrast, could see only 'une vague impression des œuvres de Thomas Couture' (*EsA*, p. 472) in its 'intention mélodramatique'; and, more generally, his dismissive 'le peintre se cherchait encore' is out of sympathy with those creative contacts with tradition which Manet himself reasserts. It seems inconceivable, in respect of what Zola does *not* write, that Manet had not mentioned to him how *Olympia* reworks Titian's *Venus of Urbino*. Zola is content to claim that the painter's originality was inseparable from an awareness 'qu'il n'arrivait à rien en copiant les maîtres' and that 'il fit effort pour oublier tout ce qu'il avait étudié dans les musées' (*EsA*, pp. 474–75). With its multiple iconographic threads gesturing towards that formative dimension of Manet's work, the portrait as a whole can be seen to object to such categorical remarks, underlining instead the failure, on Zola's part, to give due weight to the art of the past.

No more than *Olympia* can the portrait be deemed to be a mere structure of colours. For it takes issue, and acutely so precisely by being that of a *writer*, with the implication that only writing can articulate meaning, or that painting in general was amenable only to formalist critical purchase. For it is in its surfeit of meanings that the portrait works between intelligibility and self-cancelling ironies, ultimately closer to Flaubert's *ne pas conclure* than to Zola's unambiguous prose, and irreducible to it. As in the case of Fantin-Latour's *Atelier aux Batignolles*, a contemporary caricature is again paradoxically helpful: Bertall's *Promenade au Salon de 1868* (Fig. 4.12) shows Zola, with a notorious long-tailed black cat at his feet, trying to read a massive book, against a background of proliferating and comically heterogeneous drawings; and inscribed down the left-hand side of the image (taking the place of Manet's screen) is a vertical Japanese 'explicatory' caption in indecipherable script. Underlying Manet's resistance to textual appropriation, we can perhaps discern a statement about his own art. For there is a sense in which it inverts Zola's ambition to 'mettre le nom de Manet sur une de mes œuvres'. For here we do have the image of the writer and the name of the painter side by side. The latter's signature (with which he had such fun in other pictures) is framed by texts, and yet both Zola and his writing about the artist are firmly within Manet's pictorial frame. Those paradoxes inform the contemporary debate, in which Zola himself is personally

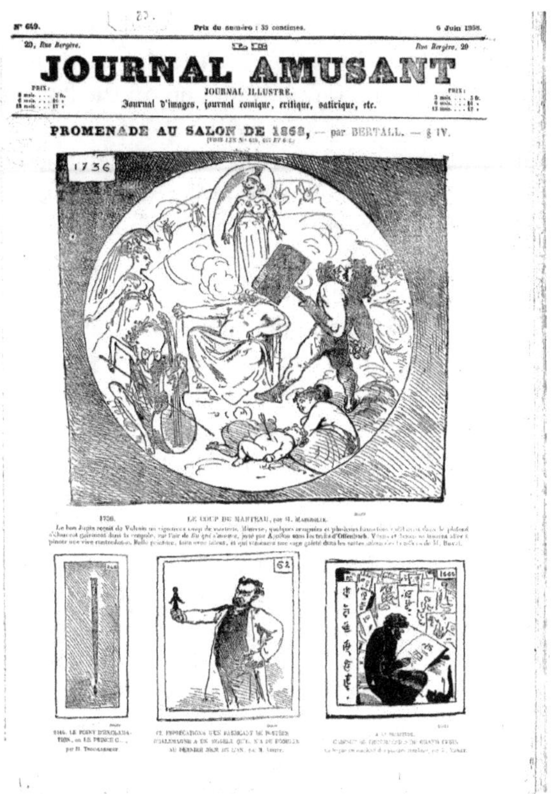

N° 649. Prix du numéro : 35 centimes. 6 Juin 1868.

20, Rue Bergère. LE Rue Bergère, 20

JOURNAL AMUSANT

JOURNAL ILLUSTRÉ.

Journal d'images, journal comique, critique, satirique, etc.

PROMENADE AU SALON DE 1868, — par BERTALL. — § IV.

1736. LE COUP DE MARTEAU

Fig. 4.12. Bertall, *Promenade au Salon de 1868* (*Le Journal amusant*, 6 June 1868).

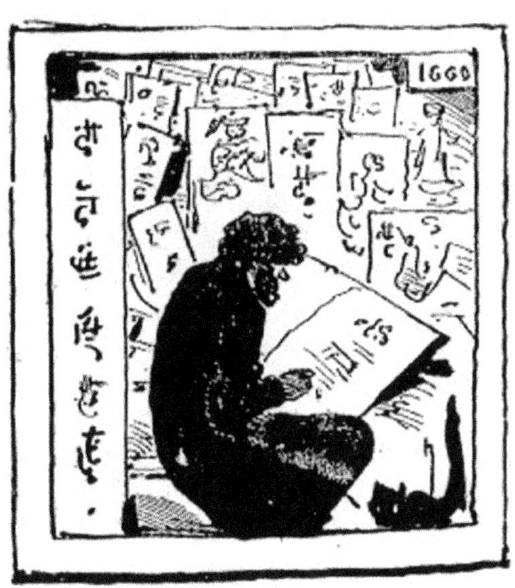

Fig. 4.13. Bertall, *Promenade au Salon* (detail). The no. 1660 in the top right-hand corner corresponds to that of the portrait in the Salon catalogue; the caption reads: 'À LA SCABIÈRE. CABINET DE CHINOISERIES DE GRAND DEUIL VISITÉ PAR UN EMPLOYÉ DES POMPES FUNÈBRES, PAR M. MANET'.

invested, about the relative autonomy of literature and painting. And where Manet ultimately stands can be gauged by following the diagonals to an originality writ large, defying massive inkwell and flamboyant pen, in the lettering dwarfing Zola's authorship.[62]

The most explicit reflection on his pictorial image remains Zola's review of his own portrait in his Salon article of 10 May 1868. At this further level of self-consciousness and objectification, he recalls the many hours of sitting for it, watching himself being pictured while sinking into a trance-like state of exhausted limbs and eyes, removed from the noise of the street and the pettiness of human toil. In this evocation of the dehumanized and dematerialized subject, we are reminded of Roland Barthes having his photo taken: 'un sujet qui devient objet'.[63] So too, Zola is reduced to the status of (in his own words, thematically anticipating the title of his later novel) a 'bête humaine quelconque' (*EsA*, p. 180) or an inanimate object copied by a fastidiously mimetic artist, the lifeless pictorial matter which a number of critics, besides Redon, had commented upon. Zola himself, however, seeks to qualify such judgements by his singling out of the detail of his painted writing hand (a quasi-Barthesian *certificat de présence*, one might say). Long before Barthes, indeed, Zola had characterized his writing on Manet as 'un acte de présence' (*EsA*, p. 468). His stress on the hand's 'real skin' and the reacting crowd refer us back to the critique of Olympia's 'dirty skin', as the highlighted hand is held in an analogous arrested relationship (with his feathery quill in florally decorated inkwell) to the courtesan's (in relation to the flowers offered for her to take). Such an allusion of his own evokes the scandalized focus of 1865 on that 'toad-like' hand at the very centre of *Olympia* — too life-like, with a life of its own, substituted for the veiled conventional coverings of *L'Origine du monde* (to borrow Courbet's title) as surely as Zola's active writing will originate his own world, in the midst of this re-visualization of Manet's looking.

Throughout his life, once he had become well known, Zola would be repeatedly portrayed, painted, etched, sketched, caricatured and photographed. But, given to him after the 1868 Salon and lent back for subsequent exhibitions, this Manet became, for contemporaries, the benchmark of a certain image of the novelist. When he lost a significant amount of weight, Edmond de Goncourt noted in his *Journal*, on 4 March 1888, that Zola had begun to resemble once again his portrait by Manet; but then, barely seven months later, Zola's having (inevitably) put all those kilos back on inspires another *Journal* entry, in the meeting of a person so unrecognizable that his face no longer looked like the one in the Manet's portrait which he had momentarily regained. Yet we might also note that the production of the portrait coincides with Zola's early *Madeleine Férat*, in which a photographic portrait of the heroine's first lover functions as a morbid and contaminating presence, precluding liberation from the past. Zola's mirroring in both negative inversion, exemplified by Cézanne, and positive recognition (at least in his writing on Manet which precedes the 1868 portrait) can be juxtaposed with this phantasmic scenario, ultimately played out in his photograph of the portrait, in which his own name is liberated from the painter's dominating signature. For the resistance to Manet's later development can be seen to be, on Zola's part, a sort of distancing from an assimilating absorption which threatens to negate his own identity. Manet is one of the models, of course, for the Claude Lantier of *L'Œuvre*. But the vicissitudes of the fictional painter's career preclude affording him the kind of unqualified admiration with which Zola had championed Manet's work in the 1860s. And it makes of the writing of the novel of 1886 a creatively affirming stepping-back from the reflective space in which Zola confronts the negatives — in the photographic sense, too — of his artistic self and imaginative practice.

Notes to Chapter 4

1. Three of which have been identified: *La Polichinelle* (*c.* 1874–76), *Lola de Valence* (1862–63) and *Le Torréador* (1868).
2. See *Manet, 1832–1883*, ed. by Françoise Cachin, exh. cat. (Paris: RMN/New York: Metropolitan Museum of Art, 1983), pp. 204–05 (hereafter cited as *Manet*, ed. by Cachin). This work was presented to Zola as a gift, not least because he had singled out the original 1864 painting for special praise.
3. *Manet*, ed. by Cachin, pp. 440–41. There may be an oblique reference to this work in Zola's later remarks on Manet's pastel portraits of this period: in the context of *Dans la serre* (1879), he writes that 'de cette époque datent aussi d'admirable pastels, des portraits d'une finessse et d'une couleur exquises' (*EsA*, p. 608).
4. Mitterand, *Zola*, III, 705, n .1. What is in fact therefore a sort of double portrait may compensate for, or be aligned with, the apparent intention that Zola himself might figure in the 1879 picture, perhaps on the model of that of Jules Guillemet and his wife (*Dans la serre*, originally entitled *M. et Mme Jules Guillemet dans la serre*) that same year. Cachin notes (*Manet*, p. 441) that Manet's letter responding to Zola's request refers to making appointments for them both. Beth Brombert claims that 'Mme Zola had wanted him to do her portrait but was too embarrassed to ask him herself, so her husband communicated her desire'; in *Edouard Manet: Rebel in a Frock Coat* (Boston: Little, Brown & Co., 1996), p. 423. This particular photograph is also consistent with Zola's attempts to reassure his wife that, notwithstanding his long-established alternative family with Jeanne Rozerot, she retained a unique and lasting place in his affections.
5. These claims are confronted in my 'Zola's Manets', in *Perspectives on Manet*, ed. by Therese Dolan (Farnham: Ashgate, 2012), pp. 97–117, from which a certain amount of material in the present chapter is drawn. Unlike his Cézannes, sold at auction in 1903, the three Manet paintings were retained and made over to the state as late as 1918, with Zola's widow retaining a life interest (i.e. until 1925).
6. Brombert, *Edouard Manet*, p. 195.
7. It is reproduced in François Émile-Zola and Massin, *Zola Photographer*, trans. by Liliane Tuck (London: Collins, 1988), p. 179. See Bertrand Éveno, 'Zola photographe', in *Mimesis et Semiosis: littérature et représentation*, ed. by Philippe Hamon and Jean-Pierre Leduc-Adine (Paris: Nathan, 1992), pp. 393–408, where it is termed a form of 'autocélébration, je dirai même d'autoglorification' (p. 404). The most sustained study of it to date is Maya Balakirsky Katz, 'Photography Versus Caricature: "Footnotes" on Manet's *Zola* and Zola's *Manet*', *NCFS*, 34 (2006), 323–35, mainly concerned with its corrective function in relation to negative images of the writer, rather than with its relation to the portrait and the painter.
8. Based on Nadar's famous 1898 photograph (see Mitterand, *Zola*, III, 475) but as Katz notes, 'in the medal the model assumes something of classical sculpture, with the heroic brow, defined jawbone, swept back coiffure, and the cowl of his monk-like cloak' ('Photography Versus Caricature', p. 329). Zola's photograph of Nadar's image is thus also a homage to the photographer whose work he and Manet so admired, not least for his photographs of paintings; see Juliet Wilson-Bareau, 'Manet et l'Espagne', in *Manet-Velázquez, la manière espagnole au XIXe siècle*, exh. cat. (Paris: RMN, 1983), pp. 170–215 (p. 194), who also refers to Manet dedicating to Nadar his *Jeune Femme couchée en costume espagnol* (1862); and *Manet*, ed. by Cachin, pp. 99–102.

9. In the manner of Berthe Morisot looking more acutely at reproductions of Botticelli's *Primavera* (of which Zola also had a copy): 'is it because I understand it better now, or does it really gain from being seen in black and white?'; cited by Anne Higonnet, *Berthe Morisot* (New York: Harper Perennial, 1990), p. 191. Uncannily, but arguing against such an enhancement, Jules Joly's review of the original portrait predicted that 'reproduced in a black and white engraving, it would evidently lose something of its outlandish appearance; What would it then retain of real originality? Nothing, absolutely nothing.' Cited by Katz, 'Photography Versus Caricature', p. 331.
10. Higonnet, *Berthe Morisot*, p. 220.
11. Éveno, 'Zola photographe', p. 404: 'il s'immortalise dans une forme de mise en abyme, il regarde et fixe sur une plaque sa propre image qui n'est déjà qu'une représentation de lui-même'.
12. Carol Armstrong refers to it as a 'painted photograph'; see her *Manet Manette* (New Haven and London: Yale University Press, 2002), p. 156.
13. Reproduced in Michael Fried, *Manet's Modernism or, The Face of Painting in the 1860s* (London and Chicago: University of Chicago Press, 1996), p. 324.
14. See Niess, 'Lantier-Manet', in *Zola, Cézanne and Manet*, pp. 113–50.
15. Armstrong, *Manet Manette*, p. 37.
16. Which is not quite borne out by the facts: regretting that he had been unable to repay a visit to the painter, Zola's letter to Guillemet of 17 October 1876 mentions having heard that Manet 'était un peu découragé' (*Corr.*, II, 495–96).
17. 'Le peintre se cherchait encore'; 'il y a forcément, pour chaque artiste, une période de tâtonnements et d'hésitations qui dure plus ou moins longtemps' (*EsA*, p. 483 and p. 474); in a letter of May 1870, Zola writes of Cézanne's continuing 'période de tâtonnements' (*Corr.*, II, 219).
18. He refers both to 'trente à quarante ' and 'une trentaine de toiles dont la plus ancienne date de 1860' (*EsA*, p. 469 and p. 482). What was originally a footnote includes a list of seventeen works not in Manet's studio at the time of his visit at the end of 1866. Altogether, he mentions another twenty-three, but eight of these by title only.
19. At one stage in the preparation of *L'Œuvre*, Zola thought about including such an 'exposition particulière' (Ms 10316, fol. 300); but whereas Manet's established him as a major figure, this idea hardly fitted with the descending curve of the career of his fictional painter.
20. '*Le Ballet espagnol* et *La Musique aux Tuileries* furent ceux qui mirent le feu aux poudres' (*EsA*, p. 485); in respect of *Le Christ mort et les anges*, Zola seizes on protests that 'ce Christ n'était pas un Christ' (*EsA*, p. 487).
21. As he would note in planning *L'Œuvre*: 'J'ai Claude, qui est au début, la tête, le chef de l'école' (Ms 10316, fol. 271) or, more accurately reflecting Manet, 'chef d'école malgré lui' (fol. 37).
22. Dominique Fernandez and Ferrante Ferranti, *Le Musée d'Émile Zola: haines et passions* (Paris: Stock, 1997), p. 34. But nor should we give much credence to reports of an interview with Adolphe Retté shortly before Zola's death in which he supposedly declared: 'Manet ne fut pas un grand peintre. C'était un talent incomplet [...]. J'étais jeune, je cherchais partout des armes pour défendre la doctrine sur laquelle j'ai basé mes livres. Manet par son souci de choisir des sujets contemporains et son effort vers le réalisme m'avait semblé bon à soutenir. Mais, pour dire la vérité, sa peinture m'a toujours déconcerté'; republished in Adolphe Retté, *Le Symbolisme: anecdotes et souvenirs* (Paris: Vannier, 1903), pp. 191–92.
23. Armstrong, *Manet Manette*, p. 49.
24. In blatant contradiction with the truer 'amabilité, 'douceur' and 'politesse exquise' of the 'homme du monde', Manet is figured as a 'lutteur convaincu', 'un homme impopulaire qui ne tremblait pas devant le public, qui ne cherchait pas à apprivoiser la bête, mais qui s'essayait plutôt à la dompter, à lui imposer son tempérament' *(EsA*, p. 153); this appears in one of Zola's very first 1866 articles on Manet, but is significantly eliminated in the 'cut-and-paste' versions of his 'Nouvelle manière' texts.
25. Brombert, *Manet*, pp. 192–93, double-edged in so far as it forms the basis for her view of the inadequacies of Zola's engagement (see pp. xiv, xviii, 104, 132, 382). On Zola's role in Manet's elevation as the 'father' of modernism, see also Armstrong, *Manet Manette*, p. 31.
26. See my 'Zola, Manet and *Thérèse Raquin*', *FS*, 34 (1980), 278–99.

27. His complicitous colleague, Louis Ulbach, did the necessary in his 'La Littérature putride' (*Le Figaro*, 23 January 1868): 'M. Zola voit la femme comme M. Manet la peint, couleur de boue avec des maquillages roses'; in his preface to the second edition of *Thérèse Raquin*, dated 15 April 1868, Zola writes: 'Je me suis trouvé dans le cas de ces peintres qui copient des nudités, sans qu'un seul désir les effleure, et qui restent profondément surpris lorsqu'un critique se déclare scandalisé par les chairs vivantes de leur œuvre' (*OC*, I, 520).
28. Léon Laurent-Pichat in *Le Phare de la Loire*, 16 June 1868.
29. There remains more legitimate doubt as to whether or not Manet's painting (begun in October or November 1876) was itself inspired by images of Nana, as Gervaise's daughter embarking on a career as a high-class prostitute, in *L'Assommoir*, the relevant later parts of which were published in instalments between 9 July 1876 and 7 January 1877. But it is not merely the juggling of chronology which is at issue. Virtually every serious analysis of the painting invokes Zola's novel of 1880. See, in particular, Hollis Clayson, *Painted Love: Prostitution in French Art of the Impressionist Era* (New Haven and London: Yale University Press, 1991), pp. 67–75.
30. Nowhere in Zola's art criticism is Manet's *Nana* ever mentioned. Whether the two 'de facto surrogates' (Clayson, *Painted Love*, p. 75), named by critics as *Nana à sa toilette* and referring to *Nana* in its absence, form part of a campaign is another question. They were shown, in April 1880, at the *Vie moderne* gallery of Zola's publisher, Georges Charpentier, who organized unprecedented publicity for the launch of the novel in volume form on 14 February. And let us not entirely forget Pascal Dagnan-Bouveret's *Nana* at the Salon of 1879 or Georges Bellenger's *Nana au miroir* (for the 1882 illustrated edition of the novel) which may be quoting Manet's *Devant la glace* (1876) shown in 1880 as one of the 'two *nanas* at their toilettes' (Armstrong, *Manet Manette*, p. 228); nor the theatrical adaptation of *Nana* at the Théâtre de l'Ambigu (29 January–31 May 1881); see Mitterand, *Zola*, II, 573–82; and Janice Best, 'Portraits d'une "vrai fille": *Nana*, tableau, roman et mise-en-scène', *CN*, 66 (1992), 157–66. Nana's initial relation (in 'La Belle Hélène') to the prettified eroticism of Salon tradition so deplored in Zola's art criticism was recognized by André Gill's caricature, 'La Naissance de Nana-Vénus: motif à tableau pour les BOUGUEREAU futurs' (*La Lune rousse*, 19 October 1879).
31. Peter Brooks, 'Nana at Last Unveil'd? Problems of the Modern Nude', in *Body Work: Objects of Desire in Modern Narrative* (Cambridge, MA: Harvard University Press, 1991), pp. 123–61 (p. 145).
32. Janet Beizer's term, in 'Uncovering *Nana*: The Courtesan's New Clothes', *L'Esprit créateur*, 25 (1985), 45–56.
33. For a more detailed analysis of Zola's differentiation, see my 'Zola's Transpositions', in *Translation and the Arts in Modern France*, ed. by Sonya Stephens (Bloomington: Indiana University Press, 2017), pp. 131–47 (on *Nana*, pp. 135–37); this essay includes the further example of Renoir's *La Balançoire* (1876) and the corresponding scene in Zola's *Une page d'amour* (1878).
34. See Brooks, 'Nana at last Unveil'd', p. 134; and Brombert (*Manet*, p. 132), who writes, of *L'Œuvre*, that 'the painting to which [Zola] devotes singular attention is *instantly recognizable* as Manet's *Le Déjeuner sur l'herbe, only its title altered, Plein Air*' (my emphases). One of the few to note the differences is Fried (*Manet's Modernism*, p. 249) who argues that the fictional painting is made more 'Courbet-like', or at least an amalgam of Courbet *and* Manet, by virtue of the elimination of that 'facingness' which is specific to Manet's achievement in the 1860s. The more plausible amalgam, it could be argued, is *Cézanne* and Manet, Zola having originally entitled the invented painting *Baigneuses*, with its 'quatre femmes, l'une nageant encore, l'autre sortant de l'eau, deux couchées sur l'herbe' (Ms 10316, fol. 31); 'des femmes nues dans une clairière très ensoleillée' (fol. 80). This could be compared with Cézanne's series of three, four and five *baigneuses* dating from 1879–82, as well as those of 1874–75. On the other hand the amalgam has many layers: Zola's note here that one of the women should be a blonde and the other a brunette, together with the intention that the former 'servira la gorge [substituted for 'les seins'] et la tête de Christine', when juxtaposed to the further detail that she should be depicted by Claude as 'nue jusqu'à la ceinture' (fol. 63), conjures up Manet's dyptich, *La Brune aux seins nus* (1872) and *La Blonde aux seins nus* (*c.* 1878; in Manet's possession until his death).
35. 'Tout cela, les figures, les étoffes, la nature morte du déjeuner, s'enlevait gaiement en plein soleil, sur les verdures assombries du fond' (*RM*, IV, 28).

36. Richard Shiff, *Cézanne and the End of Impressionism* (Chicago and London: University of Chicago Press, 1984), p. 376.
37. Sandoz's exhaustion ('brisé par sa pose') may also reflect the apparently endless sittings which Manet imposed on Zola between November 1867 and February 1868.
38. His remarks on his own portrait, in *L'Événement illustré* of 10 May1868, include: 'je recommande particulièrement la main placée sur un genou du personnage; c'est une merveille d'exécution. Enfin, voilà donc de la peau, de la peau vraie, sans trompe-l'œil ridicule. Si le portrait entier avait pu être poussé au point où en est cette main, la foule elle-même eût crié au chef-d'œuvre' (*EsA*, p. 181). This was also a challenge to the repeated critique of Manet's painting of hands; on 'Manet's long-standing obsession with hands', see Griselda Pollock's observations in *12 Views of Manet's 'Bar'*, ed. by Bradford R. Collins (Princeton, NJ: Princeton University Press, 1996), p. 300 and p. 312, n.55.
39. Ms 10316, fol. 287; 'Sandoz n'est là que pour donner mes idées sur l'art' (fol. 226); 'Le mieux, ce sera de ne me prendre que comme théoricien' (fol. 278). On how the original intention to 'me laisser à l'arrière-plan' is gradually eroded by Sandoz's involvement in the narrative, see my 'L'Homme et *L'Œuvre*: Zola et la déformation romanesque', in *Lire/Dé-lire Zola*, ed. by Jean-Pierre Leduc-Adine and Henri Mitterand (Paris: Nouveau Monde Éditions, 2004), pp. 135–52.
40. The hesitations in Zola's preparatory notes (Ms 10316) are instructive in this respect: 'Claude chef d'École, lancé par Jory' (fol. 77); 'Je me prendrai moi-même pour me mettre de la bande, un journaliste' (fol. 271) ; on the one hand, 'pas moi avec Manet'; on the other, 'je pourrais même en faire écrire [une étude sur Claude] par Sandoz, la mienne' (fol. 223). But he subsequently transfers this role, indicating Alexis as the model for Jory and his 'article sur Claude et qui fait scandale et qui le met en avant' (fol. 290).
41. Reiterated time and again in the novel's work notes (Ms 10316): 'd'un côté la femme, de l'autre l'art, et la femme sera vaincue' (fol. 309) ; Christine is 'la victime anéantie de l'art' (fol. 203); and Zola's virtually automatic recourse to a contemporary *idée reçue*, 'que le génie doit être chaste, toute la virilité gardée pour l'œuvre' (fol. 199), adding here that Claude 'ne coïte qu'avec son œuvre'. On the durability of the trope encoding the rivalry between writers and painters, see Alexandra Wettlaufer, *Pen vs Paintbrush: Girodet, Balzac and the Myth of Pygmalion in Post-Revolutionary France* (New York. Palgrave, 2001).
42. See Zola's letter of 26 April 1860 (*Corr.*, I, 149) cited in chapter 2. In the work notes for *L'Œuvre*, such a naïve approach is viewed with contempt: 'le sujet surtout existent (*sic*) pour les visiteurs bourgeois' (Ms 10316, fol. 330).
43. Alexandra Wettlaufer, 'Metaphors of Power and the Power of Metaphor', *Nineteenth-Century Contexts*, 21 (1999), 437–63. The discourse moves from analogy to metaphorical continuity: 'Il avait sur le bout de la langue, comme on dit, le mot nouveau qu'il apportait, et il ne pouvait le prononcer. [...] Il parla un langage plein de rudesse [...] un langage entièrement nouveau [...] une langue qu'il avait fait sienne' (*EsA*, p. 474).
44. George Mauner, *Manet, 'Peintre-Philosophe': A Study of the Painter's Themes* (University Park, PA: Pennsylvania State University Press, 1975), p. 149.
45. In his letter to Valabrègue of 8 Januart 1866, Zola acknowledged sardonically that 'les Aixois préfèrent la bergerade de mes *Contes à Ninon* à l'eau-forte de ma *Confession* (*Corr.*, I, 435). On the specific objections aimed at the latter, see my 'L'Accueil critique à l'œuvre de Zola avant *L'Assommoir*', *CN*, 54 (1980), 214–23.
46. *Corr.*, I, 496–97.
47. The dedicatory note to Manet, dated 19 December 1868, affixed to Zola's *Madeleine Férat* (1868) served the same purpose.
48. 'La bouche mobile, un peu railleuse par instants' (*EsA*, p. 152); 'mobile, un peu moqueuse dans les coins' (*EsA*, p. 472).
49. Theodore Reff, 'Manet's Portrait of Zola', *Burlington Magazine*, 117 (1975), 35–44 (p. 40). This has also been described as a 'joyful mockery that makes contempt barely perceptible' (Brombert, *Manet*, p. 42).
50. Henri Mitterand writes of the portrait that 'on ne saurait mieux signaler la consubstantialité du scriptural et pictural' ('Le Musée dans le texte', *CN*, 66 (1992), 13–22 (p. 15)). The more negative reading of it is Nicole Savy's 'Un étranger vu par Manet: Émile Zola', *CN*, 66 (1992), 23–32.

51. House, *Impressionism: Paint and Politics*, p. 24, n. 39.
52. Françoise Cachin, *Manet: The Influence of the Modern* (New York: Harry Abrams, 1995), p. 218.
53. See, in this respect, George Heard Hamilton, *Manet and his Critics* (New Haven: Yale University Press, 1954), p. 75.
54. By Paul Lefort, 'Essai d'un catalogue raisonné', *GBA*, no. 22 (1 February 1867). This was identified by Katherina Schmidt, 'Zu Édouard Manets Porträt Émile Zola', in the exhibition catalogue *Manet, Zola Cézanne: das Porträt des modernen Literaten*, ed. by Katharina Schmidt (Basel: Kunstmuseum/Ostfildern-Ruit: Gerd Hatje, 1999), pp. 21–47 (fig. 14).
55. Theodore Reff, 'Manet and Blanc's *Histoire des peintres*', *Burlington Magazine*, 112 (1970), 456–68.
56. 'Il a traversé l'Espagne en 1865 seulement, et ses toiles ont un accent trop individuel pour qu'on veuille ne trouver en lui qu'un bâtard de Vélasquez et de Goya' (*EsA*, p. 482).
57. Armstrong, *Manet Manette*, p. 166.
58. Fried, *Manet's Modernism*, p. 323.
59. Wettlaufer, 'Metaphors of Power', p. 456. It might just be a semantic step too far, however, to relate *piper* (to deceive) and *pipée* (a bird-call) to Zola's unlit pipe, to be contrasted instead with smoke-wreathed dreamers like Mallarmé, in Manet's 1876 portrait of the poet.
60. This suggestion is made by Wilson-Bareau, 'Manet et l'Espagne', p. 210.
61. Alan Krell's hypothesis in 'Manet, Zola and the "Motifs d'une exposition particulière", 1867', *GBA*, 99 (1982), 109–15.
62. It is difficult to subscribe to Armstrong's view that Manet's signature is a 'validation' of Zola's critical writing on him (*Manet Manette*, p. 49).
63. *La Chambre claire* (Paris: Seuil, 1980), p. 30.

CHAPTER 5

❖

Painters of the Landscape: From the Barbizon School to the Impressionists

'Il est curieux de penser combien notre école historique est faible et combien notre école paysagiste s'élève chaque jour.' This insight of Zola's in 1862, in a letter to Cézanne,[1] underlines his early recognition of a fundamentally important inversion of a long-established pictorial hierarchy. In this, even academic landscapes were placed beneath history painting. But the definitive demise of the former, exemplified by Nicholas Poussin (1594–1665) and Claude Lorrain (1600–1682), was signalled by an 1863 decree removing such compositions, established in 1816, from the annual competition for the Prix de Rome. For these Italianate or mythological landscapes now seemed unacceptably artificial compared to the representation of nature by painters inspired by a real rural location rather than an imaginary site. The consequence was a decisive break in the history of landscape as a genre, transforming what had previously served as a mere background into the very subject of a painting.

This was driven not merely by aesthetic imperatives, for these new kinds of domestically-sized and charming pictures of a recognizable countryside catered for a newly enriched urban bourgeoisie.[2] As Zola somewhat ironically wrote in 1875, 'peu de personnes ont des galeries; mais il n'est pas un bourgeois à son aise qui ne possède quelques beaux cadres dans son salon, avec de la peinture quelconque pour les emplir' (*EsA*, p. 269). In reworking this statement for his review of the Salon of 1881, he added that the 'embourgeoisement de l'art' could be seen in the ubiquity of 'des toiles dont les dimensions sont calculées à tenir dans un panneau de nos étroites pièces modernes'; 'les portraits et les paysages dominent, parce qu'ils sont d'une vente courante' (*EsA*, p. 399). He himself shared a preference for a genre to which the contemporary art market, as he noted, gave further impetus, at least judging by those decorating the walls of his own homes: four Cézanne landscapes; Baille's *Montagne*; a Boudin *Coucher du soleil sur la mer*; *Paysage* by Henri Bouvet (1859–1945); Coste's *Le Barrage de Jaumegarde* and *L'Estaque*, both from 1862; *Le Port de Dieppe, la nuit* by Henri Guérard (1846–1897); Guillemet's *La Campagne à Aix* (1866), *Temps gris* (1872) and *Les Chaumières*; Monet's *Promenade en rivière* (1876); Jongkind's *Bords de la Seine* (1872); Pissarro's *Au bord de la rivière* (1866) and *Le Bocage* (1867); and images of the natural world by Béliard and Léon-Paul Robert. In due course, notwithstanding such evidence of his personal tastes, Zola's disenchantment with Impressionism would be inseparable from the commercialization of the genre. Long before this, however, the prescient Durand-Ruel, as the most important dealer in landscapes, had begun to assemble a significant stock of works by the so-called 'école de 1830', which included Théodore Rousseau, Corot, Millet and Charles-François Daubigny (1817–1878).[3] Otherwise associated, either as members or intermittent visitors, with what is more commonly known as the Barbizon School, such painters would be seen in retrospect as the precursors of the Impressionists themselves, a continuity which Zola's writing about them underscores. But he also suggests in due course, more significantly, that their work represented an ideal from which their successors had deviated.

In the antithetical conceptions of landscape painting, he could exploit once again what he saw as the irreconcilable opposition between academic tradition and modern art. In 1867, Zola had already evoked 'nos paysagistes modernes [...] se contentant de traduire le premier coin de forêt venu' (*EsA*, p. 481). Almost a decade later, institutional prejudice in this respect remained a potent theme:

> Malgré l'éclat dont on fait briller le paysage de grands artistes comme Corot, Jules Dupré, Théodore Rousseau et d'autres moins connus, l'Académie a toujours rejeté les paysagistes au deuxième rang. C'est à eux que notre siècle doit son originalité [...] le premier débutant venu [...] se croit en droit de siéger plus haut dans la hiérarchie de l'art que les paysagistes. C'est tellement le cas que jamais le jury ne donnera une première médaille à un paysagiste. (*EsA*, p. 331)

These painters camped out in the forest north of Fontainebleau, 'à Barbizon, cette thébaïde de l'art parisien',[4] were for Zola and other critics of similar persuasion an avant-garde to the extent that they portrayed the countryside outside Paris in its unmediated state, unadorned, neither enhanced by intimations of the sublime nor, for the most part, encroached upon by human figures. As early as 1868, he alerts his readers to the fact that amongst 'nos paysagistes modernes', several are 'de véritables maîtres que les autres s'efforcent de suivre' (*EsA*, p. 172). And he mentions certain other painters only because their 'obstination' in remaining wedded to the neo-classical and manicured 'paysage historique' served to better highlight the originality of those no longer subscribing to its principles: 'il faut dire que Paul Flandrin et de Curzon nous rendent un grand service, en nous rappelant dans quelles aberrations s'étaient fourvoyés les paysagistes classiques' (*EsA*, p. 570).[5] But of equal importance is that modern landscape paintings, evacuated of potential narrative significance which a 'littérateur' might have overlaid on a pictorial image, allowed him to adhere to his oft-repeated, if not always respected, dictum ('parlons peinture') in contradistinction to those 'autres paysagistes' dismissed as 'des poètes qui riment sur la nature des odes, des fables, des madrigaux', those 'littérateurs fourvoyés [qui] se servent d'un pinceau comme d'une plume' (*EsA*, p. 183).

The Barbizon School

As far the Barbizon School itself is concerned, it is not merely in Zola's art criticism that he evokes its members. His reading of *Le Paysagiste aux champs*, by the critic and painter Frédéric Henriet (1826–1918), coincides with his commentary in his *Salon* of 1866, a link explicitly declared in the opening lines of his book review in *Le Salut public* of 18 July: 'Le Salon de peinture est fermé, les paysagistes apprêtent leurs chevalets et leurs boîtes de voyage.' And his enthusiastic remarks about this 'bon livre, dont les eaux-fortes sont excellentes' (*OC*, x, 553–54), can also be juxtaposed with his 1878 text entitled 'Aux champs', subsequently included in *Le Capitaine Burle* (1882). Henriet had published a widely hailed article, in two instalments, in an 1857 issue of *L'Artiste*, in which he had celebrated the work of his friend Daubigny,[6] one of whose engravings (of the painter's 'bateau-atelier', *Le Botin, à Conflans*) he included in his general survey of the genre. Zola's 1866 review of *Le Paysagiste aux champs* cites 'l'anecdote qui me servira de mot de la fin', in which a baffled farm labourer, comparing himself to 'cet oisif', comes across 'un paysagiste qui peignait une vue des bords de l'Oise, et s'efforçait de fixer sur sa vivante ébauche, les chatoiements de la lumière sur les eaux nacrées [...]. Or ce paysagiste était Daubigny'. The 1878 text, devoted 'à toute une bande de peintres [...] qui ont découvert la banlieue parisienne' harks back to the period when 'Français, Corot, Daubigny abandonnèrent la formule classique, pour peindre sur nature'.[7]

What is striking about Zola's commentary on these 'Barbizonniers' (to adopt Léo Hoek's term)[8] is the way in which reservations about certain of them are subordinate to the necessity of grouping such painters under the banner of a common opposition to the criteria of academic landscape. His first mention of Théodore Rousseau, for example, labels him as 'un romantique endurci', 'un des plus acharnés contre les réalistes, dont il est pourtant le petit cousin' (*EsA*, p. 145), unforgiving of his role in the 1866 Salon jury which had rejected the submissions of Cézanne, Manet and Renoir. The following year, Zola's analysis of his paintings, occupying a prominent place in the Universal Exhibition of 1867, swerves between qualified admiration and nuanced contempt. On the one hand, he refers to the painter's earliest canvases (refused admission to the Salon year after year between 1837 and 1847 to the extent of earning him the sobriquet of 'le grand refusé' and thus another victim of the Académie des Beaux-Arts), as being 'vraiment supérieures et traitées avec une largeur tout à fait magistrale', confirmed by a subsequent visit to the Musée du Luxembourg to view again his *Sortie de forêt à Fontainebleau, soleil couchant* (1850–51) (Fig. 5.1), its elements 'interprétés par un esprit vigoureux qui nous a communiqué en un langage étrange les sensations poignantes que la campagne faisait naître en lui' (*EsA*, p. 165); on the other, 'le persécuté de la veille n'a pas tardé à devenir le triomphateur du lendemain', as honoured by the State as any 'adepte du paysage classique', rendering the natural world 'en esprit despotique' as a result of a preconceived systematization of its optical effects: 'De tout cela naissent des œuvres maigres et raides, grincheuses' (*EsA*, pp. 538–39). But, by 1875, Rousseau has been promoted to the ranks of 'des créateurs du paysage moderne' (*EsA*, p. 270), a status retained in all subsequent references to him in Zola's art criticism.

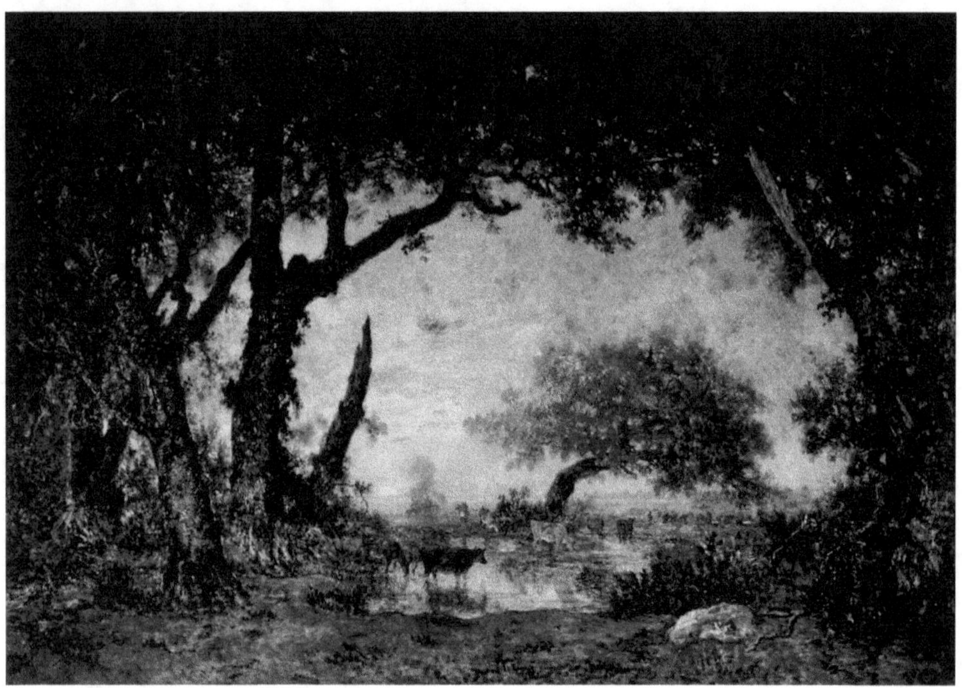

FIG. 5.1. Théodore Rousseau, *Sortie de forêt à Fontainebleau, soleil couchant* (1850–51), oil on canvas, 142 × 198 cm. Grand Palais, Paris.

Millet is another one of these. In 1866, Zola had relegated him to the category of 'Les Chutes', alongside other painters in apparently terminal decline. His *Un bout de village de Gréville* (Fig. 5.2) struck Zola as 'une peinture molle et indécise'. It is not the case, however, that this reflects a more general negative assessment of Millet's work.[9] For, in this same article, Zola nostalgically refers to paintings (conjuring up for us *L'Angélus* (1855–57) or *Les Glaneuses* (1857)) in which 'les horizons s'étendaient larges et libres; il y avait sur la toile comme un souffle de la terre. Une, deux figures au plus, puis quelques grandes lignes de terrain, et voilà qu'on avait la campagne ouverte devant soi, dans sa poésie vraie' (*EsA*, p. 164). And accordingly he too is completely rehabilitated in June 1875, remembered in the year of his death for his 'paysages spacieux' and the 'grandeur épique' of his ploughed fields stretching to the horizon, his profile defined for posterity as one of 'les trois principaux héros de la lutte' (*EsA*, p. 291) alongside Rousseau and Corot. In his obituary notice five months earlier, Zola's tribute to Millet is not in the least ambivalent:

> Sa grande originalité est sa rudesse pleine d'une mâle poésie; le monde des paysans dans lequel il s'est enfermé a une grandeur biblique, une simplicité du plus haut caractère; il a peint la campagne, avec sa largeur d'horizon, son odeur puissante, sa beauté souveraine. Il était un des trois ou quatre maîtres vraiment originaux de l'époque. (*EsA*, p. 638)

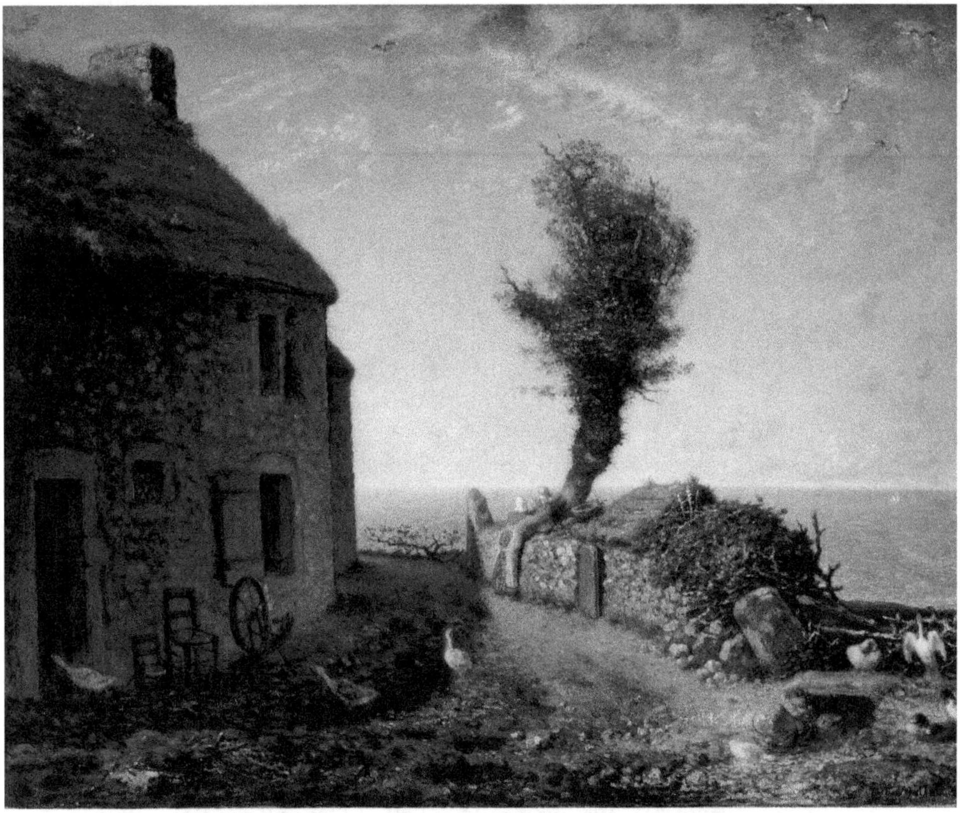

Fig. 5.2. Jean-François Millet, *Un bout de village de Gréville* (1866), oil on canvas, 81.5 × 100.5 cm. Boston Museum of Fine Arts. Gift of Quincy Adams Shaw.

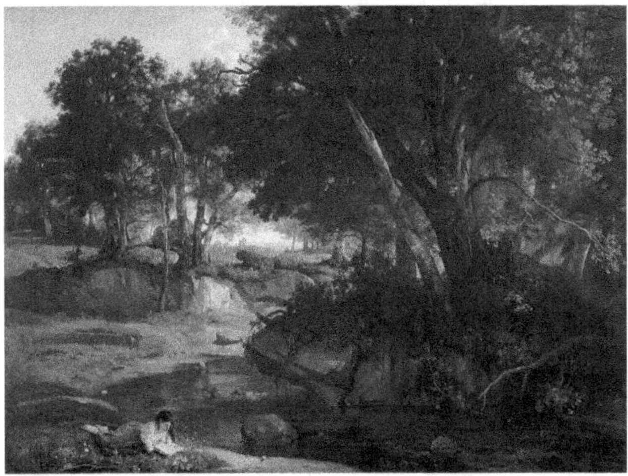

Fig. 5.3. Camille Corot, *Forêt de Fontainebleau* (1834), oil on canvas, 175.6 × 242.6 cm. National Gallery of Art, Washington DC. Chester Dale Collection.

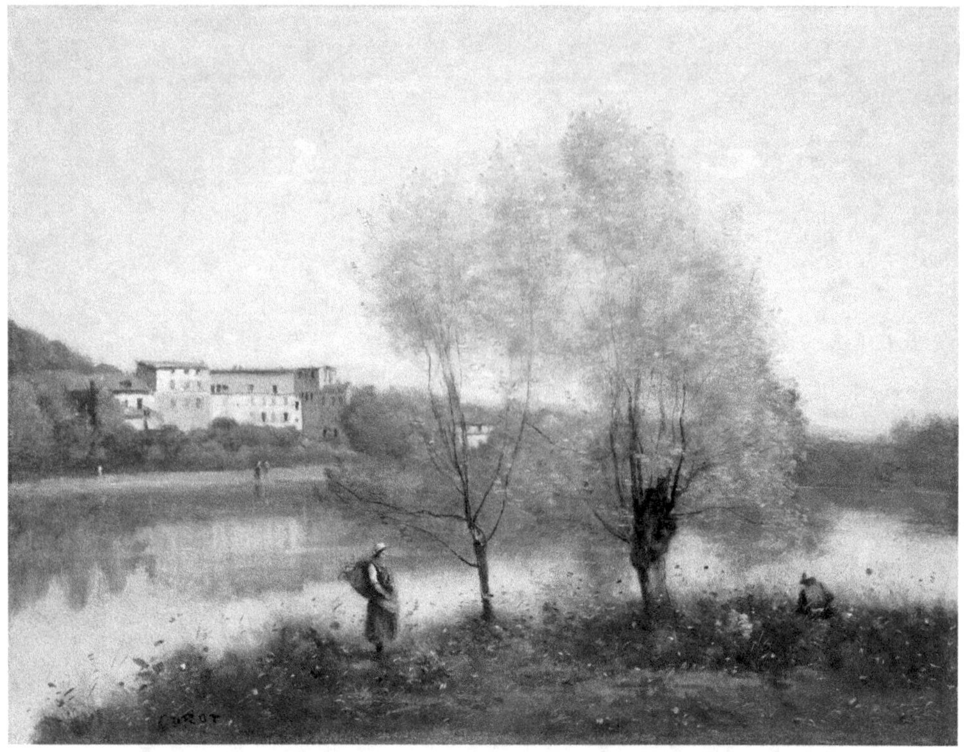

FIG. 5.4. Camille Corot, *Ville d'Avray* (*c.* 1865), oil on canvas, 49.3 × 65.5 cm. National Gallery of Art, Washington DC. Gift of Count Cecil Pecci-Blunt.

That Corot, another of the founding members of the group, 'un des maîtres du paysage moderne' (*EsA*, p. 246), should coincidentally die in the same year, only a month later,[10] doubtless enhanced Zola's revaluation of the Barbizon School: 'Théodore Rousseau, Millet, Corot, les coryphées du paysage se sont suivis coup sur coup dans la tombe. En quelques années, notre école moderne a été comme décapitée' (*EsA*, p. 267). While not being able to resist a gentle admonishment, in respect of paintings such as *Une Matinée, la danse des nymphes* (c. 1850) ('si M. Corot consentait à tuer une fois pour toutes les nymphes dont il peuple ses bois, et à les remplacer par des paysannes, je l'aimerais outre mesure' (*EsA*, p. 168)) (cf. Fig. 5.3), that did not preclude admiration for the 'toiles exquises' (*EsA*, p. 241), however diaphanous, consistently produced by 'notre grand Corot' (*EsA*, p. 323). In 1868, there were reservations about his 'prédilections pour les effets de brouillard' and his 'tons vaporeux' characteristic of 'les rêveurs et les idéalistes', just about compensated for by 'la fermeté et le gras de sa touche, le sentiment vrai qu'il a de la nature' (*EsA*, p. 196). His contemporary prestige, however, demanded a reverence further enhanced by his death on 22 February 1875: 'Aujourd'hui', as Zola wrote in *Le Sémaphore de Marseille* four days later, 'c'est un concert d'éloges universel' (*EsA*, p. 638). Even with the odd nymph and residual classical ruin, Corot's silvery rendering of *Les Plaisirs du soir*, his posthumous submission to that year's Salon, 'laisse une

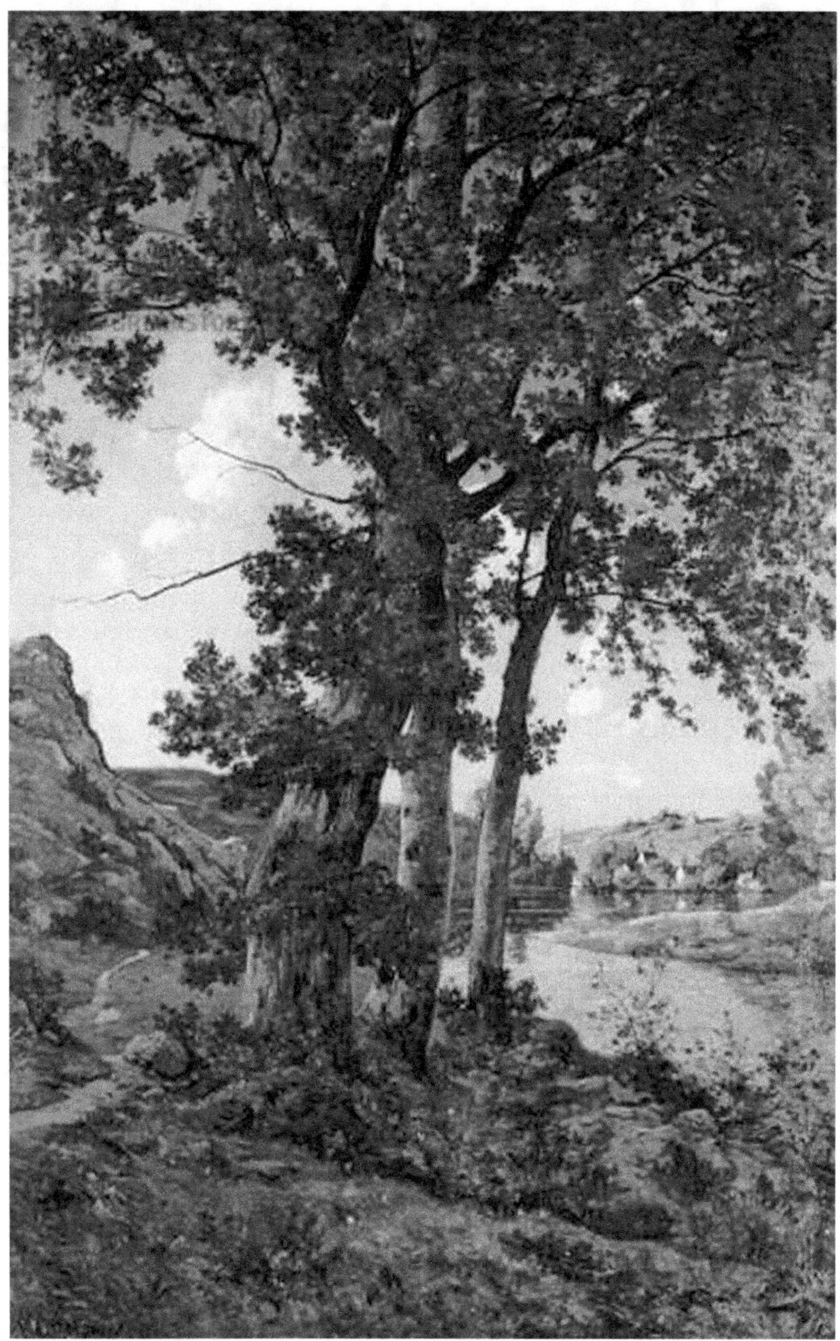

Fig. 5.5. Henri Harpignies, *Les Chênes de Château-Renard* (1875), oil on canvas, 167 × 109 cm. Musée des Beaux-Arts d'Orléans.

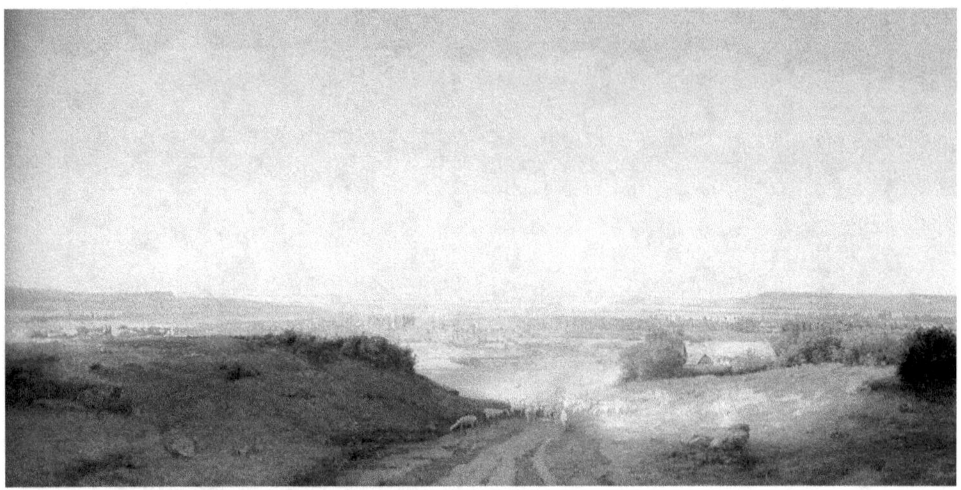

FIG. 5.6. Antoine Chintreuil, *L'Espace* (1869), oil on canvas, 102 × 204 cm. Musée d'Orsay, Paris.

profonde impression. Derrière le masque mythologique se dresse devant nous un des bois des alentours de Paris, à cette heure mélancolique où les étoiles se mettent à briller dans le ciel.' Admitting his preference in the next paragraph for paintings in which 'la nature est représentée dans toute sa simplicité', Zola nevertheless concluded that 'aucun peintre jusqu'ici n'a rendu la nature avec autant d'exactitude et de fidélité' (*EsA*, p. 546).

Following his lament in respect of the loss to French art of these three 'coryphées du paysage', Zola added: 'Aujourd'hui, les élèves seuls demeurent.' But he is so insistent on extending an unbreakable lineage that, unlike his habitual belittling of artistic successors, he is also generous to now less well-known painters following in the footsteps of the leading members of the Barbizon School. François Français (1814–1897) had blotted his copybook as surely as Rousseau by adopting the same conservative stance in the deliberations of the 1866 Salon jury,[11] but is ultimately 'un peintre qui s'est chargé d'enterrer le paysage classique' (*EsA*, p. 594). Another 'des disciples de Corot' was Henri Harpignies (1819–1916), 'le plus actif des paysagistes', with his 'toiles puissantes [...] nettes et colorées', 'un artiste que les jurys refusaient hier encore et qui est en train de devenir un maître' (*EsA*, p. 260) and whose *Les Chênes de Château-Renard* (Fig. 5.5) was described by Zola as 'magnifique de vérité' (*EsA*, p. 292). Guillemet, who had given Zola his *La Campagne à Aix* at the writer's request,[12] is also named as one of Corot's distinguished pupils. Another was Antoine Chintreuil (1814–1873), whose originality had consigned three of his paintings to the Salon des Refusés of 1863; Zola's comments on his work in 1878 are unusually detailed in singling out pictorial effects, in his *L'Espace* (Fig. 5.6),[13] anticipating with the wisdom of hindsight those of the Impressionists: 'Il s'efforçait de rendre des impressions qui échappent en partie au pinceau' such as 'une aurore trempée de rosée, ou un orage, ou un rayon de soleil filtrant à travers la pluie': 'certaines de ses toiles sont magnifiques: la nature revit en elles avec ses sons, ses parfums, ses jeux

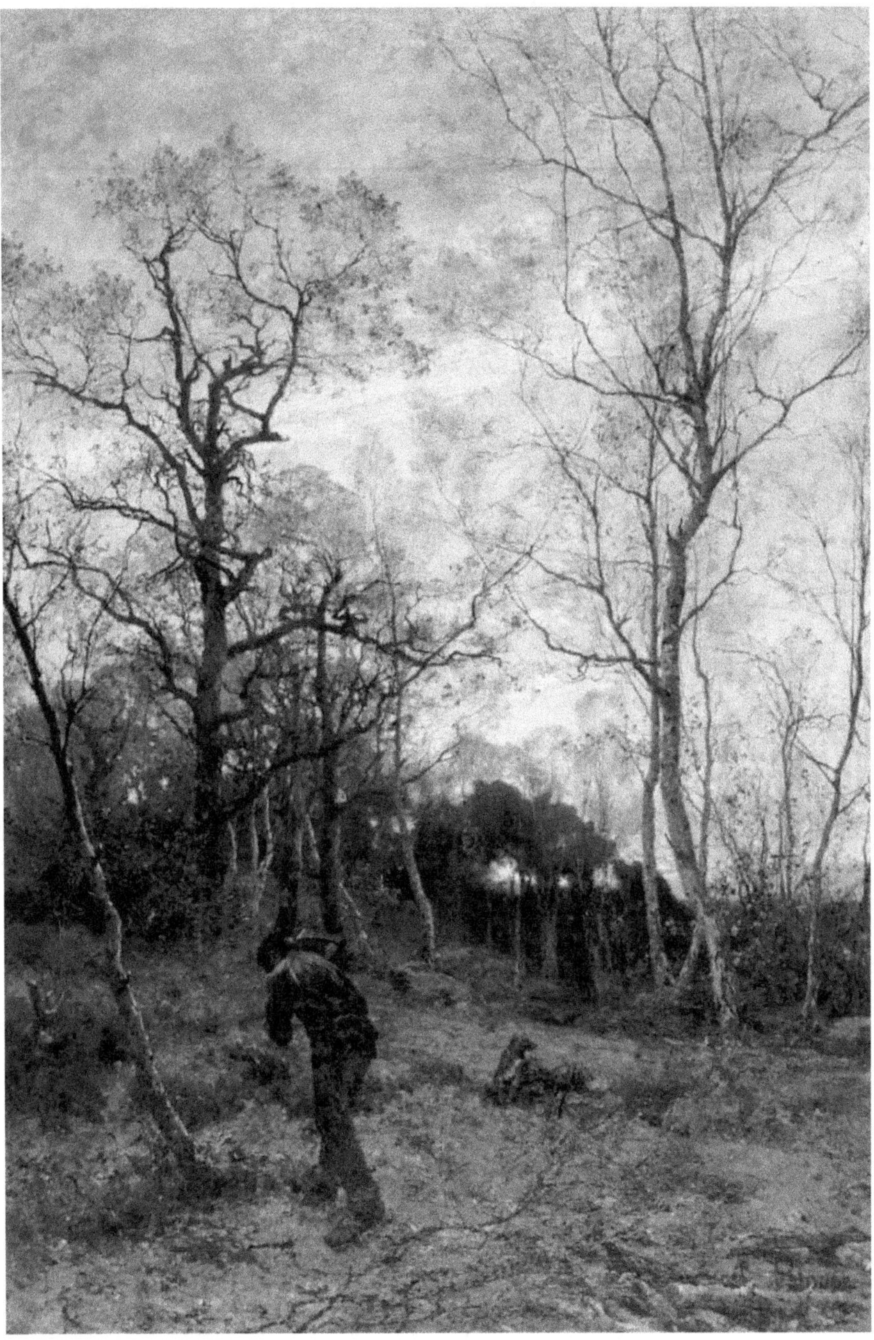

Fig. 5.7. Léon Pelouse, *Une coupe de bois à Senlisse* (1876), oil on canvas, 240 × 160 cm. Mairie de Pierrelaye, Seine et Oise.

d'ombre et de lumière' (*EsA*, p. 549). Berthe and Edma Morisot had worked with Corot at Ville d'Avray (see Fig. 5.4) in the summer of 1861, before he passed them on for further study with the Barbizon painter Achille Oudinot (1820–1891), whose work resembled his own. Although Zola may have mentioned them in his *Salon* of 1868 to please Manet, he was clearly aware of their artistic provenance: 'Corot est leur maître, à coup sûr', noting in Berthe's *Ros-Bras (Finistère)* 'une fraîcheur et une naïveté d'impression' (*EsA*, p. 197). Former members of the Barbizon School cited admiringly in Zola's art criticism include the Belgian artist César de Cock (1823–1904) and Léon Pelouse (1836–1911) whose 'tallis superbes' (Fig. 5.7) mark him out as 'un débutant d'hier en train de se mettre au premier rang' (*EsA*, p. 241), who 'peint à merveille les forêts' (*EsA*, p. 571). Even Paul Huet (1803–1869), in spite of his excesses, 'fut un des premiers à changer de manière', three of his paintings of the late 1860s testifying to the fact that 'l'amour et le respect de la nature brillent déjà chez lui à travers quelques excès romantiques' (*EsA*, p. 570). And such is the new-found dominance of the genre that Zola makes a point of referring, in the context of the Salon of 1875, to 'encore quatre ou cinq paysagistes de talent' (*EsA*, p. 292), exemplified by those working far from Fontainebleau, notably in the seascapes of Boudin, Charles Lapostolet (1824–1890) (yet another of those whose 'martyrdom' was assured for posterity by having been relegated to the Salon des Refusés), and Karl Daubigny (1816–1886).

In Praise of Daubigny

The accolade given to the last of these is instructive: 'un digne élève de son père qui fut un paysagiste des plus doués'. For there is no doubt that the father in question was by far the most important, in Zola's eyes, of the generation of landscape artists immediately prior to the emergence of the Impressionists. Daubigny *père*, an exceptionally close friend of Corot since 1849,[14] had originally gained the trust of the 'nouvelle école' of young painters by mounting in vain a rearguard action defending those of them rejected by the Salon of 1866 jury: 'Lui seul a lutté contre certains de ses collègues, au nom de la verité et de la justice' (*EsA*, p. 142). Zola must have appreciated, in particular, his much-publicized, if failed, efforts to secure the admission of Cézanne's portrait of Valabrègue, their mutual Provençal friend.[15] When he re-published in volume form his articles devoted to that year's exhibition, he prefaced *Mon Salon* with a long open letter, 'À mon ami Paul Cézanne', as mentioned in Chapter 2, designed to counter any discouragement in the face of such resistance to their shared aesthetic ideals. Nor does it seem a coincidence that, only a couple of months after Daubigny's interventions on behalf of artists whom Zola was also supporting, he should foreground his name by way of the 'anecdote', cited above, closing his review of Henriet's book. 'Cette figure sympathique' had subsequently been instrumental in persuading the jury of the 1868 Salon, much to the displeasure of the fine arts administration,[16] to admit works by Bazille, Monet, Pissarro, Renoir, Degas, Sisley and Berthe Morisot in an exhibition widely, if perhaps prematurely, seen as a revolutionary moment in the history of modern art, marking the advent of a new generation of painters: 'Le Salon de 1868', as one of the most authoritative critics of the day summatively put it, 'sera le Salon des jeunes'.[17] Daubigny, on the other hand, was already an established artist, benefitting from official approval as well as huge popular success.[18] Such a status qualified most of his peers for Zola's critical scorn. Daubigny was an exception in his ironic awareness that his best paintings were commercial failures: unlike Zola's later condemnation of Monet's 'peine de la hâte, de son besoin de vendre' (*EsA*, p. 380), 'M. Daubigny a contenté la foule sans trop se mentir à lui-même' (*EsA*, p. 168).[19] Over and above such evidence of strategic solidarity and artistic integrity, however, Daubigny's importance for Zola remained his seminal role in the development of landscape painting itself, reflected in his own distancing from an early adherence to tradition, such as his *Campagne romaine* of 1836:

> Si Corot conservait encore comme un faible écho des anciens paysages historiques, Daubigny par contre [...] hâta la révolution réaliste dans notre école. L'un des premiers, après Paul Huet qui, malgré tout, gardait dans une certaine mesure le bric-à-brac romantique, il alla dans les champs et copia le premier paysage venu. [...] Daubigny fut un déchiffreur, un maître. (*EsA*, p. 547)

The past tense, reminding his readers of Daubigny's death on 19 February 1878, further reinforced Zola's sense of the end of an era. Two years earlier, he had been described as the last survivor of the great pioneers of modern landscape: 'de la bande héroïque des conquérants il ne reste que Daubigny' (*EsA*, p. 331). The year 1878, which saw the mounting of the first Universal Exhibition since 1867, thus provided Zola with the opportunity to engage in a retrospective account of the genre's development during that interval, fortuitously bookended by the deaths of Rousseau and Daubigny. In also listing the other deceased members of the 'grande école de paysagistes', Zola stressed that 'de 1867 à 1878 ces artistes marchèrent toujours à l'avant et constituèrent la force et la beauté de notre école' (*EsA*, p. 542). While himself using, for his long review of the section devoted to French painting, the official catalogue of the 'Exposition universelle internationale', such an assertion was an absolute contradiction of its own euphoric preface which maintained that 'plus le retour des études vers la peinture historique s'accentue et se généralise, moins le salon annuel donne une idée complète de l'activité des ateliers'. But 1878 also coincided with the intensification of Zola's campaigns on behalf of Naturalism, aggressively pushing back against critics of an aesthetic increasingly dominant since the publication of *L'Assommoir*. There emerges in both his literary and art criticism a teleology dependent on an ascending line of precursors: for the novel, Balzac, Stendhal and Flaubert; for painting, artists leaving behind Romanticism and moving towards the verisimilitude of his own representation of the external world. Accordingly, Zola's quasi-Darwinian conception that 'notre école de paysage a *tué* l'école historique'[20] finds expression in a series of equivalences and analogies recruiting painters of a realist kind under the banner of a militant Naturalism. This would reach its semantic and spatial triumph in the very title of *Le Naturalisme au Salon* (1880). The landscape artists of the Barbizon School fit perfectly into Zola's signposting of that apotheosis, with its 'paysagistes innovateurs' forming a pictorial

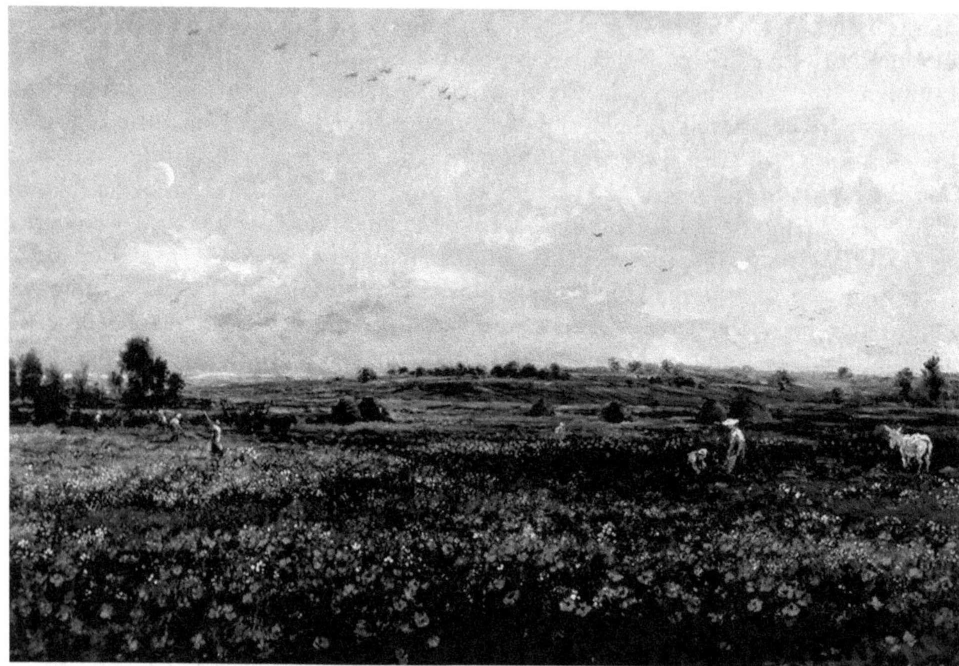

FIG. 5.8. Charles-François Daubigny, *Les Champs au mois de juin* (1874), oil on canvas, 135 × 224 cm. Herbert F. Johnson Museum of Art, Cornell University, Ithaca, New York. Gift of Louis V. Keeler, Class of 1911, and Mrs Keeler.

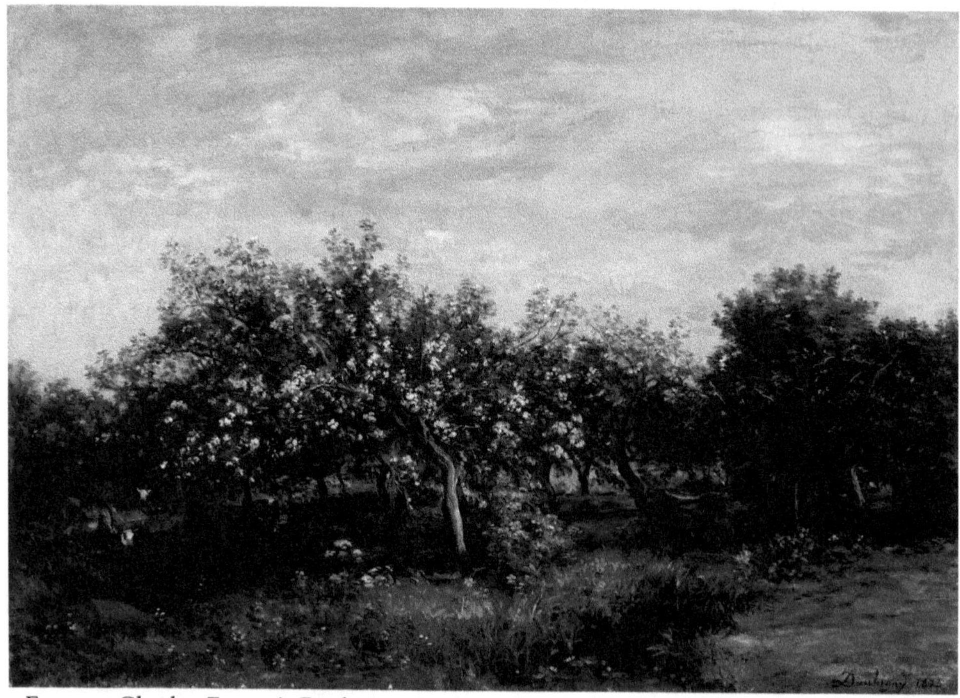

FIG. 5.9. Charles-François Daubigny, *Le Verger* (1873–76), oil on canvas, 58.7 × 84.8 cm. Metropolitan Museum of Art, New York. Bequest of Collis P. Huntingdon.

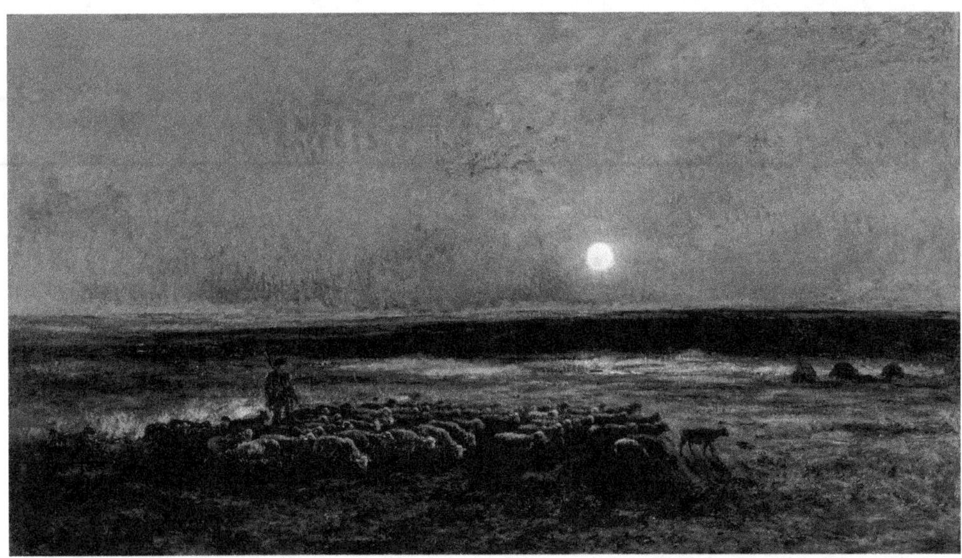

FIG. 5.10. Charles-François Daubigny, *Lever de la lune, à Auvers (Seine et Oise)* (1877), oil on canvas, 106.5 × 188 cm. Montreal Museum of Fine Arts. Gift of Lady Drummond in memory of her husband, Sir George Drummond.

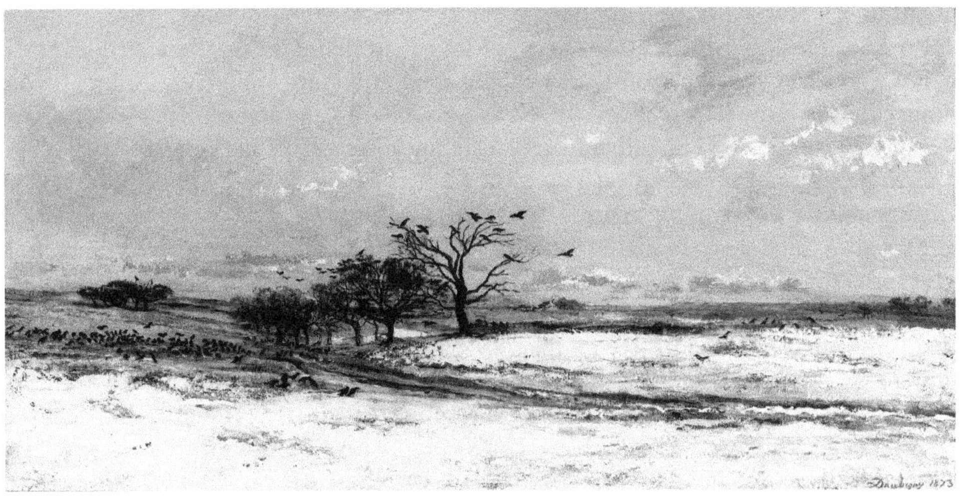

FIG. 5.11. Charles-François Daubigny, *La Neige* (1873), oil on canvas, 100.5 × 201.5 cm. Musée d'Orsay, Paris.

avant-garde in their own right. In 1875, 'le paysage classique se mourait de phtisie', its last practitioners and institutional guardians fearful lest 'le mouvement naturaliste peut s'étendre du paysage au reste de l'art' (*EsA*, p. 291). In 1878, Français, Corot and Daubigny are all inserted into 'l'histoire de notre école naturaliste du paysage' (*OC*, IX, 617), synonymous with the origins of Naturalism's irreversible advance: 'la grande révolution dans la peinture a débuté par le paysage. C'était fatal' (*EsA*, p. 569).

While it was true of some of them, it was something of a polemical sleight of hand to implicitly associate Daubigny with all modern landscape artists subject to the hostility of the Académie des Beaux-Arts. But Zola's commentary on some of his pictures suggests a genuine appreciation of 'le peintre merveilleux et véridique des bords de la Seine et de l'Oise' (*EsA*, p. 331) rather than being content with referencing him as one notable example in an extended line of precursors. As far back as 1866, long before proposing a Naturalist hegemony, Zola had alluded to his habit of painting 'avec vigueur la terre forte, le ciel profond, les arbres et les flots puissants' (*EsA*, p. 168),[21] however misleading it was to add that such an unembellished rendering of the countryside displeased the viewing public. In 1874, he singled out for praise Daubigny's *Champs au mois de juin* (Fig. 5.8), 'un champ de coquelicots, trempé de rosée' which had provoked as much enthusiasm as one of Corot's paintings 'devant lequel le public s'écrase' (*EsA*, p. 241). For his Russian readers, in a long study generated by the Salon of 1876, Zola provided details of Daubigny's favourite sites: 'Il nous a révélé les charmes des environs de Paris; il ne s'est guère éloigné à plus de trente kilomètres de la capitale, sauf pour des rares fugues en Normandie', contrasted with painters who had visited more exotic locations, such as Spain and Italy,[22] but who had 'fait moins de découvertes que lui'. Zola then waxes lyrical about his *Verger* (Fig. 5.9), with it being perhaps 'un peu noir', the only reservation he ever enunciated about any of Daubigny's paintings; 'mais quelle maîtrise dans le rendu de la verdure, quelle science de la vie arboréale. Des pommiers et des poiriers lourds de fruits se dressent devant nous, leurs troncs couverts de mousse et penchés d'un côté, leurs branches tordues.' Zola underlines its arresting realism as well as its appeal to the senses: 'Il faut connaître les petits jardinets de la banlieue Parisienne pour savourer l'impression de la vérité qui se dégage de ce tableau où l'on croit respirer la fraîcheur du feuillage, où l'on croit entendre de temps en temps, au milieu d'un profond silence, la chute étouffée d'un fruit.' Such a stress suggests the extent to which Zola's innately sympathetic response to such pictures, not vitiated by critical point-scoring, goes beyond their invulnerability to the temptations of narrative provoked by human figures: *Le Verger* invites instead a contemplation of stillness and silence. And he ends by declaring that it is 'la feuille la plus large arrachée au livre de la nature qu'on puisse voir au Salon' (*EsA*, p. 331). This kind of response is equally evident in his viewing of two of Daubigny's works displayed at the Universal Exhibition: *Lever de la lune, à Auvers (Seine-et-Oise)* (1877) (Fig. 5.10.), his very last canvas, and *La Neige* (1873) (Fig. 5.11), though both here offset, as he had to remind his Russian readers, against the sterility of conventional landscape. In the first of these, 'un tableau magnifique', 'on sent là le frémissement silencieux du soir, les derniers bruits des champs qui s'endorment. Cela donne l'impression d'une grandeur limpide, d'une tranquillité pleine de vie' (*EsA*, p. 547). *La Neige* too, with the 'points noirs' of its black crows 'immobiles et tournoyants' and gnarled trees the only focus in the featureless 'nappe blanche' of snowy foreground and background, is emotionally resonant: 'l'hiver tout entier est là devant nous. De ma vie, je n'ai rien vu de plus mélancolique: le pinceau de Daubigny, délicat plutôt que puissant, a acquis cette fois-ci une force exceptionnelle pour rendre la vue morne de nos pleines en décembre' (*EsA*, p. 548).

Towards Impressionism: Daubigny as Precursor

What is retrospectively illuminating is the relationship between the Barbizon School, and in particular Zola's privileging of Daubigny's landscapes, and his writing on Impressionism. Daubigny had been labelled as 'le chef de l'école de l'impression' as early as 1865, not least by virtue of his paintings becoming increasingly sketch-like, his fragmented brush strokes anticipating those of the Impressionists themselves, and accordingly criticized for being 'unfinished'.[23] He is today, indeed, considered their most important precursor. Even contemporary critics were aware of it: reviewing the inaugural Impressionist exhibition of 1874, Castagnary stressed that 'le non fini, après Courbet, après Daubigny, après Corot, on ne peut pas dire que les *impressionnistes* l'aient inventé'.[24] And in 1882, Huysmans was still relating Sisley's pictures at the seventh such exhibition to Daubigny.[25] Though never formally associated with the group at the time of the drafting of the founding statutes of the *Société anonyme coopérative des artistes-peintres, sculpteurs, graveurs, etc.* in December 1873 and their subsequent organizing of the three Impressionist exhibitions held between 1874 and his death in 1878, Daubigny's personal contacts with its members were significant. For his repeated efforts to secure their admission to the annual Salon were unsurprising. He had known Monet and Berthe Morisot since 1863. Guillemet became a close friend, accompanying him on excursions in his floating studio, as well as forming an important link between Daubigny and the painters meeting at the café Guerbois before 1870. Following the disappointments of the 1867 Salon, Bazille had the idea, never realized, of mounting a private exhibition, securing Daubigny's agreement to include some of his pictures, alongside those of Corot and Diaz. In London, to which they had retreated during the Franco-Prussian War (1870–71), it was Daubigny who introduced both Monet and Pissarro to Durand-Ruel. It is not axiomatic, however, that such artistic networks persuaded Zola to establish an evolutionary link between the older and younger generations of landscape painters. The nearest he gets to it is in allusions to the 'impression d'une grandeur limpide' (*EsA*, p. 547) or the 'impression de vérité' generated by Daubigny's rural scenes. In commenting on his *Lever de la lune*, at the Salon of 1877, Zola speaks of 'une impression de grandeur et de mélancolie superbe' (*EsA*, p. 350). But it hardly seems by chance that, in his Salon of 1866, he immediately follows remarks about Daubigny with his first-ever focus on Pissarro and his talent for representing 'franchement la nature', introduced by way of a prefatory 'trois paysagistes que j'aime: MM. Corot, Daubigny et Pissarro' (*EsA*, pp. 167–68).

Pissarro

Although the thematic and stylistic continuities between the work of Daubigny and that of the early Pissarro were more explicit than Zola probably knew,[26] they do serve to explain why it should have been that, at such an early date, he set himself up as the first critical champion of the latter: 'M. Pissarro est un inconnu, dont personne ne parlera sans doute' (*EsA*, p. 168). It is doubly ironic that this claim ignored the fact that, seven years before, Astruc had complemented substantive remarks on Daubigny by sketching a couple of pages inspired by Pissarro's *Paysage de Montmorency*, without mentioning the artist by name, at the Salon of 1859.[27] Zola had overreached himself much in the same way as he did in declaring his originality in writing about Manet, when in fact it was Astruc who had preceded him in that case too. Pissarro posed a different problem for the polemicist in the sense that he was far less controversial, having had his submissions accepted for the Salons of 1859, 1864, 1865 and 1866. Two more of his paintings were shown at that of 1868. Zola could only highlight at that point the apparent inconsistencies in the criteria applied by the admissions jury which had led to his exclusion from those in between, 'refusé à certains Salons, reçu à certains autres' (*EsA*, p. 182).

What is certain is that Zola's praise for Pissarro's early landscapes is, except contextually, as devoid of polemical intent as his enthusiasm for Daubigny's pictures, contrasting the arbitrary processes of the Salon jury with the consistency of Pissarro's perspective: 'c'était toujours la même interprétation austère de la nature'; 'ses toiles manquent de tout pétard, de toute sauce épicée relevant la nature trop puissante et trop âcre dans sa réalité' (*EsA*, pp. 182–83). In looking briefly at Pissarro's *Bords de Marne en hiver* (1866) (Fig. 5.12), he had been struck by its structural simplicity: 'un simple bout d'avenue, puis un coteau au fond, des champs vides jusqu'à l'horizon' (*EsA*, p. 169). What he underlines in the painter's two submissions to the Salon of 1868, *La Côte du Jallais* (Fig. 5.13) and *L'Hermitage* (also known as *L'Hermitage à Pontoise*) are again their 'aspect presque triste' and their refusal to indulge in signifying detail, 'sans chercher à y mettre le moindre régal de son invention, il n'est ni poète ni philosophe'. In other words, their excellence lies in their refusal to indulge in a 'peinture à idées'. Their surfaces are 'ternes, grises, mal léchées, grossières et rudes'. They are distinguished by 'l'austérité des horizons' and their 'nudité désolante'. And Zola's response to the 'ampleur magistrale' of their verisimilitude is almost exactly that inspired in him by Daubigny's sentient landscapes: 'On y entend les voix profondes de la terre, on y devine la vie puissante des arbres [...], et l'on se croirait en face de la large campagne' (*EsA*, p. 184). When it comes to looking at the two paintings in greater detail, Zola states his preference for *La Côte du Jallais*, notwithstanding the 'verdure pleine de sève' and the 'horizon vaste' of *L'Hermitage*. The former, it has been pointed out, explores 'the full compositional possibilities of a type of landscape essayed by Corot [...] and by Daubigny',[28] the latter as recently as 1866. For Zola, it was less its format than its evocative power which was worthy of note: 'on sent que l'homme a passé, fouillant le sol, le découpant, attristant les horizons'. Zola concludes this extended analysis by stating that 'c'est là la campagne moderne', precisely of the kind that he had contrasted to the anachronisms of academic landscape in his commentary on the painters of the Barbizon School (*EsA*, p. 186).

The two Pontoise landscapes given to Zola by Pissarro were not merely a token of a personal friendship stretching back to 1863, but almost certainly a gesture of gratitude for the pioneering public support which did much to establish his profile. Writing to Duret the day after his article devoted to Pissarro's two submissions to the Salon of 1868, Zola could not resist asking: 'Avez-vous vu les tableaux de Camille Pissarro, et êtes vous de mon avis?'[29] More curious, at first sight, is that

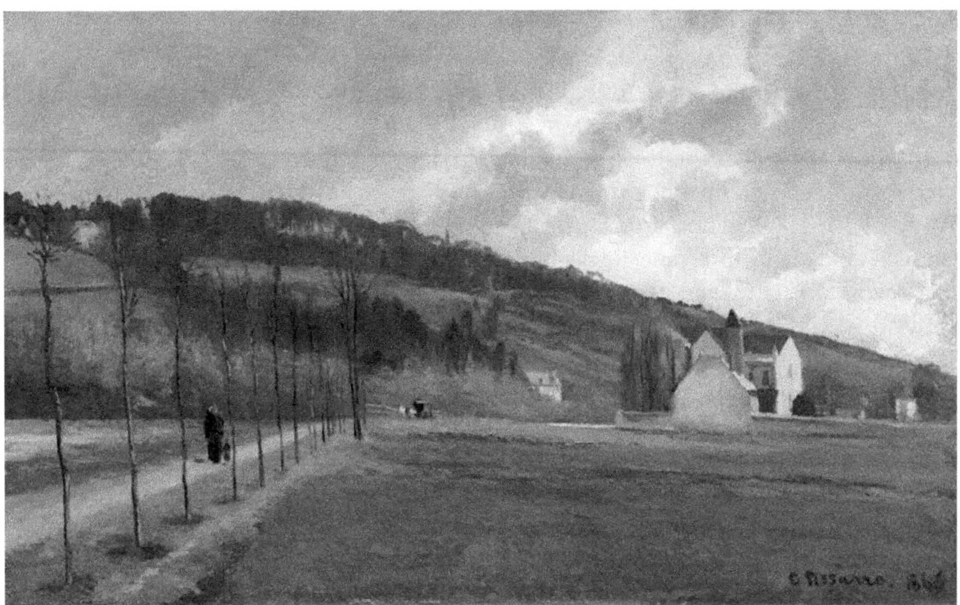

FIG. 5.12. Camille Pissarro, *Bords de Marne en hiver* (1866), oil on canvas, 91.8 × 150.2 cm. Art Institute of Chicago. Gift of Mr and Mrs Lewis L. Coburn.

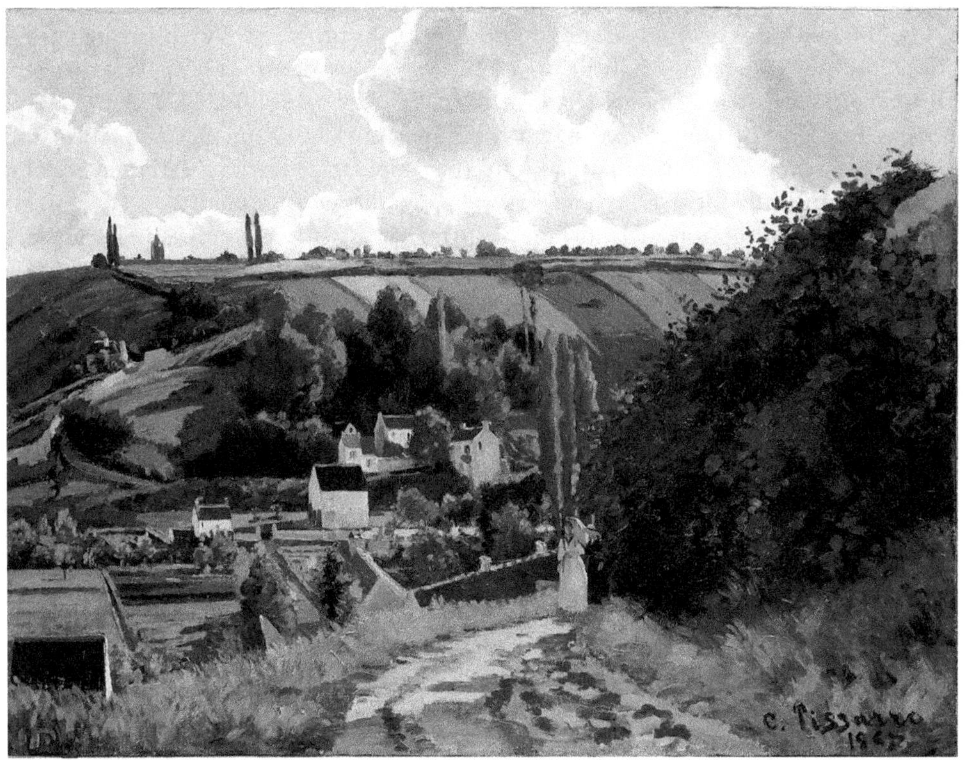

FIG. 5.13. Camille Pissarro, *La Côte du Jallais* (1867), oil on canvas, 87 × 114.9 cm. Metropolitan Museum of Art, New York. Bequest of William Church Osborn.

over the next three decades, Zola would never again focus on the qualities of a specific Pissarro painting. His name appears intermittently as one of the group of Impressionists. And Zola seems content to have recourse to generalizations about his departure from pictorial convention, some of which are ambiguous enough to place a question mark over the hypothesis that Pissarro had been so successfully recruited to the Naturalist campaign that there was no further need to illustrate his adherence to it.[30] In an 1876 article in *Le Messager de l'Europe*, he writes of Sisley having des 'moyens plus équilibrés que Pissarro', at the same time as insisting that the latter is 'un révolutionnaire plus farouche encore que Monet' (*EsA*, pp. 342–43). In 1879, he briefly alludes to 'Pissarro, dont les recherches scrupuleuses produisent parfois une impression de vérité hallucinante' (*EsA*, p. 355). As the notion of 'recherches scrupuleuses' barely disguises an antipathy to theoretically-grounded innovation which other critical texts elaborate more explicitly, that of 'vérité hallucinante' signals the distance from the 'vérité pure et éternelle' (*EsA*, p. 184) which, a decade earlier, Zola had highlighted in Pissarro's prosaic representation of reality. For the reference to Pissarro's 'revolutionary' status is primarily aimed at his increasingly *pointilliste* manner. And Zola could hardly have been unaware of Pissarro landscapes in the 1870s being very different from those like *La Côte du Jallais* and *L'Hermitage*. Ideologically inflected, the horizons previously admired by Zola for their 'austérité' were now stained with the markers of an encroaching capitalist society; and, as well as his indicative factory chimneys polluting the sky, Pissarro's waterways are a hive of industrial activity. Daubigny, by contrast, progressively eliminated from his landscapes such signs of disturbance. What had disappeared from Pissarro's was that timeless 'grandeur épique' (*EsA*, p. 184), the very term used of Millet (*EsA*, p. 291), which Zola had found in Pissarro's paintings of 1866–68 indebted to Corot and Daubigny, a quasi-Arcadian realm akin to that popularized by the Barbizon School, with its uninhabited forests, tranquil rivers and shimmering ponds.[31]

For Zola's conception of landscape painting (the genre encompassing seascapes and cityscapes as well as depictions of the countryside) is simple or, alternatively, simplistic. His advocacy of working *en plein air*, with artists registering an authentic optical experience of the external world rather than one merely imagined within the confines of a studio,[32] finds its most unproblematic and nostalgic expression in his evocation, as late as 1878, of the Barbizon painters setting off with their palettes and easels, 'plantant des chevalets en pleine campagne' (*EsA*, p. 392), as he had ten years earlier evoked them, 'la boîte sur le dos, heureux comme des chasseurs qui aiment le plein air' (*EsA*, p. 193), 'pour peindre sur nature [...] en quête de nouveaux horizons' (*EsA*, p. 617). The painters he continues to celebrate are those faithful to such an ideal. And this hierarchy is indirectly confirmed, it can be suggested, by his personal tastes[33] — testifying to a residual Romantic vision of the countryside[34] shared by so many contemporary inhabitants of an ever-expanding, and unbearably crowded, Paris — at least judging by the titles of works in his possession such as those by Robert (*Route dans la campagne*) and Béliard (*Dans le parc*), both of whom had participated in the inaugural Impressionist exhibition of 1874.[35] Béliard, a painter now more or less forgotten,[36] also contributed to the second such exhibition two years later, offering Zola the opportunity to praise yet again pictures by 'un copiste soigneux de la nature', characterized by their timelessness, not least riverbank scenes clearly indebted to Daubigny: 'Certains de ses paysages: *La Rue de Chaufour à Étampes*, les *Bords de l'Oise*, *La Rue Dorée à Pontoise*, sont des pages excellentes, solidement bâties, d'une tonalite extrêmement juste, qui arrivent jusqu'au trompe-l'œil, tant elles sont fidèles' (*EsA*, p. 584).[37]

Jongkind

Equally revealing in this respect is Zola's admiration for the cityscapes of Johan-Bartold Jongkind (1819–1891). The one he owned was given to him by the artist as a way of thanking Zola for the long study he had devoted to the painter in *La Cloche* of 24 January 1872.[38] He had earlier included Jongkind, lodged between Pissarro and Corot within a survey of innovatory landscape painting, in his *Salon* of 1868. The term 'impression' is used twice in underlining that 'il voit un paysage d'un coup, dans la réalité de son ensemble, et il le traduit à sa façon, en conservant la vérité et en lui communiquant l'émotion qu'il a ressentie'. It is this stress on a sentient landscape, *not* found in Béliard's provincial scenes, which reminds us of Zola's response to the Barbizon School. In Jongkind's submission to that year's Salon, Zola finds evidence of 'un maître intime qui pénètre avec une rare souplesse dans la vie multiple de la nature', marvelling at his ability to 'rendre le ciel et la terre avec cet apparent désordre': 'Ici, tout est original, le métier, l'impression, et tout est vrai parce que le paysage entier a été pris dans la réalité avant d'avoir été vécu par un homme' (*EsA*, pp. 195–96). Zola's 1872 essay, prefaced by his rehearsal of the context ('le paysage classique est mort, tué par la vérité') without which Jongkind's originality could not be understood, amplifies the thrust of his earlier commentary, but now energized by a recent visit to the painter's studio. He finds in his canvases 'cet amour du Paris moderne' which he shares. But, and crucially, Zola is drawn to the fact that the painter 'a compris que Paris reste pittoresque jusque dans ses décombres', the anecdotal details of his *Saint-Médard et la rue Mouffetard* (1868), for example, both registering historical specificity and conjuring up, in its emotional resonance, the spectator's own urban experience not limited to a particular moment or location. Zola's response is grounded in both affinity and absorption: 'Cette œuvre me va au cœur. Le grand ciel nuageux a l'odeur des pluies de Paris. J'y respire la vie de nos jours, je me rappelle des après-midi attristés, de longues courses faites à travers la ville, toute mon existence de Parisien.' Amongst the works Zola singles out for comment is yet another of Jongkind's returns (Fig. 5.14), in an 'étude' seen in his studio, to the iconic site of Le Pont-Neuf: 'au fond, la Cité; des chevaux se baignent dans l'abreuvoir, au pied de l'escalier du quai; on devine Paris bourdonnant au-dessus de cette rivière tranquille.' For that is what most of the painter's evocative cityscapes do: often focused on Notre-Dame, viewed from the banks of the Seine (Fig. 5.15), [39] and devoid of narrative or critical intent, they create an *atmosphere*, 'un poème de joie ou de mélancolie', capturing the *essence* of the city. And that achievement, Zola reminds himself more than once, is inseparable

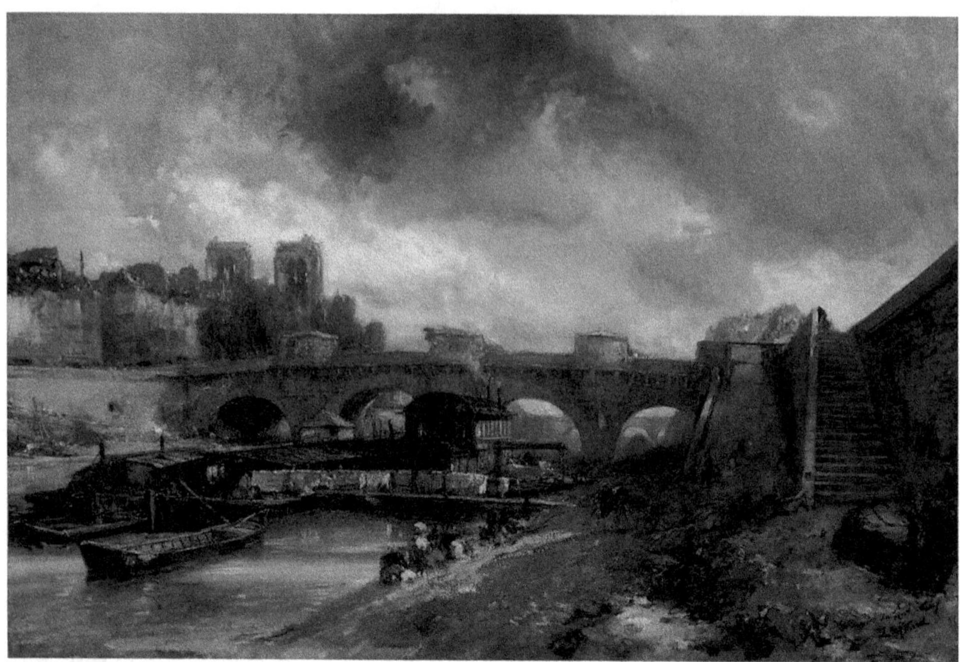

FIG. 5.14. Johan-Barthold Jongkind, *Le Pont neuf* (1849–50), oil on canvas, 54.6 × 81.6 cm. Metropolitan Museum of Art, New York. Gift of Mr and Mrs Walter Mendelsohn.

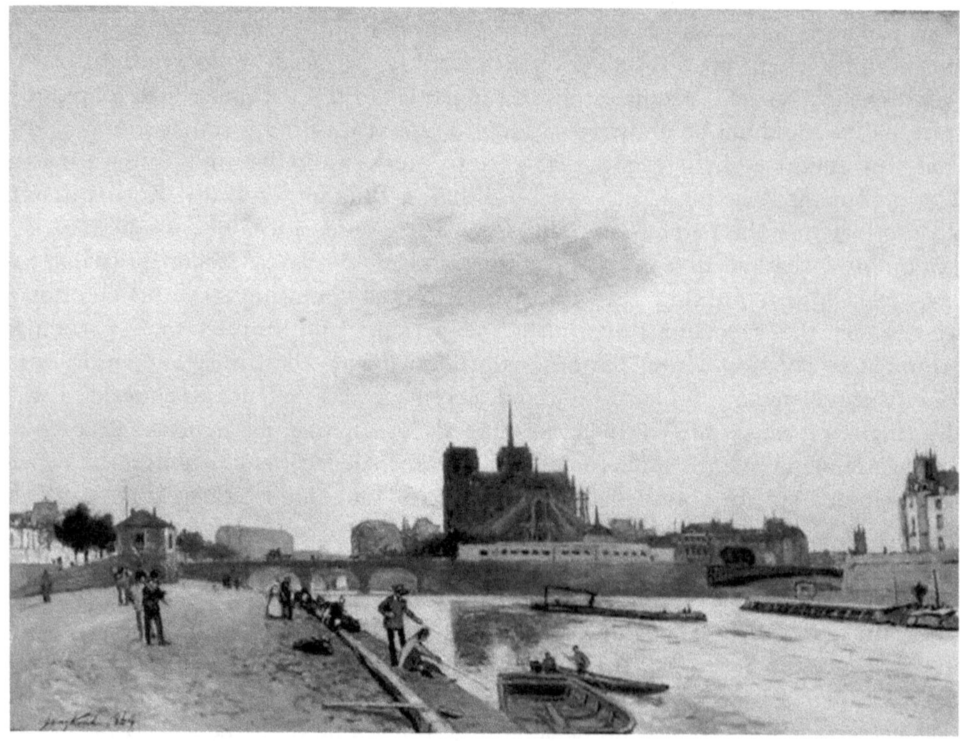

FIG. 5.15. Johan-Bartold Jongkind, *Notre-Dame de Paris, vue du quai de la Tournelle* (1864), oil on canvas, 42.5 × 56.5 cm. Private collection.

from Jongkind's 'largeurs étonnantes, des simplifications suprêmes', the apparent 'ébauches jetées en quelques heures, par crainte de laisser échapper l'impression première', in fact the result of precisely what he would in due course accuse the Impressionists of lacking: 'La vérité est que l'artiste travaille longuement ses toiles, pour arriver à cette extrême simplicité et à cette finesse inouïe' (*EsA*, pp. 502–04).

Zola's Landscape Preferences: From Corot to Monet

Another recurrent feature of Zola's writing on landscape is his focus on the elements, the 'éternelles sources de l'observation et de l'analyse' (*EsA*, p. 392): unchanging nature, the sky and the clouds. Foregrounded in his study of Jongkind is the attention he pays to the effects of light on water. He makes a special note of such technical brilliance exemplified in a range of painters: Corot's 'eau dormante' (*EsA*, p. 196); Daubigny's 'vapeurs argentées des brouillards s'élevant du fleuve' (*EsA*, p. 547); Guillemet's 'marines admirables' (*EsA*, p. 571) and his pictures of the Seine; Sisley's *Inondation à Port-Marly* (1876); Béliard's riversides; Boudin's 'horizons humides de l'eau' (*EsA*, p. 199); Berthe Morisot's seascapes 'exécutées avec une finesse étonnante' (*EsA*, p. 342), one of which (*Femme et fillette au bord de la plage*) he would secure in 1877; even the 'reflets exquis dans la rivière' (*EsA*, p. 201) occupying the bottom third of Degas's *Portrait de Mlle E. F.: à propos du ballet de 'la Source'* (1867–68).[40] In Jongkind's depictions of his native Holland, Zola is charmed by 'les eaux blafardes des temps gris et les eaux gaies et miroitantes des jours de soleil' (*EsA*, pp. 502–03); in those of Paris, 'la bande moirée de la Seine dont l'eau verdâtre est tachée du noir de suie des chalands'. His submission to the Salon of 1868 (*Vue de la rivière d'Overschie, près Rotterdam*) is, in Zola's estimation, simply marvellous: 'l'eau bavarde et miroite au premier plan', while the red tiles of the houses 'se reflètent dans la rivière transparente qui prend des tons roses' (*EsA*, p. 195).

But it is in the early work of Monet, above all, that Zola gives the fullest expression to such enthusiasm. While he makes a point of defending paintings of other kinds against contemporary criticism (*La Femme à la robe verte*, for example, at the Salon of 1866), it is the artist's rendering of rivers and the sea which most engage him. Within the argument informing this chapter, it seems wonderfully apt that the one Monet painting which Zola owned was his *Promenade en rivière* (1876), otherwise known as *Le Bateau-Atelier* (Fig. 5.16), indebted in more ways than one to Daubigny; all the more so, one might add, given Monet's only intermittent acknowledgement of such a debt.[41] It was in 1868 that Zola started to look at Monet's work with serious attention (*EsA*, pp. 187–92). Given his preference for pristine landscapes uncluttered by human figures, satisfying 'nos besoins de nature vierge', and although he makes amends by subsequently praising the dappled trees and play of light in the artist's gardens and orchards, one detects a certain irony in the remark that 'Claude Monet préférera un parc anglais à un coin de forêt [...], ne peut peindre un paysage sans y mettre des messieurs et des dames en toilette. La nature paraît perdre de son intérêt pour lui, dès qu'elle ne porte pas l'empreinte

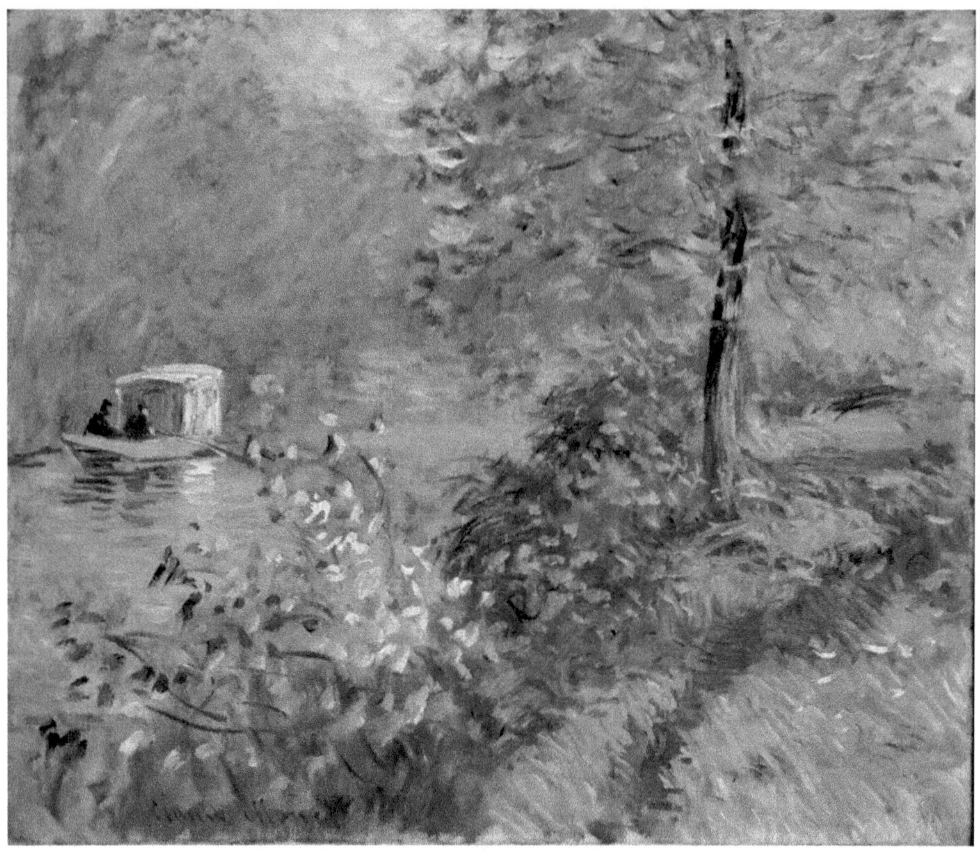

FIG. 5.16. Claude Monet, *Le Bateau-atelier* (1876), oil on canvas, 54.5 × 65.3 cm. Musée d'art et d'histoire de Neuchâtel. Gift of Yvan and Hélène Amez-Droz.

de nos mœurs'.[42] On the other hand, Zola was so permanently enchanted by his depiction of flowing water that, in taking notes on the view of the Île de la Cité in *L'Œuvre*, more than fifteen years later, he visualized 'la Seine vide, verte, petites vagues *à la Monet*, flot dansant, fouetté de blanc, de gris, de rose, reflets multicolores' (Ms 10316, fol. 436; my emphasis). As he wrote in his *Salon* of 1868: 'il y a en lui un peintre de marines de premier ordre'; 'il est un des seuls peintres qui sachent peindre l'eau; sans transparence niaise, sans reflets menteurs. Chez lui, l'eau est vivante, profonde, vraie surtout.' Contemplating the Monet painting admitted to that year's exhibition, *Navires sortant des jetées du Havre* (1867), Zola is immersed in a *sensory* experience akin to that provoked in him by the other landscape artists he likes best: 'l'eau est âcre; l'horizon s'étend avec âpreté; on sent que la haute mer est là, qu'un coup de vent rendrait le ciel noir et les vagues blafardes, [...] nous entendons la voix sourde et haletante du vapeur qui emplit l'air de sa fumée nauséabonde. J'ai vu ces tons crus; j'ai respiré ces senteurs salées.' The water itself is the very opposite of 'l'eau factice [...] des peintres de marine en chambre': 'elle

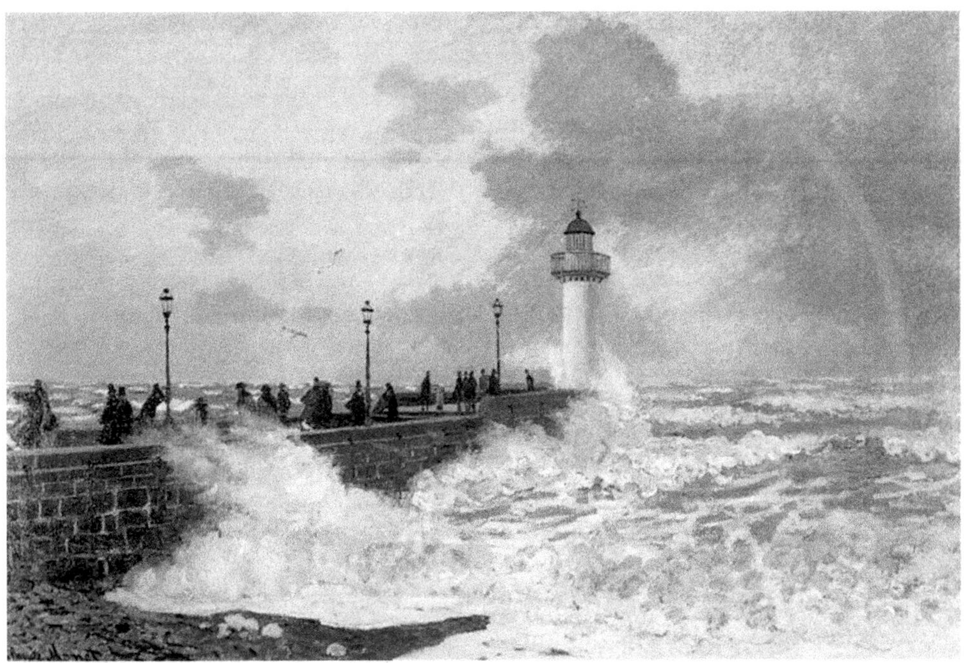

FIG. 5.17. Claude Monet, *La Jetée du Havre* (1868), oil on canvas, 147 × 226 cm. Private collection.

clapote autour des barques avec de petits flots verdâtres, coupés de lueurs blanches, elle s'étend en mares glauques [...]; elle allonge les mâts qu'elle reflète en brisant leur image, elle a des teintes blafardes et ternes qui s'illuminent de clartés aiguës' (*EsA*, pp. 188–89). And, inevitably (given the polemical stakes), Zola claims that Monet's *rejected* submission, *La Jetée du Havre* (1868) (Fig. 5.17) is even more characteristic of his talent, with its 'vagues sales, ces poussées d'eau terreuse qui ont dû épouvanter le jury habitué aux petits flots bavards et miroitants des marines en sucre candi'.

From this point onwards, Monet's status, in Zola's eyes, seems assured. By the time of the second Impressionist exhibition, in 1876, 'M. Claude Monet est certainement un des chefs du groupe' (*EsA*, p. 342), not least, of course, as a result of his unwillingness to seek admission to the official Salons of 1872 and 1873 while simultaneously plotting the independent exhibition mounted in April 1874. It was probably this laudatory comment of 1876 which occasioned Monet's gift of the painting, mentioned above, which remained in Zola's private collection until his death. In his review of the third such exhibition, in 1877, Monet is 'la personnalité la plus accentuée du groupe' (*EsA*, p. 589). By 1880, he is 'le chef des impressionnistes' (*EsA*, p. 372). Of those shown in 1876, justifying these claims on Zola's part, the picture which generates the most sustained appreciation is the painter's *La Prairie*, 'une petite toile, rien qu'une nappe d'herbe avec deux ou trois arbres se découpant sur le bleu du ciel' (*EsA*, p. 585), exemplifying more generally the stunning particularities of his landscapes. Even when Zola begins to voice reservations about his work, notably in *Le Naturalisme au Salon*, where he writes that Monet 'n'a pas la note distinguée de M. Manet, il peint lourdement les figures', he adds: 'mais c'est un paysagiste incomparable, d'une clarté et d'une vérité de tons superbes. Il y a surtout en lui un peintre de marines merveilleux; l'eau dort, coule, chante dans ses tableaux, avec une réalité de reflets et de transparence que je n'ai vue nulle part' (*EsA*, p. 380).

Disenchantment: Zola and the (In)directions of Impressionism in the Late 1870s

The inadequacy of Monet's painting of human figures, however, are the least of Zola's reservations. To be sure, he parenthetically expresses his admiration for his *Lavacourt* (1880), the painting marking Monet's return to the official Salon, 'un bout de Seine, avec une île au milieu, et les quelques maisons blanches d'un village sur la berge de droite', with its 'note exquise de lumière et de plein air' (*EsA*, p. 379). But this comes immediately after a devastating passage, in this same text of 1880, devoted to the Impressionist movement as a whole: 'j'entends m'occuper ici plus de l'impressionnisme que des impressionnistes'. Cast in the past tense, justified by its members now going their separate ways ('leur groupe paraît avoir vécu'), Zola's overview affords him the opportunity to provide an abbreviated critical history of the movement's origins and development. This starts, of course, with the 'revolutionary' quitting of the studio 'où les peintres se sont claquemurés depuis tant de siècles, et d'aller peindre en plein air, simple fait dont les conséquences sont considérables' (*EsA*, pp. 373–74). And it is the stress on those consequences which reveals how far Zola's attitude had shifted since 1876. In his review of that year's Impressionist exhibition, he had underlined that the true originality of the 'nouvelle école' was to be found in 'une décomposition de la lumière s'irisant de toutes les couleurs du prisme' and 'dans l'étude de la vraie lumière et du plein air', citing Monet's *La Prairie*, in which 'la décolorisation des verts et des bleus au grand soleil [...] prend une intensité de lumière aveuglante' (*EsA*, p. 585). Four years later, in repeating this explanation of 'ses milles décompositions et recompositions', Zola's perspective on a transitory light's 'effets multiples qui diversifient et transforment radicalement les aspects des choses et des êtres' is more double-edged. The most overt concern is the unfinished and sketch-like qualities of paintings which, ironically enough, had long been the target of Impressionism's detractors. As Zola admitted in 1880, 'les plaisantins de la presse' had caricatured 'le peintre impressionniste saisissant au vol des impressions, en quatre coups de pinceau informes; et il faut avouer que certains artistes ont justifié malheureusement ces attaques, en se contentant d'ébauches trop rudimentaires'. Without denying the validity of capturing 'la nature dans l'impression d'une minute; seulement, il faut bien fixer à jamais cette minute sur la toile, par une facture largement étudiée. En définitive, en dehors du travail, il n'y a pas de solidité possible' (*EsA*, p. 374). Monet seemed to Zola the most culpable in this respect: his leadership of the movement

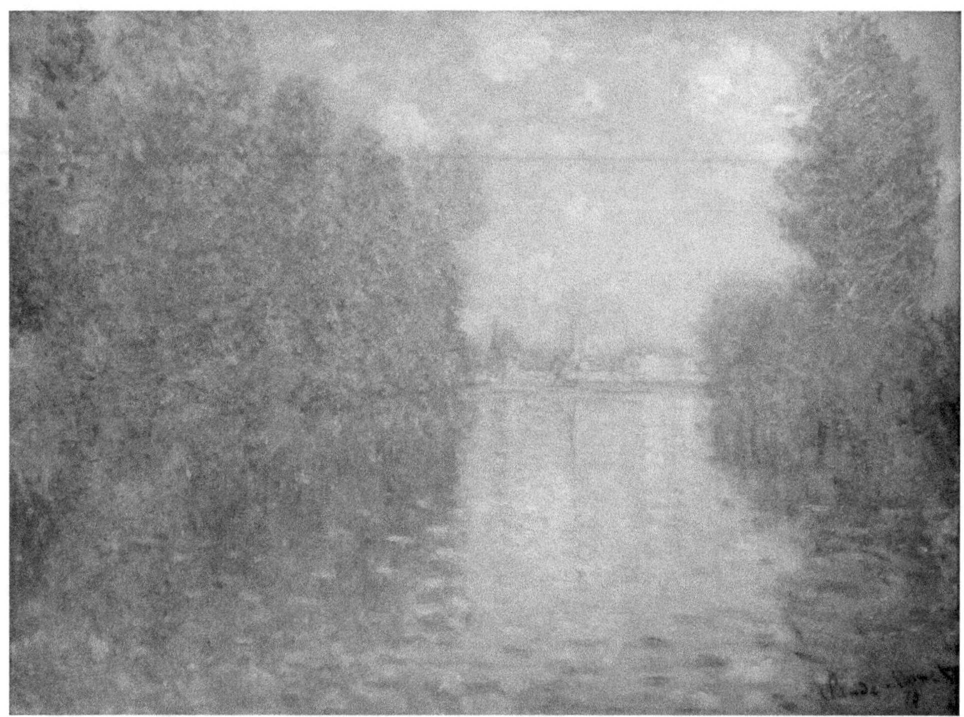

FIG. 5.18. Claude Monet, *Effet d'automne* (1873), oil on canvas, 55 × 74.5 cm. Courtauld Institute of Art, London.

'n'avait pas été heureuse pour lui'; he had 'trop cédé à sa facilité de production'; his 'esquisses à peine sèches' were at odds with 'le goût des morceaux longuement étudiées'; his own 'ébauches' revealed him to be 'sur la pente de la pacotille' (*EsA*, p. 380).[43] We need only look at a couple of Monet's paintings between 1873 (Fig. 5.18) and 1885 (Fig. 5.19) to understand Zola's increasingly severe remarks. Guillemet, by contrast, whose 'technique s'est perfectionnée et son amour de la vérité est resté le même', had had the good sense, according to Zola, to distance himself from 'un groupe de jeunes artistes révolutionnaires qui se piquaient de n'exécuter que des esquisses; plus le côté technique était maladroit et plus bruyamment on vantait le tableau' (*EsA*, p. 332).[44]

But this emphasis on the Impressionists' technical insufficiencies barely masks a more fundamental objection, namely the erosion of verisimilitude. Such a criterion informs Zola's assessment of landscape artists from his characterization of Daubigny as the 'peintre merveilleux et *véridique*' of the Seine and the Oise, to Guillemet's consistent 'amour de la *vérité*' and 'la religion du *vrai*' (*EsA*, p. 392, my emphases). The Impressionists' apparent abandonment of this pictorial principle was perceived by Zola as a betrayal as much as a disappointment. All the more so, it can be argued, because it coincided with the most militant phase of his Naturalist campaign, itself intensified by an awareness of a contemporary *mise en question* of the aesthetic he

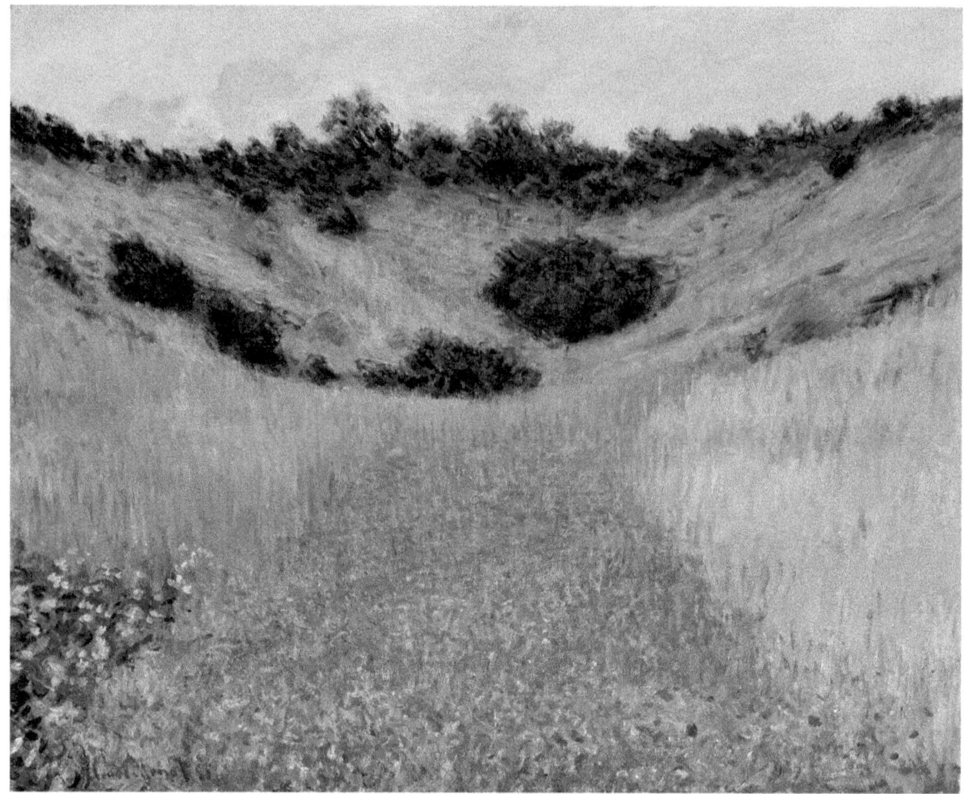

FIG. 5.19. Claude Monet, *Champ de coquelicots dans un creux près de Giverny* (1885), oil on canvas, 65.1 × 81.3 cm. Boston Museum of Fine Arts.

had propounded in both his critical writing and his fiction. Landscape had seemed to Zola the genre which heralded the ultimate dominance of that aesthetic. Its decreasing prevalence at the annual Salon, noted by Zola from 1876 onwards, was a matter of regret. 'Ce que Corot a fait pour le paysage, il faut que quelque grand artiste le fasse pour le reste de l'art: aujourd'hui déjà', he wrote in 1875, 'on peint des arbres vivants; bientôt on peindra des hommes vivants' (*EsA*, p. 271). Suggesting that not even Manet had achieved that yet, he repeated that this remained the challenge: 'Maintenant, il reste à opérer une révolution semblable dans les autres domaines de la peinture' (*EsA*, p. 293). He would repeat this word for word in his review of the Salon of 1881, still adding that 'c'est à peine si la lutte s'engage, et il faudra peut-être encore toute la fin du siècle' (*EsA*, p. 400). In *Le Naturalisme au Salon*, provisional victory had already been declared, referring specifically to the painters of the landscape: 'ici, la bataille naturaliste est gagnée depuis longtemps'. But such is Zola's triumphalist confidence in 'ce souffle de naturalisme qui transforme les lettres et les arts' (*EsA*, p. 391), that he indiscriminately extends its reach to the majority of artists of his time.[45] Even Bastien-Lepage had left behind his academic training 'pour se

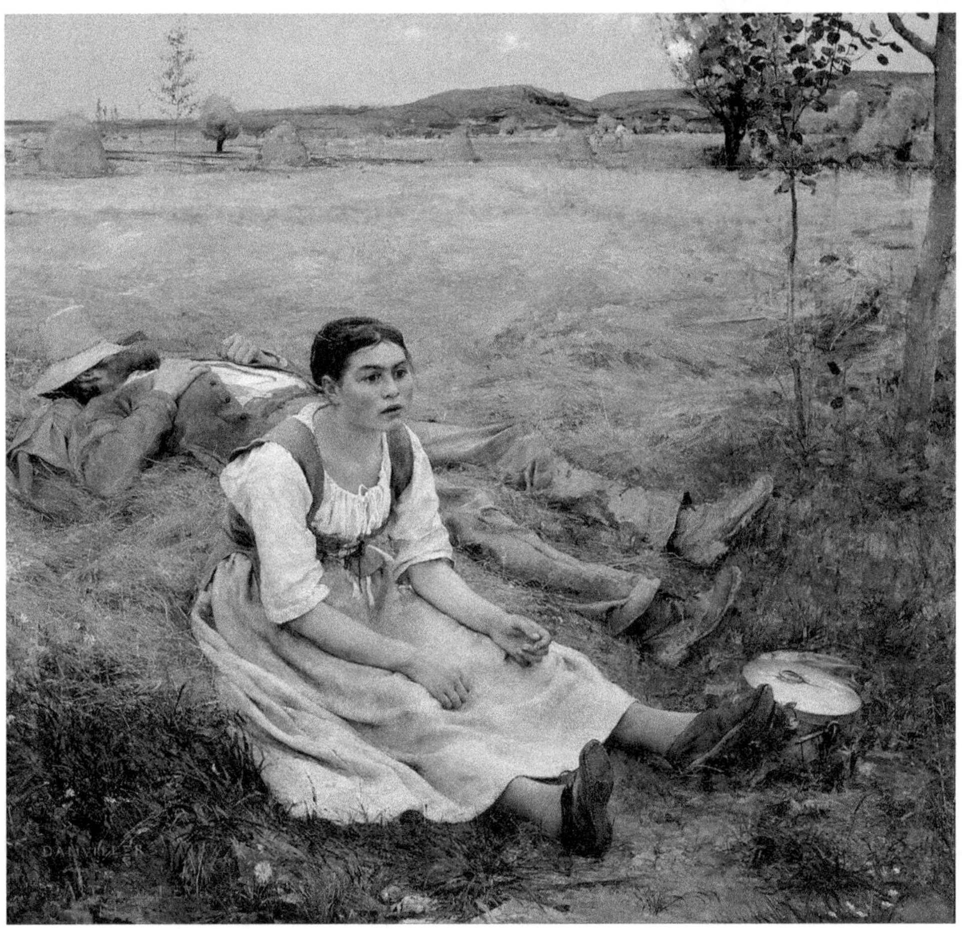

Fig. 5.20. Jules Bastien-Lepage, *Les Foins* (1877), oil on canvas, 160 × 195 cm. Musée d'Orsay, Paris.

donner amoureusement à l'étude de la nature', his *Les Foins* (Fig. 5.20) and *Saison d'octobre* (Fig. 5.21), shown at the previous year's Salon,[46] being described by Zola as 'deux pages où l'on a respiré le grand air avec une surprise d'admiration' (*EsA*, p. 381), confirming Bastien-Lepage's status, along with Gervex, 'à la tête du groupe des artistes qui se sont détachés de l'École pour venir au naturalisme' (*EsA*, p. 384).

Whether in relation to Bastien-Lepage or other artists testifying to this Naturalist advance by virtue of the exactitude of their representation of the external world, Zola never fails to underline the enormous and lasting influence of the Impressionists. But whereas they had once been championed as the heroic protagonists of a pictorial revolution, in 1880 they are demoted to the ranks of mere precursors. They fail the Naturalist 'test'. Renoir is exempt because Zola had long considered him as 'un peintre se spécialisant dans les figures humaines' (*EsA*, p. 343).[47] Degas escapes Zola's censure in contradistinction to 'les œuvres peu bâclées des autres impressionnistes' (*EsA*, p. 372). But also, no doubt, because he too was

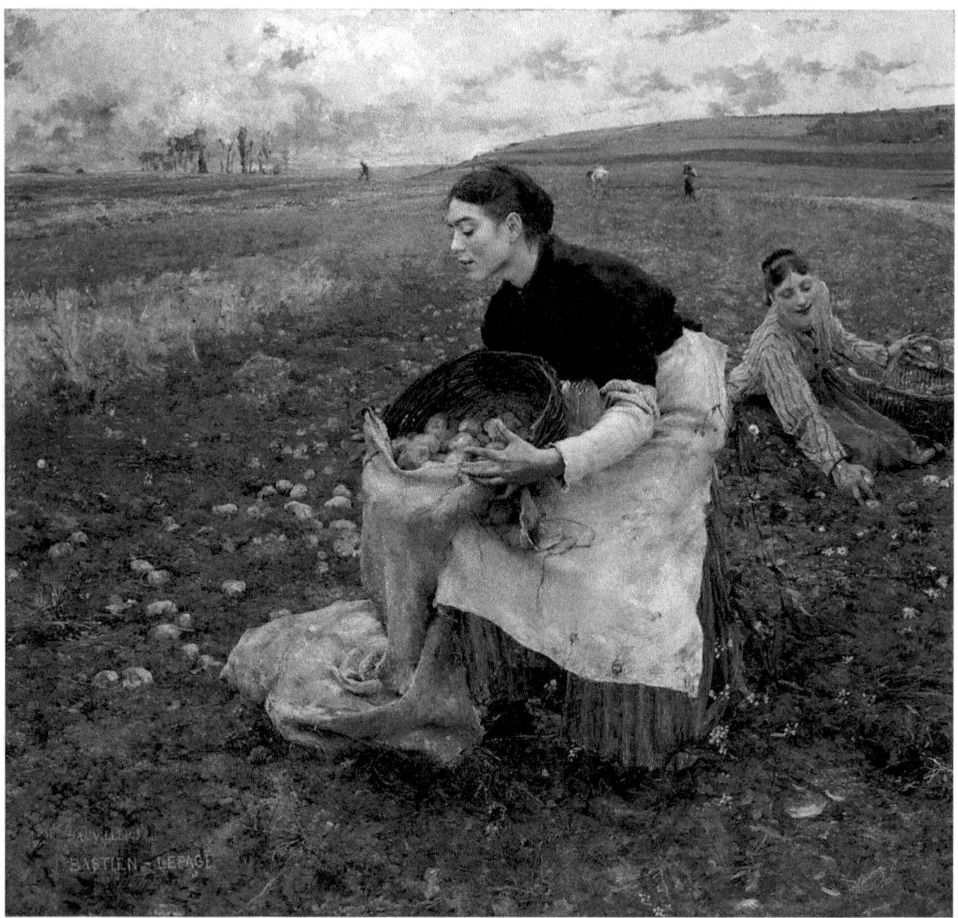

FIG. 5.21. Jules Bastien-Lepage, *Saison d'octobre* (Salon of 1877), oil on canvas, 180.7 × 196 cm. National Gallery of Victoria, Melbourne. Felton Bequest.

not one of the recognized exponents of landscape. Significantly perhaps, while associated with 'nos grands paysagistes', the Impressionists are no longer viewed as the direct heirs of the Barbizon School. Instead, to better distinguish their practice, they are seen as the wayward successors of Courbet whose 'solidité' is implicitly compared with their own lack of it: 'en dehors du travail, il n'y a pas de solidité possible' (*EsA*, p. 374). If Monet, who 's'agite dans le vide', because of his lack of direction ('dans les sentiers de traverse' (*EsA*, p. 372)) is Zola's exemplary target, it is not simply because of the unfinished quality of his work. Of his anti-naturalist colour values ('des herbes bleus, des terrains violets, des arbres rouges, des eaux roulant toutes les bariolures du prisme'), Zola, notwithstanding his earlier reliance on Duret's explanation of complementary colours,[48] cannot resist commenting that he had perhaps 'exagéré un peu les tons nouveaux que son œil a constatés'. More generally, Zola laments the fact that not a single one of the Impressionists had been able to realize 'définitivement la formule nouvelle'; instead, in rendering the decomposition of light, 'la formule est là, divisée à l'infini'. And his conclusions are damning: 'ils restent inférieurs à l'œuvre qu'ils tentent, ils bégayent sans trouver le mot'; 'ils lâchent trop souvent leur facture, ils se satisfont trop aisément, ils se montrent incomplets, illogiques, exagérés, impuissants', Zola taking it upon himself to advise the Impressionists to correct these weaknesses by returning to what he still thought (or desperately hoped) were their original realist ambitions: 'il leur suffit de travailler au naturalisme contemporain pour se mettre à la tête d'un mouvement et pour jouer un rôle considérable dans notre école de peinture' (*EsA*, pp. 376–77).

'J'ai plus de confiance dans l'observation directe que dans la théorie'

In this litany of perceived defects, one term stands out: 'illogical'. Zola had never before used it in relation to the Impressionists. And, in tracking an evolutionary dynamic ('dans la seule évolution possible, ils marchent à l'avenir') from their innovatory *plein air* painting to the *mouvement*'s loss of momentum ('la lutte des impressionnistes n'a pas encore abouti' (*EsA*, p. 376)), this notion of illogicality is more telling than remarks about compositional structure or *facture*. It would be rehearsed in *L'Œuvre*. For this is a key trope in Zola's demonstration of these painters' increasing distance from mimetic imperatives, more obviously discernible in their landscapes than in the depiction of urban sites still securing his approval, by virtue of being historically anchored and thereby (apparently) less vulnerable to pictorial experimentation.[49] He delegates to the hypothetical spectator the stupefied reaction ('il reste béant') provoked by Monet's prismatic effects, but charges of exaggeration are his own. The catalyst for such reservations can be identified in the preceding statement that the Impressionists, in painting outside, were 'comme le chimiste, comme le physicien qui retournent aux sources, en se plaçant dans les conditions mêmes des phénomènes' (*EsA*, p. 374). This obliquely refers his readers to contemporary thinking about the mechanics of visual representation — in the context of an astonishing range of inventions in the field of optical instrumentation.[50]

That Zola was aware of this is not in doubt. In this respect, indeed, the publication of Duranty's *La Nouvelle Peinture* in April 1876, timed to coincide with the second Impressionist exhibition,[51] represents an instructive moment, paradoxically, in Zola's increasing disenchantment with the painters he had championed over the previous decade. Repaying an explicit citation from his 1867 study of Manet, headed 'Une nouvelle manière en peinture' (its original title in *La Revue du XIXe siècle*), Zola appears to endorse 'une brochure écrite par un critique au jugement solide, Duranty' (*EsA*, pp. 338–39) and cites amongt its 'aperçus' a long quotation explaining the Impressionists' discovery that 'la grande lumière décolore les tons, que le soleil reflété par les objets tend, à force de clarté, de les ramener à cette unité lumineuse qui fond ses sept rayons prismatiques en un seul éclat incolore, qui est la lumière'. As Zola would just as cryptically do in 1880, Duranty adds that 'le plus savant physicien ne pourrait rien reprocher à leurs analyses de la lumière',[52] thereby signalling a debt to Michel-Eugène Chevreul (1786–1889), the influence of whose

De la loi du contraste simultané des couleurs (1839) was by now generally accepted by even the most conservative of art critics.[53] Zola would not confront Chevreul in any detail until his preparation of *L'Œuvre* in 1885. Other writers on the visual arts already had a far more informed sense, whether second-hand or not, of a new culture of vision, given added impetus by the debates provoked by the Impressionists' exhibitions. In precisely the same month of 1876 as Zola's review of the second of these, Émile Blémont, for example, while also qualifying his enthusiasm (Monet has occasionally 'poussé trop loin la décomposition du rayon solaire, le papillonement des couleurs, l'irisation de la lumière') develops the analogy between science and pictorial vision in precise terms: Monet, he asserts, 'ni plus ni moins qu'un chimiste, [...] tirerait d'un morceau de charbon noir tout l'éblouissement de l'écharpe d'Iris, toutes les couleurs et les nuances complémentaires'.[54] Zola's grappling with this new phenomenology in his 1880 summative account of the Impressionists' development is more ambivalent than it might seem at first sight. Given his sustained advocacy of scientific methodology, ever since his confident espousal in 1864 of 'Du *Progrès* dans les sciences et dans la poésie' (*OC*, x, 310–14; my italics), culminating in the approximation of the natural sciences to Naturalism itself, Zola could hardly be seen to repudiate further evidence of an advance registered in his very first *Salon*, in 1866: 'le vent est à la science' (*EsA*, p. 156); in this case as a result of the ophthalmic research establishing the verifiable principle that colour was not an innate feature radiating out of an object but rather the marker of the light bouncing off it. Accordingly, Zola's own analogy between the Impressionists and physical scientists can only serve as a validation of the painters' 'recherche plus exacte des causes et des effets de la lumière, influant aussi bien sur le dessin que sur la couleur'. On the other hand, however, 'cela paraît simple à énoncer, mais les difficultés commencent avec l'éxécution', leaving unmet the challenge of 'tout ce que l'on doit vaincre, si l'on veut accepter la nature avec sa lumière diffuse et ses variations continuelles de colorations' (*EsA*, pp. 374–75). This will be picked up in *L'Œuvre*, its narrator commenting that Claude Lantier's 'obstination à peindre sur nature compliquait terriblement son travail, l'embarrassait de difficultés presque insurmontables' (*RM*, IV, 204).

The trajectory of Zola's disenchantment with the Impressionists can be tracked: in 1876, Zola is still asserting that 'la plupart d'entre eux s'efforcent visiblement de communiquer avant tout l'impression véridique donnée par les choses et les êtres' (*EsA*, p. 339); by 1879, however, there are reservations: 'tous les peintres impressionnistes pèchent par l'insuffisance technique' (*EsA*, p. 356). In 1880, their laudable intentions are seen as even more compromised by the excesses of 'les effets de coloration les plus imprévus' and the resultant *pointillisme* (or *divisionnisme*) of the 'formule [...] divisée à l'infini' (*EsA*, p. 376) increasingly characteristic of the work of Monet and Pissarro. Zola's article in *Le Figaro* of 23 May 1881, nominally inspired by that year's Salon, does not mention the Impressionists at all.[55] In the absence of published art criticism by Zola during the next fifteen years, it is only in relation to *L'Œuvre* (1886), both in its preparation and in its definitive text, that one finds elaborated his subsequent thinking about the landscapes of the Impressionists. And, as one contemporary reviewer of the novel underlined, that thinking highlights 'toutes les contradictions qu'on a relevées entre les théories et les œuvres de M. Zola'.[56]

The authorial monologue driving the preparatory notes for his novels, as this book illustrates time and again, often gives us the most immediate access to a pre-fictionalized discourse. Unsurprisingly, there are numerous instances in those for *L'Œuvre* which reproduce, occasionally almost verbatim, some of his earlier writing on the visual arts: the constraints placed on originality by the narrow-minded deliberations of the Salon jury; the philistinism of the viewing-public; elements of the synoptic art history, traced back through Courbet and Delacroix but only as far Ingres, so often rehearsed in his exhibition reviews; comments on individual painters; the references to the Impressionists: 'et en arriver à l'école du plein air elle-même, aux efforts éparpillés, ébauches, impressions bâclées',[57] and in the idea that Claude Lantier, his fictional painter, 's'élèvera contre leur travail hâtif, le tableau fait en deux heures, l'esquisse qui contente, la vente hâtive de Monet'.[58] These references are subsequently amplified, in more or less stilted discussions between the novel's characters. The most sustained such digression is the passage in chapter 9 which reads like a page of art criticism in its own right, in which Zola carefully demonstrates how 'la science entrait dans la peinture' (*RM*, IV, 248) by staging a long conversation between Claude and Gagnière, the novel's landscape artist, devoted to the *theory* of complementary colours in all its arcane technicalities. Its *practice*, contrarily and as will be seen below, is dramatized in the novel's scenes set at Bennecourt, just along the Seine from (and substituted by Zola for) Vétheuil, a favourite site of landscape artists from Daubigny to Monet. As far as the theoretical dimension of 'la nouvelle peinture' is concerned, Zola's successive allusions to it since its retailing by Duranty leave their mark. In a novel consciously designed, and documented, to mirror the artistic world of his time, it was inevitable that this dimension should be included, notwithstanding the potential anachronism of inserting its 1870s context into *L'Œuvre*'s supposed Second Empire timeframe:[59] 'Je prendrais en outre pour Claude quelques théories des impressionnistes, le plein air, la lumière décomposéee, toute cette peinture nouvelle qui demande *un génie pour être réalisée*.'[60] Zola's own underlining here exactly corresponds to reservations to which he had given expression in his art criticism.

In the process of transposing those theories into the novel itself, he would receive unsolicited corrective advice, however courteously prefaced, in relation to his understanding of complementary colours. In response to Signac's letter to him of 8 February 1886 pointing out that, in the text of *L'Œuvre* appearing in serial instalments in *Gil Blas*, he had noticed an error ('pour que le drapeau devint violet [...] il aurait fallu que le ciel soit orangé ou jaune'), Zola accordingly modified to this effect the definitive version of the novel published in volume form at the very end of March. More substantively, he preserved within his work notes a letter sent to him by the neo-Impressionist painter Léo Gausson, then aged only 25 and describing himself as a landscape artist, who went on at some considerable length about 'les travaux du savant Chevreul', offering Zola an explanation of 'le côté mécanique et pratique de la couleur raisonnée [...] en dehors du tempérament artistique'. 'Pour l'harmonie des couleurs', he added, in a further implicit critique of Zola's approach, 'les influences si diverses de l'homme deviennent nulles en face des lois physiques': 'nous entrons dans une logique, cela est fait de déductions qui s'emboîtent mécaniquement les unes dans les autres'. Declaring that 'Chevreul pose ces bases toutes scientifiques', Gausson then proceeded to spell out for Zola's benefit the eminent scientist's theory of complementary colours. Upon receiving a second missive from Gausson, the novelist belatedly replied on 28 November 1885, suppressing what must have been his irritation, claiming to have no need of the synopsis sent to him earlier and which he professed to have read 'malgré sa longueur': 'toute ma jeunesse s'est passée au milieu des théories que vous reprenez aujourd'hui. J'ai des personnages qui disent absolument ce que vous dites.'[61] This was disingenuous on two counts: Zola had *not* been familiar with Chevreul's theories until well past his 'jeunesse'; and his characters had *not* yet been charged with voicing them, given that, at this juncture, he had barely completed half of the twelve chapters of the novel.[62] Only in the plan drawn up immediately before drafting chapter 9 is there a reminder to himself to include 'les couleurs complémentaires, avec Gagnière'. In any case, the correlation between the passage in question and Gausson's detailed scientific advice makes it clear that Zola borrowed from it in some detail. But it is equally clear that Zola was very far from sharing its enthusiastic tenor. Signac's polite intervention in such matters is of anecdotal interest. Zola's reply to Gausson, on the other hand, is revealing. For in its objection to the 'importance trop grande peut-être donnée à la technique de l'art, car en somme deux bons yeux suffisent. J'ai plus de confiance dans l'observation directe que dans la théorie', one could hardly invent a more succinct summary of Zola's unreconstructed approach to pictorial representation.

For Zola's recognition of Chevreul's eminence, widely celebrated on the occasion of his hundredth birthday (in the very year *L'Œuvre* was published),[63] did nothing to mitigate his resistance to advances in optical science justifying the Impressionists' radical transformation of landscape painting. It can be traced back to his oft-quoted definition of a work of art as '*un coin de la création vu à travers un tempérament*' (*EsA*, p. 161; underlined by Zola himself in his *Salon* of 1866), precisely the notion which Gausson rejects in his insistence that the mechanics of vision operate 'en dehors du tempérament artistique'. But this was the founding principle of Zola's aesthetic, first articulated in his 1865 essay on Courbet. His championing of Manet underlines, in the necessarily subjective representation of external realities, the psycho-physiological individuation of the artist. His lexical choices in writing about the visual arts reveal the extent to which he clings to this premise: his texts consistently prioritize personality, individual sensitivity and originality of vision as the *sine qua non* of the accurate depiction of the world. Observation and exactitude are also the key tropes of *Le Roman expérimental*, the collected essays published in October 1880 and complementing the text of *Le Naturalisme au Salon* appearing in *Le Voltaire* between 18 and 22 June of that same year. Which is not to deny that, either intuitively or registering an awareness of new thinking about perception, there are instances where we can discern a less stable version of pictorial mediation. In *Le Ventre de Paris*, Claude Lantier, in his first incarnation, is both the spokesman for 'le positivisme de l'art, l'art moderne tout expérimental' (*RM*, I, 776) — refuting the view, nevertheless reinforced in *L'Œuvre* as well as in Zola's art criticism, that 'on ne fait pas de l'art avec de la science' (*RM*, I, 800) — and also, by contrast, illustrating Zola's own work note for that novel that 'les jeux de lumière change [*sic*] à chaque instant l'aspect des Halles' (Ms 10338, fol. 296). And to restore the importance of 'vu' in 'vu à travers un tempérament' is to return with a somewhat different emphasis to Zola's own 'Théorie des écrans' cited in my Introduction. For this text's ultimate emphasis on an invariable external world itself points to the limits of Zola's assimilation of 'discredited "spectatorial" epistemologies'.[64] As Émilie Piton-Foucault has put it, he ignores the problematic fact that 'le passage d'une physiologie de la vision passive à la vision projective et subjective, ainsi que l'essor des arts optiques engendrent alors une mise en crise et une redéfinition même de la notion du réel, remis en cause dans la philosophie schopenhauerienne comme une simple représentation illusoire'.[65]

In respect of landscape, the implications of the contradiction between an invariable nature and its subjective representation are discernible in *L'Œuvre*. Its fictional painter and his wife, Christine, relive the rural experience which Zola himself had enjoyed in the 1860s, as was mentioned in Chapter 1, in the company of many of those painters who would in due course become the leading Impressionists. In the novel, the excursions to Bennecourt provide the context for Claude's most fulfilling creative period. But an unease about his landscapes is registered by Zola in Christine's objections to them. For in his preparatory notes she already incarnates the 'réalité' from which Claude increasingly loses sight.[66] 'Interdite parfois, devant un terrain lilas ou devant un arbre bleu, qui déroutaient toutes ses idées arrêtées de coloration', she acknowledges in her 'critique' ('à cause d'un peuplier lavé d'azur') of her husband's paintings the veracity of the optical impression, but remains wedded to empirical fact: 'il ne pouvait y avoir des arbres bleus dans la nature' (*RM*, IV, 155). The extent to which she voices Zola's own reservations can be gauged from an earlier text in which he nostalgically recalled watching his painter friends at their easels beside the Seine. That lived riverside idyll, headed 'La Rivière', forms the last part of 'Aux Champs' (1878), which had begun, as noted earlier, with an evocation of the Barbizon School. Another part, headed 'Le Bois', is equally autobiographical in its reminiscences of excursions to Verrières with Cézanne. Initially appearing in *Le Messager de l'Europe*, but before being collected in *Le Capitaine Burle* (1882), these texts were published in *Le Figaro* between October 1880 and July 1881. And it is not beside the point that this virtually coincides with *Le Naturalisme au Salon*. What is striking about Zola's descriptions of the settings of these texts is that, unlike in *L'Œuvre* — where he notes in its preliminary *dossier* 'les difficultés de peindre sur nature' (Ms 10316, fol. 214) — their visualization is uncomplicated. His verbal landscapes are full of colour and 'les tons les plus délicats' (*OC*, IX, 630): a scene of fields and woods 'étalant une veste d'arlequin bariolée de toutes les nuances du vert et du jaune' (*OC*, IX, 621); the shimmering reflections in the water of the overhanging trees ('des nappes de verdure'), the 'rideaux de peupliers', the white mist hovering above the surface of a pond and the pantheistic 'sérénité de la campagne' serve to conjure up an atmosphere: 'On songeait au bain de la Diane antique, trempant ses pieds de neige dans les sources ignorées des bois' (*OC*, IX, 622). Introduced by 'l'œil distingue...', such a descriptive fabric is optically recuperable (in the reader's 'mind's eye'). In every sense of the phrase, and from Zola's admiring perspective, these landscapes are as *true to nature* as those of Corot or Daubigny.

Without tendentiously blurring the distinction between verbal and pictorial representation, it is equally instructive to explore the preparatory dossier of *La Terre*. Long before finishing *L'Œuvre*, on 23 February 1886, Zola was already imagining how he would include pictures of his next novel's rural setting. It is significant that, amongst the newspaper clippings he appended to his notes were: an article by the novelist René Maizeroy, best remembered from his portrait (*c*. 1882) by Manet, devoted to the Salon of 1884, headed 'Voyage au pays des peintres'; and, even further back, one by Louis de Fourcaud, in *Le Gaulois* of 11 May 1882, in which the Salon of that year provoked its reviewer to consider the challenges involved in depicting the 'vérité' of the countryside: 'c'est l'observation sincère et passionnée qui la dévoile. Celui-ci s'inspire de Millet'. Praising Bastien-Lepage, as Zola had done, Fourcaud stressed the necessity 'de donner l'impression de la nature elle-même, directement étudiée en dehors des œuvres antérieures'. When Zola followed that exhortation, visiting the potential setting for *La Terre* in May 1886, the resulting 'Notes sur la Beauce' are much closer to Millet's landscapes than Pissarro's. Indeed, the novel's opening description of Jean sowing bears un unmistakeable resemblance, even in its colour values, to Millet's iconic *Le Semeur* (1850).[67] Although he had only seen the Beauce in spring, Zola consciously interpolated at intervals each of the seasons within his text, reminding himself 'pas de paysages longs' (Ms 10329, fol. 378). Though whether or not, in describing the 'paysage de désolation' of winter ('description du pays d'hiver. Terres noires, prairies, arbres dépouillés' (Ms 10328, fols 195 and 1)), he remembered his similar response to Daubigny's *La Neige*, is a speculative parallel too far. It is interesting that Huysmans's 'votre cadre de paysages est superbe' is echoed in the conclusion of Arsène Alexandre, the art critic, that Zola's descriptions were those of 'un maître peintre' (both cited in *RM*, IV, 1533). For this seems to have been Zola's intention: 'La Beauce par tous les temps, l'été. Le vent dans les blés, une pluie sur eux, un orage qui passe' (fol. 221) with an oft-repeated metaphor originating in the note that 'la Beauce est la mer' (fols 124 and 131) and his picturing of infinite horizons as delineated and as resonant, and as beautiful, as in those landscape paintings he had admired in his art criticism.

Zola's representations of the landscape, and notably his cityscapes, in *L'Œuvre* are similarly 'legible'.[68] They are so differentiated from those of his fictional painter that one is reminded of Degas's alleged remark, cited earlier, that Zola had written the novel as a demonstration of verbal superiority. What is certain is that the passage in chapter 9 devoted to the theory of complementary colours accommodates a concept of vision which is the obverse of Zola's prioritizing of the 'deux bons yeux' sufficient to record a scene. It is not by chance that it should be Gagnière whose theoretical proselytizing is thus treated with irony. It has been shown that he is a composite character, modelled on a variety of artists with whom

Zola was familiar.[69] Charged with delivering an abbreviated explanation of the theory of complementary colours,[70] his character traits alone are not designed to inspire confidence. Zola's conception of him tells us much about his opinion of the theories Gagnière so enthusiastically propounds: he is a dreamer, with his head in the clouds; distracted by the latest fad; always late; and an interminable bore.[71] More significant is that Gagnière is himself a *failed* landscape painter. This is made explicit in both Zola's preparatory notes and in the text of the novel, 'lui qui aurait pu avoir un talent si conscientieux de paysagiste' (*RM*, IV, 164).[72] His pictorial tastes are infantile: he is transfixed by the 'petit chef-d'œuvre', which could be the work of a four year-old, not unlike Christine's 'petits paysages d'écolière' (*RM*, IV, 108), of 'une petite maison au bord d'un petit chemin, avec un petit arbre à côté'. Hanging next to it is one of the tiny landscapes he submits to the annual Salon, but virtually identical to each other year after year: 'un paysage d'un gris perlé, un bord de Seine soigneusement peint, joli de ton quoiqu'un peu lourd, et d'un parfait équilibre, sans aucune brutalité révolutionnaire' (*RM*, IV, 122). Stuck in this mode, absurdly blaming Claude for his failures ('il a volé mon originalité' (*RM*, IV, 333)), by the end of the novel Gagnière has given up painting altogether. 'Quel raté!', as Mahoudeau confirms (*RM*, IV, 336). But some of Zola's most interesting notes about Gagnière do not survive their elaboration in his definitive text. He had initially imagined him being an 'élève de Corot' (Ms 10316, fol. 298). In the light of his mediocrity, this must have seemed at odds with Zola's genuine admiration for an artist 'qui a inventé le paysage' (*RM*, IV, 136).[73] Instead, in the novel itself, he is self-taught: 'il avait appris la peinture tout seul dans la forêt de Fontainebleau' (*RM*, IV, 80). At the same time, however, the work notes had indicated an exemplarity which is highly revealing as far as Zola's view of contemporary landscape painting is concerned. For he writes of Gagnière that 'cela me donne d'abord notre école de paysage, *déclinant* après Rousseau, Corot, Daubigny, etc.'. In another note, sketching a first portrait of the character, he adds Millet to the list, but again sees Gagnière as representative, inserting between the lines an allusion to the high point of the Barbizon painters against which more recent landscape artists are found wanting: 'elle *décline* après ces maîtres'.[74] In this reference back to the Barbizon school with which this chapter began, we find the implicitly comparative dimension of Zola's disenchantment with the Impressionists.

L'Œuvre both rehearses and fills out the reasons for that disenchantment. Two kinds of landscape are invoked by Fagerolles: on the one hand, 'il ne parlait plus que de peinture grasse et solide, que de morceaux de nature jetés sur la toile, vivants, grouillants, tels qu'ils étaient'; on the other, he mocks 'ceux du plein air, qu'il accusait d'empâter leurs études avec un cuiller à pot' (*RM*, IV, 83). That last colloquialism ('in a jiffy') corresponds to the 'travail hâtif'' for which Zola had condemned Monet. 'Solide' is the quality admired in Courajod's Corot-like *Mare de Gagny*, referenced as having been painted thirty years earlier: 'on n'a encore rien fichu de plus solide... Pourquoi laisse-t-on ça au Luxembourg? Ça devrait être au Louvre' (*RM*, IV, 136). Indeed, across the whole of Zola's art criticism, this 'solidity' is the quality which determines his judgement. Claude Lantier, like the Impressionists, fails to satisfy this criterion: too many aspects of his canvases 'manquaient de solidité' (*RM*, IV, 127). But this is characteristic of his development rather than his ambitions. Zola subscribes to the latter: 'il faut peut-être le soleil, il faut le plein air, une peinture claire et jeune, les choses et les êtres tels qu'ils se comportent dans de la vraie lumière' (*RM*, IV, 45). He also accepts, up to a point, what he refers to as the 'théorie du soleil' and the 'science des reflets', the 'sensation juste des êtres et des choses dans la lumière diffuse' (Ms 10316, fols 7 and 122). As he had done in the case of Monet,[75] Zola accordingly celebrates Claude's depiction of the transluscent currents of the Seine, overlaid by his own 'danse des reflets au fil du courant' (*RM*, IV, 104). He even defends his 'bleuissement, cette notation nouvelle de la lumière' (*RM*, IV, 128) against its uncomprehending spectators.

It is when this is taken to excess, however, that Zola parts company with his fictional painter. Claude's artistic development is prefigured in Gagnière's. In an attempt to break out of a creative dead end of the kind Zola had underlined in Monet ('il s'agite dans le vide'), Gagnière 'raffinait la sensation jusqu'à l'évanouissement final de l'intelligence' (*RM*, IV, 85). Pervasive self-consciousness leads only to theoretical abstraction which is a travesty, as Zola suggests, of the pictorial legacy of the Barbizon school: 'À la suite des paysagistes français, ces maîtres qui ont les premiers conquis la nature, il se préoccupait de la justesse du ton, de l'exacte observation des valeurs, en théoricien dont l'honnêteté finissait par alourdir sa main' (*RM*, IV, 84). Even before listening to Gagnière's explanation of the theory of complementary colours, Claude's authentic vision is sufficiently destabilized to worry his supportive fellow artists: 'ce qui, surtout, rendait le tableau terrible, c'était l'étude nouvelle de la lumière, cette décomposition, d'une observation très exacte, et qui contrecarrait toutes les habitudes de l'œil, en accentuant des bleus, des jaunes, des rouges, où personne n'était accoutumé d'en voir' (*RM*, IV, 206). The next stage in betraying the simple precepts of 'une éducation de l'œil' (*RM*, IV, 109) leaves us in little doubt about where Zola stands:

> Et le cas terrible, l'aventure où il s'était détraqué encore, venait d'être sa théorie envahissante des couleurs complémentaires. Gagnière, le premier, lui en avait parlé, très enclin également aux spéculations techniques. Après quoi, lui-même, par la continuelle outrance de sa passion, s'était mis à exagérer ce principe scientifique qui fait découler des trois couleurs primaires, le jaune, le rouge, le bleu, les trois couleurs secondaires, l'orange, le vert, le violet, puis toute une série de couleurs complémentaires et similaires, dont les composés s'obtiennent mathématiquement les uns des autres. Ainsi la science entrait dans la peinture, une méthode était créée pour l'observation logique, il n'y avait qu'à prendre la dominante d'un tableau, à en établir la complémentaire ou la similaire, pour arriver d'une façon expérimentale aux variations qui se produisent, un rouge se transformant en un jaune près d'un bleu, par exemple, tout un paysage changeant de ton, et par des reflets, et par la décomposition de la lumière, selon les nuages qui passent. Il en tirait cette conclusion vraie, que les objets n'ont pas de couleur fixe, qu'ils se colorent suivant les circonstances ambiantes; et le grand mal était que, lorsqu'il revenait maintenant à l'observation directe, la tête bourdonnant de cette science, son œil prévenu forçait les nuances délicates, affirmait en notes trop vives l'exactitude de sa théorie; de sorte que

> son originalité de notation, si claire, si vibrante de soleil, tournait à la gageure, à un renversement de toutes les habitudes de son œil, des chairs violâtres sous des cieux tricolores. La folie semblait au bout. (*RM*, IV, 247–48)

Even the turgid copying-out of Gausson's synopsis is telling. But the transcription of the latter's 'nous entrons dans une logique' as a scientifically grounded 'observation logique' is important. For it refers us to the alternative 'logique' of Bongrand's realistic representations of rural life and Sandoz's negative reaction to Claude's final painting ('la cause de la logique outragée'), precisely because 'ce n'est guère vraisemblable' (*RM*, IV, 236). And this serves to explain, in retrospect, the lack of verisimilitude synonymous with Zola's characterization of the Impressionists as 'illogiques'. For Claude, this development is a catastrophic harbinger of artistic impotence. Zola's explanation of distorted representation due to 'la lésion de son œil' (Ms 10316, fol. 265) is consistent with his physiological conception of vision.[76] It fatally compromises the ambition to 'tout voir et tout peindre' (*RM*, IV, 46).

A decade after *L'Œuvre*, Zola would return to the implications of this symptomatic failure of modern art, and of landscape painting in particular. His final published article of art criticism, in *Le Figaro* of 2 May 1896 (*EsA*, pp. 401–09), is only indirectly prompted by paintings exhibited that year.[77] Claiming that 'je me suis un peu désintéressé de la peinture', he retrospectively charts the evolution of the visual arts over the thirty years since his first *Salon*. Here he focuses on the vitiated creative legacy of the once-favoured members of 'la nouvelle peinture', signalled by the experimentation of their successors, referring to the 'queue désastreuse' of Manet, Monet and Pissarro.[78] The non-descriptive tonalities in works testifying to chromatic subjectivity, the blurring of outlines and the emphasis on *sensation* rather than transcription all provoke a kind of blindness occasioned by the absence of recognizable referents: 'rien que des taches', whether in portraiture or landscape, 'des arbres, des maisons, des continents, et des mers'. The essay is punctuated by repeated indictments of 'excès', 'abus', 'extravagances' and a visceral opposition which 'tourne au dégoût et aux vomissements', as contrasted to the period when the Impressionists had worked 'délicieusement'.

In L'*Œuvre*, Zola had celebrated the incursions of *le plein air* at the 1863 Salon des Refusés: 'des paysages surtout, presque tous d'une note sincère et juste' (*RM*, IV, 164). But its ultimate ubiquity, registered towards the end of the novel with familiar reservations, is viewed in the 1896 text with further ambivalence, by virtue of a monotony at odds with artistic individuality: 'Et voilà qu'aujourd'hui il n'y a plus que du plein air.' 'Les tonalités blondes' have been replaced by 'cette file continue de tableaux exsangues, d'une pâleur de rêve, d'une chlorose préméditée'. What infuriates him most ('où ma surprise tourne à la colère') are the aberrations of 'la théorie des reflets' he had admired, as he recalls, in Monet's depiction of the glistening surfaces of rivers and the ocean: 'si l'on aborde la nature immense et changeante, la lumière devient l'âme de l'œuvre, éternellement diverse.' 'Rien n'est plus délicat à saisir et à rendre', he adds, 'que cette décomposition et ces reflets'. Pissarro too is bracketed with Monet in having, at least at one time, so wonderfully 'étudié ces reflets et cette décomposition de la lumière'. Instead, now taken to extremes by prior ratiocination, 'dès que le raisonnement s'en mêle', the results are 'ces paysages violets et ces chevaux orange':[79] 'Oh! les horizons où les arbres sont bleus, les eaux rouges et les cieux verts! C'est affreux, affreux, affreux!' Zola's rhetorical horror is by no means a reaction limited to a single genre. But an unrecognizably new kind of landscape is a recurrent target in his evocation of 'ces larves de créatures sortant des limbes, volant par des espaces blêmes, s'agitant dans de confuses contrées d'aubes grises et de couleurs de suie!' Few would dispute the fact that Zola's vituperative discourse, taken to such caricatural lengths, traduces the post- (and neo-) Impressionist works characteristic of the end of the century. Or that he is conscious of being faced with a radically inverted pictorial language, apparently devoid of structure, referent, grammar, and syntax — a science of painting manifestly at odds with Naturalist criteria. In an 1897 interview (*EsA*, pp. 700–04), Zola repeated many of the points made in this *Figaro* article the year before, not least that the apparently definitive triumph of the 'école du plein air' gave him no satisfaction, precisely because 'notre succès a ouvert le chemin aux excentriques'. There is also, however, a weary acknowledgement that each artistic movement is succeeded by another, necessitating the acceptance of 'de nouvelles façons de comprendre'. The tone of Zola's remarks is deeply nostalgic in its evocation of the battles of the past and a period of his life surrounded by the likes of Cézanne, Manet, Renoir, Pissarro and Degas 'et d'autres encore'. Of those, only Guillemet remained in touch. The landscapes of the Barbizon school had long since disappeared from view. Even those of the Impressionists were part of a world he had lost.

Notes to Chapter 5

1. Letter of 29 September 1862 (*Corr.*, I, 362).
2. On the ideological implications of this urban taste for the rural, see Nicholas Green, *The Spectacle of Nature: Landscape and Bourgeois Culture in Nineteenth-Century France* (Manchester: Manchester University Press, 1990).
3. In 1878, to capitalize on the perceived neglect of this generation of landscape artists at the Universal Exhibition that year, Durand-Ruel mounted a huge exhibition of his own (*Exposition rétrospective de tableaux et dessins des maîtres modernes*, 15 July–1 October) which included no fewer than eighty-six works by Corot, sixty-one by Millet, twenty-three by Théodore Rousseau, and eighteen by Daubigny.
4. As Zola put in his 1875 study of the Goncourts' *Manette Salomon* (*OC*, XI, 171). The phrase is taken from the novel itself, in Michel Crouzet's 'Folio Classique' edition (Paris: Gallimard, 1996), p. 337. Its chapters 71–83 are devoted to the 'École de Fontainebleau', transparently the Barbizon School, with the fictional painter Crescent ('un des premiers il avait bravement rompu avec le paysage historique', p. 360) an amalgam of Millet and Théodore Rousseau.
5. Paul Flandrin (1811–1902) is the model for Garnotelle in *Manette Salomon* (see above, n. 4); Alfred de Curzon (1820–1895) was the other contemporary landscape artist representative of the genre's academic residue.
6. Two years later, in his *Salon de 1859*, Baudelaire (still subscribing to the view that landscape was 'un genre inférieur') was not entirely persuaded, but sensed that 'M. Daubigny veut et sait faire davantage', preferring his paintings 'avec leurs défauts à beaucoup d'autres plus parfaites, mais privées de la qualité qui le distingue' (*Œuvres complètes*, ed. by Claude Pichois, 2 vols (Paris: Gallimard, Bibliothèque de la Pléiade, 1975–76), II, 660–61). A revised edition of Henriet's *Le Paysagiste aux champs* appeared in 1876. Amongst numerous other publications devoted to the artist, he went on to produce *Charles Daubigny et son œuvre gravé* (1875), enjoying such a reputation

as a Daubigny specialist that it was unsurprising that he should be the consultant *expert* at the posthumous auction (6–8 May 1878) of the contents of the painter's studio.

7. *Le Messager de l'Europe*, August 1878, reprinted in *Le Figaro* of 25 July 1881 (*OC*, IX, 617–18). In respect of the Parisian suburbs mentioned here, see my 'Les Représentations de la banlieue chez Zola et les peintres', *CN*, 66 (1992), 59–71.
8. Although differentiating myself from him on a number of points, any approach to Zola's writing on landscape painters must start with Hoek's 'Zola vis-à-vis du paysage' in *Titres, toiles et critique d'art: déterminants institutionnels du discours sur l'art au dix-neuvième siècle en France* (Amsterdam: Rodopi, 2001), pp. 255–350. Hoek's study is only concerned with the major figures of the Barbizon School (Corot, Rousseau, Millet and Daubigny), with a coda on Pissarro.
9. Hoek makes this claim (*Titres,* p. 287), in distinguishing Rousseau and Millet (as more akin to Romantic painters of nature) from Corot and Daubigny (as precursors of the Impressionists) to account for Zola's judgements. The argument that he was 'déçu' by the first two, derives largely from Zola's article entitled 'Les Chutes' within his review of the Salon of 1866. He cites Zola's 1867 about-turn ('J'ai cru très naïvement au génie de M. Théodore Rousseau, sur ce qu'on me racontait des débuts de ce peintre [et] je n'y crois plus guère', *EsA*, p. 537) as a definitive repudiation of his professed admiration for the painter's early work. But this is surely coloured by Zola's more general polemical stance in respect of artists institutionally rewarded at the Universal Exhibition of that year.
10. Millet died on 23 January, Corot on 22 February 1875. The latter had started working at Barbizon in 1828; Millet had moved there in 1849 to escape an outbreak of cholera, on the advice of (to give him his full name) Narcisse Diaz de la Peña (1808–1876). In 1878, this Spanish member of the Barbizon School was belatedly added to Zola's list of 'toute une grande école de paysagistes' (*EsA*, p. 542). At Diaz's death on 18 November 1876, however, Zola had made up for this oversight in a fulsome tribute to 'un des derniers survivants de la grande phalange, qui a fondé notre école de paysage' (*EsA*, pp. 642–43), compared to Corot not only in his inserting 'dans la nature réelle la fantaisie d'une nymphe' but also in Zola's preference for his earliest works. The lineage was also extended backwards in 1875 to preface it by another master of the genre: 'Les maîtres s'en sont allés, Troyon, Théodore Rousseau, Millet, Corot' (*EsA*, p. 260). Constant Troyon (1810–1865) had first been mentioned by Zola in a journalistic piece in the year of his death, 'las de gloire et d'impuissance' (*OC*, XIII, 22); the Prix Troyon, surviving the culling of landscape from the Prix de Rome, was virtually the only official award about which he was not scathing, evoking in *Le Sémaphore de Marseille* of 30 September 1875 'ce prix annuel que la mère du célèbre paysagiste a fondé pour honorer la mémoire de son fils et que l'Institut décerne au meilleur paysage peint sur un sujet donné' (*EsA*, p. 223). Eleven of Troyon's paintings were included in Durand-Ruel's 1878 exhibition (see above, n. 3). Nor was this lineage exclusively French: on the occasion of a gift to the Louvre in 1873 of Constable's *Weymouth Bay with Storm Approaching* (1818–19), Zola wrote of the painter, 'ce maître inconnu chez nous', that he was 'vraiment le père direct de nos paysagistes modernes' (*EsA*, pp. 618–19).
11. 'On m'assure qu'il a débuté par des paysages assez largement compris et peints avec une certaine force. Je ne connais de lui que des sortes d'aquarelles lavées à grande eau. Il a dû être très dur pour les tempéraments vigoureux' (*EsA*, p. 140). Corot too had been less than supportive ('mou dans la défense des toiles qui auraient dû lui être sympathiques'), though Zola speciously gave him the benefit of the doubt on the grounds of a self-effacing modesty integral to his much-loved personality ('le père Corot, comme on le nommait, était la bonté même', as he was to write in his obituary notice of 1875 (*EsA*, p. 639)), exempt from the more brutal comments aimed at other members of that year's jury by having been himself refused entry to the Salon in the early part of his career.
12. Inscribed 'À mon ami Zola', Guillemet having written to him on 2 November 1866 to say that it would be an honour to give him an 'étude' to decorate his walls: 'vous choisirez celle qui vous ira le mieux' (cited by Baligand, 'Lettres inédites', p. 181).
13. Doubtless helped by owning a copy of Albert de la Fizelière's *La Vie et l'œuvre de Chintreuil* (Paris: Cadart, 1874), with a preface by Jean Desbrosses (1835–1906), Chintreuil's pupil, published as a catalogue to coincide with the major retrospective of the artist's work at the École des Beaux-

Arts (see my 'Zola et ses livres', p. 196). Given the date and context of Zola's comments, he probably saw *L'Espace* at the Universal Exhibition of 1878 where it was shown alongside *Le Bosquet aux chevreuils,* the painter's posthumous submission to the Salon of 1874, both works being lent by the Musée du Luxembourg. Seven other paintings by Chintreuil were shown at Durand-Ruel's 1878 exhibition (see above, n. 3). He was another of those landscape artists finally given their due at the Salon of 1868, the highly respected Chesneau, in *Le Constitutionnel* of 1 July, praising his *Lever de soleil* as 'une page d'une vigueur d'effet, d'une réalité et par là d'une beauté saisissante' and his *L'Ondée* as 'un tour de force'.

14. Daubigny being ill at the time, his son Karl took his place as a pallbearer at Corot's funeral in 1875. But in due course he had granted his wish to be buried near to Corot's grave in the Père-Lachaise cemetery.
15. Hoek mistakenly claims that Daubigny 'réussit à faire accepter le *Portrait de Valabrègue*' (*Titres*, p. 321). In fact, 'it was submitted to the Salon in 1866 as an act of defiance rather than with any serious expectation of acceptance' (*Cézanne: The Early Years*, ed. by Gowing, p. 100), as turned out to be the case.
16. Daubigny had followed up his stand in 1866 by encouraging Cézanne to mount a campaign demanding a 'Salon des Refusés' on the model of the famous such exhibition of 1863. The only consequence of the letter to this effect, supported by Zola, was to sufficiently irritate the Comte de Nieuwerkerke, as Surintendant des Arts, as to ensure the rejection of Daubigny's own submissions to the Salon of 1867. That year, he added his signature, alongside those of Monet, Manet, Sisley, Pissarro and Renoir, to Bazille's renewal of Cézanne's initiative. By securing, in the election for membership of the jury of the 1868 Salon, the vast majority of votes from eligible artists (no longer restricted to previous winners of medals and the Prix de Rome), Daubigny was able to exert an influence for which he was never forgiven by the authorities. When Monet and Sisley were rejected once again in 1869 and 1870, Daubigny resigned from the jury on principle, as did Corot. Further evidence of his refusal to compromise was his support for Courbet during the latter's travails with the authorities after the Commune, and in December 1871, together with Corot and Daumier, his petitioning Thiers, the President of the Republic, to liberalize the regulations for the Salon of 1872.
17. Castagnary, *Salons*, I, 255. It was Castagnary who reported Nieuwerkeke's displeasure at this outcome of the jury's deliberations: 'C'est à Daubigny la faute. Daubigny a voulu faire de la fausse popularité; c'est un ambitieux, un libéral et un libre penseur' (p. 254). To the extent that this confirmed oppositional sympathies shared by Zola, his admiration for the painter was thereby further enhanced.
18. His first successful submission to the Salon had been as long ago as 1838. Both those in the Salon of 1852 were purchased by the French government. The following year, Napoléon III bought Daubigny's *Étang de Gylieu* (awarded a first-class medal at the Salon of 1853) for his personal collection at St Cloud. Leading politicians also patronized his work. His *Printemps* (Salon of 1857) went directly to the Musée du Luxembourg, shortly followed, in 1859, by the award of the *Légion d'honneur.* Daubigny's reputation was such that his work was represented at the Universal Exhibitions of both 1867 and 1878.
19. See Simon Kelly, 'Daubigny et Monet: le paysage de rivière, un produit commercial', in *Éblouissants reflets: cent chefs-d'œuvre impressionnistes*, ed. by Sylvain Amic (Paris: RMN/ Musée des Beaux-Arts de Rouen, 2013), pp. 36–41; and Lynne Ambrosini, 'The Market for Daubigny's Landscapes, or "The Best Pictures Do Not Sell"', in *Inspiring Impressionism: Daubigny, Monet, Van Gogh*, exh. cat. (Edinburgh: NGS, 2016), pp. 81–91. Zola was well aware of Daubigny's increasing wealth: in 1876, he noted that 'pendant quinze ans il n'a pas vendu ses toiles plus de cinq cents francs. Il est vrai que depuis l'heure du triomphe du paysage il a écoulé tout un ramassis de son atelier pour des sommes fort respectables' (*EsA*, p. 331). In fact, even in the late 1860s, his pictures were fetching sums of the order of 4,000 francs, and in 1872 his *Plage à Villerville* was sold for 12,000 francs. Between 1871 and 1873, he earned 369,800 francs, making him one of the most affluent painters of the period.
20. In the preface to the theatrical adaptation of *Thérèse Raquin* (1875) (*OC*, xv, 122; my emphasis).
21. An error ('les îlots puissants') crept into the 1866 edition of *Mon Salon*, whereas the original text in *L'Événement* of 20 May 1866 has the more plausible 'flots puissants' cited here.

22. Zola was probably unaware of Daubigny's Italian sojourn (1836–37) in preparation for entering the competition for the Prix de Rome, as well as of his London paintings (1865, 1866 and 1870–71) and those produced in the Netherlands (1871). In 1852, he had travelled to Switzerland with Corot. Zola's reference to his 'rares fugues en Normandie' downplays his frequent visits to its coast throughout his career, in the interests of stressing that Daubigny's subjects were recognizably local. This is the thrust of Zola's allusions to the painter in the opening section of 'Aux Champs', devoted to 'La Banlieue': 'Personne encore ne s'était douté du charme des rives de la Seine. Plus tard Daubigny explora le fleuve tout entier, depuis Meudon jusqu'à Mantes; et que de trouvailles, le long du chemin' (*OC*, IX, 618).
23. See Maite van Dijk, 'Daubigny and the Impressionists in the 1860s', in *Inspiring Impressionism*, pp. 45–79. By 1861, Gautier's initial enthusiasm had modulated into criticizing Daubigny's merely 'juxtaposed patches of colour' (Snell, *Théophile Gautier*, p. 142).
24. Cited by Riout, *Les Écrivains devant l'impressionnisme*, p. 57.
25. 'Certains réminiscences de Daubigny m'assaillent devant son exposition de cette année'; in J.-K. Huysmans, *Écrits sur l'art, 1867–1905*, ed. by Patrice Locmant (Paris: Bartillat, 2006), p. 270. Sisley, together with Renoir, had painted in the vicinity of Fontainebleau in 1866. His debt to Corot was clear. But a comparison between Corot's and his own *La Route de Sèvres* (1873) is the starting point of a study differentiating their practice; see Robert L. Herbert, 'Industry in the Changing Landscape from Daubigny to Monet', in *French Cities in the Nineteenth Century*, ed. by John M. Merriman (London: Hutchinson, 1982), pp. 139–64.
26. According to Maite van Dijk, Pissarro's *La Marne à Chennevières*, at the Salon of 1865, has 'rightly been described as a homage to Daubigny's larger version of his *Ferryboat near Bonnières-sur-Seine*, shown at the 1861 Salon' (*Inspiring Impressionism*, p. 50). On Pissarro's initial following of convention ('attentive to the expectations' of the arbiters of public taste as well as potential buyers) before liberating himself from it, thereby parting company with Daubigny's landscapes, see Richard Thomson, *Camille Pissarro: Impressionism, Landscape and Rural Labour* (London: Herbert Press,1990), pp. 12–14.
27. Zacharie Astruc, *Les 14 Stations du Salon; suivies d'un récit douloureux* (Paris: Poulet-Malassis et De Brosse, 1859), pp. 286–87. Only in the 'Errata' (p. 407) does Astruc reveal 'Pissaro' (*sic*) as being the name of the artist in question. Zola would repeat this claim in 1868: 'Il y a neuf ans que Camille Pissarro expose [...] des toiles fortes et convaincues, sans que la critique ni le public aient daigné les apercevoir' (*EsA*, p. 182). But Jean Rousseau had written admiringly of Pissarro's submission to the Salon of 1866 (*L'Univers illustré*, 14 July 1866). It remains broadly true, however, that it was from the Salon of 1868 onwards that the painter enjoyed increasing critical attention.
28. *Camille Pissarro, 1830–1903*, ed. by Christopher Lloyd and Anne Distel (London: Arts Council of Great Britain, 1980), p. 75.
29. Letter of 20 May 1868 (*Corr.*, II, 125).
30. Hoek argues that 'ce qui pourrait expliquer pourquoi Zola néglige après 1866 de revenir sur un artiste qu'il prétend apprécier tellement, c'est peut-être que celui-ci paraît si complètement gagné à sa cause naturaliste que sa défense en est devenue superflue pour un critique qui s'intéresse moins aux qualités artistiques de l'œuvre qu'à la conquête de l'hégémonie institutionnelle dans le champ artistique' (*Titres*, p. 340). Apart from anything else, it was not until much later that Zola began to associate numerous artists with his own brand of Naturalism. The section of his *Salon* of 1868 entitled 'Les Naturalistes' and wholly devoted to Pissarro refers to 'tout un groupe qui s'accroît chaque jour', of which he is not as necessarily a member as of 'Les Actualistes' (so designated in his next article) which includes Monet.
31. Zola's first novel, *La Confession de Claude* (1865), is largely set in the outer suburbs to the south-east of Paris which Zola himself had frequented. This barely disguised autobiographical text is punctuated by the use of pathetic fallacy. It nostalgically evokes 'ces paysages pénétrants de ma jeunesse' (*OC*, I, 55) and 'la campagne [...] à cet âge adorable, où la vieille nature a pour quelques jours les grâces délicates de l'enfance' (p. 73), subsequently overwhelmed by 'la tristesse indicible des contrées que la main de l'homme a déchirées' (p. 66). The factory chimneys glimpsed on the horizon speak of a contamination to which Zola returns in 'Aux Champs' in 1878.

While rejecting the idealized representation of nature in both literature and painting 'parce qu'elle n'avait pas encore été humanisée', his response to the urban depredation of its purity is contradictory: 'notre passion des champs nous vient de ce grand mouvement naturaliste du dix-huitième siècle. Nous voulons la campagne dans sa rudesse, nous y fuyons la ville, au lieu d'emporter la ville avec nous' (*OC*, IX, 616–17).

32. Zola's celebration of the *plein air* suppresses the fact that many such canvases were only completed back in the studio, as evidenced by Daubigny, right from the start of his painting outdoors in 1843, and others coping with the vagaries of the weather.
33. Late in life, in a psychological experiment, Zola responded to a question about his favourite sights, claiming these were either 'les spectacles urbains' or 'les paysages'; see Dr Édouard Toulouse, *Enquête médico-psychologique sur la supériorité intellectuelle: Émile Zola* (Paris: Flammarion, 1896), p. 259.
34. This was in spite of his progressive liquidation of his early enthusiasm for the rural novels of George Sand, her version of the peasantry definitively demystified in *La Terre* (1887).
35. Having shown two watercolours there, Robert (a pupil of Bonnat and Puvis de Chavannes, specializing in rural scenes *à la Barbizon*) subsequently, and much to their irritation, parted company with the Impressionists, returning to the official Salon between 1879 and 1883. Letters from Guillemet to Zola before 1870 make it clear that both knew Robert personally.
36. See *Édouard Béliard (1832–1912): le peintre* (the catalogue of the exhibition mounted in 2014 by the Musée intercommunal of the artist's native Étampes).
37. *Le Sémaphore de Marseille*, 30 April–1 May 1876. In another article, in *Le Messager de l'Europe* in June, this commentary is repeated almost *verbatim* ('un paysagiste dont le trait distinctif est la méticulosité', 'le copiste appliqué de la nature', etc.) as are Zola's reservations about a lack of 'flamme intérieure' (*EsA*, pp. 340–41). By the time Zola came to write *L'Œuvre*, he exemplifies artistic failure (see below, n. 72).
38. At almost exactly this moment, Zola started work on *Le Ventre de Paris*. Its cityscapes, viewed through the eyes of his fictional painter, are clearly related to Zola's admiration for Jongkind.
39. Zola would make the same point in relation to Guillemet's views of the Seine shown at the Salons of 1874 and 1875: 'tout au fond la Cité et la cathédrale de Notre Dame, se découpant sur un ciel bleu. Ceci, c'est Paris vivant' (*EsA*, p. 292). This is also the view which represents Claude's ultimate challenge in *L'Œuvre*.
40. In remarking that he would have preferred a title such as *Une Halte au bord de l'eau*, Zola revealed a misunderstanding of the painting shared by many contemporary critics. It in fact represented the stage set of a ballet!
41. The only precursors which Monet tended to cite were Courbet and Corot, thereby reinforcing his status as the pioneering *plein air* painter of the period. For the same reason, he also erased from his artistic *curriculum vitae* his working alongside Jongkind, whom he had known since 1862. On the formative influence of Daubigny, see *Monet: The Seine and the Sea, 1878–1883*, ed. by Michael Clarke and Richard Thomson (Edinburgh: NGS, 2003), pp. 40–41. But Monet's *Pommiers près de Vétheuil* (1878), painted in the year of Daubigny's death, is clearly a homage to one of his most important mentors. He had recognized Daubigny's originality at the Salon of 1859, and his 1865 pictures set in the forest of Fontainebleau testify to his artistic apprenticeship.
42. It was also a somewhat unfair remark, given Monet's landscapes of the 1860s which were clearly compositionally indebted to Daubigny and Corot.
43. There is an echo here of Zola's 1867 critique of Rousseau: 'on dirait que ce paysagiste prend à tâche d'user toute son énergie à émietter la nature' (*EsA*, p. 539).
44. In his review of Guillemet's *Villerville* at the Salon of 1879. It was not only their personal friendship which dictated Zola's consistently favourable assessments of the painter's work. As contrasted with the Impressionists, what secured his critical sympathy was the structural clarity of his landscapes: 'Ce qui constitue l'originalité de Guillemet, c'est qu'il garde un pinceau vigoureux tout en poussant à l'extrême l'étude des détails' (*EsA*, p. 332).
45. If 'le naturalisme triomphant' can embrace artists other than those representing the landscape, such as Fantin-Latour and Gervex, it is also the benchmark against which aberrations can be judged: Jules Breton's rural scenes, for example, categorize him as 'un naturaliste de la veille,

mais un naturaliste tout confit en poésie' (*EsA*, p. 385). On the other hand, certain artists are beyond the pale: Jean-Paul Laurens, in returning to history painting 'sans la renouveler par l'observation et l'analyse de la nature', cannot therefore be 'rangé parmi les naturalistes' (*EsA*, p. 389).

46. Where he had asserted that both rural scenes (the second also known as *La Récolte des pommes de terre*), bore witness to Bastien-Lepage being 'le petit-fils de Courbet et de Millet' (*EsA*, p. 357).
47. Reviewing the second Impressionist exhibition (1876), Zola repeated this contemporary cliché: 'M. Renoir est surtout un peintre de figures' (*EsA*, p. 586). Most of the eighteen Renoir works shown there were indeed portraits.
48. In 1878 (see below, note 53), Zola had transcribed Duret's remarks about Impressionist painters seeing that 'au soleil les ombres portées sur la neige ont des reflets bleus, et il peint des ombres bleues [...]. Certains terrains argileux des campagnes revêtent des apparences lilas, l'impressionniste peint des paysages lilas [...]. Par le soleil d'été, aux reflets du feuillage vert, la peau et les vêtements prennent une teinte violette, l'impressionniste peint des personnages violets' (*EsA*, pp. 575–76).
49. Zola can thus continue to praise the modernity and Naturalist accuracy of *plein air* renderings of 'des scènes mondaines ou populaires, le Bois, les Halles, nos boulevards, notre vie intime' (*EsA*, p. 377).
50. Detailed in Jonathan Crary's magisterial *Techniques of the Observer: On Vision and Modernity in the Nineteenth Century* (Cambridge, MA: MIT Press, 1990); on the 'plurality of means to recode the activity of the eye' (p. 24), see pp. 110–36. Another important study is Martin Jay, *Downcast Eyes: The Denigration of Vision in Twentieth-Century French Thought* (Berkeley: University of California Press, 1993), especially chapter 3: 'The Crisis of the Ancien Scopic Régime: From the Impressionists to Bergson' (pp. 149–209). The implications for Zola's art criticism are discussed in my 'Zola and the Science of Painting', *Nottingham French Studies*, 60.3 (2021), 295–306.
51. As its extended title makes clear: *La Nouvelle Peinture — À propos du groupe d'artistes qui expose dans les galeries Durand-Ruel* (Paris: E. Dentu, 1876).
52. Cited from Duranty's text reproduced in Riout, *Les Écrivains devant l'impressionnisme*, pp. 108–34 (p. 122).
53. Including even Charles Blanc, in his *Grammaire des arts et du dessin* (1867). Duranty had already alluded to Chevreul in his *Salon* of 1870. See Georges Roque, 'Chevreul and Impressionism: A Reappraisal', *Art Bulletin*, 78.1 (1996), 26–39. Although only belatedly translated in 1877 as part of the first complete French edition of his work, the conceptual premises of Schopenhauer's *Le Monde comme volonté et comme représentation* (1818) were also widely disseminated, from 1874 onwards, by writers like Théodore Ribot and, more significantly, Duret — from whose *Les Peintres impressionnistes* (Paris: Heymann et Perois, 1878) Zola cites directly in the year it appeared: 'c'est à eux que nous devons l'étude du plein air, la sensation non plus seulement des couleurs, mais des moindres nuances des couleurs, les tons et encore la recherche des rapports entre l'état de l'atmosphère qui éclaire le tableau et la tonalité générale des objets qui s'y trouvent peints' (*EsA*, p. 575). In his preface, Duret names Zola as one of the 'prosélytes' of Impressionist painting (p. 8).
54. *Le Rappel*, 9 April 1876. Zola's review of the exhibition appeared in *Le Sémaphore de Marseille* of 30 April–1 May.
55. Entitled 'Après une promenade au Salon' (indicative of a rather uncommitted visit to it), this text largely reworks the opening part of his review of the Salon of 1875 published in *Le Messager de l'Europe*, updated to rehearse his belief in 'la victoire prochaine du naturalisme dans notre école de peinture' (*EsA*, p. 400). The artists he cites as examples of those who had 'passé dans le camp des modernes' are Butin, Gervex, Bastien-Lepage and Ernest Duez, all of whom had works exhibited at the Salon of 1881. He refers to representations of the modern world, but to no particular paintings, even though Béliard, Guillemet, Renoir and Manet each had two canvases accepted. Monet was not represented but, given Zola's previous year's castigation of him being 'sur la pente de la pacotille', one notes his condemnation of 'les peintres qui habituent le public à la peinture de pacotille et lui gâtent le goût' (*EsA*, p. 399).
56. Marcel Fouquier, in *La France*, 2 May 1886.

57. Ms 10316, fol. 205. In the novel itself, the narrator interjects: 'Depuis le Salon des Refusés, l'école du plein air s'était élargie, toute une influence croissante se faisait sentir; *malheureusement*, les efforts s'éparpillaient, les nouvelles recrues se contentaient d'ébauches, d'impressions bâclées en trois coups de pinceau' (*RM*, IV, 197; my emphasis).
58. Monet's reputation in this respect is given anecdotal substance, thanks to Guillemet, in Zola's notes on Durand-Ruel buying up all the work of the Impressionists: '[il] se toque pour Monet, achète et achète encore. [...] Toutes les ébauches que Monet lui donne; un puits, un gouffre — Mille Monet — Aussi Monet en veut-il à Pissarro, à Sysley (*sic*) et aux autres: "Si j'étais tout seul!"' (Ms 10316, fols 355–56).
59. In response to Ludovic Halévy's remark that, in the novel, 'les dates manquent', Zola explained that it opened in 1863 and ended in 1876, while admitting 'que j'ai dû, comme dans presque tous les romans de la série, hélas! précipiter les événements et les entasser les uns sur les autres' (*Corr.*, V, 381). But Geffroy, in *La Justice* of 12 May 1886, more precisely referred to 'une acceptation évidente, et inadmissible, de l'anachronisme' (cited in *RM*, IV, 1391).
60. Ms 10316, fols 300–01; subsequently reminding himself: 'La question des impressionnistes. La formule impress. [*sic*] qui demande un génie pour être réalisée' (fol. 38); and 'L'effet des impressionnistes sur le salons. Travail trop hâtif' (fol. 173). This was a charge levelled at Monet by many critics at this stage in his career. Huysmans, for example, refers to his decreasing interest in 'cette peinture brouillonne et hâtive'; like Zola, he considered that 'l'impressionnisme tel que le pratiquait M. Monet, menait tout droit à une impasse'; see his review of the seventh Impressionist exhibition (1882) (*Écrits sur l'art*, p. 271).
61. Ms 10316, fols 343–46. See Micheline Hanotelle, 'Léo Gausson et Zola: réflexions relatives à une lettre du peintre Léo Gausson à Émile Zola et réponse inédite du romancier', *CN*, 63 (1989), 193–203.
62. In a letter to Huysmans of 13 November, and thus shortly before replying to Gausson, Zola expressed his frustration at his slow progress on the novel: 'j'en suis à peine à la moitié' (*Corr.*, V, 333). In chapter 7, but only in rudimentary terms, we are told that Gagnière, briefly explaining it to Mahoudeau, is 'enfoncé depuis quelques mois dans une théorie des couleurs' (*RM*, IV, 191); and Claude's awakened curiosity, a few pages later ('Hein? Tu pioches la théorie des couleurs complémentaires'), merely prepares its subsequent elaboration.
63. See Zola's letter of 26 August 1886, enclosing a contribution to the public homage to Chevreul (*Corr.*, V, 430).
64. Jay, *Downcast Eyes*, p. 150.
65. Émilie Piton-Foucault, *Zola ou la fenêtre condamnée: la crise de la représentation dans 'Les Rougon-Macquart'* (Rennes: Presses universitaires de Rennes, 2015), p. 1043.
66. Ms 10316, fols. 133 and 141: 'Christine est la réalité'; this goes straight into the text of the novel; 'Christine était la réalité, le but que la main atteignait' (*RM*, IV, 243).
67. Ms 10328, fol. 6: 'Débuter par Jean qui ensemence un champ sur le plateau'; 'la campagne, la semence volant toujours dans l'air' (fol. 13). In *L'Œuvre*, Chambouvard's sculpture of this epic figure is much admired: 'Étonnant, *le Semeur*! murmura Claude, et quelle bâtisse, et quel geste!' (*RM*, IV, 133). The sculptor's later *Moissonneuse* (p. 289), Bongrand's *Noce au village* ('une noce débandée à travers les blés, des paysans étudiés de près, et très vrais, qui avaient une allure épique de héros d'Homère' (p. 87)) and *L'Enterrement au village* ('un convoi de jeune fille, débandé parmi des champs de sigle et d'avoine', (p. 288)), as well as Mahoudeau's *Vendangeuse* (p. 133), all testify to Zola already having *La Terre* in mind even before finishing *L'Œuvre*.
68. The descriptive texture of his so-called 'literary impressionism' is referentially grounded. In *L'Œuvre*, to take a single example, the place de la Concorde is 'peuplée de points noirs *qui étaient des hommes*' (*RM*, IV, 75; my emphasis).
69. Because of his well-known championing of Wagner, Fantin-Latour had been envisaged as a partial model for Gagnière ('Fantin, mais plus inférieur comme peintre'), thereby arriving at Béliard (see below, n. 72); and Lapostollet whose name was inserted in the work notes relating to Gagnière, but mainly as an example of a landscape artist inexplicably rejected by the Salon jury (Ms 10316, fol. 73).
70. Zola repeats the note 'les couleurs complémentaires, avec Gagnière' (Ms 10316, fols 142 and

156); but he was also aware that this could not be expanded to fill a whole chapter: 'J'ai encore le développement des théories, mais tout cela ne me donne pas un chapitre de quarante pages' (fol. 116).

71. Ms 10316: 'rêvant, dissertant' (fols 242–43), but 'vague, sur la peinture' (fol. 108); 'rêvassant' and 'envolé ailleurs' (fol. 81); 'extasié et les théories' (fol. 242); 'distrait' (fol. 75). These traits are affixed to the character in the text of *L'Œuvre* (*RM*, IV): 'assommant' (p. 79); always 'songeant à autre chose' (p. 131); 'les regards perdus dans la nuit' (p. 84); 'en extase, philosophant et poétisant' (p. 335); 'l'air plus falot encore que de coutume' (p. 122).

72. Ms 10316: 'le raté peintre' (fol. 194); 'raté comme peintre, s'aigrissant' (fol. 113); 'raté comme peintre. Prendre là Béliard' (fol. 295); in adding to the last of these notes, 'j'aimerais qu'il soit né où il retourne', Zola cemented the identification of Béliard who had given up painting and returned to his native Étampes to pursue a career in local politics. In Zola referring to Gagnière as 'conscientieux', but whose landscapes are devoid of emotion, we are reminded of his assessment of Béliard as a 'copiste soigneux' in 1876: 'je voudrais une flamme qui montât dans toute cette conscience, même si cette flamme devait bruler aux dépens de la sincérité' (*EsA*, p. 584). Paradoxically, Béliard's last studio was the model for Claude Lantier's in *L'Œuvre*.

73. This is said of the elderly Courajod, 'notre père à tous' (*RM*, IV, 260–61), the 'maître paysagiste' (p. 137) whose *Mare de Cagny*, in the Luxembourg, is further evidence of this fictional character being at least partly modelled on Corot. On the other hand, we are told that Courajod is seventy (p. 137), in a chapter supposedly taking place in 1863, which does not fit (Corot being born in 1796), contrary to Niess's assertion that this 'would be almost exactly right for Corot' (*Zola, Cézanne, and Manet*, p. 58). At one stage, Zola had the character aged eighty (Ms 10316, fol. 144)!

74. Respectively: Ms 10316, fol. 295 and fol. 242 (my emphases in both). Their only mention in the text of *L'Œuvre* occurs in relation to the strategies of Naudet, the art dealer: 'Ses premiers gains venaient de la hausse des morts illustres, niés de leur vivant, Courbet, Millet, Rousseau' (*RM*, IV, 290), notwithstanding the anachronisms involved: the loose timeframe of the novel, anchored only by the Salon des Refusés of 1863, barely extends beyond 1866, so Rousseau (d. 1867) might just qualify, but not Millet (d. 1875) or Courbet (d. 1877).

75. Claude's return to the official Salon (*RM*, IV, 205) exactly corresponds to Monet's, which is the context of Zola's continuing admiration, prefacing his 1880 reservations, of the latter's depiction of rivers and the sea.

76. This is by no means exclusive to Zola. The prevalence of such a medical discourse is exemplified by Huysmans: he alludes (in a review of the Impressionist exhibition of 1880), to 'les expériences du Dr Charcot sur les altérations dans la perception des couleurs' amongst his hospital patients as well as to contemporary opthalmic research; and in the declaration that 'l'école nouvelle proclamait cette vérité scientifique: que la grande lumière décolore les tons', he repeats verbatim Duranty's earlier analysis of the Impressionists' decomposition of light. More damningly, he asserts that 'l'œil de la plupart d'eux s'était monomanisé', exemplified by Caillebotte's 'indigomanie', before a return to 'l'état normal'; 'leurs rétines étaient malades'; likening their idiosyncratic colour schemes to those of the 'hystériques de la Salpêtrière'; and concluding that 'ce désarroi de la vue domine tout, noie tout, dans leurs toiles' (Huysmans, *Écrits sur l'art*, pp. 164–67).

77. There were three major exhibitions in 1896: that of the Société des artistes français, mounted in the traditional venue of the Palais de l'industrie; the Salon de la Société nationale des beaux-arts, at the Palais du Domaine du Bagatelle, on the Champ-de-Mars; and the fifth Salon de la Rose + Croix, which had opened on 2 March. It has been suggested that Zola's article was a virulent response to the latter, in a poster for which he was caricatured as 'Gorgon-Zola'; reproduced in *Zola*, ed. by Michèle Sacquin (Paris: Bibliothèque nationale de France/Fayard, 2002) p. 171.

78. Zola's denigration of 'la queue' is consistent with the principle, articulated in relation to 'disciples' of every school, that imitation is the obverse of an originality further undermined by angling works towards public acceptance. This is exemplified in *L'Œuvre* by Fagerolles's success. But as early as an article in *Le Bien public* of 15 October 1877, Zola had deplored the fact that 'nos Salons annuels sont aujourd'hui plein d'impressionnistes, je veux dire de jeunes gens malins qui copient les impressionnistes en les édulcorant, pour la plus grande jouissance des bourgeois'

(*OC*, IX, 716–17).

79. This detail is anticipated in *L'Œuvre*, in the characters' ribald reaction to a painting of 'des chevaux fantastiques, bleus, violets, roses' (*RM*, IV, 121).

CHAPTER 6

❖

From *La nouvelle peinture* to the Old Masters: Zola's Revisionist Art Criticism

If, as the previous chapter argued, the publication of Duranty's *La Nouvelle Peinture* marked a decisive moment, paradoxically, in Zola's increasing disenchantment with 'la nouvelle peinture' itself, most strikingly represented by Impressionism, it is not therefore by chance that it also coincides with Zola's shifting attitude towards the Old Masters. For whereas his writing on contemporary painting initially positions the pictorial output of earlier generations in *contradistinction* to the artists he champions in the 1860s and 1870s, ultimately they serve in his thinking as a timeless *corrective* to modernist experimentation. Emblematic of Zola's distancing himself from a polemically-inflected rejection of the Old Masters, is a text he published in 1880, *Madame Sourdis*. The character of Ferdinand, who has been identified as a 'hybrid' of Manet, Cézanne, Renoir, Degas and Pissarro,[1] is perceived as a representative of 'la peinture d'une nouvelle école, qui niait Raphaël' (*OC*, IX, 1121–22). But oblique authorial irony at his expense is telling, registering at the very least a revealing ambivalence. For it has sometimes been claimed that it was only as a result of Zola's visit to Rome in 1894 that he found himself belatedly revaluing the achievements of the Italian Renaissance — too late to leave its mark on his art criticism or, indeed, his fiction. This chapter will propose instead that Zola's appreciation of the Old Masters, akin to Flaubert's, is longstanding, however effectively disguised it had to remain within the critical discourse of a self-appointed opponent of officially sanctioned pictorial tradition. With the wisdom of hindsight, we can see this prefigured in his confiding to Huysmans, in 1883, that 'plus je vais et plus je me détache des coins d'observations simplement curieux, plus j'ai l'amour des grands créateurs abondants qui apportent un monde'.[2]

Liberation from the Art of the Past

In his attacks on the dictates of the Académie des Beaux-Arts, Zola establishes an equivalence between pictorial originality and a rejection of the art of the past. Integral to such a perspective is a denial of 'le beau absolu immuable [...] dominant les âges', irrespective of whether found in the variables of 'les matinées pâles et froides de la Hollande, dans les soirées chaudes et voluptueuses de l'Italie et de l'Espagne' (*EsA*, p. 476). In one of his earliest articles, in 1866, he refers to Courbet's progressive liberation from such criteria: 'Courbet a commencé par imiter les Flamands et certains maîtres de la Renaissance; mais sa nature se révoltait, et il se sentait entraîné par toute sa chair [...] vers le monde matériel qui l'entourait' (*EsA*, p. 163).[3] In tracking Manet's development, to take an analogous example, Zola so distorts the painter's apprenticeship that he disparages the latter's visits to Italy and Holland: 'il perdit son temps'. His stress on Manet's modernity, in his pioneering study of 1867, leads him to assert that, 'sentant qu'il n'arrivait à rien en copiant les maîtres, [...] il fit effort pour oublier tout ce qu'il avait étudié dans les musées' (*EsA*, pp. 474–75). As late as 1876, Zola is still insisting, for the same reason, on his view 'qu'on n'arrivait à rien en copiant les maîtres' (*EsA*, p. 333). Writing about Impressionist landscapes in his *Salon* of 1868, Zola contrasts those of Pissarro with the sanitized 'campagne officielle' prevalent 'au temps de Poussin', with its 'belle ordonnance' and 'correction magistrale' (*EsA*, p. 193). Such charges of artifice and anachronism, levelled at painters still wedded to 'le paysage classique' like Flandrin and Alfred de Curzon, are a constant refrain: 'on croit se promener à travers la nature de Poussin, une nature créée pour les pasteurs de Virgile. Rien ne saurait être plus sublime et en même temps plus grotesque' (*EsA*, p. 332).[4]

Over and above, or underlying, such apparent opposition to the art of the past embedded in commentary on particular painters, is Zola's singling out of the continuing prestige of the Prix de Rome ('une de ces institutions que tout le monde attaque et qui subsistent quand même' (*EsA*, p. 631)) as the most nefarious impediment to the acceptance of a truly modern freedom of expression, whether pictorial or sculptural. It represented, as he put it as early as 1868, 'toute la défroque antique dont on abuse dans les arts depuis deux mille ans' (*EsA*, p. 623). 'Quand le prix de Rome a été créé', he would write in *Le Roman expérimental* (1880), 'il s'agissait de fournir à des jeunes artistes l'occasion de faire un séjour dans la ville que l'on regardait alors comme le tabernacle de l'art' (*OC*, x, 1368). Actually *copying* there the Old Masters, rather than simply being influenced by them, exemplified the fundamental principles of the Académie des Beaux-Arts, determining the training of painters as well as admission to the Salon. These were consecrated by the annual competition for the Prix de Rome, awarded to the rendering of a mythological or biblical subject which adhered most consistently to academic criteria. For avant-garde critics, this recourse to 'les mondes morts de l'antiquité' (*EsA*, p. 628) was anathema.[5] 'Dans notre art moderne', Zola had stressed in an article of 1876, 'qui se nourrit de plus en plus des réalités contemporaines, on ne comprend pas trop de quelle utilité peut être un séjour de quatre années à Rome' (*EsA*, p. 632). That four-year stay at the Villa Médicis, described by him as long ago as 1867 as 'une cage froide' (*EsA*, p. 532), was a waste of time and talent, 'une sorte de gymnastique de dessin selon les maîtres' (*EsA*, p. 632), an apprenticeship devoted to 'l'étude des langues mortes artistiques' (*OC*, x, 976). In assessing the characters in Edmond de Goncourt's *Manette Salomon* (1875), Zola had noted: 'Garnotelle, le prix de Rome, le peintre correct et médiocre' (*OC*, xi, 171). This is certainly the thrust of his remarks in *Le Bien public* of 18 June 1877: 'Rome est si peu nécessaire à nos peintres que les plus grands d'entre eux, Eugène Delacroix, Courbet, Théodore Rousseau, Millet, Corot et toute notre grande école de paysagistes, n'y ont point passé. De cette pépinière qui devait être fertile en maîtres, il n'est guère sorti que des médiocrités' (*OC*, x, 1369).

It was therefore equally unsurprising that Zola should share much topical contempt for the short-lived experiment of the Musée des copies (1873–74),[6] initiated by Thiers with the support of Charles Blanc who had never wavered in his conviction that only by studying the Old Masters could artists and critics achieve a degree of professional competence. From his conservative perspective, only the Renaissance, indeed, served as a counterweight to the destabilizing contemporary innovations which he decried. Consistent with Blanc's wider pedagogic mission, painters were dispatched all over Europe to bring back reproductions of masterpieces which could thereby be made accessible to the general public. But the 'Musée européen', as it was also known, quickly became, in the surrounding polemics (even before its opening), the 'Musée des Horreurs', as Albert Wolff termed it in *Le Figaro* of 18 April 1873. On that same date, Zola wrote in *Le Sémaphore de Marseille* that 'les grands artistes sont généralement de très mauvais copistes', referring to a painter (identifiable as Delacroix's cousin, Léon Riesener (1808–78)) who had spent a year copying Old Masters in Amsterdam from which he returned with a commission to copy Rubens's *Le Coup de lance* and his own artistic impotence confirmed: 'c'est un garçon absolument fini, et dont toute l'originalité s'en est allée' (*EsA*, p. 617).

The logic of opposing originality and imitation has, of course, a long rhetorical history. Whatever Zola's reservations about Baudelaire's art criticism, nobody had put it better than in the latter's conception, in his *Salon* of 1859, of infinite regression in academic art's investment in copying the Old Masters: 'L'imitateur de l'imitateur trouve ses imitateurs, et chacun poursuit ainsi son rêve de grandeur.'[7] In 1875, Zola remarked that representing contemporary figures was not in itself a sufficient condition of properly modern portraiture: 'Bien entendu, les modèles sont pris dans la vie, mais presque toujours l'artiste songe à imiter une école quelconque. Il veut peindre comme Rubens, Rembrandt, Raphaël ou Vélasquez. Il a dans la tête un vieil idéal' (*EsA*, p. 286). In the same review of that year's Salon, he derides Doré's *Dante et Virgile visitant la septième enceinte*, with its dimensions (10 x 4 m) approximating to those of Veronese's *Noces de Cana*: 'on dirait une caricature de Michel-Ange' (*EsA*, p. 272), a charge Zola would repeat in *Le Naturalisme au Salon* (1880) in respect of Doré's habitually huge submissions to the annual exhibitions: 'Il croit de bonne foi ressusciter Michel-Ange, d'autant plus que certains critiques ont fait la mauvaise plaisanterie de le lui persuader' (*EsA*, p. 392).

For his Russian reading public, in these extended surveys of the latest manifestations of French artistic productivity, an innate patriotism leads Zola to attenuate his critique of a derivative national culture of which reliance on the Old Masters was symptomatic: 'Nous avons à cette heure des Rubens, des Véronèse, des Vélasquez, petit-fils des génies célèbres qui, sans grande originalité personnelle, n'en donnent pas moins à nos expositions un accent d'individualité très curieux. La

France, en peinture, est en train de battre toutes les autres nations avec les armes qu'elle emprunte à leurs grands peintres de jadis' (*EsA*, p. 267). So constantly is this point made that he would repeat it almost verbatim in 1881, referring to the prize-winning orthodoxies of the day as 'petits-fils très adroits' demonstrating 'une facilité d'imitation incroyable' (*EsA*, p. 396). At the beginning of his career as an art critic, however, he simply deplored 'les plagiats dont vit notre école; nous ne possédons pas un art véritablement français; nous imitons les Italiens, les Hollandais, les Espagnols même, en leur donnant notre grâce, notre esprit, notre banalité charmante' (*EsA*, p. 174). At this same Salon of 1868, he lambasts the 'amusants farceurs' in relation to the 'maîtres de la Renaissance' whose work they profess to respect while achieving in their own right only 'une falsification de la peinture': 'Ils parlent de traditions, ils disent qu'ils suivent les règles, et je jurerais qu'ils n'ont jamais vu et compris un Véronèse ou un Vélasquez, car s'ils avaient vu et compris de tels modèles, ils chercheraient à peindre d'une autre façon' (*EsA*, p. 185).

Such irony at the expense of unthinking, or even conscious, imitation also leaves its mark on Zola's fiction. Fagerolles, in *L'Œuvre*, is mocked for his pretentious *hôtel particulier* described as 'la reproduction exacte d'une maison renaissance de Bourges' (*RM*, IV, 268), presumably the fifteenth-century Palais de Jacques Cœur. In the work notes for the novel, he is characterized by his 'très grande facilité' and as having 'une adresse de singe' visible in his 'imitation de bronzes' of every kind (Ms 10316, fols 236–37), thereby justifying his 'ferme résolution de travailler désormais à obtenir le prix de Rome' (*RM*, IV, 136).[8] These same notes highlight the contradictions of Claude's work on his *Plein air*: 'Il a voulu du nu, il en a mis du vert, vert [*sic*], jaune et or', 'y revenant dans une débauche d'art', with Zola adding between the lines 'les peintres de la Renaissance' (fol. 80). In *Germinal*, imitation results in kitsch: as in the inappropriate 'salle de recettes et une chambre de machine, arrondies en chevet de chapelle renaissance, que la cheminée surmontait d'une spirale de mosaïque' (*RM*, III, 1390); or the managerial décor, brutally contrasted to that of the miners, of Hennebeau's 'cabinet italien du dix-septième siècle, un contador espagnol du quinzième, et un devant d'autel pour le lambrequin de la cheminée [...] tout ce luxe de chapelle' (*RM*, III, 1318–19). Other domestic interiors are no less parodic: Nana's 'candélabres de zinc jouant le bronze florentin' (*RM*, II, 1122), her luxurious residence 'de style Renaissance' ('bâti par un jeune peintre, grisé d'un premier succès') with its eclectic 'mobilier artistique' (*RM*, II, 1347) and grandiose bed, prefiguring Irma Bécot's 'grand lit d'amour' in *L'Œuvre*, where this 'courtisane fauve' seems to step out of 'un vieux cadre de la Renaissance' (*RM*, IV, 304).

The Old Masters Revalued

It is almost certainly a mistake, however, to argue that such textual moments obliquely reinforce Zola's credentials as one of the most consistently oppositional art critics of the period. For they have to be set against potential contradictions and discernible ambiguities. In the name of architectural modernity, for example, Dubuche, in *L'Œuvre*, wants to sweep away 'les dentelles ouvragées de la

Renaissance, ce renouveau antique greffé sur le moyen-âge, des bijoux d'art où notre démocratie ne pouvait se loger!' (*RM*, IV, 137). But the exclamation mark prefaces even more portentous declamations: progressively 'gagné par sa fougue' as he elaborates an inter-artistic modernist manifesto, we may well ask whether he is subject to the same authorial irony as the 'nouvelle école' of *Madame Sourdis* 'qui niait Raphaël'. Even Zola's apparent distaste for inappropriately anachronistic décors is balanced by his own tastes, contrarily mirrored in the home of the autobiographically conceived Sandoz, with its 'bibelots de tous les peuples et de tous les siècles [...] des cabinets italiens et des vitrines hollandaises' (*RM*, IV, 323). And not just in fictional inventiveness, as is evident from Zola's own heterogeneous collection, including reproductions of a Botticelli, Renaissance miniatures and four bronze statuettes in the style of Michelangelo.[9] As for copying the Old Masters, his letters of the 1860s make gentle fun of Jean-Baptiste Chaillan, Zola's and Cézanne's mutual friend, the 'fort médiocre copiste' who returns from the Louvre with his 'Chaillan-Rubens [...] bien triste à voir'.[10] But to Cézanne himself, in trying to persuade the painter to join him in Paris in 1862, Zola underlined 'un avantage que tu ne saurais trouver autre part, celui des musées, où tu peux étudier d'après les maîtres [...] tu copieras, soit au Louvre, soit au Luxembourg, le chef-d'œuvre qui te plaira'.[11] For even in his most scathing denunciation of the Musée des copies, Zola was not calling into question the achievement represented by the originals: 'Sur les cent et quelques copies exposées, la plupart étaient ridicules [...]. C'est insulter les chefs-d'œuvre que de les défigurer ainsi' (*EsA*, p. 617). No less double-edged is Claude Lantier, in his first incarnation as the young painter of *Le Ventre de Paris*, comparing the younger of the two Méhudin girls 'à une vierge de Murillo', only to declare 'en se fâchant, que Murillo peignait comme un polisson' (*RM*, I, 619). Shortly afterwards, however, Zola comments in the press on the sale at auction of Murillo's *Petit Pasteur,* 'une des plus belles toiles du maître' (*EsA*, p. 652).

What is certain is that Zola's appreciation of the Old Masters distances him from Claude's militant dream, in *L'Œuvre*, to create 'une sacrée suite de toiles à faire éclater le Louvre' (*RM*, IV, 47). Nor does he share, in this respect, the incendiary remarks of Duranty or Pissarro.[12] For it is also in *L'Œuvre* that it is said of Courbet that 'la vision restait celle des vieux maîtres et que la facture reprenait et continuait les beaux morceaux de nos musées' (*RM*, IV, 45). And the narrator's attitude towards Claude's refusal to complete his Louvre apprenticeship resembles Zola's impatience with Cézanne's failure to follow to the letter his pedagogic advice cited above.[13] For although he often castigates the residual academic conformity of contemporary painters, Zola's real critical contempt is reserved for 'les faiseurs, les hommes qui ont volé un semblant d'originalité aux maîtres du passé' (*EsA*, p. 156). Between his frequent visits to the museum with Chaillan and Cézanne in the early 1860s and taking his children there forty years later, the Louvre remains for Zola both the apogee of artistic achievement and the benchmark against which the apparently 'scandalous' aspects of modern painting are judged.[14] In his *Salon* of 1866, he writes that 'la place de M. Manet est marquée au Louvre comme celle de Courbet' (*EsA*, p. 155),[15] anticipating his more specific prediction, in the provocative conclusion to his 1867 study of the former, that 'le destin avait sans doute déjà marqué au musée du Louvre la place future de l'*Olympia* et du *Déjeuner sur l'herbe*' (*EsA*, p. 497).[16]

But Zola's familiarity with the Old Masters is not limited to contemplating their works in the galleries of the Louvre, while not forgetting (as Francis Haskell reminds us) that this category 'gradually came to embrace all artists who had lived before the French Revolution'.[17] If Cézanne played a seminal role in Zola's pictorial apprenticeship, as described in Chapter 2, we can only speculate about the extent to which Zola subscribed to his oft-cited 'le Louvre est le livre où nous apprenons à lire' informing Cézanne's own admiration for the acknowledged masterpieces of the past.[18] The painter's preferences were clear-cut: 'Je n'aime pas les primitifs [...]. Je n'aime que Rubens, Poussin et les Vénitiens'.[19] On the one hand, it is not difficult to correlate such references with Zola's, always allowing for the fact that, like the profusion of Old Masters indexed across Balzac's writing,[20] many might be dismissed as little more than cultural clichés.[21] For these survive the half-century absence of relevant major exhibitions in France since 1814.[22] On the other, there are, as we shall see, significant conjunctions between those artists and works which Cézanne and Zola both privilege.

Zola's engagement with the art of the past starts early in his career, as is evident from some of those book reviews, mentioned in Chapter 1, that formed part of his artistic education: browsing through Alfred Michiels's *Histoire de la peinture flamande depuis ses débuts jusqu'en 1864*, Zola learned about the discovery of painting in oil as well as 'l'époque artistique des Van Eyck' (*OC*, x, 498); in relation to the work of Dürer, 'un vieux maître allemand' whose drawings were reproduced in a 'magnifique volume' edited by Charles Narrey (*Albert Dürer à Venise et dans les Pays-Bas*), he admitted that 'nous n'en sommes plus à cet art un peu sec et trop symbolique; mais il y a en lui une naïveté et une foi pénétrantes qui nous disent que tout cela a été vécu' (*OC*, x, 627–28); a fortnight later, in *Le Salut public* of 9 October 1866, in a double review devoted to publications concerning Rembrandt and Velázquez, 'les deux puissants génies', he criticizes both studies: *Rembrandt, discours sur sa vie et son génie*, authored by a Dutch scholar, seems to him merely preliminary erudition to what its translator (William Bürger) advocates as a book focused on 'cet attrait poétique que comporte l'originalité du Shakespeare de la Hollande'; *Vélasquez et ses œuvres*, by William Stirling ('historien conscientieux et bien informé'), is, for Zola, devoid of 'une analyse plus pénétrante du génie de Vélasquez [...] plus artistique et plus poignante' (*OC*, x, 653); and in his ferocious dismantling of the *Tableau historique des beaux-arts*, as mentioned earlier, Zola mocks its guiding principle ('dégager l'idéal du réel en ramenant chaque forme à son type', ascribed to Greek aesthetics and inherited by Raphaël) to the extent that 'les artistes [de] la Renaissance [et] Raphaël lui-même [...] vous auraient éclaté de rire au nez' in repeating it 'tandis qu'ils peignaient' (*OC*, x, 659–61).

One book which Zola did not merely skim-read, as we have seen, was Proudhon's *Du principe de l'art et de sa destination sociale* (1865), offering him a pretext for defining his own aesthetic principles. While his long study of this, in two instalments, is headed 'Proudhon et Courbet', it is seldom noted that the book itself accommodates a much wider range of artists. For, in the first part of his essay, Zola rehearses Proudhon's survey of 'l'art égyptien, l'art grec et romain, l'art chrétien, la Renaissance, l'art contemporain' (*EsA*, pp. 421–22): Michelangelo, Titian, Veronese, Rembrandt, Raphaël, David, Ingres, Léopold Robert, Horace Vernet and Delacroix, the latter as representative of the Romantic generation as the sculptors David d'Angers and François Rude. And from this range of artists, it is the Old Masters who are recruited by Zola to refute Proudhon's central thesis equating aesthetic and utilitarian values, thereby downgrading Delacroix's subjectivism, for example, relative to Courbet's social critique. 'Quant à la Renaissance et à notre époque', Zola fulminates, 'il n'y voit qu'anarchie et décadence', citing directly Proudhon's 'Plût à Dieu que Luther ait exterminé les Raphaël, les Michel-Ange et tous leurs imitateurs, tous ces ornementateurs de palais et d'églises' (*EsA*, p. 422). Countering this with 'j'aime la Renaissance et notre époque, ces luttes entre artistes, ces hommes qui tous viennent dire un mot encore inconnu hier', Zola explains that they are 'des gens qui se permettent d'avoir du génie sans consulter l'humanité: des Michel-Ange, des Titien, des Véronèse, des Delacroix, qui ont l'audace de penser pour eux et non pour leurs contemporains'. The inclusion here of Delacroix is not apparently consistent with Zola's campaigning rejection of Romanticism. But no less surprising is that his admiration for the painter exemplifying the latter's extravagant aesthetic should receive its most extended expression in an 1877 article devoted to his *bête noire*, Adolphe Thiers, Zola declaring himself stupefied that the politician, 'avec sa passivité de mouton, ait su découvrir Delacroix'. For it had been in his review of the Salon of 1822 that Thiers alone ('seul contre tous') had defended Delacroix's *Dante et Virgile aux enfers*. Zola somewhat undercuts his tribute by referring to the painting itself as 'très raisonnable et très tranquille comparée à ces tableaux merveilleux que le peintre créa plus tard', not yet having shaken off the influence of Géricault and 'pas encore rompu avec la tradition'. But in underlining 'l'énorme insolence de cet acte', Zola rehearses what Thiers had himself written in relation to Delacroix's grouping and distribution of the painting's human figures 'avec la hardiesse d'un Michel-Ange et la fécondité d'un Raphaël' (*OC*, XIV, 300).

A far less generalized invocation of the Old Masters, however, coincides with Zola's reading of Taine. This leaves an indelible mark on his own writing about the visual arts. For while Proudhon's references serve an essentially polemical purpose, Zola recognized in Taine a critic temperamentally qualified to dispense insights into the masterpieces he had viewed on a visit to Rome, Florence and Venice in the spring of 1864, collected in the two volumes of his *Voyage en Italie* published by Hachette almost two years later. Their evocation of 'les glorieuses années de la Renaissance' was immediately celebrated by Zola as exemplifying 'une esthétique toute d'observation [qui] porte sur Raphaël et sur Michel-Ange des jugements qui ont dû effrayer notre École des Beaux-Arts' (*OC*, X, 348).[23] A few months later, in *Le Salut public* of 26 October 1866, he cites Taine's remark that these artists' contemporary spectator

> sentira, sans éducation d'atelier, par une sympathie volontaire, les nudités héroïques de Michel-Ange; la santé, la placidité, le regard simple d'une

> Madonne de Raphaël; la vitalité hardie et naturelle d'un bronze de Donatello; l'attitude contournée, étrangement séduisante, d'une figure de Vinci; la superbe volupté animale, le mouvement impétueux, la force et la joie athlétique des personnages de Giorgione et du Titien. (*OC*, x, 673)

Zola had already developed this admiration in his extended study of Taine, imagined as 'vivant en pleine Renaissance', in *La Revue contemporaine* of 15 February 1866.[24] 'C'est le compagnon de Rubens et de Michel-Ange', Zola writes, 'un des lurons de *La Kermesse*, une de ces créatures puissantes et emportées tordant leurs membres de marbres sur le tombeau des Médicis' (*EsA*, p. 449). In spite of Taine's analytical methodology, his empathy is registered in 'un certain frémissement dans la phrase' which bears witness to his feeling for 'Rubens et Michel-Ange, Swift et Shakespeare. Cet amour, chez lui, sera instinctif, irréfléchi' (*EsA*, p. 453). For Taine, according to Zola, 'la Renaissance est l'anarchique réveil de la chair, et nous entendons encore aujourd'hui du fond des âges ce cri du sang, cette explosion de vie, cet appel à la beauté matérielle et agissante' (*EsA*, p. 460). Angling such paraphrase towards his assimilation of an evolutionary history of art, Zola establishes a parallel between fractures: 'C'est Michel-Ange dressant des colosses en face des vierges de Raphaël; c'est Delacroix brisant les lignes que M. Ingres redresse' (*EsA*, p. 462). But, prefiguring Zola's 1894 contemplation of the artist's *Last Judgement* in the Sistine Chapel, it is clearly Michelangelo, as explicated by Taine, who secures his own visceral attention: 'Michel-Ange, grossissant les muscles, tordant les reins, grandissant tel membre aux dépens de tel autre.' He shares Taine's preference for Michelangelo over a somewhat fey Raphaël, subscribing to his view that 'Michel-Ange est moderne et c'est pour cela que nous le comprenons sans effort'.[25] Taine's influence on late nineteenth-century appreciation of the Old Masters is seminal: Cézanne too (to take a particularly relevant example), acknowledges such a debt.[26] For Zola, it can be argued, it was a revelation with far-reaching consequences, both for his art criticism and his fiction.

From this perspective, the visit to the Louvre in chapter 3 of *L'Assommoir* (*RM*, II, 443–47) is instructive. As Gervaise's wedding party proceeds through the museum, the present tense of the narrative confirms once again Zola's familiarity with the place: 'la longue galerie où sont les écoles italiennes et flamandes'; and, as opposed to the 'ignorance ahurie' of the working-class characters, with 'des siècles d'art [...], la sécheresse fine des primitifs, les splendeurs des Vénitiens, la vie grasse et belle de lumière des Hollandais'. It is a discourse, modulated through various points of view, which is both conflated and allusive, creating in the Louvre a connotative space uneasily lodged between familiarity and an erudition which is testimony to Zola's own pictorial education. For he appears to write for a reader able to imagine what the characters feel amongst the splendours of the Gallery of Apollo; who would recognize, amongst 'les dieux de marbre noir muets dans leur raideur hiératique', *Le Nègre* situated at the entrance of the Louvre since 1603; a reader who would have, in the mind's eye, as Gervaise and her friends make their way up to the 'galerie française' on the first floor, the 'musée assyrien' assembled between 1847 and 1852, with its 'bêtes monstrueuses, moitié chattes et moitiés femmes' which so terrify

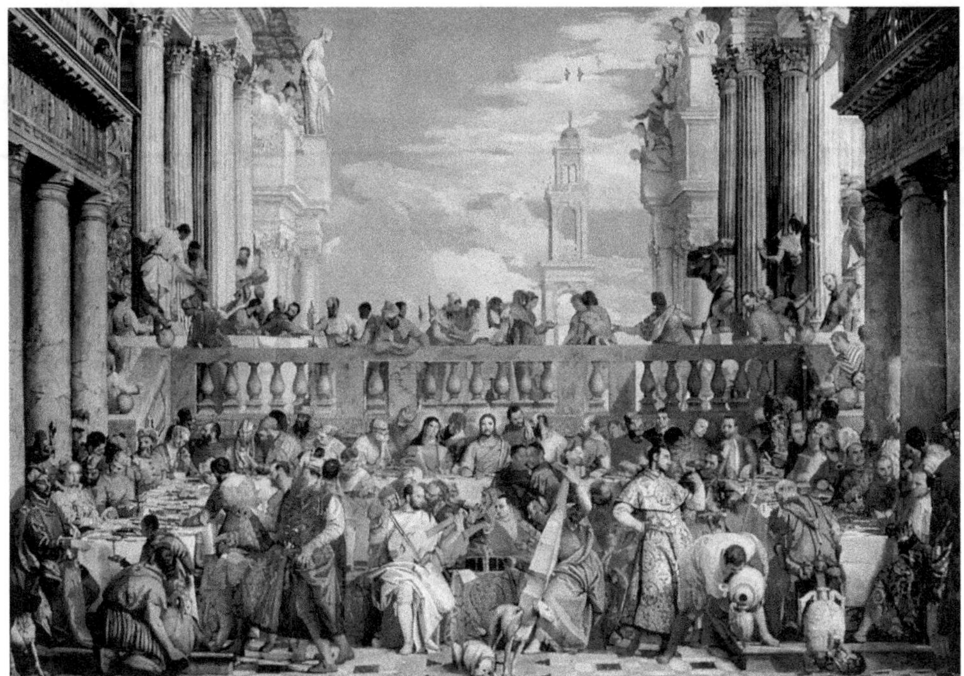

FIG. 6.1. Paolo Veronese, *Les Noces de Cana* (1562–63), oil on canvas, 667 × 994 cm. Musée du Louvre, Paris.

them; who would have no trouble answering the vague speculation about monetary value indulged in by the characters, starting perhaps with the very Murillo picture included in Zola's guided tour, purchased from the Soult collection in 1852 for so scandalous a sum that, for a generation, guides to the Louvre named the price — right up to the last of the 615,300 francs it had cost the nation.

The whole episode functions, of course, as a *mise en abyme* of fictional destinies.[27] But it is also a prime example of Henri Mitterand's remark, cited in the Introduction in relation to the *Rougon-Macquart* series, that 'rares sont les romans du cycle où ne se montre pas le point de vue du critique d'art', adding that this 'scène d'anthologie' in *L'Assommoir* reveals Zola's 'idéaux artistiques'.[28] It also illuminates his critical purchase on the masterpieces on display. For whereas Madinier, the self-appointed and unreliable guide, provides for the characters a historical commentary devoid of sensitivity to colour and form, Zola measures the emotional impact of the paintings against their power to speak directly to the intimate concerns, however unsophisticated, of the viewer overcome by the profusion of works barely glimpsed ('il aurait fallu une heure devant chacune, si l'on avait voulu comprendre'): in the *Mona Lisa*, Coupeau finds 'une resemblance avec une de ses tantes'; by virtue of the colour of the sitter's hair, Mme Lorilleux identifies herself with Titian's portrait of Laura Dianti (*Woman with a Mirror, c.* 1515), notwithstanding Madinier confusing this with Leonardo de Vinci's *La Belle Ferronnière*; the heavily pregnant Mme Gaudron 'les mains sur son ventre' (all the more ironic faced with one of the artist's

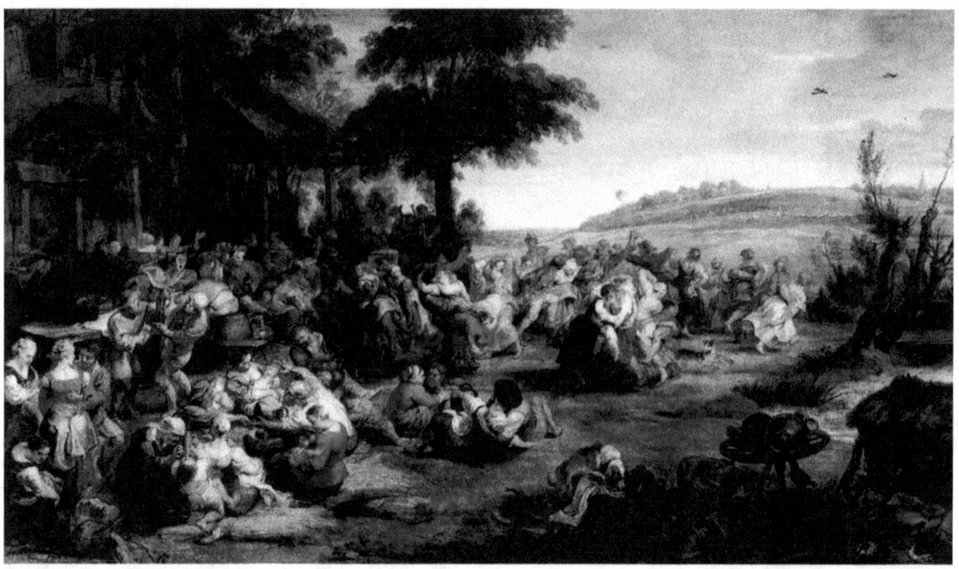

Fig. 6.2. Peter Paul Rubens, *La Kermesse* (*c.* 1635), oil on panel, 149 × 261 cm. Musée du Louvre, Paris.

versions of *The Immaculate Conception*), and her husband 'restaient béants, attendris et stupides, en face de *La Vierge* de Murillo'; even the ribald reaction to 'les cuisses d'Antiope' is not just for comic effect, Zola thereby alluding to either Titian's *Jupiter et Antiope* (1535–40) or Correggio's *Le Sommeil d'Antiope* (*c.* 1528), or both.

But what is also notable is the extent to which Zola's own 'reading' here of certain Old Master paintings is properly creative. The two most precisely aligned into a mutually informing structure are Veronese's *Noces de Cana* (Fig. 6.1) and Rubens's *Kermesse* (Fig. 6.2). Evidence of Zola's admiration for the former's 'magnificence tumultueuse', to be found throughout his work,[29] is of a purely strategic kind. It assumes its importance in *L'Assommoir* only in contradistinction to the Rubens. He had clearly been struck by Taine's interpretation of the latter's 'caractère essentiel' ('la furie de l'orgie, la rage de la chair saoule et brutale' (*EsA*, p. 464)), adopting it repeatedly in a variety of contexts.[30] The novel elaborates more ambiguously the painting's celebration of carnality and inebriation, irrecuperable to moral judgement, social forms, and temporal constraints. But whereas Madinier refrains from saying anything about it ('il ne dit toujours rien, il se contenta d'indiquer la toile, d'un coup d'œil égrillard'), Zola constructs a thematic matrix which picks up, and reinforces, the threads of Rubens's sacrilegious rendering of the Mass originally said on the anniversary of the foundation of a church. 'La plus puissante pochade qui soit au Louvre' (as the entry in the contemporary *Guide Joanne* puts it) is positioned by the novelist as an ideal of pastoral liberation grotesquely mimed on leaving it behind. Amongst the 'détails orduriers' spotted by Boche, 'un qui dégobille' looks forward to Coupeau's fateful vomiting, as the later 'figures rouges qui sautaient' (*RM*, II, 594) in the riotous feast at the end of chapter 7, seem to step out of Rubens's exuberant danse. The two textual segments are linked by the 'peu propre' reaction

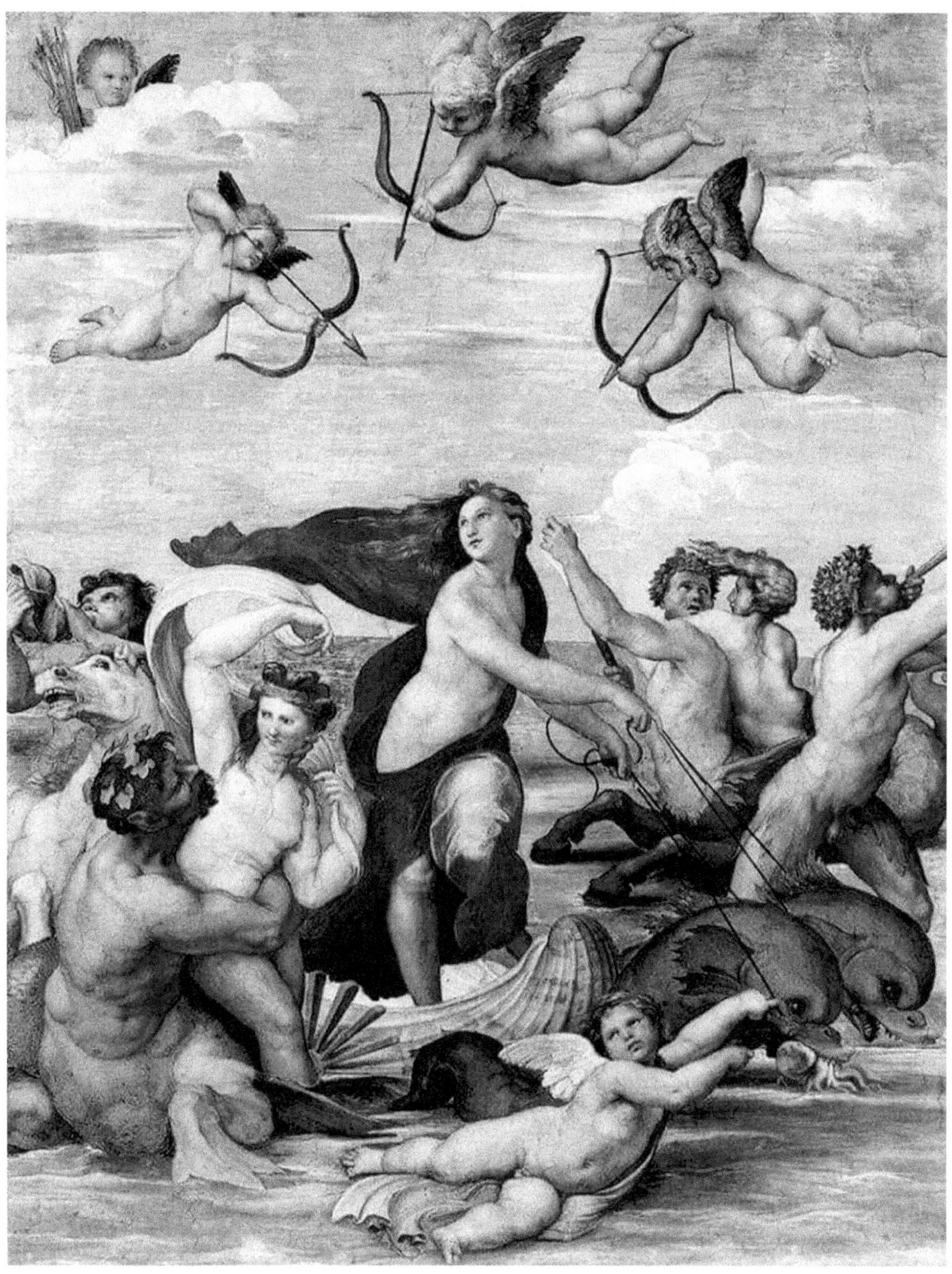

Fig. 6.3. Raphaël, *The Triumph of Galatea* (*c.* 1512–1514), fresco, 295 × 225 cm. Villa Farenisa, Rome.

to Clémence's 'baring all' there and the sarcastic 'ils sont propres' which greets the double 'voiding' of the *Kermesse*. Zola's narrative sequence thereby takes us from the upright configurations of the sacred in the *Noces de Cana* to the circular dynamic of the *Kermesse*, in a rhythm internal to both orgies of gluttony and characteristic of the degradation between and beyond them.

It is worth underlining that for Cézanne too, whether coincidentally or not, Rubens, whose work he studied and restudied all his life, occupies a special place in his pantheon. Zola's affinities seem to have been grounded, as well as articulated, in the antithesis highlighted by Taine, between the sheer materiality of Rubens and the idealization of Raphaël: after referring to the 'rage de la chair' in the *Kermesse*, Zola notes from his reading that in Raphaël's *Triumph of Galatea* (Fig. 6.3), 'au contraire, le caractère essentiel, l'idéal, est la beauté de la femme, sereine, fière, gracieuse' (*EsA*, p. 464). It is for the same reason, and again like Cézanne,[31] that he is clearly sympathetic to Taine's preference, as cited above, for Michelangelo over Raphaël. He would often rehearse this traditional opposition, but not always in absolute terms. In *Fécondité* (1899), Mathieu, his spokesman asserting that 'l'idée de beauté varie', recalls that 'pendant toute la Renaissance, elle a été dans la femme saine et forte, aux larges hanches, aux seins puissants. Chez Rubens, chez Titien, *même chez Raphaël*, la femme est robuste' (*OC*, VIII, 58; my emphasis). But returning, for the moment, to the first of the Old Masters referenced here, it can be argued that, for Zola, Rubens conjures up a set of images rather than being simply a name drawn from a fund of cultural icons. And not only in *L'Assommoir*. In *Le Ventre de Paris*, the young Marjolin is described as 'splendide, ce grand bêta, doré comme un Rubens, avec un duvet roussâtre qui accrochait le jour' (*RM*, I, 625); and in preparing the role within it played by Lisa Quenu ('ma création principale'), Zola's 'ce sera un Rubens' (Ms 10338, fol. 63) is shorthand for the portrait of her filled out in the final pages of the novel's opening chapter, 'cette belle chair de femme' amplified as 'une plénitude solide et heureuse [...] forte de la gorge, dans la maturité de la trentaine', and, bathed in the morning sunshine, *pictured*: with the 'blancheur transparente' of her 'chair paisible', the whiteness of her collar and sleeves offset by the glimpse of a black dress beneath her apron, she is 'trempée de clarté, les cheveux bleus, la chair rose, les manches et la jupe éclatantes' (*RM*, I, 637).

To a lesser extent, similar associative moves between pictorial references and visualization can be tracked elsewhere in Zola's fiction. In *Le Ventre de Paris*, Claude's contemptuous dismissal of Murillo as a painter is subsequently overlaid by the narrator's authenticating description of Claire Méhudin: with age, she gradually succumbs to 'l'avachissement d'une sainte de vitrail'; 'mais à vingt-deux ans, elle restait un Murillo [...], selon le mot de Claude Lantier, un Murillo décoiffé souvent', with her 'finesse de nature, sa peau mince que l'eau des viviers rafraîchissait éternellement, sa petite face d'un dessin noyé, ses membres souples' (*RM*, I, 715) and her chastity intact. In *Le Rêve*, Zola hesitates between Hans Memling (*c.* 1430–1494) and Van Eyck (*c.* 1395–1441) in imagining a portrait of Angélique iconographically consistent with their representations of the Virgin.[32] That of Clotilde, in the opening pages of *Le Docteur Pascal*, is substantiated by a comparison not stereotypically allusive but grounded in precise visual details: 'sa petite tête ronde, aux cheveux blonds et coupés court, un exquis et sérieux profil, le front droit, plissé par l'attention, l'œil bleu ciel, le nez fin, le menton ferme'; 'sa nuque penchée [...] d'une fraîcheur de lait, sous l'or des frisures folles', set off by 'sa longue blouse noire'; 'grande, la taille mince, la gorge menue, le corps souple, de cette souplesse allongée des divines figures de la Renaissance' (*RM*, v, 918). In *Lourdes* (1894), Sabathier (described as 'un ancien universitaire nourri de littérature et d'art') fleshes out his image of *père* Massias by indirectly pointing us to a painting of a martyr by José de Ribera (1591–1652).[33]

All such evidence (whether in fictional texts or work notes) reveals, on Zola's part, a familiarity with the Old Masters which goes beyond a mechanical or superficial recourse to a common frame of cultural reference. For this continuing reliance on, and admiration for, the art of the past also serves to contextualize a discernible shift in Zola's critical positioning. The case of Manet is symptomatic: championing him aggressively in the 1860s made it necessary to claim that he had learnt nothing from the Old Masters, and thus relegating to a footnote 'trois copies qu'il a faites au musée du Louvre: *La Vierge au lapin*, d'après Titien; le *Portrait du Tintoret*, d'après Tintoret, et *Les Petits Cavaliers*, d'après Vélasquez' (*EsA*, p. 491). As we saw in Chapter 4, Manet's 1868 portrait of the writer, with its cross-references to Goya and Velázquez, had perhaps suggested the extent to which polemical pressures had resulted in Zola's illegitimate suppression of the painter's artistic heritage. That omission did not prevent him from recommending Manet to his publisher, with a view to him illustrating his *Contes à Ninon*, on the grounds that of the two lithographs he was enclosing in his letter, his one of *Lola de Valence* 'représentant une danseuse espagnole est, à mon sens, un chef-d'œuvre d'une souplesse et d'une énergie rares. On dirait une eau-forte de Goya'.[34] By 1875, however, he can unhesitatingly declare that Manet's 'coups de pinceau heureux l'égalent parfois aux maîtres espagnols' (*EsA*, p. 278); and by the time he comes to write the preface to the catalogue of the 1884 Manet retrospective, Zola makes further amends (or, rather, engages in an about-turn) by specifically drawing the spectator's attention to 'de très intéressantes copies: *La Vierge au lapin*, le portrait de Tintoret, une tête de Filippo Lippi, qui prouvent combien le peintre, accusé d'ignorance, avait fréquenté les maîtres d'autrefois' (*EsA*, p. 608).

He had similarly placed an emphasis on Courbet liberating himself from the Old Masters. But, progressively, Zola aligns the painter with them. Even as far back as his 1865 essay on Proudhon, Courbet 'a pour frères, qu'il le veuille ou non, Véronèse, Rembrandt, Titien' (*EsA*, p. 425). If, in *L'Œuvre*, for all his 'métier absolument classique', Courbet's 'peinture noire' is deemed by Claude to be compromised by 'le moisi de l'atelier' (*RM*, iv, 45), this is not Zola's view. In 1878, he writes of Courbet that 'il a fait sienne la large brosse des artistes de la Renaissance [...]. Il est dans la ligne authentique de la tradition' (*EsA*, p. 543), promoting him to the rank occupied by distinguished artists such as Veronese. Tellingly, it is implicitly in contradistinction to the later Manet (in his more Impressionist phase), that Zola makes the parenthetical point, within his 1884 text on the Manet exhibition, that

Courbet is 'réaliste dans le choix de ses sujets, mais classique de ton et de facture, empruntant aux vieux maîtres leur métier savant' (*EsA*, p. 610). For it is this repeated emphasis on Courbet's 'facture magistrale' (*EsA*, p. 387) which makes him ultimately 'le maître le plus solide et le plus logique de notre époque' (*EsA*, p. 400). That his qualities should be transferred in *L'Œuvre* to a sculptor is not arbitrary: 'Je ferai alors de mon Dieu, de mon Courbet un sculpteur [...]. Cela irait très bien, ce gobage de soi, avec la matérialité des statues. L'épaisseur da la forme, la chair sentie. Pas très moderne, un Carpeaux solide' (Ms 10316, fols 293–94). Nor is that last comparison devoid of significance. In recalling Sunday outings with her father, Zola's daughter included the detail that 'il nous menait devant le groupe de *La Dance* de Carpeaux',[35] long admired by the novelist who considered its creator the finest sculptor of his generation. Courbet's 'solidité de facture [et] sa technique infaillible restent inégalées dans notre école. Il faut remonter jusqu'à la Renaissance pour trouver un coup de pinceau aussi large et aussi vrai' (*EsA*, pp. 354–55): 'un magnifique classique qui reste dans la plus large tradition des Titien, des Véronèse et des Rembrandt' (*EsA*, p. 373); in other words, an 'Old Master' for modern times.[36]

A more radical revision is visible in the case of Andrea Mantegna. In a fierce 1876 attack on the work of Gustave Moreau, exemplifying a 'mouvement rétrograde', Zola argues that he 'redécouvre des formes archaïques ou primitives, prend comme modèle Mantegna' (*EsA*, p. 328). This article had appeared shortly after drafting the Louvre episode in *L'Assommoir* with its passing mention of 'la sécheresse fine des primitifs'; and, in *L'Œuvre*, Chaîne's own stylistic 'minuties naïves d'un primitif' result in an exact copy: 'Le Mantegna, surtout, d'une sécheresse si naïve, avait l'air d'une image d'Épinal décolorée, clouée là pour le plaisir des gens simples' (*RM*, iv, 310).[37] In *Paris*, however, which Zola started writing in May 1896, in the very month of his *Figaro* article decrying the aberrations of contemporary painting, we find a remarkable volte-face. For, in the Louvre's 'salle des Primitifs' ignored by Gervaise Macquart's wedding party, the fictional Antoine, partly modelled on Marcellin Desboutin about whose engavings Zola had written admiringly in 1889, is 'dessinant une académie d'après Mantegna' with 'une sorte de dévotion':

> Ce qui le passionnait chez les Primitifs, ce n'était pas le mysticisme, l'envolement de l'idéal, que la mode y veut voir: c'était, au contraire, et très justement, une sincérité de réalistes ingénus, leur respect et leur modestie devant la nature, la loyauté minutieuse qu'ils mettaient à la traduire le plus fidèlement possible. (*OC*, vii, 1306)

As the 'très justement' suggests, the same present tense adopted by the narrative voice in *L'Assommoir* reveals Zola's newly admiring perspective filtered through the intensity of Antoine's absorption: 'Pendant des journées d'acharné travail, il venait là les copier, les étudier, pour apprendre d'eux la sévérité, la probité du dessin, tout le haut caractère qu'ils doivent à leur candeur d'honnêtes artistes' (*OC*, vii, 1306). For while Zola's *Figaro* article condemns a modish and debased 'retour à l'extase des Primitifs', 'et encore les Primitifs étaient-ils des ingénus, des copistes très sincères' (*EsA*, p. 406).

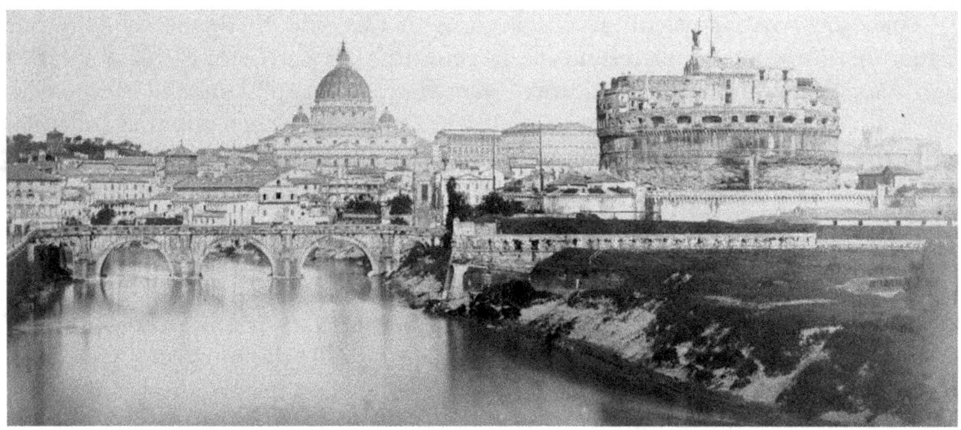

FIG. 6.4. Nineteenth-century Rome: photo by Robert Turnbull Macpherson (1814–1872).

Celebrating the Old Masters: *Rome* (1896)

That this particular about-turn should be registered in 1896 is obviously related to Zola's extended visit to Italy some eighteen months earlier (Fig. 6.4). Its prime motivation had been to undertake the research necessary for *Rome*, the second of his *Trois Villes* series, which he had had in mind since 1891, initially conceiving it as an exploration of the religious conflicts of the *fin de siècle*. But on arrival in the Eternal City at the end of October 1894, Zola's focus was partly, if significantly, displaced by the spectacle of the place and its artistic treasures. His response to the latter was not unlike Flaubert's during his 1851 pilgrimage to 'le plus spendide musée qu'il y a au monde': 'la quantité de chefs-d'œuvre qu'il y a à Rome est quelque chose d'effrayant et d'écrasant'.[38] Zola would not return to Paris until mid-December 1894, having also briefly taken in Naples, Florence, Venice and Milan. And, as well as preparing *Rome* (drafted between 2 April 1895 and March 1896), he also compiled a 400-page *Journal de voyage* which both fertilizes the genesis of the novel and provides, in the shape of an authorial monologue interspersed with comparisons with his native Provence, a day-to-day commentary on what he had seen. On a personal level, Zola's stay in Rome, extended until 5 December, revived images of long ago. More than thirty years earlier, he had waxed lyrical to Cézanne about Jean Goujon's exquisitely fashioned Renaissance *Fontium nymphis*, with its 'charmantes déesses, gracieuses, souriantes', in the Place des Innocents. In the autumn of 1894, every *piazza* offered him the sight of, as he inserted in the text of *Rome*, 'une adorable fontaine Renaissance' (*OC*, VII, 542). Having more or less shared with Taine the view that Poussin was the antithesis of modern landscape, Zola's actual contemplation from a carriage of the Roman Campagna on 14 November brought that artist to mind, now redeemed from the twin pictorial 'sins' of anachronism and artifice: 'À l'Acqua Acetosa. De là, la campagne, tout à fait du Poussin [...]. Tous les fonds des tableaux du Poussin, que nous connaissons, avec un ciel rayé' (*OC*, VII, 1077). In the novel, too, his surrogate observer closes the gap between art and life: 'en suivant la rive, il venait de voir des Poussin' (*OC*, VII, 770).

There are two far-reaching consequences of this visit to Rome. On the one hand, as Zola's notes ('un résumé de la peinture' (*OC*, VII, 1074)) make clear, it vastly expanded his artistic 'education'. On the other, it substantiated, beyond his reading or excursions to the Louvre, what had previously been admired from afar or in the abstract. Pierre Froment, his fictional protagonist, is taken along the same itinerary through the city's streets, squares, churches, galleries, palaces, museums, famous ruins and other tourist sites as (with his Baedeker in hand) Zola himself, 'où j'évoquerai toutes mes sensations, non pas de l'archéologie, mais la sensation d'un artiste lancé là-dedans' (*OC*, VII, 1028). His surrogate is also the author of a book: it is hardly a coincidence that the synopsis of his *La Rome nouvelle* ('il revécut son livre, après avoir revécu sa vie' (*OC*, VII, 529–39)) is the mirroring prelude to Zola's novel; nor that, in spite of its serious reforming and historically-based intent, it should be scornfully dismissed by the representative of conservative Catholicism as 'de la littérature' (*OC*, VII, 582) and thereby condemned to the papal Index as surely as Zola knew in advance that *Rome* itself would be. He too had initially conceived his work as primarily an exploration of the ideological infrastructure and conflictual tensions of contemporary Catholicism. But documenting himself *in situ* brought him face to face with a Rome insufficiently understood if limited to the kind of narrative which structures Pierre's *La Rome nouvelle.* For both Zola and his protagonist, Rome is an extraordinary *visual* experience. Both are accordingly introduced for the first time to a whole range of artists: Perugino, Pinturicchio, Signorelli and Bernini, to name but a few. *Rome* is a text saturated with pictorial references, even if its analogies have recourse to artists with which Zola was already familiar to a certain extent: Bramante (Donato d'Angelo Lazzari), for example, is 'le Michel-Ange et le Raphaël de l'architecture' (*OC*, VII, 672). Pierre's guide, Narcisse Habert, alerts him to 'un chef-d'œuvre des Primitifs, un Cimabue, un Giotto, un Fra Angelico' (*OC*, VII, 693). In looking at centuries-old statuary, Zola transferred directly to Pierre his own sense of 'une intensité de vie étonnante' and a necessary reappraisal, totally at odds with the antipathy he had displayed in the 1860s towards the neoclassical sculptural ideal of the Académie des Beaux-Arts: 'Comme cela vous prend autrement que l'histoire classique qui vous fait exécrer l'Antiquité, et comme on comprend, comme on sympathise' (*OC*, VII, 1033).[39] Pierre's preconceived view of Roman architecture, in the opening pages of the novel ('sans grâce ni fantaisie, sans magnificence extérieure') undergoes a similar proleptic shift: 'C'était évidemment fort beau, il finirait par comprendre, mais il devrait y réfléchir' (*OC*, VII, 517). And there is no mistaking the autobiographical weight of Pierre's definitive revaluation of the art of the past: 'il revint enthousiasmé d'avoir eu la révélation de tout un art classique, qu'il n'avait guère goûté jusque-là' (*OC*, VII, 770).[40]

Inevitably perhaps, this revisionist journey of discovery culminates in the episode which brings him through the Vatican to the Sistine Chapel. Like travellers before and since, and Flaubert in particular,[41] Zola was overwhelmed by its pictorial glories, resulting in what Henri Mitterand calls 'une de ses pages de critique d'art les plus inspirées'.[42] *Rome* repays further scrutiny for that alone, it could be argued, for nowhere else in Zola's writing on the visual arts do we find ekphrasis to such a

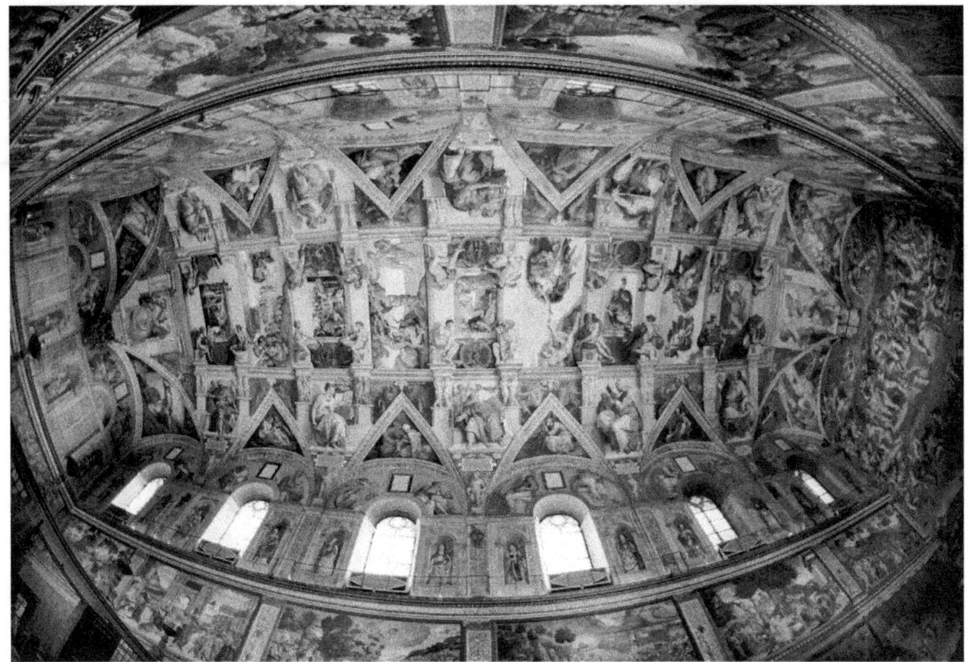

FIG. 6.5. Michelangelo, ceiling (1508–12) of the Sistine Chapel, Vatican.

degree. Equally inevitable, it can also be argued, is that it should be Michelangelo who dominates this critical discourse, to the extent that, as soon as Pierre steps into the Chapel, he is 'pris tout entier par le génie surhumain de Michel-Ange. Le reste disparut' (*OC*, VII, 664). For Zola's earlier writing, leaving aside instances of a specific debt to Taine, already testifies to the place he occupies in his imaginative frame of reference, whether obliquely or allusively: in the figure of Goujet, the 'colosse' at his anvil, in *L'Assommoir*, for example (*RM*, II, 529–34), prefigured in his 1868 text, 'Le Forgeron' ('nu jusqu'à la ceinture, les muscles saillants et tendus, semblable à une de ces grandes figures de Michel-Ange' (*OC*, IX, 396)); in his 1875 obituary piece devoted to Carpeaux, Zola refers to his 'passion pour Michel-Ange, qui demeura son dieu toute sa vie' (*EsA*, p. 640); and in *L'Œuvre*, a conversation about Wagner's originality ('le dieu, en qui s'incarnent des siècles de musique!') generates a euphoric critical conflation: 'Ah! Beethoven, la puissance, la force dans la douleur sereine, Michel-Ange au tombeau des Médicis ! Un logicien héroïque, un pétrisseur de cervelles, car ils sont tous partis de la symphonie avec chœurs, les grands d'aujourd'hui!' (*RM*, IV, 200).[43] It is no less significant, however, that such analogies had been overlaid on Zola's own texts, from Flaubert's private reaction to his reading of *Nana* ('la mort de Nana est Michelangelesque') to Jules Lemaître, the leading critic, as respected as his fellow novelist and to whose reviews Zola would often immediately respond: 'Il y a du Michel-Ange dans M. Zola', Lemaître wrote of *L'Œuvre*. 'Les figures font penser à la fresque du *Jugement dernier*.' And in singling out, to explain his 'génie', its author's 'don de la vision concrète et démesurée', Lemaître prefigures precisely the qualities which Zola would find in the self-

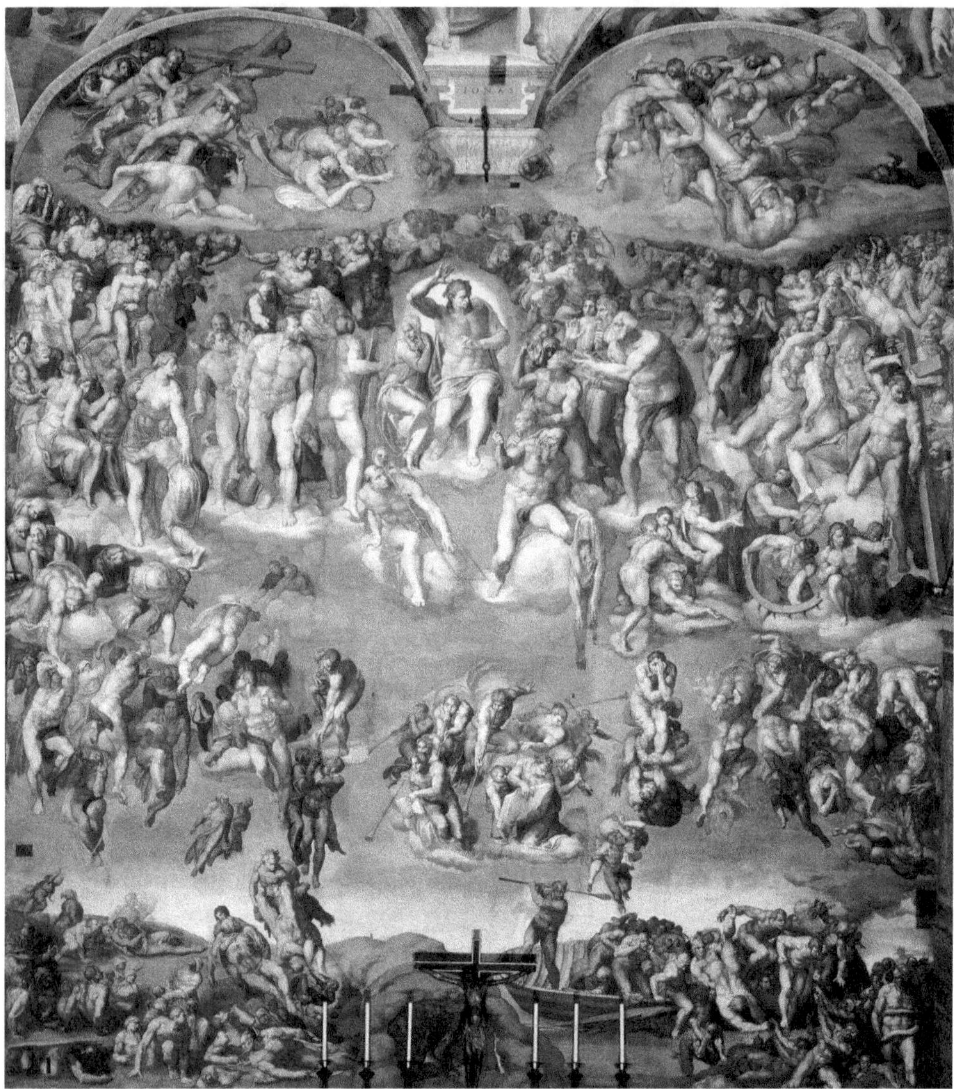

FIG. 6.6. Michelangelo, *The Last Judgement* (1536–41), Sistine Chapel, Vatican.

reflecting mirror of Michelangelo's decoration of the Sistine Chapel. In Manet, as was highlighted in an earlier chapter, Zola strategically underlined parallels with his own emerging aesthetic in the 1860s. With the *Rougon-Macquart* now complete, Michelangelo offered him the opportunity to engage in a retrospective assessment of the distinguishing qualities of a life's work.

Those qualities are highlighted in a long exchange, in chapter 6 of *Rome*, between Pierre and Narcisse Habert as they jointly survey the Sistine Chapel's frescoes and and ceiling (Fig. 6.5), the latter preferred by Zola, like Taine before him, to *The Last Judgement* (Fig. 6.6) by virtue of it being 'la première fois qu'il s'attaquait à la

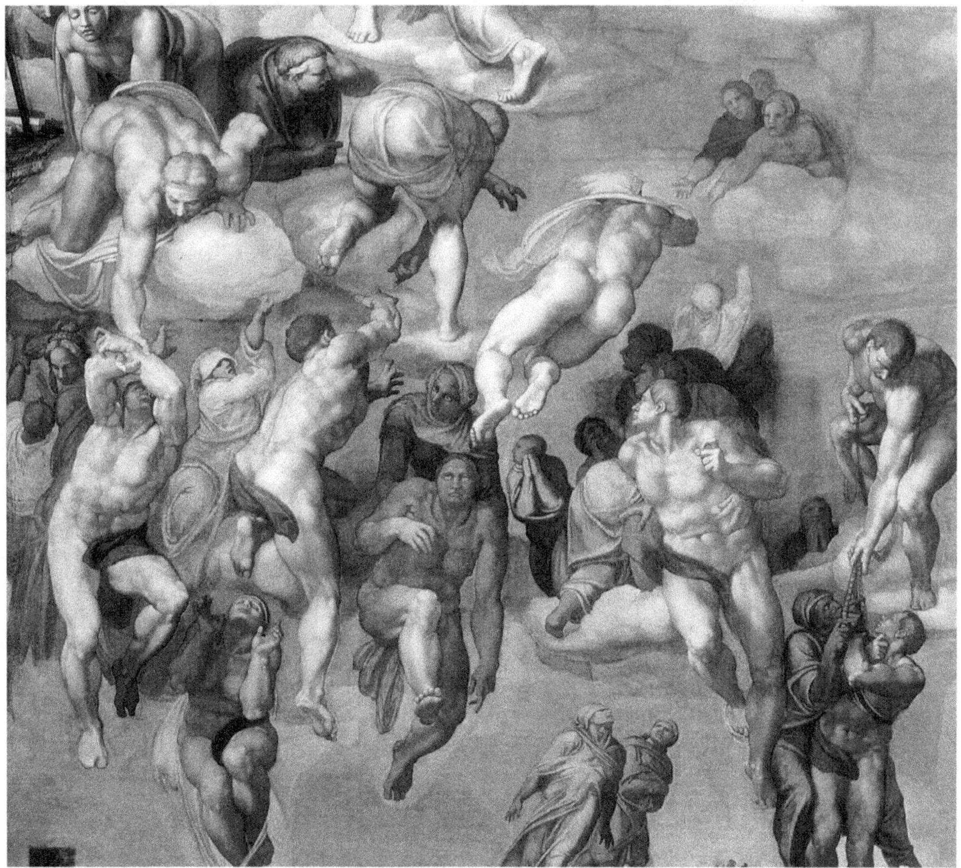

FIG. 6.7. Michelangelo, *The Last Judgement* (detail).

peinture' and thus evidence of an innate creative energy (*OC*, VII, 1071). Habert, transparently modelled on the painter Ernest Hébert (1817–1908),[44] counters Pierre's hyperbolic enthusiasm for Michelangelo by asserting the superiority of Botticelli. Pierre can hardly get a word in edgeways, reduced to 'Botticelli est un merveilleux artiste...' before being cut off. Once he gets the chance to express an opinion, the very terms of his politely 'begging to differ' are instructive: 'Michel-Ange reste le tout-puissant, le faiseur d'hommes, le maître de la clarté, de la simplicité et de la santé' (*OC*, VII, 667). For the emphasis on what Zola had called, as long ago as 1866, 'la santé plantureuse', the obverse of a collective neurosis afflicting the majority of the artists of his time, reminds us of a diagnosis fundamental to Zola's increasingly negative assessment of the art of his contemporaries. Even in this early phase of his art criticism, he had stressed that the Old Masters, by contrast, 'étaient des puissantes natures qui peignaient en pleine vie' (*EsA*, p. 148). Artistic mediocrity, he added in 1868, could only be explained in relation to 'la crise nerveuse que traversent les temps modernes. Nos artistes ne sont plus des hommes larges et puissants, sains d'esprit, vigoureux de corps, comme étaient les Véronèse et les Titien. Il y a eu un détraquement de toute la machine' (p. 174). And this is a diagnosis dramatically elaborated in *L'Œuvre*: in its preparatory notes, Zola makes it clear that, in his fictional painter's creative indirections and ultimate failure, 'je voudrais aussi que notre art moderne y fut pour quelque chose [...], notre impatience à secouer les traditions, notre *déséquilibrement* en un mot' (Ms 10316, fol. 265), the underlining being Zola's own. It is implicit here, as well as being subsequently confirmed in the grounded figure of the successful Sandoz, that Zola considers himself protected from such an aesthetic malady. A decade later, his positioning and that of the Naturalist hegemony is being eroded. So when it comes to articulating Habert's refusal to subscribe to Pierre's insistence on Michelangelo's qualities, 'sa haine sourde, inconsciente, contre la santé, la simplicité et la force' (*OC*, VII, 672), Zola associates the point of view of 'ce cerveau moderne [...] gâté par la recherche de l'original et du rare' with writers of the *fin de siècle* differentiating themselves from his own achievement: 'peindre notre moment. Un A. France, un B... [i.e. Paul Bourget], dans la haine des besognes colossales et du génial décor' (*OC*, VII, 1072). And this is equally evident in Zola's rehearsal of the traditional juxtaposition of Michelangelo and Raphaël, where he again alludes to the increasingly prevalent objections to his novels' relegating to the margins the vicissitudes of the inner life. In elaborating for *Rome* the semblance of a plot,[45] he almost unwillingly includes 'une étude de leur fameuse psychologie, puisque pour eux la psychologie consiste uniquement dans le combat du devoir et de la passion'.[46] As opposed to the materialism of Michelangelo, 'avec Raphaël', Pierre is given to declare (following almost verbatim Zola's commentary in his *Journal de voyage*), 'c'est une analyse psychologique d'une pénétration profonde, apportée dans la peinture. L'homme y est plus épuré, plus idéalisé, vu davantage par le dedans' (*OC*, VII, 668).

Inseparable from these qualities are metaphors of gendering. Pierre's comparative juxtaposition, in this same passage, of Raphaël and Michelangelo makes no claim to be original: 'C'est Racine à côté de Corneille, Lamartine à côté d'Hugo, l'éternelle paire, le couple de la femme et du mâle, dans les siècles de gloire.' As his self-confessed 'humble disciple' (*OC*, X, 563), Zola had picked up on Taine's physiological notion of 'le véritable caractère de la Renaissance' being that of 'la beauté mâle et sérieuse' and 'la vigueur virile'. Pierre accordingly finds this in what he calls, significantly, Michelangelo's 'page immense': 'une poussée continue de la virilité créatrice' (*OC*, VII, 664), most obviously visible in the sheer physicality of his figures (Fig. 6.7), 'démesurés dans la force de la musculature'.[47] A slightly more nuanced view of Raphaël is discernible in a parenthetical acknowledgement of the painter's 'élégance virile', without qualifying the summative view of him as 'un sentimental, un féminin dont on sent le frisson de la tendresse'. Notwithstanding Zola's own abiding affection for Botticelli's pictures,[48] that does not mean Pierre accepting Habert's argument that, in Botticelli, 'rien d'efféminé, ni de menteur, partout une sorte de fierté virile' (*OC*, VII, 667). Nearer to the mark is (the appropriately named) *Narcisse* Habert savouring the young masculine figures represented by the artist, 'beaux pourtant comme des femmes, d'un sexe équivoque', precisely the androgyny to which Zola would so ferociously object in his 1896 diatribe aimed at *fin de siècle* painting: 'ces vierges insexuées qui n'ont ni seins ni hanches, ces filles qui sont presque des garçons, ces garçons qui sont presque des filles' (*EsA*, p. 406). For, by contrast, Zola's own erotically charged conception of his literary ambitions is decidedly unequivocal: as he had put it in the 1874 preface to his *Nouveaux Contes à Ninon*, 'c'est l'âpre désir, prendre la terre, la posséder dans une étreinte [...]. Je voudrais coucher l'humanité sur une page blanche [...]. J'ai besoin de toute ma virilité' (*OC*, IX, 351).

In his *Journal de voyage*, Zola wondered 'comment Michel-Ange a-t-il été accueilli par ses contemporains, sa maîtrise subie ou non' (*OC*, VII, 1074). The judgement of posterity is one of the recurrent themes of his art criticism, particularly in relation to Delacroix and Manet. But it is clearly a question also hanging over his own work, especially towards the end of his writing career. In that light, Habert's expressed antipathy towards Michelangelo can be read as an abbreviated transposition of the charges levelled at Zola himself by hostile critics: 'un homme sans mystère, sans inconnu, qui voyait gros à dégoûter de la beauté, des corps d'hommes tels que des troncs d'arbres, des femmes pareilles à des bouchères géantes, des masses de chair' (*OC*, VII, 667). To which Pierre responds, on Zola's behalf, that 'le cas de Michel-Ange me paraît décisif, car il n'est le maître surhumain, le monstre qui écrase les autres, que grâce à cet extraordinaire enfantement de chair vivante et magnifique, dont votre délicatesse se blesse'. For such are the affinities with Michelangelo revealed to Zola in the Sistine Chapel that his description of its pictorial splendours becomes an *apologia pro mea sua*.

At a pragmatic level, he identifies in this section of *Rome* (*OC*, VII, 664–69) with the solitary nature of Michelangelo's labours, working on 'cette *page* immense' (my emphasis) of white plaster, 's'enfermant tout seul avec sa besogne géante [...], passant quatre années et demie solitaire et farouche, dans son enfantement quotidien de colosse'. Literally, of course, this hardly reflects Zola's Parisian experience, notwithstanding the famous inscription of *nulle dies sine linea* on the mantelpiece of his study, during the two decades spent producing *Les Rougon-Macquart*. But it does correspond to an *idea* of his writing life: projected in the preface to his *Nouveaux Contes à Ninon*, cited above ('Je me suis enfermé chez moi pour ne mettre que le travail dans ma vie'), and elaborated in Sandoz's working habits, in *L'Œuvre*, which amount to an isolated martyrdom, divested of domestic and social pleasures: 'j'ai fermé la porte du monde derrière moi, et j'ai jeté la clef par la fenêtre... Plus rien, plus rien dans mon trou que le travail et moi' (*RM*, IV, 263). Michelangelo's 'tranquille confiance en sa volonté' is manifestly a projection of Zola's: 'Si j'ai un orgueil, j'ai celui de cette volonté, dont l'effort m'a tiré lentement des besognes du métier' (*OC*, IX, 350). The immensity of Michelangelo's achievement is also figuratively assimilated, as Pierre keeps in his mind's eye the 'centaines de mètres carrés à couvrir', much as Zola had relentlessly progressed his twenty-volume series in the face of the kind of disparagement, shading into caricature, which Habert directs towards Michelangelo: 'Un homme qui s'attelait comme un bœuf à la besogne, qui abattait l'ouvrage ainsi qu'un manœuvre, à tant de mètres par jour!'

As far as formal and visual effects are concerned, all Habert is prepared to admit is that Michelangelo is 'un maçon colossal'. But, for Zola, there is nothing pejorative or double-edged in such a remark. In his study of Balzac, in *Les Romanciers naturalistes,* an extended architectural metaphor concludes that *La Comédie humaine* had been 'bâti par un maçon prodigieux' (*OC*, xi, 25). And it compellingly invites comparison with the basic principles of his own aesthetic, as (literally) underlined even in the preliminary notes for *Les Rougon-Macquart* as a whole, penned in early 1869 (*RM*, v, 1736–76): 'Tout le monde réussit en ce moment l'analyse du détail; il faut réagir par *la construction solide des masses*, des chapitres, par *la logique, la poussée de ces chapitres* se succédant comme des blocs superposés'; 'établir douze, quinze puissantes masses'; 'chaque chapitre, chaque masse doit être comme une force distincte qui pousse au dénouement'; differentiating himself from the Goncourts (thinking perhaps of the 155 very short chapters of their *Madame Gervaisais* published that February) who 'seront si bien écrasés par la masse (par la longueur des chapitres) [...] qu'on n'osera m'accuser de les imiter' (*RM*, v, 1743–45); and assuring his potential publisher that the separate building blocks of his series would add up to 'un seul et vaste ensemble'. The architectural and sculptural metaphors are rehearsed in the preface to the *Nouveaux Contes à Ninon*, where Zola writes of his dream of 'quelque coup de pouce éternel donné dans le granit' and his cosmic ambition to 'coucher l'humanité sur une page blanche, tous les êtres, toutes les choses; une œuvre qui serait l'arche immense'. That last image is repeated twice in *L'Œuvre* (*RM*, iv, 46 and 162): 'Ah! que ce serait beau, si l'on donnait son existence entier à une œuvre, où l'on tâcherait de mettre les choses, les bêtes, les hommes, l'arche immense!' As far back as 1860, Zola had been outlining such an encyclopaedic project, provisionally entitled 'La Chaîne des êtres'. In the Sistine Chapel, over three decades later, he found himself confronted by the apotheosis of an art at once narrative, pictorial, sculptural and architectural, in the service of a totalizing vision of Creation. Inspecting its dynamic, and yet structured, texture more closely, with its 'science parfaite' and 'la perpétuelle victoire technique sur les difficultés que les plans courbes présentaient', Pierre is the mouthpiece of a critical euphoria engendered by the spectacle of 'cette humanité agrandie de visionnaire, débordant en des pages de synthèse demesurée, de symbolisme cyclopéen'. It is not as paradoxical as it might seem that it was this *anti-naturalist* quality which Flaubert, 'lost for words', had also admired.[49] As Zola had noted back in 1866, Taine had said as much, Michelangelo 's'affranchissant de la réalité, créait selon son cœur des géants terribles de douleur et de force' (*EsA*, p. 464). Such a liberation from the constraints of mimesis legitimized Zola's theoretically heretical definition, in the context of *Germinal*, of his own creative processes: 'le saut dans les étoiles sur le tremplin de l'observation exacte. La vérité monte d'un coup d'aile jusqu'au symbole.'[50] Of Michelangelo's 'pages de synthèse géante, de symbolisme colossal', Zola wrote in his journal entry for 13 November, 'pas de modèle vivant possible pour cet agrandissement énorme. Tout donc tiré du cerveau' (*OC*, vii, 1071). Little wonder that he should complete the identification with this supreme artist in the most personally explicit terms: 'Une œuvre énorme qui me va au cœur, dont j'ai rêvé toute ma vie'.

The particular emphasis on solidity and structure, evident in his writing on Courbet, is equally reflected in Zola's obsessive fascination with the monumental fabric of Rome's buildings (the city itself being described by Pierre as 'cette page immense' (*OC*, vii, 664)), is signalled in a view of the masterpieces of Raphaël prior to his coming under the overwhelming influence of Michelangelo, as Pierre acknowledges the painter's 'solidité de métier admirable' (*OC*, vii, 668); and a case is even made for Botticelli's 'solidité savante' (*OC*, vii, 667). In Caravaggio, Zola admires the same 'modelé puissant' (*OC*, vii, 1074) as in the ceiling of the Sistine Chapel. This distinguishing quality of the Old Masters serves to illuminate, both retrospectively and in his writing on painting after his 1894 visit, numerous aspects of Zola's art criticism. For the implicit criteria against which works are judged are indeed those of the 'écoles de Renaissance', for which, as he writes in 1875, pictorial subjects 'n'étaient que des prétextes à une facture magistrale' (*EsA*, p. 269). Jean-Jacques Henner's *Christ mort* (1876), for example, suffers by comparison: 'on pense involontairement à la large brosse des maîtres et cette manière paraît bien tatillone' (*EsA*, p. 318). Doré's weakness is that 'l'œuvre n'est pas solide' (*EsA*, p. 441). But it is also the case that one can detect Zola's appreciation of certain artists, or aspects of their art, in spite of their exclusion from the modernist canon. He admits that, however beautified Charles Chaplin's society portraits may be, 'la facture en est robuste' (*EsA*, p. 322). François Bonvin's *La Lettre de Réception* (1868) is his finest work to date because 'la peinture en très très solide' (*EsA*, p. 200), whereas two years earlier, in the painter's *Grand-maman*, Zola would have preferred 'un visage d'un seul morceau, bâti solidement' (*EsA*, p. 160). In evoking Alexei Harlamoff's portraits of Pauline Viardot (1875) and Turgenev (1876), he comments that 'sa manière est caractérisée par une solidité de facture frappante' (*EsA*, p. 321). Less surprising, given another (if better-known) portrait painter's investment in the Old Masters, this was also seen by Zola as characteristic of Léon Bonnat:[51] 'le plus solide de nos peintres' (*EsA*, p. 555) bearing comparison with Courbet; his *Jacob luttant avec l'Ange* (1876) is 'plus solide et plus vrai' (*EsA*, p. 298) than Cabanel or Gérôme, with its two figures 'aux muscles tendus par l'effort', like Michelangelo's the work of a 'maçon' ('on croirait qu'il peint avec du mortier'); and, even with reservations, 'ce n'est pas que je me plaigne de la solidité de Bonnat qui, lui, défend les transports des peintres spiritualistes' (*EsA*, p. 318); never, in Zola's later estimation of the artist's *Job* (1880), had he painted 'une académie avec plus de solidité. Ce que j'aime moins, c'est sa facture elle-même, solide mais lourde' (*EsA*, p. 388). Fantin-Latour's portrait of *Mlle Louise Riesener*, at the same Salon, is 'un de ceux qu'il a peints le plus solidement', not least because 'il a passé des années à étudier les maîtres' (*EsA*, p. 390). Millet's best canvases are praised in retrospect: 's'il faut parler métier, j'ajouterai que la peinture de M. Millet était grasse et solide' (*EsA*, pp. 164–65). In his review of the 1878 Universal Exhibition, Zola compares Corot's *Chemin près de l'étang à Ville-d'Avray* to 'des tableaux plus francs et plus solides que je mets infiniment plus haut' (*EsA*, p. 546).

These same criteria inform Zola's assessment of the Impressionists up to their third exhibition, in 1877, differentiated from the 'métier de pacotille' to which, in his view, they later succumbed: Pissarro, 'au métier solide', contextualized in an article of 1868 by prefatory remarks on 'les maîtres de la Renaissance', 'possède la solidité et la largeur de la touche, il peint grassement, suivant les traditions, comme les maîtres', to the extent that Zola goes so far as to position him, bypassing the Barbizon School, in an artistic lineage going back to colourists like Velázquez and Veronese: 'les fils des maîtres, les artistes qui continuent la tradition, ce sont les Camille Pissarro, ces peintres qui vous paraîssent ternes et maladroits.' And, for that reason, he is favourably compared to conventional landscape artists of the period, 'encore s'ils savaient peindre, s'ils avaient le métier gras et solide des maîtres, le sujet importerait peu' (*EsA*, pp. 182–85). At the second Impressionist exhibition (1876), Sisley's *Inondation à Port-Marly*, 'd'une vérité et d'une solidité admirable' (*EsA*, p. 586) was shown alongside Béliard's 'solidité puissante qui fait de ses moindres toiles une traduction savante et littérale' (*EsA*, p. 584). Guillemet's 'toiles très solides et très puissants' (*EsA*, p. 350) were shown at the Salon of 1877, and his *Le Vieux Quai de Bercy* (1880) was considered 'très solidement peint' (*EsA*, p. 392). Renoir's portraits in the third Impressionist exhibition (1877) were preferred to many others there because they seemed to Zola 'beaucoup plus solides et d'une qualité de peinture supérieure' (*EsA*, p. 590). Zola's changing attitude towards Monet, however, brings this into sharper relief: of *Camille*, also known as *La Femme à la robe verte*, Zola writes in 1866 of the dress in question that 'elle est souple et solide' (*EsA*, p. 158); two years later, one of Monet's seascapes is 'bâti solidement' (*EsA*, p. 189); but by 1880, the painter, according to Zola, is on the slippery 'pente de la pacotille', forgetting that 'c'est l'étude qui fait les œuvres solides' (*EsA*, p. 380), driven by commercial imperatives to produce work too fast, resulting in mere sketches lacking both structure and finish. As indicated earlier in relation to Monet's later landscapes, such a critique echoes the early hostility towards Impressionism which Zola had rejected. But it is also a constant in his aesthetic preferences: in a letter as long ago as 1861, he stressed that 'j'adore religieusement la forme, la beauté pour moi est tout [...]; cet amour des lignes n'est qu'un amour d'artiste';[52] it is discernible in his remark about Bonvin: 'l'effet s'éparpille' (*EsA*, p. 160). And it serves to justify, as Sara Pappas has shown,[53] his extended focus on Bastien-Lepage, with his 'perfection du métier' and whose 'supériorité sur les peintres impressionnistes', as Zola writes in 1879, 'se résume dans ceci, qu'il sait réaliser ses impressions' (*EsA*, p. 357). Nor is Manet exempt from this, undermining the claim that he was 'le seul peintre de la nouvelle école sur lequel Zola n'a jamais avancé de réserve'.[54] In the beginning, Manet's works were structured by those 'larges masses' (*EsA*, p. 609) which his self-interested champion had proposed would be the distinguishing feature of his own writing, recalling of his *Chanteur espagnol* and *Enfant à l'épée* that 'c'était de la bonne et solide peinture' (*EsA*, p. 606). And nor was this skewed by the demands of Zola's 1884 preface, *en hommage*, to the catalogue of the exhibition mounted the year after Manet's death. For his very first article on Manet's behalf, in 1866, had pointed out that 'la toile se couvre ainsi d'une peinture solide et forte' (*EsA*, p. 154). And his major 1867 study of the painter had reiterated this particular quality: 'ses peintures sont blondes et lumineuses, d'une peinture solide'; 'vigoureux et solide'; 'fermes et solides'; his *Le Christ mort* was 'très fine et très solide', as was *Le Déjeuner sur l'herbe*, 'avec ses premiers plans si larges, si solides' (*EsA*, pp. 478–87). But when Manet becomes one of the Impressionists in all but name, despite having consistently refused to participate in any of the group's exhibitions, Zola's remarks are ambiguous at best: in *Le Linge* (1876), 'le dessin se perd dans les jeux de la lumière', the painter having 'à peine indiqué les détails de la physiologie de sa laveuse', its rejection by the Salon jury making it 'une œuvre de combat', but for Zola nevertheless one which is 'curieuse' (*EsA*, p. 335); in 1879, now categorically 'le chef du groupe impressionniste', 'sa main n'égale pas son œil'; as a result, 'ses toiles sont imparfaites et inégales'; in short, 'si le côté technique chez lui égalait la justesse des perceptions, il serait le grand peintre de la seconde moitié du XIXe siècle' (*EsA*, p. 356); of *Chez le père Lathuille*, in 1880, Zola's erstwhile crusading enthusiasm is reduced to recording its 'délicatesse de tons charmantes' (*EsA*, p. 378); and even in his 1884 essay, Zola refers to the painter's occasional 'maladresse' and 'ces lacunes brusques qui se trouvent dans ses œuvres les mieux venues. Les doigts n'obéissaient pas toujours aux yeux' (*EsA*, p. 609), revealing his own point of view in the aside that 'on peut préférer la note plus sourde et plus juste peut-être de sa première manière' (*EsA*, p. 607).

In the public domain, at least, Zola's thinking about painting, after his return from Rome, found relatively little expression. But it is clear both that, as Henri Mitterand puts it, 'il s'est gorgé de peinture' during his 1894 visit,[55] and that, as a result, his pictorial frame of reference was substantiated to a radical degree. For whether intuitive, borrowed from his own aesthetic, or adopted from an established discursive template, the criteria informing his earlier writing on the visual arts are now even more uncompromising. Prefaced by a slightly weary, if misleading, claim that 'je me suis un peu désintéressé de la peinture', Zola's article in *Le Figaro* of 2 May 1896 (*EsA*, pp. 402–09) is occasioned by that year's Salon only to the extent of providing a pretext for a retrospective analysis of the development of French painting over the thirty years since he had first engaged in art criticism. Its ambivalent tone is aptly caught in Geffroy's description of the essay as 'une sorte de fanfare de victoire jouée en marche funèbre' (cited *OC*, xii, 1064). It does evoke the heroic campaigns on behalf of Manet and the early work of the Impressionists. But its newly polemical thrust is aimed at two particular aspects of the *fin de siècle* work of their successors: the erosion, or complete absence, of delineated structures; and its individualist rather than descriptive pigmentation. For the use of colour, too, had been a decorative feature of the Sistine Chapel notable for its moderation ('quelques couleurs employées largement, sans aucune recherche d'adresse ni d'éclat' (*OC*, vii, 664)), confirming Zola's early insight that 'les grands artistes de la Renaissance ont commencé par apprendre à broyer les couleurs' (*EsA*, p. 174); even Théodule Ribot, whose *Cabaret normand* (1875) was deemed 'solide, admirablement peint, mais toujours un peu noir' (*EsA*, p. 258), exemplified 'ces peintres qui empruntent leur originalité aux écoles anciennes', the artist taking 'aux Espagnols et aux Flamands les couleurs enfumées de leurs tableaux. Il ne peint que noir, blanc et rose, et réussit des effets d'éclairage et des tons énergiques' (*EsA*, p. 280). Now, in 1896, 'devant ce Salon délavé', Zola so deplores post-Impressionist and Symbolist excesses in this respect ('ces femmes multicolores, ces paysages violets et ses chevaux orange') that 'j'en viens presque à regretter le Salon noir, bitumineux d'autrefois'. As he would underline in an interview published the following year, 'le succès de la nouvelle formule ne me satisfait pas', 'd'un excès, on est tombé dans l'excès contraire' (*EsA*, p. 704).

It is also in both these post-1894 pieces that Zola further reflects on the dynamic of artistic generations succeeding each other, invariably dwarfed by the pre-existing 'temple de génie' (*OC*, VII, 1071) of the Sistine Chapel.[56] The evolutionary model is adumbrated in *Rome*: 'Après les précurseurs [...], Michel-Ange et Raphaël; le surhumain et le divin; puis, la chute est brusque, il faut attendre cent cinquante ans pour arriver au Cavarage [...]. Ensuite, la déchéance continue jusqu'au Bernin' (*OC*, VII, 671). It is 'l'absence du génie' which obstructs the forward momentum of 'tout ce que la science de la peinture a pu conquérir'. This commonplace in writing about the fine arts, as Norman Bryson has explored,[57] transposes Zola's oft-repeated threnody: 'Tous les maîtres de notre époque sont morts. [...] Ingres et Delacroix ont laissé l'art en deuil. On les regrette toujours car il n'y a personne pour les remplacer' (*EsA*, p. 267). After his own death, in 1877, Courbet is definitively positioned next in line to these two 'génies obstinés', with Zola rehearsing the cliché of a subsequently interrupted artistic heritage: 'Ingres, Delacroix, Courbet, n'ont point trouvé des remplaçants. Il n'y a plus de génies, il ne reste que des élèves camouflés de façon plus ou moins adroite' (*EsA*, p. 563); using the same image he would apply to Michelangelo, 'le sol épuisé' after his unsurpassable achievement (*OC*, VII, 1072), 'Ingres, Delacroix, Courbet ont laissé derrière eux un champ épuisé' (*EsA*, p. 574). Following them is a creative 'vide', and their 'disciples' are a pejorative 'queue', viewed with the same disdain as Zola had overlaid on 'la queue romantique' (*OC*, XIV, 508) that followed in the footsteps of Chateaubriand and Hugo. He returns more forcefully to this sense of artistic decadence after his visit to Rome. In blaming Puvis de Chavannes for 'un débordement lamentable de mysticisme', his point about artistic successors is extended more generally: 'Sa queue est désastreuse, plus désastreuse encore peut-être que celle de Manet, de Monet, de Pissarro' (*EsA*, p. 405). Zola had noted in his *Journal de voyage* that 'quand l'homme de génie disparaît, l'école sombre' (*OC*, VII, 1072), so directly echoed in the text of *Rome* (*OC*, VII, 668) as to leave no doubt that this logic applies to both literary history and the history of art. In his 1897 interview, such a conclusion in respect of the Old Masters informs Zola's brutally unsympathetic perspective on the development of modern painting, 'le troupeau de ce qu'on appelle l'école nouvelle': 'Tout cela prouve [...] que dans les écoles, il n'y a de vrai que les Maîtres. Les autres, la suite n'existe pas'; 'une école surgit, elle remplit plus ou moins son rôle [...], doit disparaître quand elle a rempli sa mission' (*EsA*, p. 704). It is difficult to resist the temptation to see in what Zola's interlocutor called a gravely pronounced 'verité scientifique', a mirror held up to his own 'school' and its practitioners, labelled by literary history as 'les petits Naturalistes', working in his gigantic shadow. For somewhere between sadness and bitterness, the tone of these remarks cannot but remind us of a number of examples of the vicissitudes of artistic leadership: Manet's refusal to accept that of the Impressionists; the break-up of Claude's 'bande' in *L'Œuvre*,[58] reflecting that of the latter fractious grouping of painters; and of the analogous dissolution of the collective purpose celebrated in *Les Soirées de Médan* in 1880, the very year in which Naturalism itself seemed, at least for a moment, to be invulnerable to competing aesthetics.

'Il faudrait un peintre de génie'

Of his fictional painter in *L'Œuvre*, Zola concluded in his work notes for the novel that while he had the potential to become an artist, 'Claude seul qui l'aurait pu, n'a pas été le génie nécessaire', accounted for by the fact that his practice, akin to that of the Impressionists, was 'une formule qui n'a pas encore son homme, son génie, qui l'aura sans doute plus tard' (Ms 10316, fols. 205–06). A decade later, that confident prediction had been abandoned once and for all. The notion, and nature, of genius is a constant preoccupation in Zola's writing, leaving aside the fact that *Le Génie* was one of the titles he considered for *L'Œuvre* itself: by virtue of the quasi-architectural immensity of their work, Balzac is one ('le génie du siècle'; *OC*, XI, 65), and Hugo another ('un homme de génie'; *OC*, XI, 58), Zola himself all too aware of being, as Sandoz laments in *L'Œuvre*, 'né au confluent' of them both (*RM*, IV, 48). In his art criticism alone, there are some 150 instances of the term: it is used witheringly in relation to artists with unjustifiably inflated reputations: Cabanel (*EsA*, p. 276); Jean-Paul Laurens (*EsA*, p. 360); Théodore Rousseau (*EsA*, p. 538); Carolus-Duran (*EsA*, p. 553); or as a benchmark against which they can be judged, Firmin-Girard's *Le Marché aux Fleurs* (1876) being 'une gifle donnée au génie' (*EsA*, p. 324). He also uses it elsewhere, sometimes indiscriminately, as in an 1860 letter to Cézanne referring to Ary Scheffer as a 'peintre de génie', a youthful enthusiasm which would not survive for long: the next time he mentions him, he adds that Delacroix is 'le seul génie de ce temps' (*EsA*, p. 174). A more considered, if prolix, definition is to be found within his 'Théorie des écrans' (in the sections devoted to 'Les écrans de génie'), in which Zola elaborates the principle that 'les artistes de génie' themselves establish an artistic movement, rather than the other way round: 'les disciples les suivent à la trace'.[59] And size and scope, as he notes in 1878, matter: while acknowledging that 'on ne saurait mesurer le génie d'un peintre aux dimensions de ses tableaux', nevertheless 'il faut faire entrer en compte la largeur de la création, la grandeur de l'élan, de la conception de toute œuvre complexe' (*EsA*, p. 565). It remained to be seen whether any painters of his time could measure up to this ideal, intuitively recognizable but ultimately beyond rational explanation.[60]

Zola had initially placed his hopes in Manet. Having boldly asserted in 1866 that 'M. Manet sera un des maîtres de demain' (*EsA*, p. 151), the nearest Zola gets to the consecration synonymous with genius is in remarking of his paintings that they were 'une face inconnue du génie humain' (*EsA*, p. 475). Nor was such an accolade necessarily only posthumous (as in the remark about Delacroix, 'ce génie qui a seulement triomphé dans la mort' (*EsA*, p. 495)). Even after Manet's death, Zola equivocates: 'Si le génie est fait d'inconscience et du don naturel, il avait certainement du génie' (*EsA*, p. 607). He remains of the view expressed (and literally underlined) in the work notes for *L'Œuvre*: 'Toute cette peinture nouvelle [...] demande *un génie pour être réalisée'* (Ms 10316, fol. 301), cross-referencing the initially more precise 'la formule impress. [*sic*] qui demande un génie pour être réalisée' (fol. 38). Manet, having left behind the solidity of his early work, was thereby disqualified: 'Il n'a pas su se constituer une technique' and, unable (in implicit contrast to Bastien-Lepage in the same 1879 article cited above) to 'rendre ses impressions de façon complète et définitive', 'il lui arrive de s'égarer' (*EsA*, p. 356). In his *Salon* of 1875 (in terms repeated almost verbatim in 1881 (*EsA*, p. 399)), Manet is deemed to extend the artistic lineage of Delacroix and Courbet, 'mais la victoire, il faut l'avouer, n'est pas à prévoir dans un prochain avenir. Il faudrait un peintre de génie' (*EsA*, p. 293). In Zola's 1884 summative assessment, Manet is demoted to the status of a 'précurseur' (*EsA*, p. 611), undoubtedly of enormous influence but ultimately akin to those listed in *Rome* before the advent of Michelangelo and Raphaël ('Fra Angelico, le Perrugin, Botticelli et tant d'autres', (*OC*, VII, 668)), or, to cite the analogies with music inserted in *L'Œuvre*, Haydn and Mozart preceding the genius of Beethoven.[61]

The painter who apparently comes closest to meeting Zola's criteria is Courbet, precisely because of the pictorial qualities which Zola compared, as has been suggested, to those of the Old Masters. Delacroix and Courbet are 'des peintres de génie' *because*, as he writes in 1880, they 'traduisent la nature avec des procédés anciens' (*EsA*, p. 393). Zola had affixed the term to Courbet back in 1866 (*EsA*, pp. 162–64). This elevation to the rank of genius is temporarily interrupted by reservations inseparable from Zola's scorn for the 'le grand Courbet', 'vaniteux et bête', in the painter's commitment to the Commune. Exiled in Switzerland after it, however, 'lui aussi appartient dès aujourd'hui aux morts' (*EsA*, p. 314), preternaturally one of the 'génies défunts' (*EsA*, p. 555). Once alongside the exalted dead, Ingres and Delacroix ('Il était de leur taille', *EsA*, p. 542), Courbet's place in Zola's art history is assured , with his 'transcription puissante et fidèle de la nature telle que la création ne pourra sans doute jamais la dépasser' (*EsA*, p. 559). This is confirmed in *Le Naturalisme au Salon*, the 'maître ouvrier qui a laissé des œuvres impérissables' being inserted in an artistic genealogy 'comme il continue en littérature, derrière Stendhal, Balzac et Flaubert' (*EsA*, p. 373).

More problematic, in this respect, is the case of Cézanne, however sympathetic Zola would have been to the painter's reservations about Monet ('il faut mettre une solidité') and reported ambition 'de faire de l'impressionnisme quelque chose de solide et de durable comme l'art des musées'.[62] Although references to him in Zola's art criticism are few and far between, these are nevertheless worth pondering. On the one hand, his Provencal landscapes make him 'à coup sûr le plus grand coloriste du groupe' (*EsA*, p. 589) of the Impressionists. But, on the other, Zola distinguishes him from them in the remark that Cézanne 'reste plus près de Courbet et de Delacroix' (*EsA*, p. 376), an affinity not without significance in the light of Zola's celebration of these two painters as well as corresponding to Cézanne's own conception of his art in relation to his predecessors and contemporaries.[63] In the parallel with Courbet, in particular, there is an implied recognition, one could argue, of a compositional structuring of the kind Zola had recommended to Cézanne in the 1860s if he aspired to be 'le grand peintre futur': 'tu dois aussi travailler le dessin fort et ferme'; 'on naît poète, on devient ouvrier'.[64] Throughout his art criticism, Zola is careful to refer to him as, indeed, a 'grand peintre', qualified, however, by the conviction that Cézanne 'se débat encore dans des recherches de facture' (*EsA*, p. 376). In an article in *La Tribune* in 1868, Zola had evoked 'des images d'une naïveté étrange aux colorations crues' (*OC*, XIII, 113), behind which Cézanne is obliquely discernible, as he is in 'la naïveté enfantine du dessin [qui] avait une saveur toute campagnarde' (*OC*, I, 820), that same year, in *Madeleine Férat*. Zola assured Duret in 1870 that Cézanne 'est dans une période de tatônnements'. The injunction 'Attendez qu'il se soit trouvé lui-même'[65] is a frequent refrain in the years ahead: 'le jour où M. Paul Cézanne se possédera tout entier, il produira des œuvres tout à fait supérieures' (*EsA*, p. 589). Zola had confided to Baille in 1861 that 'Paul peut avoir le génie d'un grand peintre, il n'aura jamais le génie de le devenir',[66] already suspecting that the painter's' 'défaut de la ligne droite' (*pace* Flaubert), in his endless stylistic experimentation and discontinuous application (unlike his own, of course!), would preclude his ever achieving 'la gloire' which Cézanne disingenuously affected to disdain. Manet too, having been through his own 'période de tatonnements' and found 'une langue qu'il avait faite sienne' (*EsA*, p. 474), would be charged with losing his way 'entrâiné par son tempérament dans une évolution incessante' (*EsA*, p. 606). And, at one stage, as mentioned in Chapter 3, Courbet had also put at risk his preeminent status, according to Zola, having 'passé à l'ennemi', by submitting to the Salon of 1866 two crowd-pleasing paintings divested of 'je ne sais quoi de puissant et de voulu qui est Courbet tout entier' (*EsA*, p. 164). In this instance, Zola's disapproval is justified by 'une règle qui s'impose forcément à moi: c'est que l'admiration de la foule est toujours en raison indirecte du génie individuel' (*EsA*, p. 162). Another such 'rule' is the insidious impact of the 'anxiety of influence', of the kind Zola would detect in the contrast between 'les chefs-d'œuvre de Raphaël' before his visiting the Sistine Chapel and after doing so: 'l'artiste avait perdu la fleur de sa divine grâce, impressionné par l'écrasante grandeur de Michel-Ange. [...] C'était une chute brusque, totale' (*OC*, VII, 668). For, as the indirections of both Cézanne and Manet both suggest, the essential principle of Zola's concept of artistic genius is the consistency, once developed and thereafter resistant to alternative modes, of an individuated aesthetic.

It is against the background of Zola's reflections on the Old Masters that one might consider anew his thinking about Cézanne. The most frequently recycled of Zola's judgements on the painter remains his 1896 recollections of 'mon ami, mon frère, Paul Cézanne, dont on s'avise seulement aujourd'hui de découvrir les parties géniales de grand peintre avorté' (*EsA*, p. 402). But only that terminal adjective has been the object of scholarly focus, even if, in the text of his interview the following year, this hurtful notion is attenuated: 'Quant à ce pauvre Paul Cézanne, je suis heureux de voir que l'on commence à reconnaître enfin le côté génial de ce grand peintre resté en route' (*EsA*, p. 702). And Zola reportedly admitted to Gasquet in about 1900 that 'je commence à mieux comprendre sa peinture, que j'ai toujours goûtée, mais qui m'a échappé longtemps, car je la croyais exaspérée, alors qu'elle est d'une sincérité, d'une vérité incroyable'.[67] There is clearly an extent to which

Zola's allusion to the belated public recognition of Cézanne's 'côté génial' is a direct consequence of the critical reception of the painter's work in the aftermath of the first great exhibition of his paintings mounted by Vollard in November 1895. But even shortly before that, Geffroy, well-known to Zola and in literary circles, had characterized some of Cézanne's pictures as having 'une sorte d'apparence michelangelesque'.[68] The 1895 retrospective itself, as well as subsequent smaller exhibitions organized by Vollard in the years immediately following it, catalyzed a more general revaluation of the painter now dubbed 'le maître d'Aix', with many critics identifying pictorial qualities which had been the recurrent *sine qua non* of Zola's admiration for painters past and present: 'sincérité'; 'simplicité'; 'grandeur'; 'la peinture par masses'; and 'ses qualités magistrales de créateur' residing in 'cette qualité si solidement établie des formes'.[69]

It would be highly speculative, however, to conclude that, if only Zola had recognized it earlier, Cézanne would qualify as the contemporary artistic genius whose absence he lamented. For the substitution of 'resté en route' for the cruelly infelicitous 'avorté' is consistent with another recurrent theme of his writing on the visual arts, that of the perennially deferred advent of 'le génie de l'avenir': in 1868, he asks of the future 'quelle est la personnalité qui va surgir, assez large, assez humaine pour comprendre notre civilisation et la rendre artistique en l'interprétant avec l'ampleur magistrale du génie [?]' (*EsA*, p. 192); 'en attendant les génies de l'avenir', he writes in 1875, he explains that 'quand un génie paraîtra, il subjugera les esprits et fera l'éducation de toute une génération' (*EsA*, p. 270); the next year, Zola adds that 'les génies surgissent à raison d'un par génération, au plus' and that 'nous attendons toujours les génies de l'avenir' (*EsA*, p. 312); and, in 1879, the most valuable role given to 'précurseurs' such as the Impressionists is anticipatory in the sense of assuring that 'la place est balayée pour le peintre de génie' (*EsA*, p. 361). This theme is inseparable from the nineteenth century's larger discourse on the nature of creativity and genius. Anita Brookner's aptly titled *The Genius of the Future* identifies the contradictory emphases, within that discourse, of what she calls 'the last of the Romantic idealist critics', whose frustrated hopes are followed by a 'regression', their idealism 'projected back into the past'.[70] She specifically mentions only the Goncourts and Huysmans in this respect. Unlike theirs, Zola's entire work is riven by the tensions between the archaic implications of the title of *La Bête humaine* and a confidence in Progress, an optimism already visible at the end of *Les Rougon-Macquart* and reinforced through *Les Trois Villes* and *Les Quatre Évangiles*. But in what he calls, in the work notes for *L'Œuvre*, the uncertainties of 'notre temps de transition [...] naissante et trouble' (Ms 10316, fols 294–95) as far as 'le moment artistique' is concerned, Zola does indeed look backwards. Nor is this limited to the ideal represented by Michelangelo and the Sistine Chapel. For genius manifests itself for Zola, the reputed champion of modern painting, in the achievement of the Old Masters more generally. There is nothing uncertain or unreliable about Pierre's epiphany, in *Rome*, experiencing an illumination both literal and metaphorical in the Buongiovanni family's picture gallery, with its spectacular collection of masterpieces 'unique au monde', not based on a documentary source but brought together by the novelist: 'des Raphaël, des Titien, des Rembrandt et des Rubens, des Vélasquez et des Ribera, des œuvres fameuses entre toutes, qui soudainement, dans cet éclairage inattendu, apparaissaient triomphantes de jeunesse, comme réveillées à l'immortelle vie du génie' (*OC*, VII, 886).

Notes to Chapter 6

1. See John Christie, 'The Enigma of Zola's *Madame Sourdis*', *Nottingham French Studies*, 5 (1966), 13–28 (p. 20).
2. Letter of 10 May 1883 (*Corr.*, IV, 338).
3. This version of Courbet lineage is partly borrowed, ironically enough, from Proudhon: 'Tout continuateur qu'il est de l'école hollandaise, Courbet est novateur, radicalement novateur' (Proudhon, *Du principe de l'art*, p. 197).
4. The year before, in his review of the Salon of 1875, Zola seems to distinguish between Poussin himself and artists working in his footsteps: 'Je ne saurai exprimer jusqu'à quel degré de bêtise, de banalité, de vulgarité et de mensonge les petits-fils de Poussin étaient descendus' (*EsA*, p. 290).
5. See, for example, Huysmans's review in *La République des lettres* of 9 July 1876: 'beaucoup de travail dans tous ces envois de Rome, mais d'originalité, point' (Huysmans, *Écrits sur l'art*, p. 59).
6. Although accessible to journalists from November 1872 onwards, the Musée des copies was only opened for the public on 15 April 1873. Two weeks after the Marquis de Chennevières replaced Blanc as director of the École des Beaux-Arts on 23 December, he announced its immediate closure, a decision welcomed by Zola in *Le Sémaphore de Marseille* of 1 January 1874.
7. Baudelaire, *Œuvres complètes*, I, 613.
8. Though his failure to achieve this is the making of 'le jeune maître selon le goût du jour, ayant eu la chance de rater le prix de Rome et de rompre avec l'École' (*RM*, IV, 291).
9. Jean-Claude Le Blond-Zola recalled 'une très belle glace Renaissance' in Zola's study; see his *Zola à Médan* (Paris: Société Littéraire des Amis d'Émile Zola, 1999), p. 86. For a complete inventory, based on the auction-catalogue of Zola's personal effects, see Lucie Riou, 'Zola collectionneur: le cabinet de travail comme musée', *CN*, 93 (2019), 229–46. She cites (p. 232) Fernand Xau, the journalist invited to view Zola's domestic interior in April 1880, who remarked that it was 'garni de meubles de toutes les époques et de tous les siècles', precisely the impression left on visitors to the home of the fictional Sandoz in *L'Œuvre*. Such tastes are reflected elsewhere: in his *Nouveaux Contes à Ninon*, Zola evokes a child, so tranquil 'qu'on l'aurait pris pour un bronze florentin, une de ces charmantes figurines de la Renaissance' (*OC*, IX, p. 431).
10. Letter of 14 May to Baille (*Corr.* I, 166). To Cézanne, in July, Zola repeated this: 'Fort médiocre copiste, dès qu'il faut inventer il est complètement mauvais' (*Corr.*, I, 214). Chaillan is one of the models for the figure of Justin Chaîne, in *L'Œuvre*, who 'peignait en maçon, gâchant les couleurs, réussissant à rendre boueuses les plus claires et les plus vibrantes' and whose copying of a Mantegna in the Louvre is characteristic of his 'exactitude dans la gaucherie' (*RM*, IV, 68); in his studio, we are told that 'rien ne manquait dans l'exécrable' (*RM*, IV, 124); 'Au Louvre, devant les chefs-d'œuvre, il était uniquement persuadé qu'il fallait du temps' (*RM*, IV, 311).
11. Letter of 3 March 1861 (*Corr.*, I, 272).
12. 'Je viens du Louvre', declares Duranty's spokesman in *Le Réalisme* of 10 July 1856, adding that 'si j'avais eu des allumettes je mettais le feu sans remords à cette catacombe avec l'intime conviction que je servais la cause de l'art à venir'; and Pissarro reportedly said 'qu'il fallait brûler les nécropoles de l'art'. Cited by Theodore Reff, 'Copyists in the Louvre, 1850–1870', *Art Bulletin*, 46 (1964), 552–59 (p. 553). In dismay at the destruction of Parisian monuments by the Commune, Zola writes in *Le Sémaphore de Marseille* of 31 May 1871 about 'les misérables qui ont voulu brûler le Louvre' (*EsA*, p. 431).
13. 'Il en arrivait à déclamer contre le travail au Louvre, il se serait, disait-il, coupé le poignet, plutôt que d'y retourner gâter son œil à une de ces copies, qui encrassent pour toujours la vision du monde où l'on vit' (*RM*, IV, 43–44).
14. In response to the uproar provoked by Manet's *Déjeuner sur l'herbe*, Zola protests that 'il y a au

musée du Louvre plus de cinquante tableaux dans lesquels se trouvent mêlés des personnages habillés et des personnages nus' (*EsA*, p. 486). A similar irony targets Mme Josserand, in *Pot-Bouille*, who opines that 'au Louvre, on voit vraiment trop de nudités, et le monde y est mêlé parfois' (*RM*, III, 56). A variant is the citing of an Old Master to ridicule the philistinism of the public: in the context of the hostility provoked by Manet's 1874 submission, Zola writes that 'si l'on accrochait un Goya au Salon, on se tordrait' (*EsA*, p. 244).

15. In reporting the sale of six of Courbet's paintings, seized in the context of the prosecution aimed at the painter's alleged role in the destruction of the Colonne Vendôme during the Commune and attempts to secure the cost of reparations from his assets, Zola writes in *Le Sémaphore de Marseille* of 7 March 1876: 'J'espère bien qu'on mettra au Louvre les tableaux saisis. C'est là leur place, au milieu des chefs-d'œuvre des anciennes écoles' (*EsA*, p. 434).
16. In the original text of this study, published in the *Revue du XIX*[e] *siècle* (1 January 1867), only *Le Déjeuner sur l'herbe* appears in this prediction. *Olympia* was added in the definitive version (Paris, E. Dentu, 1867) timed to coincide with Manet's private show in 1867. Dying in 1902, Zola did not live to see his prophecy fulfilled: *Olympia* entered the Louvre in 1907, the same year as *Le Déjeuner sur l'herbe* was hung in the Musée des arts décoratifs, not being admitted to the Louvre until 1934.
17. Francis Haskell, *The Ephemeral Museum: Old Master Paintings and the Rise of the Art Exhibition* (New Haven and London: Yale University Press, 2000), p. 4.
18. In his 1905 letter to Émile Bernard (Cézanne, *Correspondance*, p. 392). See also Gasquet's 1921 recollections where the variant ('le Louvre est un bon livre à consulter; je n'y ai pas manqué' (Gasquet, *Cézanne*, p. 169)) is qualified by 'ce ne doit encore être qu'un intermédiaire'. But Gasquet also reported that, as a young man, 'sa frénésie de pensée' in the Salon Carré had Cézanne declaring that 'il faut brûler le Louvre' (p. 60).
19. Gasquet, *Cézanne*, pp. 180–81.
20. For a concordance, covering both his correspondence and *La Comédie humaine*, see the catalogue of the *Balzac et la peinture* exhibition (Musée des beaux-arts de Tours, 29 May–30 August, 1999); to take a single example, there are more than a hundred references to Raphaël in *La Comédie humaine* alone.
21. Amongst innumerable examples, see Maupassant, in *Gil Blas* of 1 August 1882, comparing 'la belle Ernestine' to 'une tête à la Rubens' (*Chroniques*, ed. by Gérard Delaisement, 2 vols (Paris: Rive Droite, 2003), I, 553); or Zola's characterization of Renoir's paintings: 'on dirait des Rubens sur lesquels a lui le grand soleil de Vélasquez' (*EsA*, p. 586; virtually repeated, p. 343); or his reference to Huysmans, in *Le Figaro* of 11 April 1881: 'Il apporte dans nos lettres françaises un tempérament de grand coloriste, qui rappelle les Rembrandt et les Rubens' (*OC*, XIII, 581). There may be a degree of self-irony, in relation to such name-dropping, in *L'Œuvre*: Naudet, the art dealer, praises a work by Bongrand in extravagantly allusive terms ('Ah! cette lumière, cette facture si solide et si large! Ah! il faut remonter à Rembrandt, oui, à Rembrandt!'), much to the painter's irritation (*RM*, IV, 187). In his 1889 essay on Marcellin Desboutin, Zola likens the engraver's self-portraits to 'Rembrandt, aimant à se reproduire à tous les âges et sous des aspects divers d'attitude et de costume' (*EsA*, p. 614). And another such *lieu commun* is evident in his remark about the autobiographical figure of Sandoz, in *L'Œuvre*: 'J'ai cru pouvoir, comme les peintres de la Renaissance, mettre mon portrait dans un coin du tableau' (*EsA*, p. 703). In a letter to Cézanne of 16 April 1860, advising him to lift his sights, he had written: 'Vois Rembrandt; avec un rayon de lumière, tous ses personnages, même les plus laids, deviennent poétiques' (*Corr.*, I, 146).
22. Haskell, *The Ephemeral Museum*, p. 39. But, as Maxime Du Camp recalled in his *Souvenirs littéraires* (1882), this did not preclude the relative popularity of the Old Masters (notably Michelangelo and Titian) in the artistic circles in which he and Flaubert moved in their youth. And Delaroche's mural *Hémicycle* (1841–42) for the École des Beaux-Arts, depicting some seventy artists from Antiquity to the Renaissance, remained the most public tribute to the continuing prestige of the Old Masters. In 1874, however, there opened a huge exhibition of works of art from the finest private collections in Paris, with nearly every major painter from Raphaël to Ingres represented. Of this exhibition in the Palais Bourbon, designed to raise funds for French

citizens forcibly exiled from Alsace-Lorraine, Zola wrote in *Le Sémaphore de Marseille* of 24 June, that 'depuis longtemps, on n'avait vu pareille réunion de chefs-d'œuvre' (*EsA*, p. 597).

23. *L'Événement*, 1 Feb. 1866; in the same newspaper, later that year (22 October), he alerted readers to Taine's *Philosophie de l'art en Italie* (published by Germer-Baillière), a work bringing together 'les leçons d'esthétique qu'il a données cette année à l'École des Beaux-Arts [...] tableau magistral des mœurs de l'Italie au quinzième siècle' (*OC*, x, 671).
24. Under the heading 'L'Esthétique professée à l'École des Beaux-Arts', and reprinted that summer as 'M. H. Taine, Artiste' (with minor variants) in *Mes haines*.
25. See the modern edition of Taine's *Voyage en Italie: à Rome*, préface d'Émile Zola (Brussels: Éditions Complexe, 1990), p. 164; by contrast, 'dans les peintures de Raphaël, l'immobilité de la couleur fanée et de l'attitude sculpturale ôte aux yeux une portion de leur vie' (p. 133). This was a contemporary *idée reçue*: in 1836, Gautier referred to Raphaël's 'airy limpidity' (cited by Snell, *Théophile Gautier*, p. 73); at the end of the century, Huysmans was more brutal about 'l'odieux Raphaël, qui, avec ses matrons douceâtres et ses nourrices purement humaines, nous conduisit par une longue filière et de lentes transitions aux épouvantables niaiseries des marchands de sainteté de la rue Saint-Sulpice et de la rue Madame!' In *Certains* (1889), he had contented himself by simply referring to 'les sourdes médiocrités de Raphaël' (Huysmans, *Écrits sur l'art*, p. 501 and p. 431).
26. 'J'aime les muscles, les beaux tons, le sang. Je suis comme Taine, moi, et de plus, je suis peintre' (cited by Gasquet, *Cézanne*, p. 182). Danchev (*Cézanne*, p. 398, n. 27) notes that there is a copy of *Voyage en Italie* in his studio. While the painter was also familiar with Stendhal's *Histoire de la peinture en Italie* (1817), read for the first time in 1869, there is no way of knowing how Zola responded to his 'tu l'as lu sans doute' in Cézanne's letter to him of 20 November 1878 (*Correspondance*, p. 223). But he did buy a copy in Rome in 1894. Even in characteristically grudging mode, the Goncourts, noted on 21 January 1866 that 'Taine a l'art admirable d'enseigner aujourd'hui aux autres ce qu'il ignorait hier' (*Journal*, II, 4).
27. See my 'A Visit to the Louvre: *L'Assommoir* Revisited', *Modern Language Review*, 87 (1992), 41–55.
28. Mitterand, 'Le Musée dans le texte', p. 18.
29. In *L'Œuvre*, 'l'air de fête' of Berlioz's *Roméo et Juliette* is likened to 'un Véronèse, la magnificence tumultuese des *Noces de Cana*' (*RM*, IV, 335). In 'La Semaine d'une parisienne', published in *Le Messager de l'Europe* of May 1875, Zola had compared the spectacle of the crowd in the lobby of the Opera to this 'tableau de Véronèse, un palais de fête avec sa rangée de colonnes, ses galeries éloignées, ses escaliers majestueux et sans fin' (*OC*, IX, 962). For other references between 1866 and 1875, see *OC*, x, 43, and XII, 859, 868, 923.
30. Writing about Huysmans in *Le Voltaire* of 15 June 1880, Zola refers to passages 'où grouillent toutes les kermesses de Rubens avec un débordement de vie, des empâtements de couleurs' (*OC*, XII, 602). In *L'Œuvre*, it is the template for Bongrand's *Noce au village* (*RM*, IV, 87), the very title of which echoes the *Fête au village* by which Rubens's *Kermesse* in the Louvre was also known. But even prior to reading Taine, Zola was obviously familiar with it: reviewing in 1863 Doré's illustrations for an edition of *Don Quichotte*, he singled out the representation of Gamache's wedding with its 'foule, enfants criards, coups de poing, vaisselles brisées, comme dans une kermesse de Rubens' (*OC*, x, 302). As Tooke remarks (*Flaubert and the Pictorial Arts*, p. 35), 'nineteenth-century views of Rubens tended to emphasize the animal exuberance of his paintings', citing the generalization which could have been included in Flaubert's *Dictionnaire des idées reçues*: 'Dans les bacchanales de Rubens on pisse par terre.'
31. 'Michel-Ange est un constructeur, et Raphaël un artiste, qui, si grand qu'il soit, est toujours bridé par le modèle. Quand il veut devenir réfléchisseur il tombe au-dessous de son grand rival' (cited by Gasquet, *Cézanne*, p. 189). Referring to Cézanne's giving up writing poetry, Zola (ironically?) urges him, in a letter of 1 August 1860, to replace 'le Lamartine naissant par le Raphaël futur' (*Corr.*, I, 217). On the displacement of Raphaël's pictures with a serious and didactic purpose by frivolous images of romance, see Francis Haskell, *Past and Present in Art and Taste: Selected Essays* (New Haven and London: Yale University Press, 1987), pp. 93–97. The Goncourts, by contrast, stressed that 'à Raphaël commencent l'Allégorie, appréciée par les critiques sérieux, les bonhommes sous lesquels on met de grands noms [...] en sorte qu'il est le

premier peintre littéraire' (*Journal*, II, 76: entry for 17 April 1867). Given Zola's antipathy to 'la peinture à idées', this was another reason for his downgrading of Raphaël.

32. In his work notes for the novel (Ms 10323): 'portrait d'Angélique malade, — émaciée — Un Memling. Reprendre son portrait de jeune fille (personnage), et le pâlir' (fol. 169); 'la sincérité de l'artiste. Memling. Van Eyck (fol. 391). See Béatrice Laurent, 'Éclairages du Nord dans les tableaux du *Rêve*', *CN*, 66 (1992), 73–81. For the same novel, Zola had imagined a church which would be 'le petit bijou de la renaissance' (Ms 10323, fol. 111), completed, as only the definitive text has it, 'vers 1430, en plein quinzième siècle' (*RM*, IV, 851), before being transformed into a cathedral during the reign of Louis XIV.
33. 'Je ne connais, au Louvre, qu'un tableau d'un maître italien inconnu, où il avait une tête de moine divinisée par une foi pareille' (*OC*, VII, 249). In the preparatory notes for the novel, Zola was more precise: 'Maigre et grand avec une figure d'ascète. Barbe pâle et en pointe, rare. Des yeux étincelants dans un visage pâle, blême, amaigri. Un Ribera, en plus clair' (cited by Riou, *Les Arts visuels*, p. 235). Although Spanish by origin, Ribera spent most of his career in Italy.
34. Letter to Lacroix of 8 May 1867 (*Corr.*, I, 496–97).
35. Le Blond-Zola, *Émile Zola racontée par sa fille*, p. 270.
36. Courbet was already thought of as such in 1867, in spite of his decision to forego official recognition at the Universal Exhibition. For as Patricia Mairnardi writes, 'he was promoted to a kind of "Old Master" status which permitted his earlier paintings, at least, to be seen outside of the partisan politics that had informed their creation and initial reception' (*Art and Politics of the Second Empire*, p. 140).
37. Elaborating his work notes (Ms 10316): 'Chaîne poignant les primitifs. Les gens, en projection, les cervelle [*sic*]' (fol. 104); 'Celui-ci peint les primitif [*sic*]. Mantegna (plus tard dans la boutique). Les gens vu [*sic*] en projection, les cervelles' (fol. 121); and again on fol. 194.
38. Letter to his mother, dated 8 April 1851 (Flaubert, *Correspondance*, I, 769).
39. On Zola's earlier contempt, see Michaël Maione, 'Zola et la sculpture', *CN*, 58 (1984), 151–62.
40. While the Goncourts characteristically, if unfairly, accused Zola of plagiarizing their *Madame Gervaisais*, there is a curious echo here of their heroine's altered perspective (on 'la Rome catholique' rather than works of art) who feels within herself, 'par une évolution de ses idées, se retourner contre ses admirations de la veille'. Zola was certainly familiar with the novel: referring to it in 1875 in the context of a study of its authors, in which he stressed that it was 'une étude de femme', while noting that 'leur heroïne lettrée leur a permis de peindre la Rome de l'Antiquité' (*OC*, XI, 172–73); he had re-read it shortly before leaving for Rome on 29 October 1894, writing to Edmond de Goncourt on 15 November that 'c'est aujourd'hui seulement que je la pénètre jusqu'à l'âme' (*Corr.*, VIII, 181).
41. For Flaubert, it relativized all other human achievements: 'J'aimerais mieux avoir peint la chapelle Sixtine que gagné bien des batailles' (*Correspondance*, I, 770). Zola's response was closer to Flaubert's than to that of the Goncourts, chapter 25 of their *Madame Gervaisais* describing St Peter's and the Sistine Chapel as a musical rather than pictorial experience.
42. Mitterand, *Zola*, III, 115. By virtue of its informing context, this is one instance of Zola following Stendhal's advice, in his *Histoire de la peinture en Italie*, that only by immersing oneself in fifteenth-century culture could one understand the Old Masters: 'Ce genre [de peinture] est difficile à voir; l'œil a besoin d'une éducation, et, cette éducation, l'on ne peut guère se la donner qu'à Rome'; cited by Ann Jefferson ('Stendhal's Art History and the Making of a Novelist', in *Artistic Relations: Literature and the Visual Arts in Nineteenth-Century France*, ed. by Peter Collier and Robert Lethbridge (New Haven amd London: Yale University Press, 1994), pp. 192–208 (p. 203)), who adds that, in this respect, 'Stendhal's engagement with painting is quite unlike that of Diderot, Baudelaire or Zola' (p. 205).
43. See my '"Le Delacroix de la musique": Zola's Critical Conflations', in *Le Champ littéraire, 1860–1900*, ed. by Keith Cameron and James Kearns (Amsterdam: Rodopi,1996), pp. 81–90. Taine effects the same kind of analogy: 'Plus on regarde Raphaël, plus on sent qu'il avait une âme tendre et généreuse, semblable à Mozart' (Taine, *Voyage en Italie*, p. 215). Zola had noted that Taine aligned four artistic 'geniuses': Beethoven, Michelangelo, Shakespeare and Dante.
44. Winner of the Prix de Rome in 1839 and twice appointed director of the Académie de France in Rome (1867–73 and 1885–91), Hébert had stayed on in the Italian capital until 1896, thus

allowing him to act as Zola's guide during his visit to Rome two years earlier. On his return to Paris, Zola would refer to 'notre éminent compatriote, M. Hébert, qui m'a fait visiter le Vatican' (*Entretiens avec Zola*, p. 145). Hébert seems not to have held it against him that his own paintings had been contemptuously dismissed by Zola in his art criticism.

45. Introducing the novel, Dominique Fernandez dismissed Zola's dénouement to that plot as 'la scène la plus colossalement ridicule de tout le roman français' (*OC*, VII, 512).
46. In the work notes for the novel, cited by Jacques Noiray, 'De la mise à nu comme principe poétique: genèse du personnage de Benedetta dans *Rome*', in *Zola: genèse de l'œuvre*, ed. by Jean-Pierre Leduc-Adine (Paris: CNRS Éditions, 2002), pp. 245–62 (p. 247). Zola had long been irked by reviews of his work in this respect: preparing *Le Rêve* in 1888, he noted that 'puisqu'on m'accuse de ne pas faire de psychologie, je voudrais forcer les gens à confesser que je suis un psychologue. De la psychologie donc, ou ce qu'on appelle ainsi (!)' (Ms 10323, fols 217–18).
47. As Flaubert put it in a letter of 15 July 1853 to Louise Colet, 'les bonhommes de Michel-Ange ont des câbles plutôt que des muscles' (*Correspondance*, II, 385).
48. In Rome, Zola reminded himself to get hold of 'le meilleur Botticelli, l'avoir en photographie' (*OC*, VII, 1072); i.e. his *La Derelitta* in the Pallavicini collection; and his portrait of Rosalie Lovatelli is conceived, with her 'air craintif, effacée', as 'un Botticelli éteint' (*OC*, VII, 1075). In his private collection, Zola retained an 1892 engraving 'd'après Botticelli' of *La Primavera*, by the Polish artist Félix Jasinski (1862–1901), as well as a photographic reproduction of this same Botticelli work, purchased in 1895. He had made a point of including this sentimental image amongst the works decorating the apartment he secured in 1889 for Jeanne Rozerot, his mistress and mother of his two children.
49. Tooke, *Flaubert and the Pictorial Arts*, p. 136.
50. In his letter of 22 March 1885 to Henry Céard (*Corr.*, V, 249), doubtless prompted by reviews such as that by Edmond Deschaumes, in *L'Événement* of 2 March, underlining that Zola 'voit énorme et son œil est rempli de visions gigantesques'. He repeats in the work notes for *L'Œuvre* this notion of 'le lyrisme, le coup d'aile qui résume la synthèse, emporte et agrandit' (Ms 10316, fol. 277).
51. Bonnat, who had served his artistic apprenticeship in Rome, was one of the few nineteenth-century collectors of Old Masters, housing in his opulent mansion a magnificent set of Italian, Dutch and Flemish drawings. In 1880, he paid 15,000 francs for one of Michelangelo's.
52. Letter of 17 March 1861 addressed jointly to Cézanne and Baille (*Corr.*, I, 275).
53. Sara Pappas, 'Reading for Detail: On Zola's Abandonment of Impressionism', *Word & Image*, 4 (2007), 474–84, though she makes no mention of criteria derived from, or confirmed by, Zola's thinking about the Old Masters.
54. Dominique Fernandez, *Le Musée d'Émile Zola: haines et passions* (Paris, Stock, 1997), p. 37.
55. Mitterand, *Zola*, III, 115.
56. As F.W.J. Hemmings pointed out in the introduction ('Zola critique d'art') to his and Robert J. Niess's edition of Zola's *Salons* (Geneva: Droz, 1959), the writer had long been looking for 'une espèce de Michel-Ange du XIXe siècle' (p. 38).
57. See Norman Bryson, *Tradition and Desire: From David to Delacroix* (Cambridge: Cambridge University Press, 1984), on Vasari's repeating and reinforcing Pliny's model of artistic progress (pp. 8–10).
58. Zola's intention was clear: 'une bande de quatre peintres, me donnant une coterie, et avec laquelle je pourrais montrer ce que devient une école' (Ms 10316, fol. 271); but Claude, in spite of the gradual lessening of respect for his leadership, fails to notice associated signs of 'une bande cassée': 'bien montrer', Zola noted in the light of his own experience in the 1880s, 'les fissures, les endroits où ça craque' (fol. 111). But even coinciding with the triumphalist moment of *Les Soirées de Médan*, there were signs of Zola's aesthetic being contested; by the time he was writing *L'Œuvre*, a contemporary referred to 'ce roi littéraire que sa suite néglige' (see Alain Pagès, *Zola et le groupe de Médan* (Paris: Perrin, 2014), pp. 333–40). By 1896, Zola had been completely left behind by developments in both literature and the visual arts.
59. Letter of 18 August 1864 to Valabrègue (*Corr.*, I, 373–82). He repeats this in his *Salon* of 1866: 'Je crois que chaque génie naît indépendant et qu'il ne laisse pas de disciples' (*EsA*, p. 157).

60. Of Shakespeare, he writes in a letter of 25 July 1860 to Baille: 'Le génie se sent, mais ne s'explique pas' (*Corr.*, I, 207). In a letter of 1 December 1900 to Maurice Le Blond, in the context of the setting up of a 'Collège d'esthétique moderne', Zola declares that 'je n'ai jamais été pour un enseignement esthétique quelconque, et je suis convaincu que le génie pousse tout seul, pour l'unique besogne qu'il juge bonne' (*Corr.*, X, 203). This was a long-held view: in 1867, Zola ironizes Isidore Pils's pedagogic responsibility, at the École des Beaux-Arts, 'de créer les génies de l'avenir' (*EsA*, p. 534). And in his review of the Salon of 1872, he satirizes the system of State medals, monetary awards and commissions: 'C'est donc bien cher, le génie, monsieur le Ministre' (*EsA*, p. 223).
61. 'Beethoven est l'efflorescence de Haydn et Mozart. Deux précurseurs' (Ms 10316, fol. 404); Berlioz, 'énorme du colorie musical (Delacroix)' and his 'énormité des moyens pour la puissance' comes close, but is too inconsistent ('construction d'opéra défectueuse') to match Beethoven (fols. 408–09).
62. Gasquet, *Cézanne*, p. 167.
63. Remarkably close to Zola's is his assessment of Courbet: 'un bâtisseur. Un rude gâcheur de plâtre. Un broyeur de tons. Il maçonnait comme un romain [...]. Il n'y en a pas un autre dans ce siècle qui le dégote [...]. Sa vision est restée celle des vieux [...], c'est la force, le génie, qu'il mettait par-dessous' (Gasquet, *Cézanne*, pp. 200–01); and superior to Manet, Courbet's work holding its own next to Titian, Velázquez and Veronese. The phrase 'broyeur de tons' is also part of Zola's critical lexicon: 'Les grands artistes de la Renaissance ont commencé par apprendre à broyer les couleurs' (*EsA*, pp. 174–75).
64. Letter to Cézanne of 16 April 1860 (*Corr.*, I, 139–47).
65. Letter to Duret of 30 May 1870 (*Corr.*, I, 219).
66. Undated (but mid-summer, 1861) letter to Baille (*Corr.*, I, 300–01).
67. Gasquet, *Cézanne*, p. 96, thereby anticipating Roger Fry's sense of a 'desperate sincerity' (cited by Danchev, *Cézanne*, p. 296).
68. 'Paul Cézanne', *Le Journal*, 25 March 1894. Geffroy would be one of the founding members of the Académie Goncourt. Zola had known him since 1883: in a letter of 1885, Zola refers to him as 'le brave Geffroy' (*Corr.*, V, 331); in 1887, he invites him to dinner with his publisher and two of his closest friends, Alexis and Céard (*Corr.*, VI, 79). In October 1897, he became one of the editorial directors of *L'Aurore*, in which Zola would publish 'J'Accuse', visiting him in London in February 1899 during the writer's enforced exile there.
69. Thadée Natanson, 'Paul Cézanne', *La Revue blanche*, 1 December 1895, pp. 496–500; he remarked of even the painter's admirers that 'sur le mot "incomplet", presque tous se trouvaient d'accord' (p. 497), which suggests that Zola's judgement of Cézanne, in the preparatory dossier of *L'Œuvre*, as 'le génie incomplet' was a critical commonplace. By 1899, parallels were being established with the 'décorateurs vénitiens' (*La Revue blanche*, 15 December 1899, pp. 627–28), which inform modern perspectives on Cézanne such as Meyer Schapiro's stress on his 'affinity with the great masters of the sixteenth and seventeenth centuries in the largeness of his forms, in his delight in balancing and varying the massive counterpoised elements'; Meyer Schapiro, *Paul Cézanne* (New York: Harry N. Abrams, 1952), pp. 10–11.
70. Brookner, *The Genius of the Future*, p. 116.

AFTERWORD

❖

'Le métier de critique', Zola complained in 1880, 'est un casse-cou.'[1] Without denying that such work had been instrumental in launching his career as a writer, he had clearly now reached a stage in which completing *Les Rougon-Macquart* was an all-consuming priority. The commercial success of *L'Assommoir* and *Nana* (in 1880, precisely) had in any case definitively liberated him from journalism's daily grind. The articles published in the period 1879–81 and collected in *Les Romanciers naturalistes*, *Le Roman expérimental* and *Le Naturalisme au théâtre* are not contracted commitments with deadlines. They are initiated by Zola and conceived as both a critical defence of his novel series and a militant proclamation of the aesthetic principles informing his fiction. Zola's final extended essays of art criticism, notably in *Le Naturalisme au Salon* but also in his more perfunctory review of the Salon of 1881 ('Après une promenade au Salon' (*EsA*, pp. 395–400)), have to be viewed in this same context.

To do so is to better understand his 1896 remark that he had rather lost interest in painting over the preceding decades. Zola's own explanation of this had been prefigured in 1878, in the assertion, mentioned in Chapter 1, that contemporary theatre offered him a more topical discursive platform for sustaining commentary on Naturalism's domination of each and every form of artistic expression. That was somewhat disingenuous. The fact is that developments in the visual arts increasingly threatened, rather than confirmed, the cultural hegemony Zola was at such pains to proclaim. The triumphalism asserted in the very title of *La Naturalisme au Salon* 'doth protest too much', as it were. For, on the pretext of reviewing here the Salon of 1880 (at the behest of Cézanne asking him to write something supportive about the Impressionists), the recruitment to his campaign of virtually every painter, alive or dead, stretches credibility to the point of almost devaluing the integrity of his critical stance.

In retrospect, the same charges could be levelled at much of his art criticism more generally. It is clear that, from his earliest incursions into the field and beyond, Zola's preferences and negative assessments are dictated by criteria related to his literary ambitions and achievements: on the one hand, dismissal of Romantic artifice, opposition to convention, and antipathy to any betrayal of verisimilitude; on the other, a stress on artistic originality measured in terms of an adherence to the imperatives of the representation of modern life. Zola's reputation as one of the most important art critics of his generation rests on the latter. For his uncompromising admirers, Zola's polemical writing on the painters of his time is testimony to an intellectual and personal courage encoded in the subtitle of Henri Mitterand's chronological survey of his journalism: *de l'affaire Manet à l'affaire Dreyfus*.[2] Whatever their occasional reservations about aspects of his interpretation of Manet's pictures, all art historians too include Zola's championing of him in the 1860s as a decisive moment in the emergence of arguably the greatest French painter, ultimately recognized as such by the time of his death, of the second half of the nineteenth century. By contrast and with the wisdom of hindsight, his failure to engage with Cézanne's work is inevitably held against him. His gradual disenchantment with Impressionism is similarly perceived as further evidence of his limitations as an art critic, resistant to the more radical dimensions of modernism patently at odds with his own definition of mimesis.[3] But accounts of Zola's later reservations about Impressionist painting risk obscuring his earlier ground-breaking writing on Pissarro and Monet. For the painters themselves, Zola's signal service was to bring to public attention (far more effectively than their letters of protest to the official guardians of orthodoxy) the revolution enacted in the period 1863–1876 by 'la nouvelle peinture'.

On reflection, however, it may be unduly pejorative to label the direction of his writing on the visual arts, distancing himself from 'la nouvelle peinture', as 'revisionist' or 'regressive'. For it exactly corresponds to the shifting perspectives of his literary criticism: from initially belittling the *Grand siècle* to comparing Flaubert to Corneille, in a move analogous, as Zola noted, to Taine's admiring juxtaposition of Stendhal and Racine (*OC*, XI, 73).[4] That he found in the Old Masters, and in Michelangelo in particular, both a corrective to pictorial experimentation and an affinity with his own compositional principles is not in doubt. But it is also significant that looking backwards is a recurrent aside throughout his art criticism: in his stated preference for the early work of Théodore Rousseau, Millet, Diaz, Courbet, the Impressionists and, from the perspective of his posthumous exhibition in 1884, even Manet himself. For it is consistent with Zola's evolutionary conception of the history of art, inseparable from an analogous literary history, tracking back to origins to better define the specificity of a modernism implicitly synonymous, of course, only with his own. Predecessors, whether the Barbizon School or Balzac, are given their due by virtue of their pioneering status. Successors, on the other hand, are often derided, as we have seen, as 'la queue': slavish imitators exploiting innovation in the interests of a specious originality or mitigating it to secure a wider appeal.

The correlative of such a focus on artistic lineage is Zola's (admittedly problematic) reliance on heredity, detailed in genealogical trees so carefully drawn in his own hand that they could be made public (heading, for example, the publication of *Une page d'amour* in 1878), by way of rationalizing, or justifying *ex post facto*, the origins of his fictional Rougon-Macquart family as well as some of its belatedly invented members. The preface to the opening frame of his novel cycle, *La Fortune des Rougon* (1871), '[qui] doit s'appeler de son titre scientifique: *les Origines*', stresses that his series will follow 'le fil qui conduit mathématiquement d'un homme à un autre' (*RM*, I, 3–4). Other drawings by him, notably in imagining the topography of his novels' settings, are further evidence of his geometric predilections.[5] To these can be related his demonstrable preference, as already highlighted, for paintings characterized by 'solidité', whether in Manet's suppression of intermediate semi-tones, Bastien-Lepage's clearly delineated agricultural workers, or Michelangelo's corporeal figurations in the Sistine Chapel. And it is the consistency of direction ('la ligne droite'), or lack of it in the case of Cézanne, which determines his judgements. A now-famous Impressionist 'blur' is manifestly at odds with the importance for Zola of the clarity of outline, whether in painting or as plotted by writers past and present.

Apart from such primarily aesthetic concerns, there are also many other ways in which Zola's art criticism can be viewed not as a supplementary, or even complementary, activity, but as integral to his vision of the modern world as it is explored elsewhere in his work and most memorably in his fiction. Perhaps the most fundamental is located in the preparatory notes for *L'Œuvre*, in which Zola interpolates an addition to the reasons why his Claude Lantier is incapable of realizing his ambitions: 'Je voudrais aussi que notre art moderne y fut pour quelque chose [...], notre impatience à secouer les traditions, notre *déséquilibrement* en un mot' (Ms 10316, fol. 265). Already cited in the previous chapter, Zola's own underlining deserves further scrutiny. For it is illuminated by Richard Thomson's recent *The Presence of the Past in French Art, 1870–1905*,[6] at the heart of which are, precisely, the 'instabilities' of the age. Those are political, social and cultural; and they serve to explain a compensatory return to pre-modern subjects and styles. Zola's entire work can be similarly contextualized. As long ago as 1868–69, in the preliminary notes for *Les Rougon-Macquart*, the series' explicit timeframe of the Second Empire is already enlarged to encompass 'la caractéristique du mouvement moderne': 'le moment est trouble. C'est le trouble du moment que je peins' (*RM*, v, 1738–39). That *trouble* speaks of a disorder and confusion both literal and psychological, a collective mood faced with the dissolution of structures both institutional and systemic. The traumatic events of the next twenty-five years, to name but a few, merely intensified such a sense of indirection and crisis: the Commune and its destructive epilogue; the vicissitudes of the Republic; a virulent nationalism (xenophobic, anti-semite and *revanchard*); working-class demands for justice; the advent of a militant socialism; murderous anarchist attacks; the irreconcilable fractures in the fabric of French life evident from the very start of the Dreyfus Affair in 1894. And those are only the most historically visible markers of a 'trouble du moment' complicated by science, medicine, secularization and what Zola calls 'une verité du temps: la bousculade des ambitions et des appétits', a feral energy unleashed by a capitalist society with its 'élan démocratique' no longer constrained by the outdated norms of acceptable human behaviour. 'Mon roman', he writes of his intended series as a whole, 'eût été impossible avant 89' (*RM*, v, 1738).

While the individual novels of *Les Rougon-Macquart* are, for the reader, free-standing, adjacent texts often coexist in Zola's mind during the preparation of the next simultaneous to correcting the proofs of the last. We saw this in the case of *La Terre*, in which its quasi-pictorial scenes and scenarios are obliquely alluded to in *L'Œuvre*, the serial publication of which coincided with Zola's starting work on his epic study of rural life. So too, it should be remembered that *L'Œuvre* itself immediately follows *Germinal*, with its authorial aim spelt out: 'Je le veux prédisant l'avenir, posant la question la plus importante du vingtième siècle' (Ms 10307, fol. 402). *L'Œuvre* is equally predictive, dramatizing artistic struggles and theoretical contradictions in anticipation of the next century. 'Le livre est en somme', Zola declared in its *ébauche*, 'la peinture de la production de notre époque naissante et trouble' (Ms 10316, fols 294–95). It begins, in his planning, with a restatement of 'l'art, historique et où l'on est' (fol. 2); but 'le moment de la peinture' (fol. 37) is actually, in spite of its supposed 1860s chronology, that of the novel's composition in 1885–86: 'Fin de siècle, art trouble, commencement d'autre chose' (fol. 214), cross-referencing the unconvincing hope, to be voiced in a conversation about the art of the future between Sandoz and Bongrand, that 'il faut que le 20ème siècle arrive, que la névrose romantique se calme, que l'éducation se fasse, que la démocratie s'installe, que nous sortions enfin de notre temps de transition' (fol. 294). 'Mais tout cela', he added, 'au "peut-être"', as provisional as an indeterminate 'autre chose'. It is not beside the point that Zola here conflates democratic, pedagogic, physiological and pictorial ideals. For the corresponding 'instabilities' in the artistic domain are not sufficiently metaphorical to be disassociated from the wider dismantling of certainties, not least on account of their ideological assumptions and ramifications: the questioning of conventions, values and traditional hierarchies; 'revolutionary' assaults on orthodoxy; opposing factions, pitting conformity against originality; but also internecine strife within the 'Intransigeants' (as the Impressionists were also known by admirers and detractors alike); what Zola repeatedly calls, in relation to divergent pictorial modes and exhibition strategies, 'l'anarchie des tendances'; and the rhetorical violence of the kind employed by Zola himself, aimed at both philistine bourgeois spectators and the entire administrative architecture of the fine arts established by the State, variously targeting appointments to the Salon jury, official awards and commissions, the selection of representative French painting for the Universal Exhibitions of 1867 and 1878, the Prix de Rome and the institutional 'dictatorship' of the Académie des Beaux-Arts.

It is perhaps necessary, therefore, to conclude by expanding Anita Brookner's insights into the retreat to the past by commentators repeatedly disappointed by the failure to locate the 'genius of the future'. For Zola's apparently surprising but continual referencing of the Old Masters, once freed from polemical intent, is inseparable from the exemplary status given to Courbet in his art criticism, as well as in both *L'Œuvre* and in its preparatory notes: 'Courbet, grand ouvrier classique' (Ms 10316, fol. 34). Without claiming the existence of a contemporary consensus in respect of the Greco-Roman implications of 'classique', Thomson's *The Presence of the Past* explores its lexical prevalence and connotations in the post-1870 period as essentially symptomatic of his central theme: 'the reassessment of past art in the light of what it can offer the present'; but he also insists that 'what the "classical" meant in terms of the visual arts was in a state of positive and stimulating flux throughout the nineteenth century'.[7]

For Zola, at least (and however imprecisely derivative his understanding of its provenance and aesthetic template may have been), the term 'classique' was unambiguous, synonymous with artistic immortality.[8] To effect such a semantic alignment with the universally recognized great (European) artists of centuries past thereby assured for a 'genius' a critical destiny subject neither to changing criteria nor to the inevitable waning of creativity. This is suggested by Zola's reflections, during the preparation of *L'Œuvre*, on the character of Bongrand, for whom Courbet was one model, conscious of 'la certitude de son déclin' (fol. 160) but 'célèbre, immortel' (fol. 207) nevertheless. In this context, however, another equally pertinent model is to be found in Zola's explanation, in the course of an 1897 interview, of Bongrand's origins, his fictional name and his concerns in respect of a perceived decline:

> Pour modèle de ce peintre, j'ai pris un écrivain. Bongrand, c'est Gustave Flaubert! La profession seule a été changée, mais le caractère est resté le même. Flaubert arrivé à sa gloire par *Madame Bovary*, souffrait de n'avoir jamais retrouvé le même succès dans ses livres suivants. Il lui semblait qu'il allait en diminuant à mesure qu'il avançait dans la vie; il sentait toutes ses œuvres écrasées par le souvenir de cette *Madame Bovary*. Et alors il regrettait le passé trop brillant qui l'obsédait. Ce sont ces sentiments que j'ai fait exprimer à Bongrand qui, lui aussi, souffre de rester l'homme de ses premières œuvres. Quand j'ai cherché un nom pour ce personnage, je me suis dit que Flaubert était un bon, grand, brave homme et j'ai fait Bongrand! (*EsA*, pp. 702–03)

If the naming is consistent with Zola's description of Flaubert's personality over the years,[9] so too is the allusion to the anxiety haunting the author of *Madame Bovary*. Of that novel, Zola had written in *Les Romanciers naturalistes* that Flaubert 'se prit à maudire cette fille aînée qui faisait un pareil tort à ses sœurs cadettes' (*OC*, XI, 142). But also discernible here are the residual traces of Zola's hesitations in finalizing the role Bongrand might play in *L'Œuvre*. Through an associative move, a fleeting initial comparison ('Un Manet très chic, un Flaubert plutôt' (fol. 289)) generates the idea that Bongrand should perhaps be an established writer (fols 274–75): 'Je voudrais, dans une figure, soit de peintre, soit d'écrivain, mettre debout l'auteur qui, après un chef-d'œuvre, lutte pour tenir son rang. La bataille est plus âpre encore, plus douloureuse, pour l'artiste qui veut se maintenir, que pour l'artiste qui veut arriver'; this desperation relativizes 'son immortalité assurée, devant ses efforts inutiles pour créer'; but when the character is imagined embarking on a new work with the 'fraîcheur d'un débutant', Zola's evocation of a 'tremblement devant la copie, plaisir de revoir des épreuves' is so unmistakeably personal that it is at this exact point in his work notes that an autobiographical step too far leads to Bongrand's assimilation with Courbet instead.

Such a substitution is no less revealing. Whether ascribed to real painters or fictional characters, the challenge of maintaining a reputation as opposed to establishing one was certainly Zola's. An obsessive preoccupation in this respect was not exclusive to Flaubert, judging by Edmond de Goncourt record of Zola's own anxiety in 1882: 'Malgré lui, l'écrasant succès d'hier est l'empoisonnement de sa carrière future. Et il laisse échapper, avec une profonde tristesse: "Au fond, je ne ferai plus jamais un roman qui remuera comme *L'Assommoir*, un roman qui se vendra comme *Nana*!"'[10] By the time he was working on *L'Œuvre* in 1885–86, it was not only the phenomenal success of *Germinal* which exacerbated such a concern. For, as was argued earlier in this book, Zola's novel about the artistic instabilities of the period also reflects an awareness of the splintering of the Naturalist movement and the beginnings of a reaction against the aesthetic hegemony he had hoped would be as permanent as the 'classic' status accorded to the likes of Courbet as well as consecrated by the Old Masters. Faced with indications to the contrary, it is significant that when asked, in 1891, about the likely future directions of French literature, Zola envisaged 'une sorte de classicisme du naturalisme'.[11] This is so vague as to be no more than an instinctive counter to developments in literary practice as unacceptable to him as those in the visual arts. But already, in 1879, Zola's reference to the incomprehension of his contemporary critics is significantly assertive: 'L'idée que je pouvais être un classique a fait beaucoup rire' (*OC*, x, 1317). And to marvel at Michelangelo's achievement as 'une œuvre énorme qui me va au cœur, dont j'ai rêvé toute ma vie' was to articulate for posterity a hoped-for judgement that has since been confirmed: of his own writing, formally counterbalancing as well as thematically accommodating the *déséquilibrement* of his time, as that of a 'grand ouvrier classique'.

Notes to the Afterword

1. This remark was reported by Fernand Xau, *Émile Zola* (Paris: Marpon et Flammarion, 1880), p. 34.
2. Mitterand, *Zola journaliste: de l'affaire Manet à l'affaire Dreyfus* (Paris: Armand Colin, 1962).
3. See Pierre Daix, 'Zola contre la révolution en peinture', in *L'Aveuglement devant la peinture* (Paris: Gallimard, 1971), pp. 117–98.
4. See Mourad, 'La Réhabilitation des classiques', in *Zola critique littéraire*, pp. 177–94.
5. See Olivier Lumbroso's remarks on such an 'esprit de géométrie' characterizing the 150 drawings spread across the preparatory notes for the novels of *Les Rougon-Macquart*: 'L'Invention des lieux', in *Les Manuscrits et les dessins de Zola*, 3 vols (Paris: Éditions Textuels, 2002), III, 314–15.
6. Its full title is *The Presence of the Past in French Art, 1870–1905: Modernity and Continuity* (New Haven and London: Yale University Press, 2021).
7. Thomson, *The Presence of the Past*, respectively, p. 245 and p. 11.
8. Zola's 1877 essay on Balzac as 'le génie du siècle' prefigures his evocation of Michelangelo: 'On croit le voir monter pesamment sur ses échafaudages, maçonnant ici une grande muraille nue et rugueuse, alignant plus loin des colonnades d'une majesté sereine' (*OC*, xi, 25); this extended metaphor is already to be found at the beginning of his article on Balzac in *Le Rappel* of 13 May 1870 (*OC*, x, 924). In relation to Flaubert, Zola writes of his 'idée d'immortalité [...] l'ambition puissante de faire éternel' (*OC*, xi, 103).
9. In *Les Romanciers naturalistes*, some fifteen years earlier, he had written of Flaubert's 'grand cœur': 'c'était un cœur très bon' (*OC*, xi, 129, 135). Coinciding with the 1897 interview cited here, Zola's evocation of him echoes its formula even more precisely: in his speech (printed in *Le Journal* of 25 October of that same year) at the unveiling of Maupassant's monument in the Parc Monceau, his memories included those of 'notre bon et grand Flaubert' (*OC*, xii, 716).
10. Goncourt, *Journal*, II, 949 (entry of 6 July 1882).
11. This response to Jules Huret's *Enquête sur l'évolution littéraire* was published in *L'Écho de Paris* of 31 March 1891, and subsequently reprinted in Zola's *Mélanges critiques* (*OC*, xii, 653–55).

BIBLIOGRAPHY

❖

ALEXIS, PAUL, *'Naturalisme pas mort': lettres inédites de Paul Alexis à Émile Zola, 1871–1900*, ed. by B. H. Bakker (Toronto: University of Toronto Press, 1971)

——*Émile Zola: notes d'un ami* [1882], ed. by René-Pierre Colin (Paris: Maisonneuve & Larose, 2001)

ALSDORF, BRIDGET, *Fellow Men: Fantin-Latour and the Problem of the Group in Nineteenth-Century French Painting* (Princeton: Princeton University Press, 2012)

ALSTON, DAVID, 'What's in a Name? *Olympia* and a Minor Parnassian', *Gazette des beaux-arts*, 91 (1978), 148–54

AMBROSINI, LYNNE, 'The Market for Daubigny's Landscapes, or "The Best Pictures Do Not Sell"', in *Inspiring Impressionism: Daubigny, Monet, Van Gogh*, exh. cat. (Edinburgh: National Galleries of Scotland, 2016), pp. 81–91

ANDERSON, WAYNE, *Cézanne and the Eternal Feminine* (Cambridge: Cambridge University Press, 2004)

ARMSTRONG, CAROL, *Manet Manette* (New Haven and London: Yale University Press, 2002)

ASTRUC, ZACHARIE, *Les 14 Stations du Salon; suivies d'un récit douloureux* (Paris: Poulet-Malassis et De Brosse, 1859)

ATHANASSOGLOU-KALLMYER, NINA, *Cézanne and Provence: The Painter and his Culture* (Chicago: University of Chicago Press, 2003)

AUFFRET, FRANÇOIS, 'Jongkind et Zola', *Les Cahiers naturalistes*, 88 (2014), 289–95

BALIGAND, RENÉE, 'Lettres inédites d'Antoine Guillemet à Émile Zola (1866–1870)', *Les Cahiers naturalistes*, 52 (1978), 173–205

BARTHES, ROLAND, *La Chambre claire* (Paris: Seuil, 1980)

BAUDELAIRE, CHARLES, *Œuvres complètes*, ed. by Claude Pichois, 2 vols (Paris: Gallimard, Bibliothèque de la Pléiade, 1975–76)

BECKER, COLETTE, 'Jean-Baptistin Baille', *Les Cahiers naturalistes*, 36 (1982), 147–58

——'Le Critique d'art', in *Les Apprentissages de Zola* (Paris: Presses universitaires de France, 1993), pp. 256–81

BEIZER, JANET, 'Uncovering *Nana*: The Courtesan's New Clothes', *L'Esprit créateur*, 25 (1985), 45–56

BERG, WILLIAM J., *The Visual Novel: Émile Zola and the Art of his Times* (University Park, PA: Pennsylvania State University Press, 1992)

BERNARD, ÉMILE, *Lettres d'un artiste (1884–1941)*, ed. by Neil McWilliam (Dijon: Presses du réel, 2012)

BEST, JANICE, 'Portraits d'une "vrai fille": *Nana*, tableau, roman et mise-en-scène', *Les Cahiers naturalistes*, 66 (1992), 157–66

BLAKESLEY, ROSALIND, 'Émile Zola's Art Criticism in Russia', in *Critical Exchange: Art Criticism of the Eighteenth and Nineteenth Centuries in Russia and Western Europe*, ed. by Carol Adlam and Juliet Simpson (Bern: Peter Lang, 2009), pp. 263–84

BLOCH-DANO, EVELYNE, *Madame Zola* (Paris: Grasset, 1997)

BRADY, PATRICK, *'L'Œuvre' de Émile Zola: roman sur les arts, manifeste, autobiographie, roman à clef* (Geneva: Droz, 1968)

BROMBERT, BETH ARCHER, *Edouard Manet: Rebel in a Frock Coat* (Boston: Little, Brown & Co., 1996)

BROOKNER, ANITA, 'Zola', in *The Genius of the Future: Studies in French Art Criticism* (London: Phaidon, 1971), pp. 89–117

BROOKS, PETER, 'Nana at last Unveil'd? Problems of the Modern Nude', in *Body Work: Objects of Desire in Modern Narrative* (Cambridge, MA: Harvard University Press, 1991), pp. 123–61

BRYSON, NORMAN, *Tradition and Desire: From David to Delacroix* (Cambridge: Cambridge University Press, 1984)

BUTLER, RONNIE, 'Zola's Art Criticism (1865–1868)', *Forum for Modern Language Studies*, 10.4 (1974), 334–47

CACHIN, FRANÇOISE, ed., *Manet, 1832–1883*, exh. cat. (Paris: Réunion des musées nationaux/ New York: Metropolitan Museum of Art, 1983)

—— *Manet: The Influence of the Modern* (New York: Harry Abrams, 1995)

CARLES, PATRICIA, and BÉATRICE DESGRANGES, '*Son Excellence Eugène Rougon* ou la métaire des Beaux-Arts', *Nineteenth-Century French Studies*, 21 (1992–93), 114–29

—— 'Émile Zola et ses peintres, essai de critique génétique', in *Lire/Dé-lire Zola*, ed. by Jean-Pierre Leduc-Adine and Henri Mitterand (Paris: Nouveau Monde Éditions, 2004), pp. 35–59

CASTAGNARY, JULES, *Salons, 1857–1879*, 2 vols (Paris: Charpentier, 1892)

CÉZANNE, PAUL, *Correspondance*, ed. by John Rewald (Paris: Grasset, 1978)

CHAMPFLEURY (pseud. Jules Husson), 'Courbet en 1860', in *Grandes figures d'hier et d'aujourd'hui* [1861] (Geneva: Slatkine Reprints, 1968), pp. 245–63

—— *Peintres et sculpteurs contemporains* (Paris: Charpentier, 1873)

CHARLES, DAVID, *Émile Zola et la Commune de Paris: aux origines des 'Rougon-Macquart'* (Paris: Classiques Garnier, 2017)

CHRISTIE, JOHN, 'The Enigma of Zola's *Madame Sourdis*', *Nottingham French Studies*, 5 (1966), 13–28

CHU, PETRA TEN-DOESSCHATE, ed. and trans., *Letters of Gustave Courbet* (Chicago: University of Chicago Press, 1992)

CLARETIE, JULES, *Peintres et sculpteurs contemporains* (Paris: Charpentier, 1873)

—— *Les Artistes français à l'Exposition universelle de 1878* (Paris: Decaux, 1878)

CLARKE, MICHAEL, and RICHARD THOMSON, eds, *Monet. The Seine and the Sea, 1878–1883* (Edinburgh: National Galleries of Scotland, 2003)

CLARK, T. J., *Image of the People: Gustave Courbet and the 1848 Revolution* [1973] (London: Thames & Hudson, 1982)

CLAYSON, HOLLIS, *Painted Love: Prostitution in French Art of the Impressionist Era* (New Haven and London: Yale University Press, 1991)

CRARY, JONATHAN, *Techniques of the Observer: On Vision and Modernity in the Nineteenth Century* (Cambridge, MA: MIT Press, 1990)

DAIX, PIERRE, 'Zola contre la révolution en peinture', in *L'Aveuglement devant la peinture* (Paris: Gallimard, 1971), pp. 117–98

DANCHEV, ALEX, *Cézanne: A Life* (London: Profile Books, 2012)

DAUNAIS, ISABELLE, 'La Réversibilité des arts: littérature et peinture au confluent de la critique (Zola, Huysmans)', *Études françaises*, 33.1 (1997), 95–108

—— 'Les Récits de la critique d'art, entre naturalisme et modernisme', *Littérature*, 107 (1997), 20–34

DEAN, CATHERINE, *Cézanne* (London: Phaidon, 1991)

DOMBROWSKI, ANDRÉ, 'Cézanne, Manet and the Portraits of Zola', in *Interior Portraiture and Masculine Identity in France, 1789–1914*, ed. by Temma Balducci, Heather Belnap Jensen and Pamela Warner (Farnham: Ashgate, 2011), pp. 101–20

DORAN, MICHAEL, ed., *Conversations avec Cézanne* (Paris: Macula, 2011)
DROST, WOLFGANG, 'Zola critique d'art et romancier: vision artistique et technique expressionniste', *Les Cahiers naturalistes*, 66 (1992), 33–46
DUFFY, JR., JOHN J., 'The Aesthetic and the Political in Zola's Writing on Art', *Australian Journal of French Studies*, 38.3 (2001), 365–78
DURANTY, EDMOND, *La Nouvelle Peinture — À propos du groupe d'artistes qui expose dans les galeries Durand-Ruel* (Paris: Dentu, 1876)
DURET, THÉODORE, *Les Peintres français en 1867* (Paris: Dentu, 1867)
——*Les Peintres impressionnistes* (Paris: Heymann et Perois, 1878)
EHRARD, ANTOINETTE, 'Zola et Courbet', *Europe*, 468–69 (1968), 241–51
——'Émile Zola et Gustave Doré', *Gazette des beaux-arts*, 79 (1972), 185–92
——'Émile Zola: l'art de voir et la passion de dire', in *La Critique artistique: un genre littéraire* (Paris: Presses universitaires de France, 1983), pp. 101–22
——'L'Esthétique de Zola: étude lexicologique de ses écrits sur l'art', *Les Cahiers naturalistes*, 58 (1984), 133–50
ÉMILE-ZOLA, FRANÇOIS, and MASSIN, *Zola Photographer*, trans. by Liliane Tuck (London: Collins, 1988)
EVENO, BERTRAND, 'Zola photographe', in *Mimesis et Semiosis: littérature et représentation*, ed. by Philippe Hamon and Jean-Pierre Leduc-Adine (Paris: Nathan, 1992), pp. 393–408
FERNANDEZ, DOMINIQUE, and FERRANTE FERRANTI, *Le Musée d'Émile Zola: haines et passions* (Paris: Stock, 1997)
FLAUBERT, GUSTAVE, *Correspondance*, ed. by Jean Bruneau and Yvan Leclerc, 5 vols (Paris: Gallimard, 1973–2007)
FLEMING, G. H., *James Abbott McNeill Whistler: A Life* (Moreton-in-Marsh: Windrush Press, 1991)
FOSCA, FRANÇOIS, *De Diderot à Valéry: les écrivains et les arts visuels* (Paris: Albin Michel, 1960)
FOUCART, JACQUES, 'Jongkind vu et compris par Zola', in *Jongkind, 1819–1891* (Paris: Réunion des musées nationaux, 2004), pp. 79–91
FRANGNE, HENRY, and JEAN-PIERRE POINSOT, *L'Invention de la critique d'art en France* (Rennes: Presses universitaires de Rennes, 2002)
FRIED, MICHAEL, *Manet's Modernism or, The Face of Painting in the 1860s* (Chicago: University of Chicago Press, 1996)
FURST, LILLIAN R., 'Zola's Art Criticism', in *French 19th-Century Painting and Literature*, ed. by Ulrich Finke (Manchester: Manchester University Press, 1972), pp. 164–81
GASQUET, JOACHIM, *Cézanne* [1921], ed. by François Solesnes (Paris: Les Belles Lettres, 2012)
GLINOER, ANTHONY, and VINCENT LAISNEY, *L'Âge des cénacles: confraternités littéraires et artistiques au XIXe siècle* (Paris: Fayard, 2013)
GONCOURT, JULES ET EDMOND DE, *Journal: mémoires de la vie littéraire*, ed. by Robert Ricatte, 3 vols (Paris: Laffont, 1956)
——*Manette Salomon*, ed. by Michel Crouzet (Paris: Gallimard, 'Folio Classique', 1996)
GOWING, LAWRENCE, ed., *Cézanne: The Early Years 1859–1872*, exh. cat. (London: Weidenfeld and Nicolson, 1988)
GREEN, NICHOLAS, *The Spectacle of Nature: Landscape and Bourgeois Culture in Nineteenth-Century France* (Manchester: Manchester University Press, 1990)
GROUIX, PIERRE, '"Je voudrais que les toiles de tous les peintres du monde": remarques sur Zola critique d'art', in *Écrire la peinture entre XVIIIe et XIXe siècles*, ed. by Pascale Auraix-Jonchière (Clermont-Ferrand: Presses universitaires Blaise-Pascal, 2003), pp. 281–93
GUIEU, JEAN-MAX, and ALISON HILTON, eds, *Émile Zola and the Arts* (Washington DC: Georgetown University Press, 1988)
HALÉVY, DANIEL, *Degas parle...* (Paris: La Palatine, 1960)

Hamilton, George Heard, 'Manet and Zola', in *Manet and His Critics* (New York: Norton, 1969), pp. 81–111

Hanotelle, Micheline, 'Léo Gausson et Zola: réflexions relatives à une lettre du peintre Léo Gausson à Émile Zola et réponse inédite du romancier', *Les Cahiers naturalistes*, 63 (1989), 193–203

Haskell, Francis, *Past and Present in Art and Taste: Selected Essays* (New Haven and London: Yale University Press, 1987)

—— *The Ephemeral Museum: Old Master Paintings and the Rise of the Art Exhibition* (New Haven and London: Yale University Press, 2000)

Hemmings, F. W. J., 'Zola, Manet and the Impressionists (1875–1880), *Publications of the Modern Language Association of America*, 73 (1958), 407–17

——, and Robert J. Niess, eds, *Émile Zola: Salons* (Geneva: Droz, 1959)

—— 'Émile Zola devant l'Exposition universelle de 1878', *Cahiers de l'Association internationale des études françaises*, 24 (1972), 131–53

Herbert, Robert L., 'Industry in the Changing Landscape from Daubigny to Monet', in *French Cities in the Nineteenth Century*, ed. by John M. Merriman (London: Hutchinson, 1982), pp. 139–64

Higonnet, Anne, *Berthe Morisot* (New York: Harper Perennial, 1990)

Hilaire, Michel, and Paul Perrin, eds, *Frédéric Bazille (1814–1870): la jeunesse de l'impressionnisme* (Paris: Fayard, 2016)

Hilton, Alison, '*Le Messager de l'Europe*: Zola's Art Criticism beyond Paris', in *Émile Zola and the Arts*, ed. by Jean-Max Guieu and Alison Hilton (Washington DC: Georgetown University Press, 1988), pp. 61–72

Hoek, Leo H., 'Le "Balais ivre" d'Émile Zola: lecture du discours esthétique dans la critique d'art et dans *L'Œuvre*', in *Rapports-Het Franse Boek* (Amsterdam), 60.3 (1989), 113–23

—— 'Zola vis-à-vis du paysage', in *Titres, toiles et critique d'art: déterminants institutionnels du discours sur l'art au dix-neuvième siècle en France* (Amsterdam: Rodopi, 2001), pp. 255–350

House, John, *Impressionism: Paint and Politics* (New Haven and London: Yale University Press, 2004)

—— 'Cézanne's Card Players: Art without Anecdote', in *Cézanne's Card Players*, ed. by N. Ireson and B. Wright (London: Courtauld Gallery, 2010), pp. 55–71

Huysmans, Joris-Karl, *Écrits sur l'art, 1867–1905*, ed. by Patrice Locmant (Paris: Bartillat, 2006)

Jay, Martin, *Downcast Eyes: The Denigration of Vision in Twentieth-Century French Thought* (Berkeley: University of California Press, 1993)

Jefferson, Ann, 'Stendhal's Art History and the Making of a Novelist', in *Artistic Relations: Literature and the Visual Arts in Nineteenth-Century France*, ed. by Peter Collier and Robert Lethbridge (New Haven and London: Yale University Press, 1994), pp. 192–208

Jurt, Joseph, *Les Arts rivaux: littérature et arts visuels d'Homère à Huysmans* (Paris: Classiques Garnier, 2018)

Katz, Maya Balakirsky, 'Photography Versus Caricature: "Footnotes" on Manet's *Zola* and Zola's *Manet*', *Nineteenth-Century French Studies*, 34 (2006), 323–35

Kelly, Simon, 'Daubigny et Monet: le paysage de rivière, un produit commercial', in *Eblouissants reflets: cent chefs-d'œuvre impressionnistes*, ed. by Sylvain Amic (Paris: Réunion des musées nationaux/Musée des Beaux-Arts de Rouen, 2013), pp. 36–41

Kloss, William, 'Zola and the Old Masters', in *Émile Zola and the Arts*, ed. by Jean-Max Guieu and Alison Hilton (Washington DC: Georgetown University Press, 1988), pp. 35–45

Krell, Alan, 'Manet, Zola and the *Motifs d'une exposition particulière*, 1867', *Gazette des beaux-arts*, 99 (1982), 109–15

KRUMRINE, MARY LOUISE, 'Parisian Writers and the Early Work of Cézanne', in *Cézanne: The Early Years, 1859–1872*, ed. by Lawrence Gowing (London: Weidenfeld & Nicolson, 1988), pp. 20–31

LAPP, JOHN C., *Zola before the 'Rougon-Macquart'* (Toronto: University of Toronto Press, 1964)

LASERRA, ANNAMARIA, 'Zola et la *Salomé* de Gustave Moreau: le défi du Sphinx', in *Simbolismo e naturalismo fra lingua e testo*, ed. by Segio Cigada and Marisa Verna (Milan: Vita & Pensiero, 2010), pp. 425–35

LAURENT, BÉATRICE, 'Éclairages du Nord dans les tableaux du *Rêve*', *Les Cahiers naturalistes*, 66 (1992), 73–81

LEBENSZTEJN, JEAN-CLAUDE, *Paul Cézanne, cinquante-trois lettres* (Tusson: L'Echoppe, 2011)

LE BLOND-ZOLA, DENISE, *Émile Zola raconté par sa fille* (Paris: Grasset, 1931)

LE BLOND-ZOLA, JACQUES, *Zola à Médan* (Paris: Société Littéraire des Amis d'Émile Zola, 1999)

LEDUC-ADINE, JEAN-PIERRE, 'Le Vocabulaire de la critique d'art en 1866, ou "les cuisines des beaux-arts"', *Les Cahiers naturalistes*, 54 (1980), 138–53

——'Zola et les arts plastiques', in *Zola*, ed. by Michèle Sacquin (Paris: Bibliothèque nationale de France/Fayard, 2002), pp. 55–61

——'Zola critique d'art: principes esthétiques', in *New Approaches to Zola*, ed. by Hannah Thompson (London: Émile Zola Society, 2003), pp. 101–09

LETHBRIDGE, ROBERT, 'L'Accueil critique à l'œuvre de Zola avant *L'Assommoir*', *Les Cahiers naturalistes*, 54 (1980), 214–23

——'Zola, Manet and *Thérèse Raquin*', *French Studies*, 34.3 (1980), 278–99

——'Zola et ses livres', *Les Cahiers naturalistes*, 65 (1991), 191–97

——'A Visit to the Louvre: *L'Assommoir* Revisited', *Modern Language Review*, 87 (1992), 41–55

——'Les Représentations de la banlieue chez Zola et les peintres', *Les Cahiers naturalistes*, 66 (1992), 59–71

——'"Le Delacroix de la musique": Zola's Critical Conflations', in *Le Champ littéraire, 1860–1900*, ed. by Keith Cameron and James Kearns (Amsterdam: Rodopi, 1996), pp. 81–90

——'L'Homme et *L'Œuvre*: Zola et la déformation romanesque', in *Lire/Dé-lire Zola*, ed. by Jean-Pierre Leduc-Adine and Henri Mitterand (Paris: Nouveau Monde Éditions, 2004), pp. 135–52

——'Zola and Contemporary Painting', in *The Cambridge Companion to Émile Zola,* ed. by Brian Nelson (Cambridge: Cambridge University Press, 2007), pp. 67–85

——'Against Recuperation: The Fictions of Art in *L'Œuvre*', *Romanic Review*, 102.3–4 (2011), 449–63

——'Zola's Manets', in *Perspectives on Manet*, ed. by Therese Dolan (Farnham: Ashgate, 2012), pp. 97–117

——'The End of the Affair: Zola and Cézanne', *French Studies Bulletin*, 133 (2014), 95–99

——'Rethinking Zola and Cézanne: Biography, Politics and Art Criticism', *Journal of European Studies*, 46.2 (2016), 126–42

——'Zola's Transpositions', in *Translation and the Arts in Modern France*, ed. by Sonya Stephens (Bloomington: Indiana University Press, 2017), pp. 131–47

——'Zola et les peintres: une interview retrouvée', *Les Cahiers naturalistes*, 93 (2019), 247–58

——'Zola and the Science of Painting', *Nottingham French Studies*, 60.3 (2021), 295–306

——'Zola and the Old Masters', *Bulletin of the Émile Zola Society*, 64 (2023), 3–10

——'Opposing Frames: Zola and Fromentin', in *Crossings and Interconnections: Essays in Honour of Barbara Wright*, ed. by Terry Dolan, Claire Moran and Mary Orr, *Dix-neuf*, 27. 2–3 (2024), 94–113

Lindsay, Jack, *Gustave Courbet: His Life and Art* (London: Jupiter, 1977)
Lloyd, Christopher, and Anne Distel, eds, *Camille Pissarro, 1830–1903* (London: Arts Council of Great Britain, 1980)
Lumbroso, Olivier, *L'Invention des lieux*, vol. III of *Les Manuscrits et dessins de Zola*, ed. by Olivier Lumbroso and Henri Mitterrand, 3 vols (Paris: Éditions textuels, 2002)
Lucbert, Françoise, *Entre le voir et le dire: la critique d'art d'écrivains dans la presse symbolique en France de 1882 à 1906* (Rennes: Presses universitaires de Rennes, 2005)
Mainardi, Patricia, *Art and Politics of the Second Empire: The Universal Exhibitions of 1855 and 1867* (New Haven and London: Yale University Press, 1987)
Maione, Michaël, 'Zola et la sculpture', *Les Cahiers naturalistes*, 58 (1984), 151–62
Mauner, George, *Manet, 'Peintre-Philosophe': A Study of the Painter's Themes* (University Park, PA: Pennsylvania State University Press, 1975)
——, and Henri Loyette, eds, *Manet: les natures mortes*, exh. cat. (Paris: Réunion des musées nationaux, 2001)
Maupassant, Guy de, *Chroniques*, ed. by Gérard Delaisement, 2 vols (Paris: Rive Droite, 2003)
May, Gita, 'Zola entre le texte et l'image: l'exemple de Diderot', *Les Cahiers naturalistes*, 67 (1993), 235–44
McPherson, Heather, *The Modern Portrait in Nineteenth-Century France* (Cambridge: Cambridge University Press, 2001)
McWilliam, Neil, 'Émile Bernard's Reactionary Idealism', in *Academics, Pompiers, Official Artists and the Arrière-Garde: Defining Modern and Tradition in France, 1900–1960*, ed. by Natalie Adamson and Toby Norris (Newcastle: Cambridge Scholars, 2009), pp. 25–50
Mérot, Alain, 'Autour de *La Derelitta*: Zola et les maîtres anciens', in *Du romantisme à l'art déco: lectures croisées*, ed. by Rosella Froissart, Laurent Houssais and Jean-François Luneau (Rennes: Presses universitaires de Rennes, 2011), pp. 125–36
Mitterand, Henri, *Zola journaliste: de l'affaire Manet à l'affaire Dreyfus* (Paris: Armand Colin, 1962)
——'Regard et modernité', in *Le Regard et le signe* (Paris: Presses universitaires de France, 1987), pp. 55–74
——'Le Musée dans le texte', *Les Cahiers naturalistes*, 66 (1992), 13–22
——*Zola*, 3 vols (Paris: Fayard, 1999–2003)
——'Mise au point: Cézanne et Zola', in *Zola tel qu'en lui-même* (Paris: Gallimard, 2009), pp. 171–204
——, ed., *Paul Cézanne, Émile Zola: lettres croisées, 1858–1887* (Paris: Gallimard, 2016)
Moore, George, *Impressions and Opinions* (London: David Nutt, 1891)
Moreira De Mello, Celina, 'Émile Zola et la critique d'art au XIXe siècle: enjeux littéraires', *Excavatio*, 20 (2005), 37–48
Morel, Jean-Paul, *C'était Ambroise Vollard* (Paris: Fayard, 2007)
Mourad, François-Marie, *Zola critique littéraire* (Paris: Honoré Champion, 2003)
Natanson, Thadée, 'Paul Cézanne', *La Revue blanche*, 1 December 1895, 496–500
Newton, Joy, 'Émile Zola and Théodore Duret: Portrait of an Art Critic', *Nottingham French Studies*, 27.1 (1988), 13–23, and 27.2 (1988), 13–24
——'Zola et Raffaëlli', *Les Cahiers naturalistes*, 66 (1992), 47–58
——, and Claude Schumacher, 'Zola et le peintre Georges Clairin', *Les Cahiers naturalistes*, 61 (1987), 194–203
Nicolle, Marcel, 'Une anthologie de la critique d'art en France', *Gazette des beaux-arts*, 817 (1931), 45–63
Niess, Robert J., *Zola, Cézanne and Manet: A Study of 'L'Œuvre'* (Ann Arbor: University of Michigan Press, 1968)

NOIRAY, JACQUES, 'De la mise à nu comme principe poétique: genèse du personnage de Benedetta dans *Rome*', in *Zola: genèse de l'œuvre*, ed. by Jean-Pierre Leduc-Adine (Paris: CNRS Éditions, 2002), pp. 245–62

NORD, PHILIP, 'The New Painting and the Dreyfus Affair', *Historical Reflections/Réflexions historiques*, 24 (1998), 115–36

NOCHLIN, LINDA, 'The De-Politicization of Gustave Courbet: Transformation and Rehabilitation under the Third Republic', *October*, 22 (1986), 76–86

OBERLE, CHRISTOPHE, 'Onze lettres inédites d'Émile Zola (1862–1902)', *Les Cahiers naturalistes*, 95 (2021), 339–47

PAGÈS, ALAIN, *Zola et le groupe de Médan: histoire d'un cercle littéraire* (Paris: Perrin, 2014)

PAGÈS, ALAIN, and OWEN MORGAN, eds, *Guide Émile Zola* (Paris: Ellipses, 2002)

PAPPAS, SARA, 'Reading for Detail: On Zola's Abandonment of Impressionism', *Word & Image*, 23 (2007), 474–84

—— 'The View from the Bridge: Zola's *L'Œuvre* and its Many Composites', *Word & Image*, 27 (2011), 234–45

PARSONS, CHRISTOPHER, and MARTHA WARD, *A Bibliography of Salon Criticism in Second Empire Paris* (Cambridge: Cambridge University Press, 1986)

PETROZ, PIERRE, *L'Art et la critique en France depuis 1822* (Paris: Germer Baillière, 1875)

—— *Un Critique d'art au XIXe siècle* (Paris: Félix Alcan, 1884)

PITON-FOUCAULT, ÉMILIE, *Zola ou la fenêtre condamnée: la crise de la représentation dans 'Les Rougon-Macquart'* (Rennes: Presses universitaires de Rennes, 2015)

POLLOCK, GRISELDA, 'The "View from Elsewhere": Extracts from a Semi-Public Correspondence about the Visibility of Desire', in *12 Views of Manet's 'Bar'*, ed. by Bradford R. Collins (Princeton, NJ: Princeton University Press, 1996), pp. 278–313

PROUDHON, PIERRE-JOSEPH, *Du principe de l'art et de sa destination sociale* (Paris: Garnier Frères, 1865)

RAGON, MICHEL, 'Zola critique d'art', *Jardin des arts*, 161 (1968), 12–21

RAPETTI, R., 'L'Inquiétude cézannienne: Émile Bernard et Paul Cézanne au début du XXe siècle', *Revue de l'Art*, 144 (2004), 35–50

REFF, THEODORE, 'Copyists in the Louvre, 1850–1870', *Art Bulletin*, 46 (1964), 552–59

—— 'Manet and Blanc's *Histoire des peintres*', *Burlington Magazine*, 112 (1970), 456–68

—— 'Manet's Portrait of Zola', *Burlington Magazine*, 117 (1975), 35–44

RETTÉ, ADOLPHE, *Le Symbolisme: anecdotes et souvenirs* (Paris: Vannier, 1903)

REWALD, JOHN, *Cézanne, sa vie, son œuvre, son amitié pour Zola* (Paris: Grasset, 1939)

—— *Cézanne, Geoffroy et Gasquet, suivi des souvenirs sur Cézanne de Louis Aurenche et de lettres inédites* (Paris: Quatre Chemins, 1959)

RIOU, LUCIE, 'La Correspondance avec les artistes: laboratoire esthétique et genèse de la création littéraire', in *Éditer et relire la correspondance de Zola*, ed. by Sophie Guermès (Rennes: Presses universitaires de Rennes, 2018), pp. 169–84

—— 'Zola collectionneur: le cabinet de travail comme musée', *Les Cahiers naturalistes*, 93 (2019), 229–46

—— *Les Arts visuels dans les romans, l'œuvre critique et la correspondance d'Émile Zola* (Paris: Honoré Champion, 2020)

RIOUT, DENYS, ed., *Les Écrivains devant l'impressionnisme* (Paris: Macula, 1989)

RIPOLL, ROGER, *Émile Zola journaliste: bibliographie chronologique et analytique, II ('Le Sémaphore de Marseille', 1871–1877)* (Paris: Les Belles Lettres, 1972)

ROQUE, GEORGES, 'Chevreul and Impressionism: A Reappraisal', *Art Bulletin*, 78.1 (1996), 26–39

SACQUIN, MICHÈLE, ed., *Zola* (Paris: Bibliothèque nationale de France/Fayard, 2002)

SANCHEZ, JEAN-PIERRE, ed., *Henri Gervex, 1852–1929*, exh. cat., Galerie des Beaux-Arts de Bordeaux (Poitiers: Paris-Musées/SPADEM, 1992)

SAVY, NICOLE, 'Un étranger vu par Manet: Émile Zola', *Les Cahiers naturalistes*, 66 (1992), 23–32
——'Arrêt sur l'image: le portrait d'Émile Zola par Édouard Manet', in *Impressionnisme et littérature*, ed. by Gérard Gengembre, Yvan Leclerc and Florence Naugrette (Mont-Saint-Aignan: Presses universitaires de Rouen, 2012), pp. 51–61
SCHAPIRO, MEYER, *Paul Cézanne* (New York: Harry N. Abrams, 1952)
SCHMIDT, KATHARINA, 'Zu Édouard Manets Porträt Émile Zola', in *Manet, Zola, Cézanne: das Porträt des modernen Literaten*, ed. by Katharina Schmidt (Basel: Kunstmuseum/ Ostfildern-Ruit: Gerd Hatje, 1999), pp. 21–47
SÉSINGER, GISÈLE, 'Le Lisible et l'invisible: Zola et les apories du naturalisme', in *Le Dialogue des Arts, II: littérature et peinture aux XIXe et XXe siècles*, ed. by Laurence Richer (Lyon: Presses de l'université Jean Moulin, 2002), pp. 105–25
SHIFF, RICHARD, *Cézanne and the End of Impressionism* (Chicago and London: Chicago University Press, 1984)
SHIH, CHIU-YEN, 'La Synesthésie dans la critique d'art de Zola', *Les Cahiers naturalistes*, 86 (2012), 267–76
SILVESTRE, ARMAND, *Au pays des souvenirs: mes maîtres et mes maîtresses* (Paris: Librairie illustrée, 1892)
SIMPSON, JULIET, 'Plenitude, Potential and Provence: Zola, Art Criticism and *Le Sémaphore de Marseille*', *Australian Journal of French Studies*, 46 (2009), 111–25
SNELL, ROBERT, *Théophile Gautier: A Romantic Critic of the Visual Arts* (Oxford: Clarendon Press, 1982)
SPEIRS, DOROTHY E., and DOLORÈS A. SIGNORI, eds, *Entretiens avec Zola* (Ottawa: Presses universitaires d'Ottawa, 1990)
SPOOR, FREYA, and ROBERT LETHBRIDGE, 'Picturing Walls: Zola's Modern Artworks', *Journal of the History of Collections*, 32.3 (2020), 503–08
TAINE, HYPPOLYTE, *Voyage en Italie: à Rome*, préface d'Émile Zola (Brussels: Éditions complexe, 1990)
THOMSON, RICHARD, *Camille Pissarro: Impressionism, Landscape and Rural Labour* (London: Herbert Press, 1990)
——*The Presence of the Past in French Art, 1870–1905: Modernity and Continuity* (New Haven and London: Yale University Press, 2021)
TILLIER, BERTRAND, *Les Artistes et l'Affaire Dreyfus* (Seysell: Champ Vallon, 2009)
TOOKE, ADRIENNE, *Flaubert and the Pictorial Arts: From Image to Text* (Oxford: Oxford University Press, 2000)
TOULOUSE, ÉDOUARD, DR, *Enquête médico-psychologique sur la supériorité intellectuelle: Émile Zola* (Paris: Flammarion, 1896)
VAISSE, PIERRE, *La Troisième République et les peintres* (Paris: Flammarion, 1995)
VALAZZA, NICHOLAS, *Crise de plume et souveraineté du pinceau: écrire la peinture de Diderot à Proust* (Paris: Classiques Garnier, 2013)
——'Peindre les ruines de l'Empire: Huysmans et Zola face à l'œuvre de Gustave Moreau', in *Huysmans et les arts*, ed. by Jérôme Solal (Paris: Minard, 2016), pp. 101–18
VALÉRY, PAUL, *Œuvres*, ed. by Jean Hytier, 2 vols (Paris: Gallimard, 1960)
VAN DIJK, MAITE, 'Daubigny and the Impressionists in the 1860s', in *Inspiring Impressionism: Daubigny, Monet, Van Gogh*, exh. cat. (Edinburgh: National Galleries of Scotland, 2016), pp. 45–63
VAN GOGH, VINCENT, *The Letters: The Complete and Illustrated Edition*, ed. by Leo Jansen and others, 6 vols (London: Thames & Hudson, 2009)
VENTURI, LIONELLI, *Les Archives de l'impressionnisme*, 2 vols (Paris: Durand-Ruel, 1939)
VERDI, RICHARD, *Cézanne* (London: Thames & Hudson, 1992)

VOLLARD, AMBROISE, *En écoutant Cézanne, Degas, Renoir* (Paris: Grasset, 2003)
——*Souvenirs d'un marchand de tableaux* (Paris: Albin Michel, 2007)
WALTER, RODOLPHE, 'Zola et ses amis à Bennecourt', *Les Cahiers naturalistes*, 17 (1961), 19–35
——'Émile Zola et Claude Monet', *Les Cahiers naturalistes*, 26 (1964), 51–61
——'Critique d'art et vérité: Émile Zola en 1868', *Gazette des beaux-arts*, 73 (1969), 225–34
——'L'Exposition universelle de 1878, ou amours et haines d'Émile Zola', *L'Œil*, 280 (1978), 35–45
WARD, MARTHA, 'From Art Criticism to Art News: Journalistic Reviewing in Late Nineteenth-Century Paris', in *Art Criticism and its Institutions in Nineteenth-Century France*, ed. by Micael Orwicz (Manchester: Manchester University Press, 1994), pp. 162–81
WETTLAUFER, ALEXANDRA K., 'Metaphors of Power and the Power of Metaphor: Zola, Manet and the Art of Portraiture', *Nineteenth-Century Contexts*, 21.3 (1999), 437–63
——*Pen vs Paintbrush: Girodet, Balzac and the Myth of Pygmalion in Post-Revolutionary France* (New York: Palgrave, 2001)
WICKY, ERIKA, 'La Peinture à vue de nez: la juste distance du critique d'art, de Diderot à Zola', *Canadian Art Review*, 39.1 (2014), 76–89
WILSON-BAREAU, JULIET, 'Manet et l'Espagne', in *Manet-Velázquez, la manière espagnole au XIXe siècle*, exh. cat. (Paris: Réunion des musées nationaux, 1983), pp. 170–215
WOOLLEN, GEOFF, 'Zola, Cézanne and *Le Château de Médan*', *Bulletin of the Émile Zola Society*, 20 (1999), 3–12
XAU, FERNAND, *Émile Zola* (Paris: Marpon et Flammarion, 1880)
ZOLA, ÉMILE, *Les Rougon-Macquart*, ed. by Henri Mitterand, 5 vols (Paris: Gallimard, 1960–67)
——*Œuvres complètes*, ed. by Henri Mitterand, 15 vols (Paris: Cercle du livre précieux, 1966–70)
——*Correspondance*, ed. by Bard H. Bakker and others, 10 vols (Montréal: Presses de l'Université de Montréal/Paris: CNRS, 1978–95)
——*Correspondance*, vol. XI (*Lettres retrouvées*), ed. by Owen Morgan and Dorothy E. Speirs (Montréal: Presses de l'Université de Montréal/Paris: CNRS, 2010)
——*Lettres à Alexandrine, 1876–1901*, ed. by Brigitte Émile-Zola and Alain Pagès (Paris: Gallimard, 2014)
——*Écrits sur l'art*, ed. by Robert Lethbridge (Paris: Classiques Garnier, 2021)

INDEX

About, Edmond 23
Alexandre, Arsène 41–43, 64 n. 19, 160
Alexis, Paul 34 n. 55, 40, 47–48, 64 n. 11 & 14, 65 n. 23 & 36, 67 n. 67, 90 n. 1, 124 n. 40, 208 n. 68
Alsdorf, Bridget 2, 8 n. 7
Alston, David 8 n. 6
Ambrosini, Lynne 166 n. 19
Anderson, Wayne 44, 65 n. 43
Armstrong, Carol 98, 101, 115, 122 n. 12, 15, 23 & 25, 123 n. 30, 125 n. 57 & 62
Astruc, Zacharie 2, 8 n. 6, 20, 112–13, 141–42, 167 n. 27
Athanassoglou-Kallmyer, Nina 67 n. 61
Aurenche, Louis 22 n. 65, 40

Baboneau, Henri 17, 33 n. 32
Babou, Hippolyte 20
Baffier, Jean 41
Baille, Jean-Baptistin 16, 45, 54, 59–60, 63, 66 n. 46, 50 & 53, 69, n. 92, 107, 127, 201, 203 n. 10, 207 n. 52, 208 n. 60 & 66
Baligand, Renée 31 n. 4, 69 n. 90, 70 n. 109, 165 n. 12
Balzac, Honoré de 11, 16, 87, 124 n. 41, 137, 178, 193, 199–200, 204 n. 20, 210, 214 n. 8
Barbey d'Aurevilly, Jules 73
Barrès, Maurice 42
Barthes, Roland 120
Bastien-Lepage, Jules 4, 87, 153–54, 160, 169 n. 46 & 55, 196, 200, 211
Baudelaire, Charles 1, 102, 106, 203 n. 7, 206, n. 42
art criticism 12, 24, 26, 175
*Curiosités esthétiques*15, 23
on landscape 164 n. 6
Baudry, Etienne 77
Baudry, Paul 85
Bazille, Frédéric 16, 45, 54, 59–60, 63, 66 n. 46, 50 & 53, 69 n. 92, 107, 127, 201, 203 n. 10, 207 n. 52, 208 n. 60 & 66
Becker, Colette 66 n. 53
Beethoven, Ludwig van 189, 200, 206 n. 43, 208 n. 61
Beizer, Janet 123 n. 32
Béliard, Édouard 20, 73, 128, 144–45, 147, 168 n. 36, 169 n. 55, 170 n. 69, 171 n. 72, 196
Béraud, Jean 5, 20
Berlioz, Hector 205 n. 29, 208 n. 61
Bernard, Émile 41–43, 46, 54, 56, 65 n. 30, 31, 33 & 41, 67 n. 60, 68 n. 67, 204 n. 18
Bernard-Lazare, (Bernard Lazare) 40
Bernhardt, Sarah 5
Bernini, Gian Lorenzo 188
Bertall (Charles-Albert d'Arnoux) 2–3, 118–19
Best, Janice 123 n. 30
Blakesley, Rosalind 35 n. 59
Blanc, Charles 14–15, 32 n. 16, 113, 115, 125 n. 55, 169 n. 53, 175, 203 n. 6
Blémont, Émile 156
Bloch, Armand 17
Bloch-Dano, Evelyne 64 n. 16
Boetzel, Ernest 17
Bonnat, Léon 4, 184, 168 n. 35, 195, 207 n. 51
Bonvin, François 195–96
Botticelli, Sandro 9 n. 14, 122 n. 9, 177, 191–92, 195, 207 n. 48
Boudin, Eugène 84, 127, 136, 147
Bouguereau, William 5, 27, 93 n. 41, 123 n. 30
Bouhélier, Saint-Georges de 37
Bouillet, Louis 70 n. 105
Bourget, Paul 192
Bouvet, Henri 127
Bramante (Donato d'Angelo Lazzari) 188
Bracquemond, Félix 20
Breton, Jules 4, 84–85, 168 n. 45
Brombert, Beth 101, 121 n. 4 & 6, 122 n. 25, 123 n. 34, 124 n. 49
Brookner, Anita 32 n. 17, 202, 208 n. 70, 212
Brooks, Peter 103, 123 n. 31 & 34
Brunetière, Ferdinand 32 n. 18
Bruyas, Alfred 71, 90 n. 2 & 6
Bryson, Norman 198, 207 n. 37
Buchon, Max 92 n. 27
Bürger, William (T. Thoré) 32 n. 16, 178
Burty, Philippe 15, 22, 32 n. 18, 85, 93 n. 42
Butin, Ulysse 5, 18, 169 n. 55

Cabanel, Alexandre 4, 8 n. 3 & 16, 27, 60, 67 n. 63, 74, 80, 84–85, 91 n. 16, 93 n. 39, 195, 199
Cachin, Françoise 112, 121 n. 2, 3, 4 & 8, 125 n. 52
Cadart, Alphonse 18, 93 n. 35, 165 n. 13
Caillebotte, Gustave 112, 117 n. 76
Caravaggio, Mersighi 195
Carles, Patricia 8 n. 16
Carolus-Duran 4–5, 85, 199
Carpeaux, Jean-Baptiste 186, 189
Castagnary, Jules 15, 23, 82, 92 n. 30, 93 n. 33, 141, 166 n. 17

Cézanne, Louis-Auguste 21, 54
Cézanne, Paul 4, 6, 16, 19–21, 37–71, 75, 78, 80, 90 n. 1 & 4, 92 n. 26 & 31, 96, 98, 100, 102–03, 106–07, 120, 121 n. 5, 122 n. 14 & 17, 123 n. 34 & 36, 125 n. 54, 127, 129, 136, 159, 164, 166 n. 16, 173, 177–78, 184, 187, 199–202, 203 n. 10, 204 n. 18, 19 & 21, 205 n. 26 & 31, 207 n. 51, 208 n. 62, 63, 64, 67, 68 & 69, 209, 211
Chaillan, Jean-Baptiste 67 n. 61, 177, 203 n. 10
Champfleury (Jules Husson) 71, 73, 75–76, 82, 90 n. 3, 91 n. 15 & 23
Chaplin, Charles 195
Charles, David 92 n. 29
Charpentier, Alexandre 95, 97
Charpentier, Georges 123 n. 30
Chautard, Joseph 67 n. 61
Chennevières, Philippe de 203 n. 6
Chesneau, Ernest 15, 73, 92 n. 30, 166 n. 13
Chevreul, Michel-Eugène 155–58, 169 n. 53, 170 n. 63
Chintreuil, Antoine 134, 165 n. 13
Christie, John 203 n. 1
Chu, Petra ten-Doesschate 92 n. 32
Clairin, Georges 5, 9 n. 12, 181
Claretie, Jules 72, 77, 91 n. 10, 93 n. 37 & 41
Clark, T.J. 91 n. 14
Clayson, Hollis 123 n. 29 & 30
Clerk, G. 24
Cock, César de 136
Colet, Louise 70 n. 105, 207 n. 44
Combes, Victor 67 n. 61
Conquet, Léon 18
Constable, John 165 n. 10
Corneille, Pierre 192, 210
Corot, Camille 7, 54, 69 n. 88, 75, 78, 86–87, 93 n. 42, 94 n. 47, 128–32, 134, 136–37, 139–42, 144–45, 147, 152, 160–61, 164 n. 3, 165 n. 8, 9, 10 & 11, 166 n. 14 & 16, 167 n. 22 & 25, 168 n. 41 & 42, 171 n. 73, 175, 195
Correggio, Antonio 182
Coste, Numa 17, 33 n. 31, 34 n. 46, 64 n. 11, 68 n. 77, 70 n. 106, 127
Courbet, Gustave 2, 4, 6–7, 8 n. 9, 17, 32 n. 21, 41, 56, 67 n. 63, 71–94, 102, 106, 120, 123 n. 34, 141, 154, 157–58, 166 n. 16, 168 n. 41, 169 n. 46, 171 n. 74, 174–75, 177–79, 185–86, 194–95, 198, 200–01, 203 n. 3, 204 n. 15, 206 n. 36, 208 n. 63, 210, 212–14
Couture, Thomas 98, 118
Crary, Jonathan 169 n. 50
Cuenot, Urbain 91 n. 32
Curzon, Alfred de 128, 164 n. 5, 174

Dagnan-Bouveret, Pascal 123 n. 30
Daix, Pierre 214 n. 3
Danchev, Alex 39–40, 43, 45, 53, 64 n. 9 & 20, 65 n. 39, 66 n. 54, 68 n. 68, 69 n. 82, 205 n. 26, 208 n. 67
Dantan, Édouard 13, 17
Dante Alighieri 175, 179, 206 n. 43
Daubigny, Charles-François 7, 8 n. 9, 75, 78, 87, 94 n. 47, 160–61, 164 n. 3 & 6, 165 n. 6, 8, & 9, 166 n. 14, 15, 16, 17, 18 & 19, 167 n. 22, 23, 25 & 26
Daubigny, Karl 136
Daudet, Alphonse 17
Daumier, Honoré 18
David d'Angers, Pierre-Jean 73, 179
David, Louis 73, 179, 207 n. 57
Dean, Catherine 64 n. 7
Degas, Edgar 2, 11–12, 18, 20, 31 n. 3, 54, 63 n. 3, 80, 97, 112, 136, 147, 153, 160, 164, 173
Delacroix, Eugène 1, 2, 8 n. 8, 56, 73, 76, 83, 89, 93 n. 41 & 42, 94 n. 47, 97, 157, 175, 179–80, 193, 198–200, 206 n. 43, 207 n. 57, 208 n. 61
Delmas, Paul 27
Desboutin, Marcellin 101, 186, 204 n. 21
Desbrosses, Jean 165 n. 13
Deschaumes, Edmond 207 n. 50
Desgranges, Béatrice 8 n. 10
Detaille, Édouard 4
Diaz de la Peña, Narcisse 87, 141, 165 n. 10, 210
Diderot, Denis 12–14, 31 n. 6 & 8, 32 n. 17, 18 & 20, 206 n. 42
Dijk, Maite van 167 n. 23 & 26
Dombrowski, André 70 n. 99
Doran, Michael 42, 65 n. 30, 32, 34 & 41
Doré, Gustave 6, 11, 34 n. 49, 47, 175, 195, 205 n. 30
Dreyfus Affair 39–43, 54, 64 n. 17, 65 n. 24 & 25
Du Camp, Maxime 204 n. 22
Dubufe, Édouard 84
Duez, Ernest 169 n. 55
Duffy, John 35 n. 62
Dupré, Jules 128
Durand-Ruel, Paul 13, 31 n. 2, 128, 141, 164 n. 3, 165 n. 10, 166 n. 13, 169 n. 51, 170 n. 58
Duranty, Edmond 2, 15, 22, 34 n. 43 & 55, 87, 94 n. 46, 112, 155, 157, 169 n. 52 & 53, 171 n. 76, 173, 177, 203 n. 12
Dürer, Albrecht 178
Duret, Théodore 15, 22, 27, 33 n. 30 & 33, 34 n. 44 & 54, 67 n. 61, 75, 83, 101, 116–17, 142, 154, 169 n. 48 & 53, 201, 208 n. 65

Ehrard, Antoinette 24, 34 n. 48, 35 n. 63, 90 n. 1
Émile-Zola, François 121 n. 7
Emperaire, Achille 67 n. 61
Enault, Louis 86, 91 n. 4
Eveno, Bertrand 121 n. 7, 122 n. 11

Fantin-Latour, Henri 1–3, 5, 8 n. 3 & 7, 20, 22, 31 n. 4, 34 n. 43 & 58, 57, 99, 111, 118, 168 n. 45, 170 n. 69, 195
Fénéon, Félix 66 n. 55
Fernandez, Dominique 122 n. 22, 207 n. 45 & 54

Ferranti, Ferrante 122 n. 22
Fiquet, Hortense 39, 64 n. 14
Firmin-Girard (Firmin Girard) 199
Fizelière, Albert de la 165 n. 13
Flandrin, Paul 128, 164 n. 5, 174
Flaubert, Gustave 24–26, 28, 34 n. 50, 59, 70 n. 105, 87, 91 n. 26, 118, 137, 189, 200, 210, 213, 214 n. 8 & 9
  Madame Bovary 75, 213
  on art criticism 15
  on illustrated editions 18, 33 n. 35
  on Proudhon 72
  on Rome and the Old Masters 173, 187–88, 194, 204 n. 22, 205 n. 30, 206 n. 41, 207 n. 47
Fleming, G.H. 35 n. 34
Forain, Jean-Louis 16
Fosca, François 15, 32 n. 17 & 20
Fouquier, Marcel 169 n. 56
Fourcaud, Louis de 160
Fra Angelico, Giovanni 188, 200
Français, François 129, 134, 139
France, Anatole 192
Fried, Michael 122 n. 13, 123 n. 34, 125 n. 58
Fromentin, Eugène 94 n. 47
Fry, Roger 208 n. 67

Gambetta, Léon 20
Gasquet, Joachim 41–43, 46–47, 54, 59, 64 n. 7, 65 n. 22, 27, 33 & 40, 67 n. 58, 64, 66, 68 n. 68, 70 n. 104, 91 n. 20, 92 n. 31, 201, 204 n. 18 & 19, 205 n. 26 & 31, 208 n. 62, 63 & 67
Gausson, Léo 157–58, 163, 170 n. 61 & 62
Gautier, Judith 23
Gautier, Théophile 8 n. 9, 12, 14, 23, 32 n. 17, 80, 117, 167 n. 23, 205 n. 25
Geffroy, Gustave 16–17, 65 n. 22, 170 n. 59, 197, 202, 208 n. 68
Gérôme, Jean-Léon 4, 8 n. 3, 17, 84, 93 n. 41, 195
Gervex, Henri 4, 17–18, 28–29, 33 n. 28 & 30, 60, 153, 168 n. 45, 169 n. 55
Giacomelli, Hector 24
Gill, André 18, 123 n. 30
Gill, Philippe 44
Girardin, Émile de 5
Glaize, Léon 67 n. 63
Glinoer, Anthony 34 n. 41
Gœneutte, Norbert 18
Goncourt, Edmond and Jules de 72, 90 n. 1, 120, 202, 205 n. 31, 213, 214 n. 10
  Madame Gervaisais 194, 205 n. 26, 206 n. 40 & 41
  Manette Salomon 164 n. 4, 174
Gonzalès, Eva 101
Gowing, Lawrence 66 n. 46 & 55, 68 n. 69, 70 & 71, 69 n. 83, 166 n. 15
Goya, Francisco de 113, 125 n. 56, 185, 204 n. 14
Grandville (Jean Gérard) 24
Green, Nicholas 164 n. 1
Greuze, Jean-Baptiste 46
Gudin, Théodore 167 n. 63
Guérard, Henri 127
Guigou, Paul 67 n. 61
Guillaumin, Armand 20
Guillemet, Antoine 11–12, 14, 19–20, 31 n. 4, 47, 59–60, 68 n. 72, 69 n. 90, 80, 88, 122 n. 16, 127, 134, 141, 147, 151, 164, 165 n. 12, 168 n. 35, 38 & 44, 169 n. 55, 170 n. 58, 196

Halévy, Daniel 31 n. 3
Halévy, Ludovic 170 n. 59
Hamilton, George Heard 125 n. 53
Hamon, Jean-Louis 67 n. 63
Hanotelle, Micheline 170 n. 61
Harlamoff, Alexei 5, 195
Harpignies, Henri 133–34
Haskell, Francis 178, 204 n. 17 & 22, 205 n. 31
Haydn, Franz Joseph 200
Hébert, Ernest 4, 191, 206 n. 44
Hemmings, F.W.J. 207 n. 56
Henner, Jean-Jacques 4, 60, 84, 195
Henriet, Frédéric 129, 136, 164 n. 6
Herbert, Robert L. 167 n. 25
Hervilly, Ernest d' 28, 34 n. 58
Higonnet, Anne 122 n. 9 & 10
Hilton, Alison 9 n. 14
Hoek, Léo 129, 165 n. 8 & 9, 166 n. 15, 167 n. 30
Hoschédé, Ernest 16, 33 n. 24
Houssaye, Henry 91 n. 32
House, John 1, 8 n. 4, 41, 65 n. 26, 112, 124 n. 51
Huet, Paul 136
Hugo, Victor 53–54, 69 n. 84, 77, 192, 198–99
Huot, Joseph 67 n. 63 & 65, 90 n. 4
Huret, Jules 214 n. 11
Huysmans, Joris-Karl 11, 16, 31 n. 2 & 3, 141, 167 n. 25, 170 n. 60 & 62, 171 n. 76, 173, 202, 203 n. 5, 204 n. 21, 205 n. 25 & 30

Ibels, Henri-Gabriel 18
Impressionism 11, 22, 31 n. 1 & 2, 56–57, 59, 87, 89, 106, 128, 141, 150–58, 170, 173, 196, 210–12
Ingres, Dominique 73–74, 85, 87–88, 93 n. 41, 94 n. 47, 157, 179–80, 198, 200, 204 n. 26

Japonisme 18, 33 n. 33
Jasinski, Félix 207 n. 48
Jay, Martin 169 n. 50, 170 n. 42
Jeanniot, Pierre-Georges 18
Jefferson, Ann 206 n. 42
Joly, Jules 122 n. 9
Jongkind, Johan-Barthold 25, 127, 145–47, 168 n. 38 & 41
Jourdain, Frantz 43, 54, 69 n. 89
Jouvin, B. 90 n. 7
Jouy, Jules de 101
Jurt, Joseph 31 n. 7

Katz, Maya Balakirsky 121 n. 7 & 8, 122 n. 9
Kelly, Simon 166 n. 19
Kloss, William 9 n. 14
Krell, Alan 125 n. 61
Krumrine, Mary Louise 48–49, 68 n. 71 & 74

Lacroix, Albert 69 n. 96, 93 n. 37, 109, 206 n. 34
Lagrange, Léon 73
Laisney, Vincent 34 n. 41
Lamartine, Alphonse de 54, 192, 206 n. 31
Lanoye, Ferdinand de 24
Lapostolet, Charles 136, 179
Lapp, John 68 n. 75
Latouche, Gaston 18
Laurens, Jean-Paul 4, 84, 169 n. 45, 199
Laurent, Béatrice 206 n. 32
Laurent-Pichat, Léon 123 n. 28
Leonardo da Vinci 180–81
Le Blond-Zola, Denise 39, 63 n. 4, 206 n. 35
Le Blond-Zola, Jean-Claude 203 n. 9
Lebensztejn, Jean-Claude 66 n. 47
Lefort, Paul 125 n. 54
Legros, Alphonse 20
Lemaître, Jules 189
Lindsay, Jack 91 n. 9
Lippi, Filipp 101, 185
Lorrain, Claude 127
Lumbroso, Olivier 214 n. 5

Magnard, Francis 92 n. 30
Mainardi, Patricia 9 n. 11
Maione, Michel 206 n. 39
Maître, Edmond 2
Maizeroi, René 160
Mallarmé, Stéphane 31 n. 2, 97, 125 n. 59
Manet, Édouard 1–4, 6–7, 8 n. 5, 6 & 9, 15–20, 22–23, 25–28, 31 n. 1 & 2, 32 n. 31, 33 n. 30 & 34, 34 n. 46, 35 n. 60, 37, 43–44, 46, 55–59, 66 n. 44, 70 n. 98 & 100, 76, 80, 83, 85–87, 93 n. 37, 95–125, 129, 136, 142, 150, 152, 155, 158, 160, 163–64, 166 n. 16, 169 n. 55, 173–74, 177, 185, 190, 193, 196–201, 203 n. 14, 204 n. 14 & 16, 208 n. 63, 210–11, 213
Mantegna, Andrea 186, 203 n. 10, 206 n. 37
Mantz, Paul 17
Marguery, Louis 32 n. 22
Marx, Roger 17
Mauner, George 124 n. 44
Maupassant, Guy de 64 n. 14, 204 n. 21, 214 n. 9
May, Gita 31 n. 8
McPherson, Heather 65 n. 43
McWilliam, Neil 65 n. 3 & 41
Meissonier, Ernest 4, 17
Memling, Hans 184
Ménard, Louis and René 24
Mendès, Catulle 67 n. 56
Mérot, Alain 9 n. 14
Meurent, Victorine 115
Meurice, Paul 32 n. 19
Michelangelo 177, 179–80, 184, 189–95, 198, 200, 202, 204 n. 22, 206 n. 41, 210–11, 214, 214 n. 8
Michiels, Alfred 178
Millet, Jean-François 31 n. 1, 32 n. 21, 75, 82, 87, 93 n. 42, 94 n. 47, 128, 130–32, 144, 160–61, 164 n. 3 & 4, 165 n. 8, 9 & 10, 169 n. 46, 171 n. 74, 175, 195, 210
Mirbeau, Octave 17, 37, 63 n. 3
Mitterand, Henri 3, 8 n. 10, 33 n. 30 & 32, 64 n. 8, 66 n. 47 & 49, 68 n. 68 & 76, 69 n. 93, 70 n. 100, 121 n. 4 & 8, 123 n. 30, 124 n. 50, 181, 188, 197, 205 n. 38, 206 n. 42, 207 n. 55, 209, 214 n. 2
Monet, Claude 1, 4, 8 n. 2, 18–20, 31 n. 2, 32 n. 21 & 24, 33 n. 30, 34 n. 39, 43–44, 56, 80, 89, 94 n. 50, 127, 136–37, 141, 144, 147–52, 154–57, 162–63, 166 n. 16 & 19, 167 n. 25 & 30, 168 n. 41 & 42, 170 n. 58 & 60, 171 n. 75, 196, 198, 200, 210
Moore, George 31 n. 2 & 3
Moreau, Gustave 4, 23, 25, 106, 186
Morel, Jean-Paul 65 n. 28 & 38, 69 n. 89
Morgan, Owen 63 n. 5
Morisot, Berthe 31 n. 3, 80, 97, 122 n. 9 & 10, 136, 141, 147
Morisot, Edma 136
Mourad, François-Marie 23, 34 n. 47, 214 n. 4
Mozart, Wolfgang Amadeus 200
Murger, Henri 32 n. 21
Murillo, Bartolomé Estaban 177, 181–82
Musée des copies 175, 177, 203 n. 6
Musset, Alfred de 54

Nadar (Félix Tournachon) 20, 121 n. 8
Napoléon III (Louis-Napoléon) 19, 28, 74, 166 n. 18
Narrey, Charles 178
Natanson, Thadée 208 n. 69
Neuville, Alphonse de 4
Newton, Joy 9 n. 12, 33 n. 25, 34 n. 44
Nicolle, Marcel 32 n. 18
Niess, Robert J. 44, 66 n. 44, 91 n. 26, 122 n. 14, 171 n. 73, 207 n. 56
Nieuwerkerke, Alfred-Émilien, comte de 74, 80, 92 n. 32, 166 n. 16 & 17
Nochlin, Linda 86, 94 n. 45
Noiray, Jacques 207 n. 46
Nord, Philip 40, 65 n. 24
Noriac, Jules 34 n. 53

Oberle, Christophe 33 n. 32, 34 n. 38
Oller, Francisco 47, 90 n. 1
Oudinot, Achille 136

Pagès, Alain 63 n. 2 & 5, 207 n. 58
Pappas, Sara 65 n. 42, 196, 207 n. 53

Parsons, Christopher 31 n. 11
Péladan, Joseph 54
Pelletan, Camille 23
Pelloquet, Théodore (Frédéric Bernard) 32 n. 21
Pelouse, Léon 135–36
Perugino, Pietro 188
Petroz, Pierre 32 n. 16
Pils, Isidore 208 n. 60
Pinturicchio (Bernadino di Betto-Benedetto di Biagio) 188
Pissarro, Camille 19–20, 22, 31 n. 2, 44, 47, 50–51, 80, 90 n. 1, 98, 127, 136, 141–45, 156, 160, 163–64, 165 n. 8, 166 n. 16, 167 n. 26, 27 & 28, 170 n. 58, 173–74, 177, 195–96, 198, 203 n. 12, 210
Piton-Foucault, Émilie 159, 170 n. 65
Pollock, Griselda 124 n. 38
Portalis, Édouard 34 n. 55
Poussin, Nicholas 127, 174, 178, 187, 203 n. 4
Prix de Rome 29, 127, 165 n. 10, 166 n. 16, 167 n. 22, 174, 176, 203 n. 8, 206 n. 44, 212
Proudhon, Pierre-Joseph 24, 41, 54, 71–80, 82, 87, 90 n. 2, 5, 6 & 8, 91 n. 9, 14, 16, 17, 18, 19, 21 & 25, 92 n. 29 & 30, 93 n. 42, 94 n. 47, 106, 178–79, 185, 203 n. 3
Proust, Antonin 20, 101
Puvis de Chavannes, Pierre 17, 168 n. 35, 198

Racine, Jean 192, 200
Raffaëlli, Jean-François 5, 16, 33 n. 25
Rapetti, R. 67 n. 60
Raphaël, Sanzio 173, 175, 177–80, 183–84, 188, 192, 195, 198, 200–02, 204 n. 20 & 22, 205 n. 25 & 31, 206 n. 43
Rappard, Anton van 31 n. 1
Redon, Odilon 117
Reff, Theodore 111, 124 n. 49, 125 n. 55, 203 n. 12
Rembrandt (Harmenz van Rijn) 12, 75, 175, 178–79, 185–86, 202, 204 n. 21
Renoir, Auguste 1–2, 4, 8 n. 8, 13, 18, 20, 31 n. 5, 34 n. 37, 47, 54, 56, 80, 97, 123 n. 33, 129, 136, 153, 164, 166 n. 16, 167 n. 25, 169 n. 47 & 55, 173, 196, 204 n. 21
Retté, Adolphe 122 n. 22
Rewald, John 38, 56, 63 n. 6, 65 n. 22, 66 n. 47, 67 n. 65, 69 n. 93
Ribera, José de 185
Ribot, Théodore 169 n. 53
Ribot, Théodule 197
Riesener, Léon 175
Rimbaud, Arthur 35 n. 58
Riou, Lucie 31 n. 4, 66 n. 57, 203 n. 9, 206 n. 33
Riout, Denis 94 n. 46, 167 n. 24, 169 n. 52
Ripoll, Roger 34 n. 57
Rixens, André 17
Robert, Léon-Paul 128, 144, 168 n. 35
Robert, Léopold 32 n. 21, 73–74, 179
Robinson, Lionel 33 n. 34
Rochefort, Henri 41–43
Rodin, Auguste 16
Roque, Georges 169 n. 53
Rousseau, Jean 167 n. 27
Rousseau, Théodore 4, 75, 82, 93 n. 42, 94 n. 47, 128–30, 132, 134, 137, 161, 164 n. 3 & 4, 165 n. 8, 9 & 10, 168 n. 43, 171 n. 74, 175, 199, 210
Roux, Marius 69 n. 92
Rozerot, Jeanne 121 n. 4, 207 n. 48
Rubens, Peter Paul 175, 177–78, 180, 182, 184, 202, 204 n. 21, 205 n. 30
Rudaux, Edmond 18
Rude, François 73, 179

Sacquin, Michèle 171 n. 77
Sainte-Beuve, Charles-Augustin 22
Saint-Victor, Paul de 14, 23, 93 n. 36
Salon des Refusés (1863) 19, 33 n. 34, 47, 58, 66 n. 44, 67 n. 61, 134, 136, 166 n. 16, 170 n. 57, 171 n. 74
Sanchez, Jean-Pierre 33 n. 28
Sand, George 32 n. 19, 168 n. 34
Santen Kolff, Jacques van 66 n. 48
Savy, Nicole 124 n. 50
Schapiro, Meyer 208 n. 69
Scheffer, Ary 46
Shiff, Richard 124 n. 36
Schmidt, Katherina 125 n. 54
Scholderer, Otto 2
Schopenhauer, Arthur 159, 169 n. 53
Schumacher, Claude 9 n. 12
Sésinger, Gisèle 76, 91 n. 24
Shakespeare, William 178, 180, 206 n. 43, 208 n. 60
Signac, Paul 157
Signorelli, Luca 88
Signori, Dolorès 8 n. 5, 33 n. 29
Silvestre, Armand 20, 34 n. 40
Simpson, Juliet 34 n. 59
Sisley, Alfred 4, 20, 80, 136, 141, 144, 147, 166 n. 16, 167 n. 25
Sistine Chapel 16, 180, 188–90, 193–94, 197–98, 201–02, 208 n. 41, 211
Snell, Robert 167 n. 23, 205 n. 25
Speirs, Dorothy 8 n. 5, 33 n. 29
Stendhal (Henri Beyle) 87, 137, 200, 205 n. 26, 206 n. 42, 210
Stevens, Alfred 17, 20, 33 n. 30
Stirling, William 178
Swift, Jonathan 180

Taine, Hippolyte 179–80, 182, 184, 187, 189–90, 192, 194, 205 n. 24 & 30, 210
Philosophie de l'art en Italie 20 n. 23
Voyage en Italie 205 n. 25 & 26, 206 n. 43
Thibault, Jean-François 34 n. 37
Thiers, Adolphe 32 n. 14, 166 n. 16, 175, 179

Thomson, Richard 167 n. 26, 211–12, 214 n. 7
Tillier, Bertrand 65 n. 25
Tintoretto, Jacopo 101
Tissot, James 17, 33 n. 34
Titian (Tiziano Vecellio) 9 n. 14, 101, 118, 179, 181–82, 204 n. 22, 208 n. 63
Tooke, Adrienne 34 n. 50, 205 n. 30, 207 n. 49
Toulouse, Édouard 168 n. 33
Troyon, Constant 165 n. 10
Truphème, Auguste 67 n. 61
Turgenev, Ivan 5, 27, 195
Turner, J.W.M. 16

Ulbach, Louis 123 n. 27

Vaisse, Pierre 28, 35 n. 62
Valabrègue, Antony 5, 8 n. 1, 9 n. 11, 26, 93 n. 38, 124 n. 45, 136, 166 n. 15, 207 n. 32
Valazza, Nicholas 31 n. 6
Valéry, Paul 31 n. 3
Vallotton, Félix 17
Van Eyck, Jan 178, 184, 206 n. 32
Van Gogh, Vincent 11–12, 27, 30, 31 n. 1
Velázquez, Diego Rodriguez de Silva 91 n. 20, 113, 117–18, 125 n. 56, 175–76, 178, 185, 203, 204 n. 21, 208 n. 63
Venturi, Adolpho 16
Venturi, Lionello 31 n. 2 & 10
Verdi, Richard 48, 68 n. 73
Verlaine, Paul 34 n. 58
Vernet, Horace 22, 73, 179
Veronese, Paolo 75, 91 n. 20, 175–76, 179, 181–82, 185–86, 191, 196, 205 n. 29, 208 n. 63
Viardot, Pauline 5
Vigneron, Pierre-Roch 93 n. 34
Villevielle, Joseph 67 n. 61
Vollard, Ambroise 37–43, 54, 58, 63 n. 1, 64 n. 12 & 18, 65 n. 21, 33, 35, 36 & 37, 68 n. 68, 69 n. 88, 89 & 97, 70 n. 101 & 102, 202
Vollon, Antoine 5, 84

Wagner, Richard 170 n. 69, 189
Walter, Rodolphe 34 n. 39
Ward, Martha 31 n. 11 & 12
Wettlaufer, Alexandra 107, 115, 124 n. 41 & 43
Whistler, James McNeill 18, 20, 33 n. 34
Wilson-Bareau, Juliet 121 n. 8, 125 n. 60
Wolff, Albert 22–23, 175
Woollen, Geoff 68 n. 72
Wyzewa, Téodor de 17

Xau, Fernand 37, 203 n. 9, 214 n. 1

Yvon, Adolphe 67 n. 68

Zola, Alexandrine 39, 95

Zola, Émile:
L'Assommoir 8 n. 10, 16–18, 26–27, 123, 124 n. 45, 137, 180–82, 184, 186, 189, 205 n. 27, 209, 213
La Bête humaine 53, 120
Le Capitaine Burle 159
La Confession de Claude 54, 91 n. 22, 107, 167 n. 31
Contes à Ninon 18, 56, 93 n. 37, 106, 111, 124 n. 45, 185
La Curée 18
La Débâcle 18
Le Docteur Pascal 95, 184
La Fortune des Rougon 69 n. 84, 95
Germinal 18, 176, 194, 212, 214
Lourdes 41, 185
Madame Sourdis 173, 177, 203 n. 1
Madeleine Férat 56, 120, 124 n. 47, 201
Mes Haines 11, 23–24, 26, 30, 54, 73, 205 n. 24
Mon Salon 3, 9 n. 11, 11, 23, 26, 30, 31 n. 1, 54, 63, 136, 166 n. 21
Naïs Micoulin 91 n. 16
Nana 18, 103, 105, 123 n. 29, 30, 31, 32, 33 & 34
Le Naturalisme au Salon 11, 33 n. 33, 56, 150, 152, 158–59, 170, 200, 209
Nouveaux Contes à Ninon 66 n. 54, 193–94, 203 n. 9
L'Œuvre 5–6, 8 n. 5 & 9, 9 n. 14, 11–13, 17–20, 22–23, 30, 31 n. 2 & 9, 33 n. 34, 34 n. 39, 35 n. 62, 38–54, 60, 64 n. 7, 13 & 16, 65 n. 37 & 42, 66 n. 45 & 52, 67 n. 61, 65 & 67, 68 n. 68 & 76, 77, 88–89, 90 n. 1, 91 n. 23, 92 n. 29, 94 n. 50, 98, 103–07, 121, 122 n. 19 & 20, 123 n. 34, 124 n. 39 & 42, 148, 155–64, 168 n. 37 & 39, 170 n. 67 & 68, 171 n. 71, 72, 74 & 78, 172 n. 79, 176–77, 185–86, 189, 192–94, 198–200, 202, 203 n. 10, 204 n. 21, 205 n. 29 & 30, 207 n. 50 & 58, 208 n. 69, 211 n. 13
Paris 186
Les Quatre Évangiles 202
Le Rêve 8 n. 2, 18, 184, 207 n. 46
Le Roman expérimental 75, 158, 174, 209
Les Romanciers naturalistes 12, 193, 213, 214 n. 9
Rome 3, 9 n. 14, 41, 65 n. 41, 187–95, 198–202, 207 n. 40
Son Excellence Eugène Rougon 8 n. 10
La Terre 38, 40–41, 65 n. 26, 160, 168 n. 34, 170 n. 67, 211
'Théorie des Écrans' 5, 49, 102, 115, 159, 199
Thérèse Raquin 19, 31 n. 1, 48–50, 53, 58, 102–03, 105, 122 n. 26, 123 n. 27, 166 n. 20
Les Trois Villes 3, 202
Une Page d'amour 31 n. 5, 123 n. 33, 210
Le Ventre de Paris 31 n. 1, 35 n. 61, 50–54, 68 n. 76 & 78, 69 n. 84, 78, 92 n. 29, 158, 168 n. 38, 177, 184
Le Vœu d'une morte 69 n. 85, 91 n. 22

www.ingramcontent.com/pod-product-compliance
Lightning Source LLC
LaVergne TN
LVHW081259100826
845148LV00005B/914

* 9 7 8 1 8 3 9 5 4 0 8 0 6 *